EROS IN PLATO, ROUSSEAU, AND NIETZSCHE

The Pennsylvania State University Press
University Park, Pennsylvania

EROS
IN PLATO,
ROUSSEAU,
AND NIETZSCHE

THE POLITICS OF INFINITY

LAURENCE D. COOPER

Library of Congress Cataloging-in-Publication Data

Cooper, Laurence D., 1962–
Eros in Plato, Rousseau, and Nietzsche :
the politics of infinity / Laurence D. Cooper.
    p.   cm.
Includes bibliographical references and index.
ISBN 978–0–271–03330–3 (cloth : alk. paper)
1. Love.
2. Plato.
3. Rousseau, Jean-Jacques, 1712–1778.
4. Nietzsche, Friedrich Wilhelm, 1844–1900.
I. Title.

BD436.C593   2007
128'.460922—dc22
2007026338

Copyright © 2008
The Pennsylvania State University
All rights reserved
Printed in the United States of America
Published by
The Pennsylvania State University Press,
University Park, PA 16802–1003

The Pennsylvania State University Press
is a member of the
Association of American University Presses.

It is the policy of
The Pennsylvania State University Press to use
acid-free paper. This book is printed on
stock that meets the minimum requirements of American
National Standard for Information Sciences—
Permanence of Paper for Printed Library Material,
ANSI Z39.48–1992.

To BEN AND AARON

CONTENTS

Acknowledgments   ix
List of Abbreviations   xi
Introduction: The Oneness of Desire—But Which One?   3
  1 The *Republic* as Prologue   17

PART ONE: PLATONIC EROS—THE EFFECTUAL TRUTH

  2 First Truths   53
  3 What Does Eros Want?   67
  4 Love of Wisdom versus Love of the Wise: Eros in Action   95

PART TWO: ROUSSEAU AND THE EXPANSIVENESS OF BEING

  5 Between Eros and Will to Power: Rousseau and
    "The Desire to Extend Our Being"   135
  6 *Emile,* or On Philosophy?   177

PART THREE: NIETZSCHE'S NEW ETERNITY

  7 Nietzsche's Politeia, I   205
  8 Nietzsche's Politeia, II   239
  9 Will to Power versus Eros, or a Battle of Eternities   275

Epilogue: One or Many?   305
References   331
Index   339

ACKNOWLEDGMENTS

In Plato's *Symposium,* Socrates teaches his companions that men too can be pregnant, and in more than one way. Some generate children, others produce various kinds of works. This book has been the beneficiary of prenatal care from generous and thoughtful colleagues. Jeff Church, Bryan-Paul Frost, Christopher Kelly, and Joseph Knippenberg offered valuable comments on earlier versions of selected chapters. Jonathan Marks brought a careful, sympathetic, and occasionally skeptical eye to the book, for which I am grateful. I am also thankful that Penn State Press was able to recruit two wonderfully able anonymous reviewers. Happily, they are no longer anonymous: Leon Harold Craig and John T. Scott read my manuscript with great care and offered advice that made it possible for me to improve the book substantially. I hope I haven't failed to make good on some part of that possibility.

I am also grateful to Carleton College—to the administration, for its material and moral support; to my colleagues in the Political Science Department, for their friendship and encouragement; and to my students, often the first and (I think) willing recipients of my discoveries, for the joy of teaching and learning together.

Earlier versions of chapters 1, 5, and 6 appeared, respectively, in *The Review of Politics* 63, no. 2 (Spring 2001); the *American Political Science Review* 98, no. 1 (February 2004); and *Journal of Politics* 64, no. 1 (February 2002). I thank the publishers for permission to reprint this material.

Socrates claimed that his lesson on men and pregnancy was something he had learned from a woman—not his wife, with whom he'd had three sons, but the priestess Diotima, though it is doubtful such a person existed. This is one respect in which I am happy not to be like Socrates. No, two respects: the woman who has lifted and sustained me is no fiction, and she is my wife. She too knows a few things about pregnancy, and about the years of devotion that follow. That devotion is rewarded daily. Thus the dedication of this book.

ABBREVIATIONS

Primary texts are referred to either by complete name (which will always be the practice regarding Platonic dialogues) or by the following abbreviations. Where possible, textual citations refer to the English translations listed in the references; where no adequate translation is available, I have cited a standard edition in the original language. Numbers refer, in the case of Platonic dialogues, to the standard Stephanus pagination; in the case of Rousseau's books, to the page numbers of the translations cited in the references; and in the case of Nietzsche, to section numbers rather than page numbers. Some of Nietzsche's books begin their section counts anew with each new Part or Essay, in which I case provide the name or number of the part or essay prior to the section number.

From Rousseau:

Bordes	Preface of a Second Letter to Bordes
Confessions	The Confessions of Jean-Jacques Rousseau
Corsica	Constitutional Project for Corsica
Dialogues	Rousseau, Judge of Jean-Jacques: Dialogues
Emile	Emile, or on Education
Julie	Julie, or the New Heloise
Last Reply	Last Reply by J.-J. Rousseau of Geneva
LM	Lettres morales
Observations	Observations by Jean-Jacques Rousseau of Geneva On the Answer to His Discourse
OC	Œuvres complètes
Poland	Considerations on the Government of Poland
Preface	Preface to Narcissus
Reveries	Reveries of the Solitary Walker

SC   On the Social Contract
SD   Second Discourse (Discourse on the Origin and Foundations of Inequality Among Men)

From Nietzsche:

A   The Antichrist
BGE   Beyond Good and Evil: Prelude to a Philosophy of the Future
EH   Ecce Homo
GM   On the Genealogy of Morals
GS   The Gay Science
Twilight   Twilight of the Idols
UD   On the Uses and Disadvantages of History for Life
WP   The Will to Power
Zarathustra Thus Spoke Zarathustra

EROS IN PLATO, ROUSSEAU, AND NIETZSCHE

So that in the first place, I put for a general inclination of all mankind, a perpetual and restless desire of power after power, that ceaseth only in death.

—**Hobbes,** ***Leviathan***

INTRODUCTION:
THE ONENESS OF DESIRE—BUT WHICH ONE?

How inauspicious to begin a book on eros with a line from Hobbes. And how wrongheaded: Hobbes extolls self-preservation over nobler longings and traces those longings to impermanent and "curable" sources. Human beings desire power after power, but why? Not because they are naturally drawn or propelled to some kind of transcendence but simply because no matter how safe and prosperous they are today, they cannot be assured that they will enjoy the same conditions tomorrow.[1] Find a way to guarantee security through well conceived institutions and you will have reduced the desire for power to modest proportions.

Yet Hobbes's line is irresistible because it contains more truth than it knows, or at least more truth than Hobbes develops explicitly. For there are at least three senses in which we may say that the desire for power ceases only in death. The first is the obvious one: human beings, as long as they live, will always be found restlessly desiring power. Surely that is Hobbes's main meaning. Second, the restless desire for power after power will tend to *bring* death. This may not be implied in Hobbes's statement, but it is at least consistent with his teaching and is surely something he learned from his master, Thucydides, who depicted an imperialism born of will to power—or, to be true to the text, an imperialism born of eros—that ended, inevitably, in catastrophe.[2] And third, the restless desire for power finds its *fulfillment* in death. Not death in the ordinary sense (unless one subscribes to the later Freud), but in the sense of letting go of all the delusions that sustain the ego, or, more simply,

---

1. *Leviathan* xi, paragraph 2.
2. Regarding eros as the source or magnifier of Athenian imperialism, see *The Peloponnesian War*, 2.43, 6.24. As for the claim of the inevitability of defeat, it is far from clear that the Athenians were destined to fail in their grand play for Sicily, or that Thucydides thought they were. But the logic of Athenian imperialism in its extreme stages, as represented by the words and deeds of Alcibiades, suggests that even if Athens' military defeat was not inevitable, its demise as a democratic power and "school of Hellas" was.

death of the ego itself, death of the self's identification with the ego or what I will simply call egoic consciousness—which, as we will see, does in fact have a connection to death in the ordinary sense of the word, since the death of egoic consciousness occurs precisely by virtue of accepting one's mortality. This meaning is not in Hobbes, at least not to my knowledge. But it is in Plato, Rousseau, and Nietzsche, even if the former two identify something other than "power" as the object of our desire. Each of these three thinkers posits a single, overarching psychic force in human beings. Each shows that and how this force drives so much of human activity, including, especially, the most consequential as well as both the best and the worst of human activity. Each offers insight into the character and inner meaning of this force and thus speaks to the question of how it can and should be educated and governed and satisfied. And each in his way shows that Hobbes's statement is true in all three of the senses that I have described.

"*This* force"? Can one really maintain the essential identity of Plato's eros, Rousseau's "desire to extend our being," and Nietzsche's will to power? (Eros by any other name . . . ?) Not quite. The similarities I have listed above—along with others that will be encountered later—tempt one to suppose that the three philosophers give separate names to what is really the same thing. The differences between these names, one might suppose—and what a difference there is between the passionateness of Plato's label, the clinical descriptiveness of Rousseau's, and the hardness of Nietzsche's—simply reflect the different perspectives from which the three philosophers address the same thing. There is some sense to this supposition. But in the end these names reflect more than just different perspectives or lines of approach; they reflect different interpretations. These are, however, different interpretations of roughly the same phenomena; and the phenomena in turn reflect or are born of the same basic source. The phenomena include ambition, aspiration, longing, and the spirited willingness to risk life. Their underlying source, recognized by Plato, Rousseau, and Nietzsche even as they interpret it and hence name it differently, is a deep-seated expansiveness in the human soul. Each of these philosophers notes within human beings a discontent not only with this or that limit but also with finitude itself. Each sees in human beings an apparently ceaseless and insatiable reaching-out beyond the boundaries of the self, a disposition not just to have more but to *be* more—to be *infinitely* more. The three philosophers' shared recognition is what accounts for the similarities noted above; it places them in company with one another and distinguishes them from

Hobbes. However one reads them, Plato, Rousseau, and Nietzsche emerge as poetic and musical and, yes, particularly erotic philosophers. Their company may or may not be harmonious. Family members don't always get along with one another, and the record among poets, musicians, and erotic rivals is even worse. But noble minds love nobly, and if they love their truths it is because they love truth as such. Thus an encounter between them should be a fruitful dialogue. Such, at least, is the animating hope of my inquiry.

If politics is "the art whose business it is to care for souls"[3]—and Plato, Rousseau, and Nietzsche all think that it is—then a dialogue among them on the nature and meaning of the soul's expansiveness will be fraught with political significance. One of the virtues common to the three philosophers is their appreciation of the political dimension and implications of this apparently apolitical but in actuality *pre*-political—and thus in a sense *simply* political—subject. In this they are wise but no wiser than most other political philosophers and thinkers of note. The history of serious political thought is the history of thinking about the consequences of existential longing and discontent, and only the most unimaginative or the most method-driven of "rationalists" haven't seen the challenges of politics in this light.[4] But Plato, Rousseau, and Nietzsche are unusually if not uniquely wise (and they *may* be uniquely wise) in bringing together a penetrating insight into the thing itself (eros, extended being, will to power) and a shrewd and subtle political sensibility—or, rather, bringing *to bear* the former on the latter. There have been gifted philosophic and psychological thinkers who have addressed the nature of this psychic force and gifted political thinkers and actors who have addressed its implications. Few if any other thinkers, however, have penetrated as deeply into the psychic recesses from which eros takes flight and have then

---

3. Plato, *Laws* 650b.
4. "Existential longing and discontent"—not a very felicitous phrase, but at least an impartial one in the contest between Plato, Rousseau, and Nietzsche. In order not to be too cumbersome, however, I will occasionally refer simply to "eros," as I did in the opening line of this introduction and in the title of this book. When I do identify the matter in question simply as eros (apart from when I am speaking specifically about Plato), it is not because I mean to endorse Plato's view over Rousseau's and Nietzsche's but simply because the word, admitting as it does of many varied interpretations (Plato himself gives us seven competing interpretations in the *Symposium*), can be used in a neutral way—and because it sounds right. (To hold that "eros" sounds right does represent something of an endorsement of Plato, I suppose, but no more of an endorsement than either Rousseau or Nietzsche could accept: whatever their ultimate stance toward Plato's interpretation, they recognize the kinship between the force to which they have given their own non-erotic names and what everyone recognizes as erotic.)

thought through the implications of these insights for politics—for politics, moreover, both as it has been and as it might be. Plato, Rousseau, and Nietzsche, alone and in dialogue, show us that all politics, at all levels (from psychic to international), is at bottom the politics of infinity.

Yet before I create a mistaken impression, I must hasten to add that another common feature of these three philosophers is their appreciation of the limits of politics. The highest peaks of human attainment are, for all three thinkers, heights that depend on or are even constituted by the proper cultivation and expression of the soul's primary force (eros, desire for extended being, will to power); and all three stipulate further that the accessibility of these heights has something to do with the shape of the regime under which one lives: one's regime cannot help but influence whether one will be well or poorly educated, well or poorly governed, and hence well or poorly prepared to ascend or even discern the peaks. Yet these heights themselves are essentially transpolitical even if the one who occupies them is "called" to some kind of political task (e.g., Plato's philosopher-kings or Nietzsche's "genuine philosopher" as "commander" and "legislator"). And in fact, while the accessibility of these peaks depends somewhat on the shape of one's regime, no regime can guarantee that any, let alone many, will ascend them. Thus, the political teachings of Plato, Rousseau, and Nietzsche, for all that they stimulate eros or aspiration and for all that they teach about the relation between life's peaks and the character of one's regime (or between one's inner or psychic regime and one's outer or societal regime), concern themselves, insofar as they are practically prescriptive, more with avoiding dangers than with bringing happiness. And this is especially so where the greatest or most capable individuals are concerned, such individuals being *particularly* susceptible to corruption and in any event beyond the reach of necessarily earthbound officeholders and institutions.[5] That politics should serve nonpolitical ends

---

5. All three philosophers see the development of the finest human beings as beyond the reach of politics in any ordinary sense. Plato has Socrates explain that those few gifted natures who have managed to grow well owe their good fortune to having *escaped* the political (*Republic* 496a–e). True, he imagines a city that would successfully do through politics what until now has required freedom from political involvement, but in this respect, as in others, the *kallipolis* is clearly impracticable; if gifted young people are to be governed successfully, it will be through an intimate politics that takes place beneath the notice of the city (à la Socrates, who says in the *Gorgias* that he alone of the men of his day practices politics [521d]). Rousseau memorably states near the end of the *Discourse on the Sciences and Arts* that the greatest minds need no teachers and would only be restricted in their development were they subjected to tutelage by ordinary teachers (such as the state, presumably, would assign). And Nietzsche denounces the modern state as the coldest of cold monsters and characterizes the whole spirit of democratic enlighten-

will sound right to loyal citizens of liberal regimes. That the same view should be advanced by philosophers whom one would not call liberal in any modern sense will surprise some. But it stands as the first indication of the relevance of such alien thinkers to our own situation. Liberalism, to survive, depends on the successful management, the taming, of existential longing and discontent. To flourish (and perhaps in the end to survive), it needs to resist its inherent tendency to want to tame this longing too much. Thus liberalism in particular stands to benefit—where it most needs benefiting—from a dialogue between thinkers whose "elitism" or "authoritarianism" might have seemed to place them beyond liberalism's rightful notice.

If the common ground between these philosophers creates the opportunity for a dialogue, it also *limits* the opportunity. Why only Plato, Rousseau, and Nietzsche? Why not Hobbes, too, or some other thinker who recognizes the phenomenon at issue and its importance (which would constitute enough common ground for a reasoned engagement)—without, however, believing it to be as intractable a feature of the soul or as important an ingredient of human excellence as Plato, Rousseau, and Nietzsche? Might Hobbes not be right? He might. My contention, though, is that it is those thinkers who see eros as natural and who embrace it as something to be educated rather than just tamed who have, perhaps for just that reason, developed the deepest insights into it. In saying that, I am to some extent taking their side against Hobbes. Yet in defense of this approach I might point out that Hobbes himself isn't entirely true to his position. For if he treats political eros or will to power as something that can and must be reduced and controlled, he still embraces as the crown of human experience the very thing that Plato, Rousseau, and Nietzsche embrace as the crown of human experience *for being the highest fulfillment of eros or extended being or will to power*—namely, philosophy. And Hobbes embraces it in terms that sound, well, awfully erotic.[6] So perhaps he

---

ment, which increasingly prevails in modern politics, as inimical to the development of the noblest human beings. Like Plato, he speaks of a new politics that would be more favorable to the best natures, but for him, too, the refined work of educating the best would necessarily fall to those who stand apart from (more precisely, *above*) politics in the everyday sense.

6. "Voluptuous men" who neglect philosophy, wrote Hobbes, do so "only because they know not how great a pleasure it is to the mind of man to be *ravished in the vigorous and perpetual embraces of the most beauteous world.*" Hobbes, *The English Works,* vol. 1, "Epistle to the Reader." Emphasis added. Regarding my claim that Plato, Rousseau, and Nietzsche all embrace philosophy as the crowning human experience, it is certainly true that they characterize philosophy differently from one another and, in the case of Rousseau, with apparent ambivalence. But

is not as far apart from the erotic trio as he appears. And perhaps he would concede that those who insist on investigating this dangerous phenomenon would learn most from those who had not been deterred by prudence, as perhaps he was, from writing about it.

As a provisional matter it is possible to state the common ground between Plato, Rousseau, and Nietzsche as follows. Each of the three philosophers identifies a single psychic force as the predominant force within the soul. Each sees this force as a fact, arguably the most important fact, of what one can rightly call a given human *nature,* even if that nature owes something to history or evolution. (Neither Rousseau nor Nietzsche presents human nature as so plastic as to be something less than a given nature: hence Rousseau's comments on the intractability of man's "present nature" and Nietzsche's effort to uncover and hearken to the "basic text of *homo natura.*")[7] Each extols as the highest activities or states of being things that are explicitly or implicitly shown to be peak expressions of this psychic force. Indeed, in his approach to the whole range of human phenomena each praises and blames, interprets and prescribes, so much in accord with his understanding of this force that he propounds the basis for a unified moral, political, and spiritual naturalism. Each, in other words, articulates a coherent political philosophy based on a monistic depth psychology.

Within the ambit of this common ground, however, Plato, Rousseau, and Nietzsche each offer something distinct and uniquely valuable. Each approaches the soul and society from a distinct perspective and thus sees, or at least highlights, things that the others do not. Many of their respective insights will prove complementary, which is satisfying and perhaps useful from a constructive or political point of view: where the ideas of great thinkers fit to-

---

as we shall see, Rousseau's ambivalence results partly from the fact that he sometimes speaks of what calls itself philosophy but falls short of its claim, and partly from the rhetorical demands imposed by a situation in which to speak well of philosophy would be to encourage the debased or false version. *Genuine* philosophy is for all three philosophers the highest human activity as well as—indeed, because it constitutes—the peak expression and fulfillment of eros or extended being or will to power.

7. Rousseau refers to "the present nature of man" at *SD* 92–93. The fixedness of this nature is implied by all of Rousseau's constructive projects, each of which takes into account, for example, the inevitable appearance of *amour-propre.* This fixedness is also implied by Rousseau's practical pessimism. Regarding Rousseau's pessimism, see Melzer, *The Natural Goodness of Man,* pp. 253–82. I have offered a more extensive argument for "The Fixedness of Man's 'Present Nature'" in *Rousseau, Nature, and the Problem of the Good Life* (pp. 41–47). On Nietzsche and the "eternal basic text of *homo natura,*" see *BGE* 230 as well as Part Three, below.

gether we may well be receiving knowledge from which to build policy or practice. Other insights will be in conflict, which will be satisfying and useful from what we perhaps should call a dialectical or philosophic point of view: where great thinkers clash we are called upon to deepen our reflection by thinking things through for ourselves. Sometimes the conflicts will be less comprehensive than they first appear. Let the lover of the *agon* not be discouraged, though, for, interestingly, the *deepest* conflicts are those which come to light precisely within, and precisely as we discover, hitherto unrecognized commonalities. This is another reason for looking only at philosophers with as much in common as these three have. My reading of Nietzsche, for example, builds on a Platonic dimension to his work that I do not believe has been demonstrated before; yet this revelation of the increased closeness between Nietzsche and Plato at the same time renders the decisive *difference* between them more sharply and allows us better to apprehend its depth.

The differences between Plato, Rousseau, and Nietzsche will become clear only when we address each philosopher carefully and in turn. For besides the common ground that I have mentioned, they also have in common an exquisite care and precision. The power of their thought is matched by its delicacy. Thus the "dialogue" that I hope to construct—alas, the scare quotes may be necessary—must proceed somewhat more in the manner of a series of monologues. The best I can do to create a real dialogue will be to guide the reader's attention, here at the beginning, again (more substantially) at the end, and a few times along the way, to what seem to me to be the fruitful points of engagement among the three philosophers. Yet the experience should be dialogical after all: for even if I must treat the three figures singly, the latter two are so clearly impressed by and replying to Plato as to make their thought, and hence my monological reconstructions, dialogical in themselves. (To uncover the extent to which Rousseau and Nietzsche are responding to Plato is one of my purposes.) On that more redeeming note, let me now offer a brief provisional sketch of Plato's, Rousseau's, and Nietzsche's respective approaches to the matter at hand and, to begin with, a few words about how we will approach *them*.

Plato, Rousseau, and Nietzsche are perhaps no more alike as writers than any other group of philosopher-poets. Then again, membership in this exclusive group implies a deep kinship, or so at least the three men themselves would say. By "philosopher-poet" I mean a number of things, but particularly the following. All three figures delve deeply into life's basic questions and have proven powerfully enchanting to many kinds of readers: they are philosophers whose poetry forms and moves, or, more precisely, legislates. And deliberately so. What to make of this? How should one read philosopher-poets? Exactly as one reads other great poets, which is to say, in whatever ways their works demand—which is not the same from poet to poet, though a few basic principles are common to every case. All great writers demand to be read with care and with sympathy. With respect to the latter I need only say that in approaching these three philosophers I have presumed coherence and given the benefit of the doubt where any doubt arises, that is, I have never presumed that an apparent contradiction was unnoticed or unintended by the author; rather, I have attempted to understand contradictions as reflections of competing intentions or representations that are grounded in an underlying unity. To those who, reading this, suspect that I have conceded too much, I say only that I believe my presumptions of coherence have been borne out by my subsequent discovery of the unity I had presumed from the start—and that I would not have looked hard enough to find that unity had I not approached the texts as sympathetically and respectfully as I did. About the meaning of reading with care I can say even less, for it will depend on the particular character of the individual writing. I have attempted to be mindful of this in my inquiry and will offer reflections on the question of how to read these philosophers as we proceed.

The chapters that follow are grouped into three parts and an epilogue, preceded by Chapter 1, a sort of prologue addressing the text that somehow stands behind all else that I'll be examining in this book. That text is the *Republic*, with which both Rousseau and Nietzsche wrestle in their own works and which has a special and revealing relation with the *Symposium*, which will be the focus of my treatment of Plato. Chapter 1 is a prologue to what follows because the *Republic* is itself prologue to the texts I'll be addressing more extensively in the subsequent chapters.

Platonic eros is the subject of Part One. In the *Symposium*, Plato outlines a comprehensive and what one might call a vertically oriented account of eros: he articulates the highest or truest expression of eros and shows us how to interpret lower or defective expressions in light of that peak. Platonic eros is known to point beyond politics, toward philosophy—or, rather, *through* philosophy to the good and/or the beautiful. Yet I will try to show that Plato teaches extensively about eros *in* politics, and particularly so where he seems to many readers not to be concerned with politics at all, that is, in his treatment of various characters in the *Symposium*. Chapter 2 begins by addressing necessary preliminaries. The "first truths" that it discovers are first in the phenomenological, not the ontological, sense—that is, they are the things that first come to light when looking at Plato on eros. It is precisely these truths, though, that will give us whatever access we can hope for to those other first truths.

Having tried to prepare the way in Chapter 2, in Chapter 3 I take up the question of eros itself. "The question of eros" is of course many questions, but at bottom, like the question of "the desire to extend our being" and the question of will to power, it is one: What *is* eros? Or, since we know it is a desire, What does eros want? Plato's answer, it turns out, is multipartite and multilayered, if indeed it is a single answer at all. The focus of the first half of Chapter 3 is the teaching propounded by Socrates in the *Symposium* and the *Republic*. Not that he says the same thing in each dialogue, but what he says in these two settings does, I believe, add up to a single, coherent, and—in outline anyway—comprehensive account. Of course what Socrates says, or what he wants to teach his interlocutors in a given moment, may or may not be what Plato believes. More important, it may not be the teaching that Plato wishes to impart to all of his readers. Indeed, I argue that it *is not*, though I do think that what Socrates teaches his interlocutors is what Plato wishes to teach at least some, in fact most, of his readers. Thus I call the teaching that I reconstruct in the first half of Chapter 3 Socrates' *overt* account. The grounds for supposing that this is not in fact the whole of Plato's teaching, as well as what the other elements might be, is the subject of the second half of the chapter.

A fuller understanding of Plato's teaching, however, requires that one investigate eros as it appears in and guides living human beings. This is the task of Chapter 4, which examines the characters in the *Symposium* who not only speak about eros—or perhaps don't even speak of it—but who *act* on it within the dialogue. I refer to these figures—Apollodorus, Aristodemus, Alcibiades, and Socrates—as the dialogue's "manifest lovers." How better to learn the meaning of a desire, and how better to take account of the dramatic form of Platonic writing, than to examine that motive in action? Simply by taking note of the widely divergent characters of the men I have just named, one sees that eros manifests itself in widely divergent ways. Yet on investigating more deeply we will find that these ways can be interpreted, indeed *need* to be interpreted, as versions of a single desire and, consequently, that they need to be judged by the standard of true or perfect eros. Such a judgment, if it is not quite political in itself, has enormous political implications. For as I will show, each of the *Symposium*'s manifest lovers represents a distinct political inclination: the *eros* of each lover carries powerful and, in three of the four cases, worrisome political tendencies (and even the fourth, as the object of the others' eros, is an ambiguous influence). These tendencies, in fact, prove to be of particular relevance to our own time. So not only is the *Symposium* as political a dialogue as the *Republic,* its lessons are in some ways more urgent and needful than those of the *Republic.*

If Plato's account illuminates eros' "vertical" extremes, that is, right eros and defective eros and the relation between them, Rousseau is particularly instructive on eros' pervasiveness and multifariousness of expression and, correspondingly, on the question of how to translate the recognition of a single comprehensive good into a hierarchy of greater and lesser goods. (Plato allows for lesser goods but insists strongly on their defectiveness if not falseness: civic or demotic virtue, for example, is something less than true virtue. Rousseau, on the contrary, emphasizes the goodness of lesser goods, as seen in his praise of rustic goodness and civic virtue.) These are the themes of Chapter 5, which establishes that "the desire to extend our being" is indeed Rousseau's counterpart to Plato's eros and Nietzsche's will to power and which investigates the ways that, according to Rousseau, this desire can and cannot gain satisfaction and how people ought to be governed accordingly. "Accordingly" does not mean that Rousseau advocates that people simply be steered toward the peaks. The knowledge that would lead the best prepared to the greatest heights would lead the unprepared to abysmal depths. Like Plato and Nietzsche, he is mindful of the all too real connection between the highest and the lowest, not only theoretically but in practice as well.

The paradigmatic instance of Rousseau's caution in this regard is his relatively harsh treatment of philosophy. Although he is careful to cite exceptions, Rousseau generally paints philosophy, or at least philosoph*ers,* with a broad brush and in not very appealing colors. Nowhere does Rousseau seem more distant from Plato than in this. Yet Plato, too, offers a critique of philosophers, of false or pseudo-philosophers, even while placing the genuine philosopher at the peak of human possibility. (The same combination also appears in Nietzsche.) Indeed, the critique is a necessary part of the apology. And presumably if Plato thought that a public apology on behalf of philosophy would only strengthen the appeal of false or damaging philosophy—and thereby damage the cause of genuine philosophy—he would speak of philosophy rather more like Rousseau does. My contention is that just such considerations account for Rousseau's public stance toward philosophy, and that Rousseau regards true philosophy as a supremely good thing. Yet if these considerations prevent Rousseau from publicly endorsing philosophy, they do not prevent him from a more subtle kind of exploration and endorsement. In Chapter 6, I present a reading of book 5 of *Emile* as an essentially affirmative reply to book 5 of the *Republic*—that is, as an embrace of the psychic teaching of the latter amid, or beneath, the obvious *rejection* of the *Republic*'s ostensible political teaching. Thus does Rousseau crown his rich account of erotic development with a Platonic teaching, even if the crown is quite well hidden.

Nietzsche might seem the philosopher with whom we should begin. Not only is he nearest to us (in more ways than one), but he is also clearest and most insistent in interpreting all of life in terms of a single force, in defining good and bad in terms of this force (good being what develops or expresses power, bad being the reverse), and, accordingly, in ordering the manifold expressions of this force hierarchically. Nietzsche's clarity and insistence may or may not be virtues—certainly they depart from the practice of Plato and Rousseau, who are so much more circumspect in revealing their own comparable thoughts—but they do orient the reader's mind toward themes that define Plato's and Rousseau's projects as well as his own. Yet this philosopher who is so much nearer to us turns out to be read most effectively in light of the farthest. In ways both widely known and hardly known at all, Nietzsche seeks to take on Plato—and seeks to *rival* Plato by following Plato's way in the pursuit of a decidedly non-Platonic end. Thus one does well to approach Nietzsche and will to power after first having encountered Plato and eros in a serious way. This is especially true of *Beyond Good and Evil*, which will be the focus of my inquiry into Nietzsche.

Chapters 7 and 8 are devoted to a commentary on *Beyond Good and Evil* the purpose of which is to establish the book as Nietzsche's response, both in the aggregate and in its parts (and sometimes even subparts), to Plato's *Republic*. To state what I take to be the central thematic correspondence: as the *Republic* concerns itself with the question of the best regime, so does *Beyond Good and Evil*; and as Plato's best regime requires above all the right education and governance of eros, Nietzsche's requires the same with respect to will to power. This realization makes possible not only a deeper reading of *Beyond*

Good and Evil, which is the immediate goal of Chapters 7 and 8, but also, through an analysis presented in Chapter 9, a better grasp both of will to power and of the "thing" in which it finds fullest satisfaction, Nietzsche's good, namely, (willing) eternal recurrence of all things. (It may even make possible a deeper reading of the *Republic* and a better grasp of eros, at least if there is anything to Nietzsche's skeptical reading of Plato.) And by better understanding eternal return as the crowning good, we will be better positioned to understand goodness as such, or the goodness of all goods, as Nietzsche conceives it. With this last step, Nietzsche's political teaching, however contrary to the tenets of modern liberalism, will emerge as somewhat more humane than it is normally thought to be. And Nietzsche himself may emerge as a somewhat less forbidding figure—one might almost say, a more Platonic figure.

Critics will find my Nietzsche too "orthodox," for implicit in my reading of *Beyond Good and Evil* is the view that Nietzsche has a specifiable teaching (something contested probably by most of Nietzsche's interpreters), indeed a positive political teaching (which is contested by even more interpreters). Worse yet, I take this teaching to be based on an understanding of nature and thus not nihilistic, at least not in the sense of denying the possibility of nonarbitrary bases and standards of judgment. My Nietzsche, in fact, is formally identical to Nietzsche's Plato. In various places, including several places in *Beyond Good and Evil,* Nietzsche depicts Plato as a legislator who meant to and in fact did put an entire civilization on a certain track. I see Nietzsche as attempting nothing less himself. And since it is in the *Republic* that the grounds and meaning of Plato's legislative project are revealed, it is in *Beyond Good and Evil*—Nietzsche's own *Politeia*—in which the grounds and meaning of Nietzsche's project are revealed. Since that project is centered on the education and governance of will to power (as Plato's is centered on the education and governance of eros), an analysis of *Beyond Good and Evil* seems a good way of trying to understand will to power. Hence my decision to approach Nietzsche, and only Nietzsche, by way of a single textual commentary.[8] From

---

8. Readers might find this singular emphasis on *Beyond Good and Evil* unsatisfying for violating the demands of parallelism: my treatment of Plato deals extensively with *two* dialogues. But Nietzsche did not write a *Symposium*, at least as far as I am aware. Or perhaps I should say, he did not *complete* his *Symposium*, for, substantively if not formally, his planned *Hauptwerk, The Will to Power*, was to have given a fuller account of its subject than is available in any other work.

the standpoint of Nietzsche's postmodern legacy, my Nietzsche is indeed too orthodox. But if this is orthodoxy, it is also radicalism, for a Nietzsche with a coherent, specifiable, and constructive teaching about the soul and about politics is a Nietzsche that we need to reckon with and not someone we can admire for his critical acumen (or be scandalized by it) and then forget about. The "standard" political Nietzsche, moreover, that is, Nietzsche as mere critic, is frankly a weak critic by virtue of his hypocritical recourse to the venerable concepts and vocabulary of the philosophic tradition: that he is driven to words and ideas that his critique should have rendered out of bounds shows that his critical stance is ultimately unsustainable and therefore, again, not something we need to take too seriously. But if Nietzsche's recourse to "orthodox" words and concepts like nature and justice are not hypocritical relapses into a discredited mode of philosophy but rather part of a specifiable teaching with a positive program, then it strengthens his challenge and commends his thought to us.

Like Plato and Rousseau, Nietzsche highlights things that the others don't. Nietzsche does the most to explain and make plausible the motivating power of a single psychic force and hence the existence of a single, comprehensive good. (Will to power is *more* than a psychic force, but it *is* that.) In this he can perhaps help us understand not only his own thought but also Plato's and Rousseau's better, whether or not one accepts his assessment of his predecessors. One need not accept Nietzsche's critique of Plato or the whole of his teaching on will to power in order to learn from his insights into the links between the high and the low (e.g., the sublimation of cruelty), into pathology (e.g., the decisive role of vengefulness), and even into health (e.g., health as the affirmative-spirited deployment of great power). And of course the conflict between Nietzsche and Plato is itself a gateway to deeper understanding. That conflict, as I will try to show, centers on competing understandings of "eternity."

Chapter 10 explores some of the ways in which the three philosophers' accounts are different and alike, asking with respect to the differences from where they arise and how one might begin to judge among contending positions, and seeking in the similarities the ground for practical, political wisdom on the presumption that where three such figures agree, there is likely to be some truth. When dealing with figures spaced apart in time and viewed as initiators of new epochs, one might be expected to seek a trajectory that helps make sense of their work. That is a very problematic demand, not least because the legacies of these three philosophers have often gone far afield from the original teachings. Nevertheless, Chapter 10's analysis yields a few observations on this count. It might be useful, though, to offer at this juncture one observation on the subject of trajectory. Not, however, a trajectory that describes the relations between the three philosophers' projects, but one that is described by each of them individually—and one that is perhaps their most basic similarity: as I read them, Plato, Rousseau, and Nietzsche each seek to ascend to nature, both in thought and in the way one lives, or perhaps more precisely, in thought and *therein* in the way one lives.

It is neither a pro forma disclaimer nor an attempt to escape criticism for me to say that the following studies are not comprehensive but rather essays, attempts, to gain some insight into an issue of real importance—*general* importance. Specialization is necessary, and the following chapters are a series of specialized inquiries into a handful of texts. My hope, however, is that, as a combined whole, these inquiries will point us toward the heart of things and allow progress toward a richer understanding of politics and life. This, too, is necessary. That one may not know the good does not change the fact that all political activity is based on some understanding of the good. And that one may not know the true character of eros does not lessen eros' political importance.

Modesty is a virtue for scholars. But the central demand of scholarly modesty, it seems to me, is not that one look away from important questions but that one recognize one's own limits by always questioning oneself and treating one's findings as provisional. This I have tried to do, and I don't imagine that I have even put the questions I have addressed on their proper footing, let alone settled anything. My greatest hopes are that I have helped clarify the questions and offered up a few rough insights. Perhaps, though, modesty in this case is not so remarkable a thing. For if modesty comes most naturally in the face of the divine and the infinite, it may come almost as naturally—certainly it should—to one who inquires among divine minds on the politics of infinity.

1

THE *REPUBLIC* AS PROLOGUE

If it's possible to regard the Western philosophic tradition as a series of footnotes to Plato, then it's at least as plausible to regard the history of *political* philosophy as a series of footnotes to the *Republic*. And no more so than where political philosophy looks at the soul.

In the present study our attention will be given more to the footnotes than to the *Republic* itself. We begin with that dialogue, though, because a certain awareness of it—of what it does and what it is thought to do—is useful for understanding the texts that will be occupying us. Nietzsche means to accomplish in and with *Beyond Good and Evil* something comparable to what Plato did (as Nietzsche sees it) in and with the *Republic*. Thus Nietzsche orders his book in accordance with the architecture and dimensions of Plato's. Or so I will try to establish. Rousseau gives us to understand at the start of what he took to be his best and greatest book that he regards the *Republic* as a revered source and a kind of model. What the *Republic* has done in the public sphere, he tells us, his *Emile* will do in the adjoining private or domestic sphere. Yet it becomes clear before long that the two spheres more than adjoin, they overlap; and so Rousseau, too, offers a direct response to Plato: he propounds a teaching that both rivals and supports the teaching of the *Republic*. Even Plato's *Symposium*, the major focus of Part One, can be fruitfully approached by way of a preceding encounter with the *Republic*, the depths of that shorter, lovelier dialogue, including its political depths, coming all the more clearly to light by virtue of first having looked at eros through the eyes of the city, as the *Republic* leads one to do. The *Symposium* isn't a response to the *Republic*, let alone a footnote; rather, the two dialogues are complementary. Each in some vital ways completes the other by highlighting what is only quietly present in it. The *Symposium* is the primary Platonic document with respect to the soul-force it calls eros. The *Symposium*, as I will try to show, is the dialogue that affords the most direct and probably the most comprehensive insight into eros. But if the *Symposium* is first in this sense, our approach to it will nevertheless be aided by a prior if brief reckoning with the *Republic*, which is primary in a different sense: the *Republic*, it seems to me, shows us eros as it most typically comes to light objectively, that is, for those who set out to understand it and who are not already intoxicated with or otherwise invested in it. It may seem odd for a dialogue whose perspective is so thoroughly political to do this. Isn't eros an apolitical thing? And doesn't the political perspective therefore distort our view of it? It may indeed, but only if our typical view of eros is already distorted. For the *Republic*'s political perspective is in key respects *our* perspective, the perspective of political beings.

To be more precise: The *Republic* looks at eros from a political perspective, from the perspective of the city and its concerns, casting light thereby not only on eros but also on the particular and partial character of the political perspective itself. The political perspective as it regards the soul is notable for three features in particular. First, it tends to conceive of the soul in almost tangible terms, using physical language, most especially the language of structure or parts—or, to use a more political term that Socrates himself uses, factions. Hence its conception of the soul as a tripartite structure. As evidence that the structural or tripartite view belongs specifically to the political perspective, consider that in the *Republic* the soul is at first viewed as embracing multiple *forms* and is only said to have *parts* once the focus of the conversation has become the action of these forms or parts and the relations among them, that is, when the conversation has turned to intrapsychic *politics*.[1] Second, the political perspective tends to regard eros with suspicion and a certain obtuseness on account of eros' antinomianism and its connection to the body, the body being the one thing that will always resist the city's attempts to achieve the unity that it sees as its greatest good. Both these features can be seen as the natural outgrowth of the third feature, namely, that the political perspective is, *essentially*, a *thymotic* or spirited perspective. What this means will become clear only as we proceed with our examination of the *Republic*.

The *Republic* also shows us the limits of the political perspective and effectively points us beyond them. This is the pedagogical benefit of its partiality. After showing us the soul from the political or structural perspective— precisely *by* showing us the soul from the political perspective and therewith

---

1. Compare 435c and 437d to 436a and 439d–441c; the latter is the famous demonstration that the soul is tripartite.

the limits of that perspective—the *Republic* indicates what lies beyond it, what lies beyond—or better, *within*—the soul's structure: namely, its erotic essence, its permeation or saturation by eros. (By "after" I do not mean to suggest that Plato proceeds in a linear fashion from structure to dynamics—though there is some truth to that—but that our learning from the dialogue is apt to proceed in this direction.)

The three features of the *Republic*'s political or thymotic perspective on the soul will structure this chapter's exploration of the dialogue. We will look first at the structural perspective and what it does and does not reveal about the soul; then at the outlines of eros as they come to light in the dialogue; and finally at *thymos* and its surprising "true identity" (surprising from the political perspective, at least). In each case Socrates relates plausible insights from which we, like his interlocutors, can learn. But in each case a teaching also emerges that is contrary to the starting point or what appear to be the presuppositions of the inquiry. These teachings emerge, in fact, from recognizing and understanding the *inadequacies* of the starting points or presuppositions. (1) By exploring the soul from a structural perspective, the *Republic* not only reveals things that lend themselves (perhaps exclusively) to structural representation but also helps us see the import of that which resists structural characterization, namely, the soul's *dynamics*. Thus, both the virtues and the limits of the structural perspective are illustrative and worthy of note. (2) Something comparable is true of the dialogue's treatment of eros. I have already noted the *Republic*'s suspicion of the body. This suspicion leads to a distortion of eros, not only from the standpoint of other dialogues but also from the standpoint of common experience. To be precise, the distortion lies not in what the *Republic* teaches about eros but rather in what *Socrates says* about it in the dialogue. This is an important distinction, for the dialogue speaks not only through Socrates' explicit remarks but also through the context of what he says. Socrates' behavior in the dialogue, and his success at stimulating and directing the interest and even the longing of his young interlocutors, indicate an understanding of eros that is broader and deeper than the one he explicitly articulates. From this (and from his treatment of eros in other dialogues) we may conclude that his underestimation of the body in this dialogue is a deliberate pedagogical tactic, and that he, or rather Plato, means to instruct as much by the inadequacies of Socrates' explicit arguments as by the arguments themselves. As I have said, the broader and deeper understanding of eros is more fully available from the *Symposium*, which is why that dialogue and not the *Republic* will be the focus of my inquiry into Platonic eros. But the *Republic*'s treatment of eros is still a useful starting point for the reasons I have indicated, and for yet another reason: there is much in Socrates' explicit account that is *not* distorted. In particular, the formal elements of the account—regarding the multiplicity of eros' objects and the singularity of its aim, for example—seem to me consistent with what emerges from a more comprehensive and balanced account. (3) Finally, with its explicit analysis of *thymos*, with its embrace of the thymotic perspective, and with its thymotic drama (e.g., Socrates' successful appeals to pride and noble longings), the *Republic* sheds much light on this most consequential psychopolitical force. And not only on this force: for reasons that will only become clear as we examine *thymos*, reasons unknown to *thymos* itself, an analysis of *thymos* will shed light on eros as well.

THE TRIPARTITE SOUL

Few philosophic devices have proved as influential or enduring as the tripartition of the soul in Plato's *Republic*. The division of the *psychē* into the rational, spirited, and desiring parts, first introduced by Socrates in book 4, established the terms of psychological thought not only for the remainder of the *Republic* but for a great part of Western thought even to the present day. Perhaps even more important than the particular content of this schema has been the mode of analysis it exemplifies. With Plato began a tradition of considering the soul as a differentiated structure whose respective parts perform specific, assignable functions.[2] But, as I have just indicated, what has proven so influential among subsequent thinkers is radically qualified by Plato himself. Plato sometimes presented his psychological thought by means of structural models and metaphors; even so, we would be mistaken to believe that any such structural representation is sufficient to convey—or was meant to convey—all the major elements of his psychological thought. The *Republic*'s tripartite model of the soul has significant virtues, not all of them imme-

2. It may well be that Plato wasn't the first to treat the soul in this way—he is said by Cicero to have borrowed this approach from the Pythagoreans—but it is surely Plato's treatment of the soul from which so much subsequent thought has taken its bearings. See Cicero, *Tusculanae Disputationes*. (The Pythagoreans are said to have divided the soul into only two parts, one rational and the other non-rational. This may call to mind Socrates' own bipartite division of the soul earlier in the *Republic*; see 410–12.)

diately apparent. Nevertheless, and inevitably, it fails to capture key elements of Socrates' account of the soul, an account that serves as the basis of his pedagogy during the long night's discussion and that thus informs the action of the dialogue as much as its speeches.

Socrates prefaces his tripartition of the soul in book 4 with the caveat that what follows should be understood as both provisional and incomplete: "know well, Glaucon, that in my opinion, we'll never get a precise grasp of it [i.e., the question of the soul's unity and diversity, or perhaps simply the soul] on the basis of procedures such as we're now using in the argument. There is another longer and further road leading to it" (435d).[3] Whether this further road is traveled to its end in this dialogue seems doubtful, for it is identified with the study of the Good (504aff), and we never hear more than *images* of Socrates' *opinion* of the Good (506b–e). And there is further reason to doubt that the dialogue's conclusions ever entirely cease to be provisional. (See, for example, 612a3–4.) But if we do not reach the end of the road, we certainly do make considerable progress. The tripartite model of book 4 is supplemented and corrected, most notably in book 9 (580d–592b). Whereas in book 4 desire seems to belong only to the third or lowest part of the soul, the part named for it, in book 9 each of the three parts of the soul is said to have its own distinctive desire and pleasure (580d). Whereas the problem of intrapsychic faction seems in book 4 to be limited to faction between the various parts, which limits the possibilities of faction to only three, in book 9 the possibility arises of faction *within* the parts, which opens an infinity of factional possibilities. (Only the desiring part is flatly said to be subject to internal conflict, but there are indications that the spirited part, too, is subject to its own internal factionalism;[4] as for the reasoning part, although I am not aware of any explicit reference to conflict within *it*, the dialogue nevertheless offers numerous examples of contradictory thinking.) And whereas the relations between the three parts are initially presented as rather unproblematic in book 4—most notably with the suggestion that spiritedness is reason's natural ally (440b)—book 9 more openly acknowledges the difficulties faced

---

3. Also see Socrates' earlier indication that the conversation in book 4 is taking place in the intellectual equivalent of darkness (427d, 432d).

4. One such indication occurs at 590b, where Socrates, having previously likened the spirited part of the soul to a lion, refers to it as "the lion-like *and snake-like* part." For much more on the different aspects of spiritedness, see Craig, *The War Lover*.

by a would-be masterful reasoning part. But in all of these cases the discussion in book 9 only corrects the earlier discussion; it does not refute or repudiate it. The tripartite model is revised and added on to; it is not scrapped.[5] And in fact the very insufficiencies of the discussion in book 4 that are made good in book 9 are quietly acknowledged in book 4 itself, where the opening proviso is supplemented by several subtle indications of what, specifically, is deficient in the account given there.[6] All of which suggests that, whatever their insufficiencies, the tripartite model and the structural perspective that is its source are useful and perhaps even necessary for understanding the soul. And it hardly matters if the tripartite model is only metaphoric and if its virtues are "only" pedagogical: it may well be—indeed, the dialogue seems to suggest—that metaphor or the language of myth is necessary to psychological exploration,[7] and if the tripartite model is useful for educating Glaucon and the others, it will more than likely prove useful in educating most of the rest of us. What, then, are the virtues of the structural perspective?

Perhaps the first virtue of the structural perspective, or at least of structural language, is that it facilitates the recognition and articulation, however inexact, of quantities or magnitudes. There is a sense throughout the dialogue, a sense that probably accords with most people's experience, that some people are, in some basic way, "larger" than others, that they seem to experience life more intensely or act with greater verve and with more of a certain kind of energy than others. Socrates suggests, for example, that the soul of one who is fit for the philosophic life must be of a certain size and strength, that the capable candidate for philosophy must be of "befitting greatness" or magnificent (*megaloprepeia*, 487a, 490c, 494b, 536a), and that the city's guardians must be "great-spirited" (375c). These examples indicate the utility and even the necessity of *physical* language, if not structural language, in speaking of the soul. (Recourse to physical language pervades our everyday speech, as when one speaks of "large" appetites or "explosive" anger or "powerful" and

---

5. David Roochnik aptly compares book 9's correction of book 4's account to a Hegelian *Aufhebung*, a sublation or transcendence that preserves the earlier account even as it negates it. See Roochnik, "Irony and Accessibility."

6. One finds indications, for example, that spiritedness is not in fact always reason's ally (440d); that the spirited part may be the source of more than just those emotions, such as anger, whose connection with spirit is obvious (439e); that spiritedness itself may be divisible into two parts (441c); and that the soul may in fact have more than three parts (443d).

7. Regarding the need for myth and mythological language in order to discover and express psychological truths, see Segal, "'The Myth Was Saved.'"

"penetrating" intellect. If we typically fail to appreciate that such language is borrowed from the physical realm, that only proves how automatic and, probably, how necessary is our recourse to physical metaphor when speaking of psychological phenomena.) Physical language, of course, is not always structural language. But for the same reasons that physical language is useful and even necessary, the language of structure is particularly useful, especially among interlocutors with no precise vocabulary for energy quanta. And the tripartite structure in particular allows one to speak of the relative magnitudes of each of the soul's "parts."[8]

Another virtue of dividing the soul into separate "parts" is that such a schema makes it easier to avoid the mistake of conflating psychic activities that are similar but not quite the same—for example, desire and will. Early in the discussion devoted to determining whether the soul is in fact tripartite, Socrates mistakenly conflates these two.[9] The mistake is effectively corrected by his introducing the soul's spirited part into the discussion. Only then is it possible to distinguish clearly between them. But the mistake is revealing (and is no doubt deliberate) for precisely that reason: until the third part is introduced—until *thymos* is distinguished from *epithymia*—our efforts to understand our inner lives are hampered by the failure to see important distinctions, a failure all the greater when the purpose of those efforts is to rank activities and experiences in an effort to determine the makings of a good life.

Something more than just a correct ranking of activities and experiences is necessary to achieve the good life, however, and it is just this something that reveals what is perhaps most useful about the tripartite model and the structural perspective generally. Like the city, the soul is subject to faction; and just as is the case for the former, so for the latter, too: faction is the primary source of ills and harmony is the essential condition of health, or

---

8. It should be clear from reading the dialogue that references to this or that "part" (*meros*) or "form" (*eidos*) of the soul should indeed be taken metaphorically, that is, that these words refer to functions or principles of action and not to material substances. Yet even such metaphorical usuage reflects, and serves, a certain way of conceiving of the soul. For analyses of Plato's use of such language not only in the *Republic* but throughout his corpus, see Robinson, *Plato's Psychology;* and Zakopoulos, *Plato on Man.* For an extensive list of examples that would seem to confirm "the—seemingly inescapable—necessity of our speaking and thinking of intelligible but insensible things [i.e., psychological phenomena] in terms of the perceptible realm," along with a brief discussion of the implications of this necessity for the philosophic quest, see Craig, *The War Lover,* pp. 85–86.

9. Craig, *The War Lover,* pp. 86–87.

justice. So the city believes, at least. Also, and again like the city, the source of the soul's factionalism is not that the separate factions exist or that they want different things but rather that they each want the same thing, namely, rule. The soul is a polity whose parts interact in ways that are analogous to the ways in which the city's different classes and factions interact. This is evident both from the city–soul analogy and from the political (which also means, inevitably, military) language Socrates uses to describe various psychic phenomena.[10] If the psyche really is a polity—if it is beset by contending factions, and if its health depends on overcoming this contention—then it calls for the political language, the *structural* language, of separate and contending "parts."

For all that the tripartite model expresses, however, there is much that it cannot represent, at least not well. Nor, it bears repeating, is there reason to think that it was meant to do more than it does. (When I say that the tripartite model fails to represent everything about the soul, I mean that it is incomplete vis-à-vis Socrates' teaching, not that Socrates' or Plato's teaching is incomplete vis-à-vis the soul.[11]) One possibility that the structural perspective, with its thymotic presuppositions, seems incapable of entertaining is that factionalism under some circumstances might be healthful. But chief among the elements that elude adequate representation by the tripartite model is eros, the soul's preeminent and pervasive energic presence, which, being energic, does not admit of structural representation.[12]

The tripartite model serves well to illustrate the soul as factional battleground. And it would be much more nearly adequate as a representation of the soul if this battling were comprehensible without reference to anything beyond itself. But in fact the contending parts do more than just either battle or get along, and they seek more than just rule or order. Socrates' is an erotic psychology: not just one but all three parts of the soul have desires (580d). All

---

10. Political language is applied to the soul throughout the dialogue, from Cephalus' reminder that eros can be a savage "master" (329c–d) to the mention of intrapsychic "battle" in book 10's renewed discussion of poetry (603c–d).

11. Other commentators have taken the opposing view, criticizing Plato for the failings of the structural model. See, for example, Annas, *An Introduction to Plato's Republic*, p. 125.

12. My concern in the following section is to illuminate some of what remains dark from a strictly structural perspective, not to catalogue all the interpretive limits and paradoxes presented by that perspective. There is clearly much more to be said on the latter than I shall be able to say, especially regarding what Plato may have meant for those limits and paradoxes to signify.

three, in fact, can be essentially characterized by what they *love* (581a–c). Thus their respective desires for rule are incomprehensible without reference to these objects of eros. The intrapsychic politics that the tripartite model represents so well arise at least in part from apolitical desires. And if each of the parts is erotic, so is the soul as a whole, and perhaps especially when justice (i.e., healthy harmony) has been established within it. The significance of eros emerges most clearly when we consider the two largest-souled figures of the dialogue, the two who embody more eros than anyone else—that is, the philosopher and the tyrant.

Eros is disparaged throughout the *Republic*. From book 1, where it emerges on the telling of Cephalus but with the invoked authority of Sophocles as "a sort of frenzied and savage master" (328c), through book 9, where it is said to characterize the tyrant and to be a tyrant itself (573b–579d), eros is primarily associated with unreason and injustice. Yet amid this disparagement of eros for its injustice, the philosopher, the preeminently *just* man, emerges as essentially erotic. Or at least he is described as such by Socrates. (The odd feature of the philosopher's eros, as described by Socrates, is its evident lack of connection to the body. That his interlocutors apparently accept this depiction without hesitation is testimony to the character of the political or thymotic perspective from which they are viewing eros. Evidently the city *can* embrace eros, but only if eros is detached from its origins in the personal and antinomian body.) The two human types portrayed as most opposite each other in terms of ruling parts of the soul (the philosopher being ruled by a well-developed intellectual part, the tyrant by the lowest kind of desires) are shown to have a deep, premoral similarity—a similarity, moreover, that is essential to their moral or "structural" opposition. The philosopher's eroticism is treated at length in books 5 and 6. It is said of the philosopher that he "loves" whole classes of things and that he "desires" wisdom. (See, for example, 475b–c; also see 485b–e, where Socrates says of those with philosophic natures that "they are always in love [*erosi*] with that learning which discloses to them something of the being that *is* always and does not wander about, driven by generation and decay.") The same erotic words are used to describe the tyrant. He is said to be relentlessly driven by desires; Socrates describes the tyrant's soul as a prisoner oppressed by "a tyranny . . . established by love" (574e). In their shared eroticism the philosopher and the tyrant stand together on the other side of a divide from such comparatively unerotic types as the democratic man. They are animated by "their sense of their radical incompleteness and their longing for wholeness."[13] Which longing, in turn, leads them to especially intense passion and single-mindedness.[14]

There is a strong suggestion in the *Republic* that the basis of the kinship between the philosopher and the tyrant, their shared eroticism—or at least the capacity for it—is inborn. Everyone has a certain degree of eros or eroticism within him- or herself. This is implied by the application of the tripartite structure to all souls and by Socrates' claim that everyone experiences the lawless—which is to say, undeniably erotic—desires (572b). But to have a measure of eros in one's soul is not necessarily to be what we would normally characterize as an erotic person, any more than the presence of *thymos* in all our souls makes us all "great-spirited." What seems to distinguish especially erotic individuals from unerotic ones is quantity: the former have more eros, or greater desire, than the latter.

According to Socrates' account in the *Republic*, this quantitative difference translates into a qualitative one. More accurately, it translates into a special and limited range of qualitative options or potentials. We are given to understand that one who begins life with an erotic nature is destined for one kind of qualitative (erotic) extreme or another, either very good or very bad. To have a great capacity for good is also to have a great capacity for evil,[15] and there seems to be precious little room for compromise, as the following exchange between Socrates and Adeimantus suggests:

> "Concerning every seed or thing that grows, whether from the earth or animals," I said, "we know that the more vigorous it is, the more it is deficient in its own properties when it doesn't get the food, climate, or place suitable to it. For surely bad is more opposed to good than to not-good."
>
> "Of course."
>
> "So I suppose it is reasonable that the best nature comes off worse than an ordinary one from an inappropriate rearing."

---

13. Allan Bloom, "Interpretive Essay," in Bloom, trans., *The Republic of Plato*, p. 424. Bloom's characterization is as unexceptionable a shorthand characterization of eros as I have encountered.

14. Its veiling of the kinship between the philosopher and the tyrant might well be another virtue, a politic and therefore a political virtue, of the structural perspective. (Compare to Nietzsche's striking insistence that the philosopher is himself a tyrant [*BGE* 9]).

15. Love may be beyond good and evil, as Nietzsche claims (*BGE* 153). But good and evil are always concerns of the city, its primary categories of judgment. (It should also be noted, lest such a statement be interpreted too idealistically, that good and evil are also *determined* by the city.)

"Yes, it is."

"Won't we say for souls too, Adeimantus," I said, "that, similarly, those with the best natures become exceptionally bad when they get bad instruction? Or do you suppose an ordinary nature is the source of great injustices and unmixed villainy? Don't you suppose, rather, that it's a lusty one corrupted by its rearing, while a weak nature will never be the cause of great things either good or bad?"

"Yes," he said, "that's the case."

"Well, then, I suppose that if the nature we set down for the philosopher chances on a suitable course of learning, it will necessarily grow and come to every kind of virtue; but if it isn't sown, planted, and nourished in what's suitable, it will come to all the opposite, unless one of the gods chances to assist it." (491d–492a)

That "the best natures" are "lusty one[s]"—that it is eros which distinguishes the philosopher and the tyrant on the one hand from those with more "ordinary" natures on the other—is in itself enough to instruct readers of the *Republic* in the pressing need to understand eros. How does eroticism come to manifest itself in such utterly divergent ways? Also, what is the role of spiritedness, also a force in the soul (as well as one of the three parts), in the psychologies of these extreme human types? And how should we understand the relation between eros and spiritedness? We turn now to the dialogue's treatment of the soul's dynamics in themselves.

EROS IN THE *REPUBLIC*

Although eros figures prominently in the *Republic*, it is never taken up as a subject in itself. It is never subjected to Socratic dialectic or problematized in any other way—not for the interlocutors, at least. Yet precisely by looming so large among Socrates' *answers* to his interlocutors, eros suggests itself to Plato's readers as a question.

What Is Eros?

As seen in the tyrant and the philosopher respectively, eros in the *Republic* is both bodily and more than bodily—indeed, bodily and nonbodily. How can it accommodate such radically different meanings?

A useful starting point in ascertaining the meaning of eros is the psychoanalytic distinction between the aim of a drive or longing and its object(s). "The object is that from which the attraction emanates or which the lover finds attractive; the aim is that toward which the instinct of eros strives."[16] On the basis of Socrates' treatment of eros in the *Republic* we may understand eros to be a sort of force or drive that is characterized by—indeed, whose every version is characterized by—a single aim, but that can manifest itself in desires for a multitude of objects ranging (at least) from the sexual to the contemplative. The aim of eros is a kind of wholeness or unity. The lover senses that the object of his or her desire promises "comprehensive satisfaction."[17] And an object always *is* present in any "instance" of eros: eros is not simply an intense desire or need; it is "a striving for wholeness or perfection, a combination of poverty and contrivance, of need *mitigated by a presentiment of completeness.*"[18] And there can be no such presentiment except where there is an object of desire. Although eros is not explicitly characterized in terms of "wholeness" or "perfection" or "comprehensive satisfaction" in the *Republic,* such an understanding can be discerned at the core of each of the particular kinds of eros. (Socrates suggests the same thing somewhat more explicitly in the *Symposium,* as we will see.)

What is the specific character of the wholeness that is sought? Or, rather, to begin with, what is the character of the seeking? (These are separate questions. What eros ultimately or *really* wants is one thing; what it *thinks* it wants, or what we think we want, may be, and in fact usually *is,* something else.) Socrates' account in the *Republic* suggests that whatever the specific object(s) of eros, the character of its seeking is acquisitive and expansionist. Eros seeks wholeness not through constriction, mastery or homogenization but through the possession or incorporation of more and more objects of desire (or else through the more and more complete possession or incorporation of the same

---

16. See Santas, *Plato and Freud,* p. 31; also see 52 n. 31, for an explanation of why it is not anachronistic to apply the terminology of "aim" and "object" to Plato. My use of psychoanalytic terminology does not imply a Freudian interpretation of Plato or the soul.

17. The phrase is Jacob Howland's; see his *The Republic: The Odyssey of Philosophy,* p. 38. His characterization is worth quoting in full: "The root meaning of *eros* is sexual desire; more broadly, *eros* designates other kinds of passionate desires as well. Just as the depths of human sexual desire contain more than mere lust, so that *eros* is often translated as 'love,' *eros* in its distinctly human forms transcends mere appetite. *Eros* is definitive of the human condition: it is not a specific, discrete desire of a part of the soul or body, like thirst, but a mysterious longing of body and soul as a whole for whatever it is that will provide us with comprehensive satisfaction."

18. Rosen, "The Role of Eros in Plato's *Republic,*" p. 453; emphasis added.

object of desire). Eros seeks wholeness not through elimination or control of desire but through the *satisfaction* of desire, and such satisfaction always entails the acquisition of an object of desire.[19] Both the tyrant and the philosopher, the two preeminent erotic types, are characterized by their longing to have more, to expand the realm of their possessions. Each, moreover, believes or senses that in *having* what is wanted he will *be* more—not simply in the sense of rank, but in a more quantitative sense: satisfaction of erotic desire promises a fullness or plenitude of felt being.[20] What distinguishes the tyrant and the philosopher from each other are the particular objects of this shared longing. What the philosopher erotically desires is knowledge and truth, or at least the sight of the truth (475e), objects through which he seeks (and attains) greater being.[21] What the tyrant erotically desires is the satisfaction of perverse

19. The acquisition is by and for oneself, even if the goods one seeks can be shared, and *are* shared, with others. Eros always involves an object, an other, and the lover is often prepared to sacrifice for the sake of the beloved. Nevertheless, being eros, its primary concern is for one's own wholeness or comprehensive satisfaction, which means that a sacrifice for the sake of the beloved is, in the end, not really a sacrifice at all. That all goods are desired ultimately for the sake of one's *own* good is also one of the major themes of the *Lysis*, where it is perhaps highlighted more than it is in the *Republic*; see 218c–220e. For a fine analysis, see Bolotin, *Plato's Dialogue on Friendship*, pp. 159–76. For that matter, even the lowest objects of erotic desire, those which clearly can be possessed only by one person, are possessed at least in part through knowledge and sight. What varies as one "ascends" or "descends" among eros' objects are (1) the degree to which the objects can be shared without compromising their erotic worth and (2) the degree to which the object is possessed through knowledge and sight. The latter variable is the determinant of the former.

20. This emphasis on acquisition, on being-through-having, seems to be linked to the *Republic*'s political or thymotic perspective. As we shall see in Part One, this emphasis is offset in the *Symposium* by a quieter but powerful countervailing emphasis on the lover's yielding to and even in a sense dissolving into the beloved.

21. One is tempted to say that wisdom, too, is an object of the philosopher's eros, and perhaps it is. We are never told that it is, however; and the very term *philo*sophos should give us pause. As we saw above, cognates of "eros" are used in association with "that learning which discloses to them [i.e., to those with philosophic natures] something of the being that *is* always and does not wander about, driven by generation and decay" (485a–b; also see 490a–b). As far as I am aware, the closest we get to an "eros" of "sophia" is in Socrates' reiteration of the "third wave" in book 6: neither our city nor regime nor a man will become perfect, he says, until either philosophers take charge, "or a true erotic passion [*alethinos eros*] for true philosophy [or true love of wisdom; *alethines philosophias*] flows from some divine inspiration into the sons of those who hold power or the office of king, or into the fathers themselves" (499b–c; also see 501d). Some scholars have concluded that wisdom *is* an object of eros for Plato. Craig, citing the erotic language and imagery with which Socrates describes the philosopher's love of truth and of that which *is*, finds in the *Republic* "repeated hints that *philia* for *sophia* entails—and may even essentially be—a *sublimation of eros*" (Craig, *The War Lover*, p. 54; emphasis in the original). And Laurence Lampert concludes that "for Plato," as for Nietzsche, "'philosophy' could be thought a misnomer: Sophia demands not philia but eros; the lovers of wisdom are the supreme erotics." Lampert, *Nietzsche and Modern Times*, p. 324.

bodily and egoic appetites, though strictly speaking the *Republic* defines the tyrant by enslavement to bodily appetite alone. (That the tyrant's lawless bodily appetites are rooted in the appeal of lawlessness itself and hence in some kind of will to power or longing to transcend limitations, i.e., in what I have called egoic appetites, may well be implied—indeed, I'd say it's strongly implied—but it is not stated. True to form, the *Republic*'s critique of eros focuses on the body—even when that means ignoring legitimate nonbodily grounds of critique.) Moreover, the respective desires of each of them are never permanently satisfied. They never stop desiring—which is to say, they never stop being erotic. Eros does not transcend itself.[22]

That the philosopher and the tyrant, the most just and unjust of men, are both intensely erotic underscores as powerfully as possible the moral ambiguity of eros. But this ambiguity is even more complex and problematic than we have yet seen. Socrates indicates that an individual has not ceased to be at moral risk after he has started down the right path. Even "the naturally right kind of love [eros]," that is, a moderate and musical love of what is orderly and fine (403a), is vulnerable to corruption by that which is "mad or akin to licentiousness." The same individual in whom "the right kind of love" is present remains susceptible to the wrong kinds. (Note, however, that what is called "the right kind of love" in book 3 [403a] proves to be right only from the city's perspective. As I will argue in Part One, from the most comprehensive perspective only philosophic eros is right eros. Whether they who have ascended to philosophy remain subject to corruption is not clear.) Eros, we learn from the *Republic*, is plastic, or, to employ Socrates' own metaphor, divertable (485d). It can be corrupted and so cause moral decay, as is indicated by the role of the Nuptial Number in the decline of kingship (546a–47a). And it can be improved, or sublimated. The latter can be seen in the action of the

---

22. The philosopher-kings of the middle books of the *Republic do* seem to transcend eros, if indeed they were ever erotic at all: they seem to achieve such knowledge (and wisdom) that they no longer stand in need of it. These beings, however, are clearly fantastic: more godlike than human, they have no basis in the dialogue's subsequent portrayals of the philosophic quest and need only be contrasted with the palpably (albeit ambiguously) erotic Socrates. (The question of Socrates' eros will be addressed below, both in this chapter and, more extensively, in Chapter 4.) For somewhat disparate interpretations that nevertheless agree on the deliberate unrealism of the portrayal of the philosopher-kings, see Howland, *The Republic*, pp. 116–17 and 148–49; Rosen, "The Role of Eros in Plato's *Republic*," p. 466; Hyland, "Plato's Three Waves and the Question of Utopia"; M. P. Nichols, "The *Republic*'s Two Alternatives," 252–74; and idem, "Spiritedness and Philosophy in Plato's *Republic*." Many more commentators, however, have accepted the portrayal of the philosopher-kings as a serious even if perhaps unreachable goal.

dialogue: young men whose eros had been directed to spectacle and perhaps appetitive gratification at the beginning of the evening are soon enticed by dialectic. Howland puts it well: "By giving free reign to speech about erotic satisfaction, Socrates has allowed philosophic desire to grow out of prephilosophic eros."[23] And not only can eros itself be improved, but it also proves to be the means by which the individual and perhaps even the city are improved, as Socrates indicates at the culmination of his discussion of musical education: "Surely musical matters should end in love matters [*erotika*] that concern the fair [or the beautiful and noble]" (403c). For all its dangers, eros is also a lever—as far as we know, the only lever—by which one can be elevated to the noble. But first it must itself ascend.

Sublimation

Socrates' portrayal of the soul in the *Republic* includes an appreciation of the limits of desire—limits imposed not by qualitative constraints (i.e., not by an inability to maintain certain *kinds* of desires), but by quantitative realities. The soul has only so much force. Hence the direction of its force, of its eros, toward one object necessarily reduces the amount of eros available for others: "we surely know that when someone's desires incline strongly to some one thing, they are therefore weaker with respect to the rest, like a stream that has been channeled off in that other direction" (485d). This sort of channeling, when directed "upward,"[24] might fairly be characterized as "sublimation."[25]

---

23. *The Republic*, p. 39. Howland, however, sees Socrates as first provoking and only then channeling the eros of his interlocutors, rather than channeling that which already was awake, as I have suggested. That Socrates' young interlocutors were already erotically enlivened is suggested by their eagerness to view the festival of Bendis, whose celebration, as Eva Brann puts it, "is to culminate that night in a torch-race and an 'all-nighter' [328a8], an orgiastic affair which the young men are clearly waiting to join." Brann, *The Music of the Republic*, p. 144.

24. A word about my use of vertical descriptors. "Higher" objects of eros are those, such as the *eidē*, that yield the lover more of the satisfaction that eros seeks. "Lower" objects are the reverse. But why speak of "high" and "low" or "upward" and "downward" instead of, say, "true" and "false" or "real" and "fake"? Because this is how most of us think about these things—and how Socrates, perhaps in recognition of this fact, speaks about them (see, e.g., the vertically oriented images of the Sun, the Divided Line, and the Cave). *Why* this is the case is an interesting question that I cannot pursue here, except to suggest that it may arise from—certainly it is consistent with—the political (or moral or thymotic) perspective and its penchant for ranking and hierarchy.

25. Although "sublimation" often signifies the upward channeling of something that is by nature gross or low (as it does for Freud), the word can also refer to upward channeling of that which by nature ought to be high. In its broadest sense it denotes the phenomenon of upward

Despite the absence of an equivalent term in the *Republic*, the word seems fitting to describe the education of eros as described by Plato.

The tyrannic man, too, undergoes a channeling within his soul. And, just as with the philosopher, this channeling concentrates eros in a single direction. As Socrates tells it, the process whereby an erotic man becomes a tyrannic one involves the "dread enchanters and tyrant-makers . . . contriv[ing] to implant some love in him—a great winged drone—to be the leader of the idle desires that insist on all available resources being distributed to them" (572e). This drone, this single love, draws to itself all the energy and longing that had been attached to the other desires. The concentrated channeling of eros in the tyrant is not directed upward, however, and is therefore not appropriately conceived of as sublimation (unless perhaps we think of it as negative sublimation). Sublimation can be understood as a kind of transcendence. As already noted, however, it is a transcendence *by* eros, not *of* it. What is left behind are lower objects of desire. The true aim of eros does not change; Rather, its manifestations, its objects, are displaced by "higher" ones—by the *eidê*.[26]

We have been observing that, on Socrates' account in the *Republic*, eros has a single aim but many objects. The case of the philosopher, though, reveals that we must amend that formula: however numerous its objects, eros as Socrates depicts it in the *Republic* has a limited number of proper or true objects, indeed, in the deepest sense just *one* true object. That object is the Good: "this is what every soul pursues and for the sake of which it does everything" (505d–e). Socrates never specifically identifies the Good as *eros'* object; but surely the universality of his claim ("*every* soul," "*everything*") includes eros. How, though, can one square the claim that eros has a single object with the observation that the objects of the philosopher's eros are plural, that is, the *eidê* or forms? The answer would seem to be that objects of

---

channeling without any presupposition that the lower is either the truer or the more natural state of desire.

26. The classic statement of the process of sublimation appears not in the *Republic* but in Socrates' account of Diotima's discourse on love in the *Symposium* (210a–212b), which I shall treat extensively in Part One. A large part of my treatment will be devoted to examining features of that account that depart from Socrates' treatment of eros in the *Republic*. But the outlines of that account, at least "on the surface," square with and lend support to the account Socrates gives in the *Republic*. Among the features of the *Symposium*'s account that seem to support and elaborate the account in the *Republic* are that eros ascends to successively higher objects and that the ascent is accomplished by the apprehension, by reason, of successively higher or truer or more complete instances of beauty.

eros are satisfying to the extent that they are close to or participate in the Good, and that the *eidê* are quite close to or participate quite considerably in the Good—certainly more considerably than any of eros' more common objects. But what does it mean to be close to or participate in the Good? It is difficult to know, and this difficulty (impossibility?) may itself be a subtle part of the *Republic*'s teaching. But most readers assume that there is an answer, and a plausible answer—perhaps the only plausible answer, in light of the *Republic*'s focus on levels of Being—is that to be close to or participate in the Good (which is the source of Being) means to apprehend Being and thus to *be* more (or to experience life more deeply or greatly) oneself.[27] And to participate in the Good *more than* something else does or to participate *considerably* means to experience *more* or *considerable* being. By apprehending the *eidê* the philosopher apprehends Being: recall that in apprehending the *eidê* the philosopher is gaining sight into *what is*. The *eidê* may be plural, but what makes them attractive to eros is this single defining feature, that is, their great share in Being. And in apprehending the *eidê* the philosopher gains for himself—"fills" himself with (586b)—more being.

None of what I am arguing presupposes knowledge of the character of the Good, though it does rest in part on Socrates' claim that the Good is the source of Being (509b). That claim, combined with Socrates' ranking of objects in accord with the "degree" of Being they embody and hence the degree of being they yield to those who apprehend or possess them, suggests that what human beings seek when they are seeking the Good—or what human beings seek simply, since they are always seeking the Good—is more being, or maximum being. To the extent that people pursue false goods it is not because they wish for evil or for lesser pleasures but because of ignorance about what would deliver the being they seek. (Unlike justice, the Good is universally wanted in and for itself.) They misapprehend the final object of their desires; such is one meaning of corruption, arguably the essential meaning. The *Republic* exhibits this most vividly in the person of Glaucon, whose "wishes are always contradictory . . . for he always mistakes all of his great longings for bodily desires but cannot find satisfaction for them thus understood."[28]

---

27. In the present discussion, "being," when referred to in lowercase, signifies something subjective, something *felt* or *experienced*. The uppercase "Being" refers to *what is*, objectively.

28. Bloom, "Interpretive Essay," p. 347. It might be objected that ignorance is not the only reason one would pursue lesser or false goods, and that insufficient strength of soul is also a reason. (Recall, though, that in Socrates' terms what we call insufficient strength of soul really

A question—and a challenge—arise as we consider the *Republic*'s treatment of the higher reaches of eros. I have observed that one cannot transcend eros. Even those who have ascended to true philosophy have not ceased loving—*wanting*—sight of the truth. So Socrates says. But what Socrates says on this matter is surely no more important, and is arguably much less important, than what he is and does. And what he is and does do not necessarily comport with the typical look of eros. *Is* Socrates erotic? The question will be addressed extensively in Chapters 3 and 4, where I will try to reveal something of the erotic character not only of Socratic philosophizing but also of Socrates' related but extraphilosophic pursuits as these are revealed in the *Symposium*. But it is possible to say something—not definitive, but suggestive—on the basis of the *Republic* alone. And it is *necessary* to say something, since its erotic characterization of philosophy has been one of the dialogue's more influential teachings.

Most who have addressed this question, even those who concede that the philosopher-kings are not at all erotic (i.e., even those who know that not all who are called philosophers are erotic), see Socrates as the very embodiment of philosophic eros. Indeed, it is precisely that which distinguishes Socrates from those fantastic beings that is said to reveal his eroticism—his incomplete wisdom, his consequent need for dialogue, and most especially his embrace of and delight in *all* that is, including images and opinions, and not just the *eidê* (488a).[29] But it is not clear that that which evinces Socrates' humanism and his humanity—that is, that which constitutes the *precondition* of eros—necessarily indicates the *presence* of eros. Whatever his insufficiencies, it is not clear that Socrates suffers for them: it is not clear that he experiences the neediness that would seem a central characteristic of eros. And so while he does indeed delight in the beauty of this world, and while he may even exemplify divine madness, it is not entirely certain that Socrates exemplifies philo-

---

means insufficient strength of a certain *part* of the soul, the *finest* part or the part that ought to be ruling [431a].) This seems to be implied by the assertion that most people are incapable of living the philosophic life and would be made miserable by it (486c, 536e). Undoubtedly, insufficient strength *is* a source of our being attracted to lesser and false goods. But it is so precisely because it keeps us from knowing what we really want or what would really satisfy us. In other words, weakness of soul is a source of ignorance, and it is as such that it causes us to pursue lesser goods.

29. This case has been made with considerable persuasiveness by both Howland and Nichols. See, respectively, *The Republic*, pp. 144–45 and 148–49, and "The *Republic*'s Two Alternatives."

sophic (or any other kind of) eros. Indeed, some have argued powerfully that he does not.[30]

A more complete answer will be available once we turn to the *Symposium*. But perhaps a tentative answer can be found even now by considering the self-negating character of eros and indeed all desire. A person who had grasped the Good and made it his own would have transcended human nature. Such a person's eros would be completely satisfied; he would enjoy the perfection and self-sufficiency of a Platonic god. Now in my view Socrates is not portrayed as such a one; indeed, there is ample evidence to the contrary, as noted above. (If Socrates is a god, he is not a Platonic god but a *Nietzschean* god, one who lacks final wisdom and thus philosophizes [*BGE* 295].) Nor is it clear that the total fulfillment of eros is held out even as a possibility. Consider, in this regard, Socrates' avowal that he does not have knowledge of the Good (505a, 506c). But Socrates does have an opinion about it, and one that, to judge from its incommunicability to his interlocutors, seems to be based on experience rather than speculation. Thus, to borrow the *Symposium*'s perhaps idealized terms, it may be that Socrates has climbed *partway* up Diotima's ladder. Indeed, if there is any truth to the *Republic*'s account of philosophy and if we accept Socrates as a philosopher, we are bound to conclude as much. And it may well be that the character of his eros, that is, the character of philosophic eros, is such that it appears similar to the condition in which eros has been fulfilled or overcome.

On the basis of ordinary experience, one might expect the person who is nearer to final satisfaction to be even more avidly erotic than anyone else. Desire typically reaches its peak intensity precisely when we near the wanted object. But what is true of most desire may not be true of the philosopher's desire. When we want to hold or possess something physically, we are apt to become most intensely desirous when it is nearby: there it is, just beyond one's grasp; one can "almost touch it." But when it is knowledge or sight of

---

30. See, for example, Rosen, *Plato's Symposium*, p. 320 (see also p. 317). Externally ugly and erotic, Socrates, according to Rosen, is *internally* beautiful and (by virtue of not needing anyone) *unerotic*. And the same is true of his speech. According to Rosen, Plato criticizes Socrates' unerotic nature while giving evidence of his own erotic one (p. 5). Others seem to see Socrates (and philosophy as such) as anerotic for a reason that reflects well on Socrates, namely, that eros is fundamentally delusional and Socrates is not. Indeed, Socrates is thought to lead his more promising interlocutors precisely *away* from eros. There is much to be said for this view, but as I will argue in subsequent chapters, Plato does not indicate that eros is inherently delusional even if most eros *is* delusional; and Socrates is the rare exemplar of non-delusional, indeed *true* or undistorted, eros.

the beautiful or the Good that one wants, one's desire is apt to be *calmed* as one nears it: there it is; I see it; and by seeing it, *I already have it.* Thus the philosopher's eros may be the eros of one who loves and desires, but who also, to some considerable extent, abides with that which he desires. This would make him more content and less avid a lover than most, and might well make him appear unerotic, at least by certain measures. If the satisfaction of eros would entail the negation of eros, then perhaps the partial satisfaction of eros entails a moderation of eros.[31]

In this discussion of sublimation I have concentrated on those elements of Socrates' account in the *Republic* that accord with his account in the *Symposium*. Most of these have been what I referred to earlier as formal matters, beginning with the idea of a hierarchy or tiered ascent. Each dialogue propounds the notion that it is possible and desirable for the individual to ascend these tiers through good education—desirable for the individual and the city alike. (That an individual's erotic ascent can have unwelcome effects on the city is acknowledged only very subtly, as we will see in Chapter 4.) Yet we still know little about the relations among these stages, apart from the fact of their constituting an ordered hierarchy. Most particularly, we have yet to ask whether the higher stages are inclusive of the lower ones, which may be the most important practical question on the matter. Or, to put the question in its most concrete form, does the philosopher have, and if so does he fulfill, sexual eros, or is his eroticism exclusively philosophic? It is here, as we enter into the "substance" or the experience of eros as it ascends, that Socrates' two accounts most clearly diverge, and that the character if not the meaning of the *Republic*'s political perspective comes to light.

In the *Republic* Socrates says that the philosopher experiences more real pleasure than anyone else—and not only because philosophy is itself the most

---

31. But doesn't the Cave allegory speak against my claim that the philosopher abides to a considerable extent with the objects of his desire? If the philosopher were able to keep company with the objects of his desire, why would a return to the cave be experienced as a painful separation from the objects of his eros? But the force of this objection dissipates if one interprets the painful return to the cave not as a simple or physical return to the city but as a return to the prevailing *mentality* of the city or the ascent to a position of rule, either of which conditions would indeed have the effect of depriving the philosopher of contact with the *eidê*. Indeed, if the allegory is to have any relation to Socratic philosophic practice, the return to the cave *must* be interpreted otherwise than as a simple return to the city's walls. After all, Socrates chose to dwell in the city, and there is ample reason to conclude that this choice served, rather than hindered, his philosophic inquiry.

pleasurable thing, its objects having more Being than the objects of lower desires (585b–e), but also because the rule of reason in the soul permits the other parts more pleasure than they would have if they themselves ruled (587a). That the philosopher experiences maximum pleasure from all parts of the soul does not mean, however, that his eroticism finds expression anywhere else than in philosophy. Indeed, his pleasure from those lower parts may stem precisely from a disinvestment of eros from their faculties. (One can take pleasure in the sight of physical beauty, for example, without one's passion being ignited.)[32] Socrates describes the development of a philosopher, that is, the process of sublimation, as a shifting of one's eros upward. The lower parts of the soul are thereupon abandoned by eros, of which, we might recall, there is a fixed amount in a given soul: "So, when in someone [the desires] have flowed toward learning and all that's like it, I suppose they would be concerned with the pleasure of the soul itself with respect to itself and would forsake those pleasures that come through the body—if he isn't a counterfeit but a true philosopher" (485d–e).

The body, the original focus of eros, is de-eroticized. Or so Socrates "suppose[s]" in the *Republic*. Given the dialogue's forgetfulness of the body, however, and given the fact that both the *Symposium* and the *Phaedrus* offer very different views—the *Phaedrus* especially: there, the higher stages of eros seem to include the lower ones within them (249d–51c)—we should treat this view with some skepticism.[33] But even if we remain skeptical of the *Republic*'s asceticism, it invites us to consider once more the ambiguity of eros. And not only ambiguity, but turbulence as well. The *Republic*'s political perspective has its uses: insofar as we are political beings we are well advised to look at things from a political perspective, even if we also wish to transcend that perspective. It may well be that the *Republic*'s apparent teaching regarding eros and the body is unrealistic and that it needs to be considered alongside the quite different teachings of the *Symposium*, which balance it. But to balance is not to erase. Even after bodily eros has been rehabilitated in light of the *Sympo-*

---

32. One can take pleasure in the sight of physical beauty without being erotically attracted to it: think of a landscape. Whether attraction to beauty can be altogether disconnected from passion is a more contentious question. Do we enjoy the landscape disinterestedly, or because it stimulates passion and promises fulfillment? Nietzsche offers the classic argument for the latter position, in reply to Schopenhauer, who had argued the former.

33. Regarding the *Republic*'s forgetting of the body, see Strauss, *The City and Man*, pp. 50–138. Strauss sees the *Republic* as "abstracting" not only from the body but also, and accordingly, from eros.

sium, it stands forth as powerfully explosive and in need of reason's governance. Which takes us to the means by which such governance is accomplished—and to the phenomenon, not coincidentally, into which the politically minded *Republic* offers uniquely penetrating insight.

SPIRITEDNESS

Unlike eros, spiritedness is presented in the *Republic* as one of the three "forms" or "parts" of the soul. But spiritedness is also a force that permeates the soul more generally. The soul in the *Republic* has two primary forces, each of which aims at some kind of wholeness or unity but whose objects and specific characters seem to be opposites. This *dynamic* bipartition of the soul is glimpsed in the dialogue before the more famous tripartition. Discussing the education of the guardians in book 3, Socrates speaks of the need to harmonize two of the soul's "things" or natures. What he has in mind are not the rational and the appetitive parts of the soul, which one might have expected, but rather "the spirited and the philosophic" (411e–12a).[34] These elements "might be harmonized with one another," he says, "by being tuned to the proper degree of tension and relaxation," such tuning being accomplished by music (which would tame the spirited nature) and gymnastic (which would harden the philosophic nature). (Also see 376e.) Socrates' instruction regarding the need to harmonize these two elements, the second of which is later shown to be an expression of eros, signals that the soul's higher development, and therefore human psychology more generally, need to be understood in terms of eros and *thymos*. This instruction is also the first explicit treatment of the interplay between eros and *thymos*, a theme that permeates the dialogue's treatment of the soul from beginning to end.

Like eros, *thymos* is both ambiguous and complex. In his initial discussion of the tripartite soul, Socrates seems to introduce the soul's spirited part as the natural ally of reason in the latter's struggle to control the desires:

> [D]on't we . . . notice that, when desires force someone contrary to the calculating part, he reproaches himself and his spirit is roused against that in him which is doing the forcing; and, just as though

---

34. This bipartition is foreshadowed in book 2's discussion of the nature of the guardians-to-be (375a–76c).

there were two parties at faction, such a man's spirit becomes the ally of speech? But as for its making common cause with the desires to do what speech has declared must not be done, I'd suppose you'd say you had never noticed anything of the kind happening in yourself, nor, I suppose, in anyone else (440a–b).

Soon, however, a proviso is inserted into the discussion. The spirited part is said to be an auxiliary to reason "if it's not corrupted by bad rearing" (441a). The evidence of everyday life, of course—including the political life amid which the action of the *Republic* is set—suggests that this "bad rearing" is far more the rule than the exception. A consequence of this bad rearing is a weak or defective reasoning part. If Socrates' interlocutors have never seen spiritedness "making common cause with the desires to do what speech has declared must not be done," that is surely because spiritedness regularly instructs speech and bends it to its own will. *Thymos* can be instrumental in achieving the greatest good, both in the soul and in the city. But it needs to be *made* so, for it can just as easily be enlisted into the service of lower and even lawless desires, or else simply run rampant and resist subservience either to reason or to the lower desires, in either of which cases it becomes the stuff of tyranny, both in the soul and in the city. The tyranny that results from *thymos* being subservient to lawless desire is the tyranny described as such in book 8; the tyranny that results from *thymos* taking charge of the soul and commanding the other parts is the tyranny that is presented *as the just regime* in book 5.[35] This connection to tyranny underscores, if any underscoring is needed, how vitally and how broadly important *thymos* and the education of *thymos* are from the standpoint of the greatest political concerns.

It is less the moral ambiguity of *thymos,* though, than its extraordinary range of manifestations that concerns us now. For our hope is not so much to determine how *thymos* can be made to manifest itself in this way or that as to determine what, exactly, it *is.* The range of spiritedness's manifestations includes but is not limited to anger, courage, shame, reverence, the desire for recognition, pride, vanity, contempt, envy, idealism, and fanaticism. Even if one were to disregard all of its expressions besides anger, which is perhaps its primary expression, that still would leave a wide range of phenomena: anger,

---

35. Here I follow Nichols, "Spiritedness and Philosophy," p. 48, who interprets the communism of book 5 as the consequence of *thymos*' takeover and perversion of philosophy.

after all, is a category whose members range from "the most noble indignation about injustice, turpitude, and meanness down to the anger of a spoiled child who resents being deprived of anything, however bad, that he desires."[36] One way to ask what *thymos* is would be to approach it as one would approach eros and to ask, accordingly, what it *wants*. There are solid grounds for this approach. Socrates says in book 9 that each of the soul's three parts, including the spirited part, has desires (580d). And in fact Socrates provides an answer to the question. What spiritedness loves, he says, is victory and honor (581b). Now this answer is not without problems. For one thing, the pursuit of victory and the pursuit of honor may not always be consistent with each other. Moreover, it is not clear that all the emotions, inclinations, and aspirations that are associated with spiritedness are necessarily implied or subsumed by the love of honor or the love of victory. But this latter difficulty is usually more apparent than real. There is always at least a plausible connection between the many psychic phenomena that are associated with spiritedness, on the one hand, and the love of honor or the love of victory on the other. And usually the connection is more than merely plausible once it is examined. It is not difficult to discern a connection between, say, a waspish disposition (586c) and the love of honor, or between fanaticism and the love of victory. Such things as waspishness and fanaticism, while not necessarily implied or subsumed by the love of victory or the love of honor, nevertheless are dispositions that are rightly associated with one or both of those loves. And yet this very fact, the fact that many of spiritedness's manifestations are dispositions rather than discrete desires, points to the incomparability of *thymos* and eros. Like eros, *thymos* manifests itself in desires for specific things. But unlike eros, it does not *only* manifest itself thus. To seek the essential character of *thymos* by asking what *thymos* wants or loves may therefore risk overlooking at least some part of what *thymos* is.

But the most important indication of the incomparability of *thymos* and eros has less to do with their phenomenology than with their respective origins and ends. Phenomenologically, *thymos* and eros are more comparable than not, even taking into account what was just said. Each can be correctly conceived as having numerous manifestations and objects of desire that can

---

36. Strauss, *The City and Man*, p. 110; cf. 441a–b. For more on the breadth of spiritedness's expressions, see Robinson, *Plato's Psychology*, p. 45; Thomas L. Pangle, "The Political Psychology of Religion in Plato's *Laws*"; and H. W. B. Joseph, *Essays in Ancient and Modern Philosophy*, pp. 65ff.

be interpreted and ranked with respect to some final object, or aim. With respect to their origins and ends, though, *thymos* and eros are not comparable. One, in fact, is subsumed by the other: We are given reason to conclude that *thymos is itself a part or variant of eros,* albeit eros "negatively inflected"[37]: it is born of frustrated eros and, whether it knows it or not (and usually it does not), it seeks, as its ultimate end, the very same thing that eros seeks, in the sense that the greatest victory and the greatest honor, properly understood, lie in the very thing that eros ultimately wants. This conclusion is not decisively stated or implied at any one place. But ample suggestive evidence emerges upon considering the way that *thymos* is ordinarily experienced and its correlation and covariance with eros among the dialogue's personages.

On its face, spiritedness is portrayed in the *Republic* as anerotic or even antierotic. Eros, as I have already noted, is (apparently) disparaged throughout the dialogue: it is presented as a threat to order and justice and consequently in need of severe and comprehensive governance. Spiritedness, as the means of such governance, emerges as an opponent of eros. Whereas eros is apolitical or even transpolitical and therefore (in the city's eyes) antipolitical, spiritedness is *the* political passion,[38] the passion whereby every political good is gained, not only order and justice but also patriotism, valor, and the like. Nor is it only in politics that spiritedness seems intrinsically antierotic. The same hostility is evident in the soul. As desire, eros bespeaks insufficiency, neediness, weakness. Spiritedness, on the other hand, rebels against just such vulnerability. If not always or by virtue of its nature, spiritedness generally seeks mastery and invulnerability.[39] This is seen in the story of Leontius, whose spiritedness rebelled against his desire to view corpses, that is, against the sight of human mortality (439e–40a). (The rebellion of Leontius' spiritedness may also have been a reaction against the impiety of his desire, which, too, might be viewed as a reaction against eros.) Finally, the opposition between *thymos* and eros would seem to be confirmed by the character and self-presentation of Socrates. At least if we associate spiritedness with the likes of the prickly Thrasymachus or the bold Glaucon or Polemarchus, Socrates cannot but seem athymotic in his coolness and lack of anger. And indeed he

---

37. The phrase quoted is from Rosen, "The Role of Eros in Plato's *Republic.*"
38. Strauss, *The Rebirth of Classical Political Rationalism,* pp. 165–66.
39. See Nichols, "Spiritedness and Philosophy in Plato's *Republic,*" pp. 53–57. My view is somewhat more qualified than that of Nichols, for whom spiritedness, apparently by its nature, "seeks absolute control." Regarding spiritedness's love of mastery, see especially 581a.

suggests as much when he speaks of the rare moment in which he acted "as though [his] spiritedness were aroused," a remark that implies that he normally is not spirited, and that philosophy, eros' highest expression, is at odds with spiritedness (536b–c).

None of this evidence can be rightfully dismissed. It dominates the characterizations of eros and *thymos* at the surface of the dialogue and therefore deserves to be taken seriously. If spiritedness seems opposed to eros, that is because it *is* so. But the surface is not the whole of the dialogue; and if *thymos* is indeed opposed to eros at one level—let us say, *phenomenologically*—it nevertheless proves (1) to be born of and (2) to point toward a return to eros. And the evidence for this, like the evidence for anything that is found beneath the surface, lies on the surface itself.

Origins

We do not receive from Socrates an account of spiritedness's first appearance in human beings, such as we receive from Rousseau. Spiritedness is in effect assumed to be a part of human nature as such, from the start; indeed, it or something like it is seen among the beasts, in addition to being likened to a beast itself (441b; 589d, 590b).[40] Nor is any account given of the first awakening of spiritedness in the individual. As Glaucon observes, children evince spiritedness "straight from birth" (441b). This accords with the common understanding, and indeed it is in this common understanding of spiritedness that we begin to catch sight of its origins. Spiritedness, we all perceive, arises out of the frustration of desire, even if it often grows well beyond the scope demanded by the immediate provocation. This view is the basis of Glaucon's initial association of spiritedness with desire (439e), an association that is not refuted by Socrates' subsequent effort to establish spiritedness as reason's natural ally against desire. And Glaucon's *was* the common understanding, we may be sure. That the cause of spiritedness's arousal is the frustration of desire is not a conceit of modern, mechanistic psychology but rather a long-standing view that finds voice in Homer, the most important source of the common

---

40. Seth Benardete points out that by Plato's time, the word *thymos* was decreasingly applied to human beings and increasingly reserved for describing spirited beasts. See Benardete, *Socrates' Second Sailing*, p. 55. Not that Plato simply revived an older usage: he also gave the word a more definite and perhaps a narrower sense than Homer had given it. See Koziak, *Retrieving Political Emotion*, chap. 2.

understanding of such things in ancient Greece: one need only recall the event that precipitated the main action of the *Iliad*.[41]

Thus if there is an antipathy between *thymos* and eros, there is also a sympathy between them. This may be a contradictory situation, but it's not without a certain sense. As Strauss points out, the antipathy emerges from the sympathy: "Spiritedness arises out of the desire proper [i.e., the desire belonging to the so-called desiring part of the soul and not to the spirited or calculating parts] being resisted or thwarted. Spiritedness is needed for overcoming the resistance to the satisfaction of the desire. Hence spiritedness is a desire for victory. Whereas eros is primarily the desire to generate human beings, spiritedness is the *derivative* willingness to kill and to be killed, to destroy human beings."[42] And yet how much sense is there really in this state of affairs, in which the servant is untethered from the served? That which is aroused by the frustration of desire might well be expected to limit its aim to the satisfaction of desire. Or if, once born, it is intent on pursuing a life of its own, one might at least expect it to be neutral toward desire. And yet this is not the case, as we have already seen. Spiritedness not only breaks free of the desire or eros on whose behalf it has been aroused, but also defines itself precisely by its opposition—if not to desire as such, then to unchecked desire and to the weakness and insufficiency that desire reveals. (That is why spiritedness tends to be particularly scornful toward that which is thought to *increase* this weakness and insufficiency, e.g., addiction.) Even when it is comparatively well-disposed toward desire, as it is in the soul of the just man (in whom spiritedness enforces a moderation that allows for satisfaction of lawful desires), spiritedness always represents an effort to transcend mere desirousness.

And yet there *is* sense to the being of *thymos* from the point of view of eros. Eros cannot ascend to higher objects, to greater and more comprehensive satisfaction, without the help of *thymos*, if only because ascending these peaks

---

41. Spiritedness can be provoked by any number of slights, and perhaps Achilles' wrath would have been kindled all the same had Agamemnon taken, say, some coveted instrument of war. But what actually instigated Achilles' epic anger was the theft of Briseis, an object of desire, and erotic desire at that. (Consider, too, the event that precipitated the war of which the *Iliad*'s action was but a part: again one finds offended eros at the heart of the matter.) For more on the Homeric portrait of spiritedness and the echoes of this view in Plato, see Zuckert, "On the Role of Spiritedness in Politics," in *Understanding the Political Spirit*. Regarding Homer's ongoing influence on Athenian culture in this and other regards, see Koziak, *Retrieving Political Emotion*, p. 68; and MacIntyre, *Whose Justice? Which Rationality?* pp. 48–50.

42. Strauss, *The Rebirth of Classical Political Rationalism*, p. 166; emphasis added.

requires a prior foundation in thymotically informed discipline or demotic virtue. *Thymos* is born of and for the sake of eros. And this happens naturally, by anyone's definition of nature. What eros needs, of course, is for *thymos* to remain true to the purpose implied by its origins. And while this might seem an unrealistic demand, it nevertheless is not an unreasonable one. For it is not only in its origins but also in its ends, in its greatest satisfactions, that *thymos* finds itself at one with eros.

Ends

According to Socrates' account in the *Republic* (as in the *Symposium*), eros finds full satisfaction only in philosophy. (As will be discussed in Chapter 2, the two dialogues give differing accounts of the objects of philosophic contemplation and the philosopher's response to them. But this difference does not diminish the general point, and in fact the different accounts can be reconciled.) What *thymos* is said to want, by contrast, is victory and honor. These objects are at once both more and less concrete than eros' objects. We all know at least something about what victory and honor are. But what is the greatest victory, and what is the greatest honor? If *thymos* not only arises from but also points toward a return to eros, as I am suggesting, then the greatest honor and victory must somehow entail either the *eidê*, or the Good, or philosophy. As indeed they do.

As Bloom observes, Socrates presents the philosophic life not simply as the best of lives but also as the highest embodiment of virtues that have not traditionally been associated with philosophy: "In the *Republic*, he tries to show that the philosophic life is the most just life, and elsewhere, that the philosophic life is also the most pious life and the most scientific life. He tries to present philosophy as the true fulfillment of all the other lives that men esteem and pursue."[43] But in making such claims, Bloom notes, Socrates must conceive of these virtues in unorthodox ways, and in pursuing the philosophic life one is forced to give up much of what is normally associated with them. "The philosophic life may contain all the other ways of life, but in a way that is completely alien to those who lead them. It is justice without the city, piety without the gods, and Eros without copulation or reciprocity." I would add to Bloom's formulation that for Socrates the philosophic life is also the most

---

43. Bloom, "The Ladder of Love," p. 147.

thymotically accomplished life. It is *thymos* without bloodshed or scorekeeping; it is *thymos* in its only non–zero sum manifestation.

That philosophy entails spiritedness is indicated in a number of ways in the *Republic*. First, philosophy and spiritedness are each mentioned for the first time in the same passage (375e–76c). Second, the philosophic quest is likened more than once to hunting (435d, 451b–c, 504b–d). Even if the references to hunting only represent Socrates' attempt to make philosophy appealing to a certain kind of audience, they still underscore the relation between philosophy and spiritedness: that philosophy *can* be made appealing to spirited young men says something about its nature. Third, a key element or moment of philosophy—namely, separating the kinds of beings by means of what is called *dianoia* (in the *Republic*) or *diaresis* (e.g., in the *Statesman*)—seems an essentially thymotic activity insofar as it involves division and (cognitive) mastery rather than wonder or experience of beauty.[44] Fourth, it is difficult for a careful reader to overlook the philosopher's need for courage, the virtue that is singularly associated with spiritedness. Candidates for philosophic training are to be drawn from the auxiliary class, a class whose members are characterized by a spirited nature. But if the auxiliaries need courage, there is reason to think that the philosophers need it even more. Twice courage is placed at the center of a list of characteristics necessary for a worthy candidate for philosophy (485a–86e, 489e–490c), and the philosopher himself appears as one who fears neither death, which is no great thing to him, nor truth, being one who hates the lie in the soul (490b, 535e). And while his

---

44. The *Republic*'s estimation of the place of *dianoia* or diaretic activity is an overestimation from the standpoint of the *Symposium,* and there is good reason to suppose that this representation is offered by Plato as a deliberate distortion in accordance with the political, which is to say the thymotic, perspective of the *Republic*. The error of overestimating the power of division in our efforts to know the natures of things is shown both in the *Statesman*, in which a method like the *Republic*'s *dianoia* is shown to lead to ridiculous results (i.e., the definition of man as featherless biped), and in the *Symposium*, which, with its inclusion of wonder and beauty and sudden illumination, offers the clearest completion of the *Republic*'s distorted presentation. The *Republic*'s distortion, it seems to me, is a matter of taking an *important* part of philosophy for the *crowning* part: *dianoia* clearly belongs to Platonic philosophy, and to that extent the activity of philosophy has a thymotic dimension. But *dianoia* seems too confined and too sterile to constitute philosophy's highest or most rewarding activity. (However—if rigorous analysis isn't the highest part of philosophy, it may be the final stage, as indicated by the fact that the Cave narrative ends not with sight of the sun but with reckoning. Having been struck by beauty or wonder, having arrived at what seems to be marvelous insight and freedom, we want to know that we are not deluding ourselves.) For a succinct summary of the view that the *Republic* and the *Statesman* both give a distorted picture of philosophy, a view developed by Strauss, see Zuckert, *Postmodern Platos*, 314–15 n. 65.

equanimity in the face of death rightly impresses everyone as courage, fearlessness in the face of the pursuit of the truth is perhaps even *more* indicative of courage, for many who face death with courage are able to do so precisely because they hold fast to cherished and unquestioned myths. And fifth, there is the evidence found in the character of the discussion as such. Whether or not we accept Alcibiades' interpretation of Socrates as eristic (*Symposium* 213e), we can hardly miss Socrates' relish for challenge, his boldness, his sure grasp of effective strategy and tactics, and his obvious delight in the clash of ideas. Consider, too, the delight that accompanies and thus presumably motivates learning: the pedagogical genius of Socratic conversation (and Platonic writing) is that it prompts the interlocutor (or reader) to make discoveries for him- or herself. The presupposition is that people understand and remember best what they have discovered for themselves, in part because of their delight in discovering things for themselves.[45] What is this delight if not prideful and masterful—or, in a word, thymotic? Clearly spiritedness has a place in the philosophic life, however much its form has changed from its original, unsublimated state.

But the philosophic life does not simply involve or depend on spiritedness. It is, to repeat, the most thymotically accomplished life, that is, the life in which the love of victory and the love of honor are most gratified. And it is such because there is no greater victory or honor than those won by the philosopher. There is no greater victory because philosophic insight does indeed need to be won, because it requires extraordinary courage, because it is the rarest of victories, and because it is the most satisfying of victories, the latter being partly due to the preceding factors and partly due to the fact that the philosopher's quarry has more being than any other kind of prize (585b–e). And there is no greater honor because nothing else is as honorable, even if this is rarely seen to be so. Obviously philosophy is not *widely* honored; but if we measure the magnitude of honor by the stature of those by whom it is bestowed, then philosophy is indeed the most highly honored of enterprises, at least by Socratic standards. Although they would never believe it, those who pursue victory and honor outside of philosophy will never satisfy that quest as well as the philosopher does. When the soul is ruled by its philosophic part, says Socrates, "the result is that each part may, so far as other

---

45. This interpretation of the psychological sources of learning is consistent with the account of pedagogy given in Plato's *Seventh Letter* (241). See also Leibowitz, "The Moral and Political Foundations of Socratic Philosophy," pp. 25–26.

things are concerned, mind its own business and be just and, in particular, *enjoy its own pleasures*, the best pleasures, and, to the greatest possible extent, the truest pleasures" (586e–87; emphasis added). Certainly "each part" includes the spirited part.

That the philosophic life is thymotically accomplished and that philosophic insight is the most satisfying kind of victory does not mean that philosophy is *primarily* a spirited activity. Philosophy is so thymotically accomplished precisely because it satisfies thymotic longing in the latter's highest and truest form, the form in which its focus is the same or nearly the same as that of erotic longing. It is with philosophy that we encounter *thymos*' return to and subsumption by eros. Thus this most thymotically accomplished activity is nevertheless primarily erotic, just as, and because, *thymos* itself is erotic in both origin and goal. Indeed, paradoxically, because it satisfies thymotic striving in its highest and truest (i.e., erotic) form, philosophy can be said in the end to *transcend thymos*. Let us keep in mind, though, that transcendence does not mean noninvolvement. If *thymos* is transcended, that is only because it is engaged, satisfied, and elevated—sublimated—to its (erotic) peak.[46]

Among nonphilosophers eros and *thymos* remain separate and at odds. Yet even in such individuals—and in cities, too—one sees a consistent covariation of eros and *thymos* that itself testifies to their kinship if not to their ultimate identity. (Only in the philosopher is their identity revealed.) Consider the *Republic*'s cities first. In Adeimantus' "city of pigs," both eros and *thymos* are absent; in the feverish city that follows that more placid one, both eros and *thymos* are rampant and disordered; and in the *kallipolis*, eros and *thymos* are both present but are severely regulated to the point of denaturing. As for covariation within the souls of individuals, we might take note not only of Socrates, whose spiritedness has already been discussed (implicitly, in my comments on spiritedness and philosophy) and whose eros will be treated extensively in Chapters 3 and 4, but also of Glaucon, who is repeatedly described as both highly erotic and highly spirited. Regarding Glaucon's erotic nature, see for example 474d, 468b, and 468c. For indications of his spiritedness, see especially 357a, where he is said by Socrates to be "always most courageous in everything"; also see 368c, 414c, 451b, and 506d: in each of these passages we see Glaucon forcefully asserting himself, either to compel Socrates

---

46. In this sense, the present interpretation is not inconsistent with Strauss's proclamation that "Philosophy is not spirited." Strauss, *The Rebirth of Classical Political Rationalism*, p. 167; see also *The City and Man*, pp. 110–11.

to fulfill his obligation, or to encourage or defend some particularly bold part of the argument.[47]

That Socrates presents philosophy as the peak of thymotic activity is not only my observation, and that the respective magnitudes of eros and *thymos* tend to covary in people is not difficult to see. Thus I need not belabor these points.[48] My purpose, rather, has been to adduce these observations as support for my claim (and this has *not* been advanced by other commentators, to my knowledge) that *thymos* points toward a return to eros—or, to put it more strongly, that *thymos is* eros, that it is born of, that it peaks in a return to, and that it is therefore a part or aspect of, eros.

To see *thymos* thusly allows us to appreciate both the multiplicity and the unity of the soul—or, rather, the multiplicity within the unity. Indeed, by the end of the *Republic* the soul proves to be both more manifold and more unified than it at first appeared, especially in book 4. More manifold because the possibility is raised of more parts than just the three that are named, and because the three parts themselves prove to be divisible into subparts. More unified because each of the three parts is characterized by desire and because at bottom there is but a single psychic force in pursuit of a single Good. Recall that there is something, some *one* thing, "which every soul pursues and for the sake of which it does *everything*" (505d-e; emphasis added). In this simultaneous multiplicity and oneness the soul proves to be analogous not only to the city but also to Being itself. As is the case with Being, the multiplicity strikes us before the unity. Also, and again as is the case with Being, the discovery of unity should not be understood as obviating the multiplicity.

---

47. For more on both Socrates and Glaucon, see Craig, *The War Lover;* Howland, *The Republic;* and Rosen, "The Role of Eros in Plato's *Republic.*" One point that needs to be added, though, is that while those who are highly erotic always seem to be highly thymotic, there are some who appear highly thymotic without giving much evidence of eroticism—Thrasymachus, for example. Such cases may reflect a reactive sensibility born of weakness, a condition addressed with clinical precision by Rousseau in an extraordinary passage of the *Dialogues* (112) that we will examine in Chapter 5. The likes of Thrasymachus also remind us that, while philosophy may indeed entail *thymos* in the ways indicated above, a poorly educated *thymos* inhibits philosophy as much as does a poorly educated or unsublimated eros. For that matter, even a well educated *thymos*—well educated from a strictly civic point of view, that is—inhibits philosophy, indeed is *hostile* to philosophy. See Lutz, *Socrates' Education to Virtue,* for a fine discussion of a *thymos* that, reflecting weakness, inhibits philosophy by preventing the development of philosophic eros. (Note, though, that what I say of "poorly educated *thymos*" Lutz says of *thymos* as such.)

48. Regarding philosophy as the peak of thymotic activity, see especially Craig, *The War Lover.* Note, though, that Craig sharply separates the love of victory from the love of honor and sees the philosopher as exemplifying the former but not the latter (pp. 76-78).

Rather, it is precisely by understanding the distinct role of each part of the whole—the beings that are part of Being, the *thymos* that is part of eros—that unity is properly apprehended. *Thymos* cannot return to eros and bring about psychic unity unless it is educated and developed *as thymos*, as it is in the philosopher. Which is why it makes sense—for Socrates in the *Republic* and therefore for us in considering the *Republic*—to persist in speaking of *thymos* as a discrete psychic force and even as a discrete psychic part and not *simply* as a variety of eros, even if it is ultimately that.[49]

Eros and *thymos* are each tumultuous forces, both within the psyche and in their effects on the world. It might therefore seem strange that they should reach their respective peaks and even realize their unity in the person of the philosopher, who is notable perhaps above all (at least in the eyes of outsiders) for his equanimity and apparent inner harmony. But perhaps this is not so contrary to our experience and intuition as it might seem, at least if Greek myths about the gods reflect that experience and intuition. "The one who first told the myth was not unreasonable in pairing Ares and Aphrodite," writes Aristotle,[50] and most of us would be inclined to agree. For all that we distinguish between loving and fighting, most of us have probably noticed that eros and spiritedness tend to be found together; a person who claims to be "a lover, not a fighter" is bound to incite doubt about his eroticism even as he convinces us of his lack of spirit. But the union of Ares and Aphrodite is not the end of the story, nor even the most instructive part. Aristotle neglected to mention that the union of Spiritedness and Love produced a child—a daughter, named Harmonia.

With the discovery that *thymos* belongs to eros, the *Republic*'s apparent psychic dualism resolves into a monism, albeit a tiered and variegated monism. The implications of this discovery are difficult to overestimate. The magnitude and multifariousness of eros, not to mention its ambiguity and its sus-

---

49. Plato does seem to suggest in the *Republic* that we might cease thinking of *thymos* as a discrete force and part and instead divide all desire into three primary types corresponding to the soul's three parts—call them, say, noetic eros, thymotic eros, and somatic eros. (Thanks to Leon Craig for suggesting the terms.) But that suggestion emerges from a long dialogue in which the interlocutors never altogether cease to treat *thymos* as a separate force and part. Hence my usage in this chapter. (The same effort at fidelity that has kept me talking about *thymos* as a discrete psychic force and part in connection with the *Republic* will lead me to speak very little about it by that name as we proceed to the *Symposium*. In the *Symposium*, that which the *Republic* calls *thymos*—that fraction of it that is even recognized—is referred to as a variety of eros.)

50. *The Politics*, trans. Carnes Lord, 1269b27–28.

ceptibility to inner conflict, come more clearly to sight; and eros proves even more important a thing, both theoretically and practically, than one had yet seen. In this above all the *Republic* readies us to explore the nature and the political implications of eros, whether called by that name or another, and whether by Plato or his great successors and rivals.

PART ONE

Platonic Eros—the Effectual Truth

[A]s soon as one adopts the habit of measuring oneself against others and moving outside oneself in order to assign oneself the first and best place, it is impossible not to develop an aversion for everything that surpasses us, everything that lowers our standing, everything that diminishes us, everything that by being something prevents us from *being everything*.

—**Rousseau to the Frenchman in**
***Rousseau, Judge of Jean-Jacques: Dialogues* (emphasis added)**

But, blessed one, do consider better: Without your being aware of it—I may be nothing.

—**Socrates to Alcibiades in Plato's *Symposium***

2

FIRST TRUTHS

Desire and longing—what the Greek world called eros—don't fare too well in Plato's political dialogues. In the *Republic* and the *Gorgias,* the dialogues in which the relation between eros and politics is most extensively addressed, eros is presented as a tyrannical passion that easily leads to political tyranny and almost always leads to civically destructive selfishness and injustice. Eros is disparaged even in the private sphere, in which it is depicted as enslavement to insubstantial and evanescent pleasures. The possibility of a more benign eros is acknowledged, but such an eros turns out to be unlike anything to which most of us would attach that name and unlike even what the Greeks, with their broader conception of the term, would have recognized as eros. For a happier view of eros we need to turn to two of Plato's nonpolitical dialogues, the *Phaedrus,* in which Socrates sings the praises of eros as "divine madness," and the *Symposium,* Plato's most extensive and sustained treatment of the subject in which six and arguably seven speakers eulogize Eros.

Or so it seems at first glance. In fact, things are more complicated than this. First, the dialogues' respective stances toward eros are considerably more ambiguous than I have suggested. Eros is not altogether denigrated in the political dialogues, nor is it simply lauded in the other two. Second, the themes of the dialogues are less simple than the labels I have affixed to them. The *Republic* is not simply about politics. The *Symposium,* conversely, *is* about politics, in part. (So, for that matter, is the *Phaedrus.*) Yet the initial impressions do reflect something real, having to do with the dialogues' respective perspectives or starting points. The *Republic* views even the nonpolitical from the standpoint of the political, so that, for example, philosophy comes to light as "justice" in the soul and enters the conversation because of the question of political rule. The *Symposium,* by contrast, views the political from the standpoint of the nonpolitical, from the standpoint of individual need or longing. Indeed, the *Symposium* views the political from the standpoint of the most fundamental need or longing, and for this reason it enables us to see things about politics that a reading of any of the more overtly political dialogues, including the *Republic,* does not so readily reveal. In this way the *Symposium* not only introduces new themes, but also leads us to view those of the *Republic* in a new light. (Perhaps it will lead us, or should lead us, to view those post-Platonic works that owe so much to the *Republic* in a new light as well.) My goal in these next chapters is to discern from the *Symposium,* sometimes in conjunction with the *Republic,* important features of Plato's political teaching, features of what one might call the effectual truth of Platonic eros—that is, the political implications of this not-essentially political passion. And because the political is addressed from the perspective of the needs of the soul, we may also hope to learn something about those needs themselves. The present chapter will be devoted to opening the question of eros and preparing for Chapter 3's analysis of what I take to be the most far-reaching of Plato's responses: Socrates' speech in the *Symposium.* Chapter 4 will turn to persons—particular persons, though exemplary ones. Whether divine or daemonic, after all, eros is emphatically a human thing, and it needs to be understood as a powerful practical and political force in the world. This exploration should better prepare us to raise the question whether and how the Platonic teaching on eros provides or points to a principle by which we might determine and rank human goods. This question will be treated in Chapter 10, where I will also put the same question to our other two thinkers. Understanding that the question of goods inevitably turns on the vexed question of *the* Good, we mustn't hope for much more than a few provisional and incomplete observations. But if the Good as such is too bright for most of us to look at or even to see, there still might be a possibility to judge the brightness of life's many particular goods.

No one dialogue contains the whole of Plato's teaching on eros or even on the political ramifications of eros. A full understanding of these teachings would require a full understanding of many dialogues if not the entire Platonic corpus. Yet such is Plato's artistry that what is absent or "abstracted from" in a particular dialogue normally turns out to be present after all, in the shadows, as it were. Thus while I would never suggest that one could discern all that follows without familiarity with other dialogues (particularly the *Republic*), I would claim that the following points, which seem to me to constitute the essential outlines of Plato's teaching on eros and politics, are present in the *Symposium*—if not explicitly articulated, then at least pointed at or presupposed but in any event discernible: first, that human beings long to overcome their finitude—especially, but not only, their mortality; second, that this longing, when intensified, leads them into various kinds of political ventures; third, that these ventures cannot but fail to deliver what is wanted; and, fourth, that a satisfactory life and a securely decent politics require the overcoming of the delusional pursuit of immortality through politics. This much one might learn, as Plato perhaps learned, from Thucydides.[1] But there's more: fifth, that the love of beauty arises or at least gains its force from the longing for immortality; sixth, that, despite this connection with a hopeless passion, the love of beauty can be the vehicle to real well-being, and how; and, seventh, that this is so because the love of beauty is ultimately based, as is the delusional longing for immortality itself, on a nondelusional divination of the eternal. The tragic error of humanity is to translate a love for *eternity* into the desperate and unsure longing for *immortality*. A decent life, not to mention political sanity, requires an overcoming of this error, either through a confidently held (normally religious) faith in immortality or through philosophic resignation to mortality, a resignation that need not be bitter and can indeed be joyous if it is accompanied by experience of the eternal. But this nontragic possibility represented by philosophy is rare and difficult and carries its own tragic possibilities, tragic *political* possibilities. The latter point is indicated by the three characters in the dialogue who not only talk about eros but unambiguously demonstrate or *act* upon it before our eyes. I will refer to these erotic actors as the dialogue's "manifest lovers." My focus in the following chapters will be precisely on these three figures—and (even more so) on a fourth, who, I will argue, also demonstrates eros, albeit somewhat more ambiguously, or at least more atypically, than the three. The first three lovers, in the order in which the characters appear, are Apollodorus, Aristodemus, and Alcibiades. (The names themselves are introduced in a different order, with Alcibiades in the central place.) The fourth and stranger lover is Socrates, who exemplifies the philosophic acceptance of mortality referred to above.

In the case of the three nonphilosophers my focus will be less on speeches than on actions (indeed, two of them don't offer speeches at the symposium), or, perhaps better put, their *activity*, by which I mean their customary ways of being, which manifest themselves and are discernible in both actions and

---

1. For an illuminating analysis of Thucydides' view of the ever-present and devastating political consequences of the desire for immortality, see Ahrensdorf, "The Fear of Death and the Longing for Immortality."

speeches—hence the title of this Part. Plato is not normally associated with the notion of "effectual truth." His dramas are dialogues; rather than action, he offers speeches, and, more often than not, edifying speeches. It was precisely with this in mind that he who gave currency to the idea of "effectual truth" argued for the need to break with the classical tradition for the sake of a true and useful understanding of politics. Yet that same critic quietly admitted that the ancients communicated things of great practical import,[2] and we who have no need to discredit any intellectual authorities can openly acknowledge even more: namely, that there *is* activity in the dialogues and that in this activity—in the *way* in which things are said; in the way in which they are heard or received; in the character of the relationships between the interlocutors; in the characters' actions "offstage," either prior or subsequent to the dialogue itself, remembering that these were real people—Plato teaches the truth of human experience. An important part of the truth of human experience and one that Plato particularly illuminates is humanity's resistance to and distortion of the truth—both of which, as we shall see, are on display in the *Symposium*. I certainly do not believe that the following investigation will definitively establish all or even any of what I have called the essential outlines of Plato's teaching. I do believe, though, that an investigation such as I intend can illustrate and lend support to these outlines and thus constitute a kind of interpretive pencil sketch of Plato's teaching.

I do not suppose that many readers need to be convinced of the importance of eros to Plato's thought, and this importance cannot be truly established in any case except through investigating eros and determining what it is and what it wants. In what follows I will argue for a very broad interpretation, according to which eros is not only the most powerful force in the *psychē* but the soul of all desire and therefore, directly or indirectly, the motor of all human endeavor. Platonic eros is comparable in its reach and its power to Nietzsche's will to power and Rousseau's desire for being. It is both a desire and a metadesire: a desire in that one can speak intelligibly of its object and aim, a metadesire in that it admits of many manifestations in the form of narrow disparate desires. Eros proves to be the soul of the soul, the animating nerve of human life. To my knowledge none of Plato's characters quite makes

---

2. Machiavelli, *The Prince* trans. Harvey C. Mansfield. Regarding the "effectual truth" (*la verità effettuale*), see p. 61. For the subtle acknowledgment of the ancients' wisdom, see p. 69.

this claim, let alone argues for it. Indeed, the *Republic* seems to present eros as one of *two* powerful and opposing psychic forces, the other being *thymos*, or spiritedness. And the *Republic*'s apparent psychic dualism only gains credibility from the dialogue's perhaps uniquely scientific approach to the soul, that is, its orderly and comprehensive way of investigation. Yet we have already seen that the *Republic*'s apparent dualism dissolves into erotic monism upon discovering that *thymos* is itself a variant of eros.

Another reason for supposing that Plato sees eros as the soul's single, preeminent force arises from Socrates' professions of knowledge and ignorance. His famous professions of ignorance notwithstanding, Socrates clearly knows a lot about the *psychē*.[3] Yet in numerous dialogues, including the *Symposium* (177d, 212b), he claims to be expert only in erotics. Perhaps the confessions of ignorance are simply disingenuous. But perhaps the irony is more complicated than that: perhaps Socrates does know a lot about the soul (and about much else besides) yet knows it precisely by virtue of his knowledge of eros. If that is the case, then he is effectively identifying everything he knows as knowledge of eros[4]—in which case eros must prove to be *the* thing to know about the soul, the source of all our passions and desires, or, as I said above, the soul of the soul.[5] (The same logic is yet another argument in support of my claim in Chapter 1 that *thymos* is subsumed by eros. For Socrates clearly knows a lot about spiritedness. Indeed, his uncanny ability to incite and then manage anger and indignation in his interlocutors suggests that he has a particular expertise in this area.)

TALKING ABOUT EROS

We turn now to the *Symposium*—where, having announced an inquiry into action, I must nevertheless first speak about speeches. For it is manifestly the

---

3. "Socrates is famous for saying, in the *Apology*, what he never quite says—that he knows he knows nothing. A study of the dialogue reveals that the more qualified disavowals of knowledge he in fact offers are accompanied by indications that he knows a very great deal—about politics, law, and punishment, about virtue, devotion, and moral experience, and about the gods and divine revelation." Leibowitz, "The Moral and Political Foundations of Socratic Philosophy," abstract.

4. See Lutz, *Socrates' Education to Virtue*, p. 55.

5. A related piece of textual evidence: A striking claim of Diotima's teaching, to which Socrates ostensibly subscribes, is that the erotic love of immortal fame inspires all human action (208d–e). As Strauss notes, this is a preposterous assertion—taken literally. But it is hardly preposterous if Diotima uses "love of fame" to stand in for or represent eros as such, of which the love of fame is a "high" expression. See Strauss, *On Plato's Symposium*, p. 224.

case, in the dialogues as in the larger world, that speeches prompt and are often directed toward actions and vice versa. Indeed, if by "action" one means behavior that directly affects the world, speech often *is* action. But there is a simpler reason to take up speeches. Based on the encounter depicted in the *Symposium*, perhaps the primary effectual truth about eros, the thing that first comes to light, is that people talk about it. More specifically, they talk in a certain way and on account of a certain need. The outstanding characteristic of the speeches offered by the symposiasts is self-justification. Even in this freest and most amiable and apolitical of settings the participants apparently feel the need to justify their own erotic lives, whether as expressed in actual behavior or merely as desired. Closely linked to this truth is another, namely, that the need to justify tends to produce views that are based less on objective analysis than on one's own felt needs or interests. There is not a speech among the *Symposium*'s seven eulogies that is not fundamentally self-interested. Not even Socrates' is an exception, though, unlike most of the other speakers, his interest is neither unconscious nor merely self-serving. Perhaps it is the interested origins of their views on the subject that make the participants in the dialogue so nearly impervious to rational persuasion.[6]

Reason tells us to look askance at interested or self-serving analysis. But it is an excessive and therefore dubious rationalism that would teach us to invalidate such analysis altogether. If his depiction of Socratic dialectic is any guide, Plato teaches that the way to approach the disinterested truth is precisely through a dialectical inquiry that begins with interested opinion—not only because one can infer much from the particulars of the interest, for example, the felt need to validate this or that opinion, but also because such opinion is apt to be based on at least a part of the truth.[7] There is apt to be some truth

---

6. Agathon alone is moved from his original position, for he alone is explicitly subjected to Socrates' dogged dialectical critique. The preceding speakers, though just as decisively refuted by Socrates' logic, are apparently able to maintain their original views, so great is "the power of Eros to convince each lover that his interpretation of his experience is necessarily the truth of his experience." Benardete, "On Plato's *Symposium*," p. 180. And who knows whether Agathon's conversion is sincere; or, even if it is sincere, whether it will last. Indeed, in light of the self-interested bias of erotic opinions generally and Agathon's soft character in particular, one might well suspect that his conversion by Socratic logic expired as he finally fell asleep at the end of the long night's discussion.

7. Such a view is characteristic of the entire tradition of classical political philosophy. One discerns it not only behind Platonic dialogues, which depict searches for truth via consideration of faulty but not altogether false common opinions, but also in Aristotle, whose treatises are in this sense as dialectical and dynamic as Plato's dialogues.

in such opinion precisely *because* of the interestedness of human inquiry: we all want what's good, what's *truly* good (*Republic* 505d), and for that reason alone (i.e., not wanting to be fooled) we exercise a certain intellectual rigor, however much that rigor is typically compromised or surmounted by wishful thinking. Moreover, speech about eros is speech made *to others*. As such it will reflect not only on the speaker but on the addressee, at least where the speaker has any skill. This is certainly the case of the speakers at the symposium, whose eulogies aim to convince, even to seduce, others.

Another "effectual truth" of eros begins to come to light when we take note of the character of the *Symposium*'s discourse. For all its ease and its eulogizing, the conversation is competitive, both formally and informally. There is a contest between Agathon and Socrates, or between tragic poetry and philosophy, for the mantle of wisdom. And he who enters the scene in the guise of Dionysus, ready to crown the victor, himself engages in a contest—also with Socrates—for the love of Agathon. There is also a contest, this one informal, between Aristophanes and Socrates: in the appropriate (i.e., the fourth, or central) part of his own speech,[8] Socrates effectively rebuts Aristophanes in all but name, thereby prompting the comic poet to try to respond. (This alone among the three contests promises to be an actual argument, with each side seeking—and able—to advance its cause. But the promise is extinguished by Alcibiades' raucous entrance.) How interesting that eros lends itself so readily to the *agon*, and that all three contests include as a participant the one who bears such an uncanny resemblance to Eros himself, at least by his own telling. And how revealing: the dialogue devoted to lovely speech about Love points to the connection between love and war, or between eros and *thymos*, even as it ostensibly ignores the latter.[9]

---

8. Regarding the number and order of parts of Socrates' speech in the *Symposium*: as Strauss observes, Socrates' speech divides into seven thematically indivisible parts that correspond, in order, to the teachings offered by the dialogues' seven speech-givers. See *On Plato's Symposium*, p. 183. Aristophanes is the fourth of the seven. Socrates responds to Aristophanes' teaching in the fourth part of his own speech.

9. Plato himself can be understood to be engaging in a kind of contest. Strauss observes that with its contest for wisdom and inclusion of Alcibiades, the *Symposium* mimics and competes with Aristophanes' *Frogs*. "In the *Frogs* . . . we have a contest between two tragic poets which is decided by Dionysus, the god of wine, with a view to Alcibiades. That is the model for the *Symposium*. . . . So you see how elegantly Plato pays Aristophanes back. The man who is made the point of reference in a contest between tragic poets decides at the *Symposium* in favor of Socrates, whom you, Aristophanes, so unfairly ridiculed and attacked in your comedy [*Clouds*]. We can say that the *Symposium* is the reply of Plato to Aristophanes' *Frogs*." And more generally: "The *Symposium* is the Platonic reply to Aristophanes and to the poets altogether, because . . . Socrates wins also against the tragic poet." *On Plato's Symposium*, p. 26.

As a dialogue whose point of view is nonpolitical, that takes place in a private setting beneath the notice of the polis, and whose participants are instructed to eulogize eros, the *Symposium* includes no explicit mention of *thymos*, which features so prominently in the emphatically political *Republic*. That is not to say that the phenomenon itself goes unaddressed, however. The *Symposium* offers no real analysis of the moral passions associated with *thymos*, chief among which are anger and the love of justice. But at least some of what the *Republic* calls *thymos*—in particular, that which the *Republic* praises as the raw material of courage and toughness—appears in the *Symposium* as a species of eros (i.e., love of honor, or eros for political fame). And we find in the *Symposium* confirmation and further elaboration of the *Republic*'s teaching regarding the origin and nature of *thymos*—that *thymos* is ignited by the frustration of eros and can be understood to be a permutation of eros, a "negatively inflected" variant of eros. This is suggested not only by the playful (but not simply playful) contests referred to above, but also in various speeches. For the most part, the speeches de-emphasize the possessiveness and defensiveness—the eruptions of spiritedness—that so regularly attend erotic passion. The task at hand is, after all, to *eulogize* eros; even Socrates, who faults others for making things up, sets out to "select[ ] the most beautiful parts of the truth" and "arrange them in the seemliest manner possible" (198c–e). Yet as I noted above, what is de-emphasized or "abstracted from" in a Platonic dialogue is frequently indicated all the same, only quietly. Phaedrus, the first symposiast to speak, gives an account of eros' connection to virtue whose key mechanisms are a sense of shame and the love of honor (178c–79b). Aristophanes' reference to Hephaestus brings to mind the fierce emotions incited by eros when it has been frustrated or insulted (192d; see *Odyssey* 8.321–43).[10] And Socrates more directly reveals the nearly inevitable shading of eros into *thymos*, irrespective of virtue, when he observes that animals fight so fiercely to protect their progeny (207a–b).

Even more interesting in this connection is what is suggested by the action of the dialogue. This will be taken up below. For now let me at least mention the evident spiritedness of the dialogue's three "manifest lovers." The first of these is Apollodorus, the great lover of Socrates, whose stance toward the rest of humanity, including himself, is one of ferocious disdain (173c–e). The sec-

---

10. Aristophanes' whole account of eros speaks to the relation between eros and *thymos*, but in its effective subordination of the former to the latter or to something like will to power, it rejects rather than elaborates Plato's teaching, according to which *thymos* is secondary to eros.

ond is Aristodemus, whose tender submission to Socrates somehow coexists with overt scorn for conventional piety and, by implication, for the human neediness that leads to such piety. The third is Alcibiades, whose Eros-emblazoned shield so nicely symbolizes what his meteoric career exemplifies, that is, the imperialistic and war-loving tendency of political eros. (All three cases will be discussed in Chapter 4.) Indeed, no other characters exhibit or are associated with spiritedness at all. Just as eros and *thymos* covary both in persons and in cities in the *Republic*, so, too, the *Symposium* locates these apparently opposite psychic forces together.

ASKING ABOUT EROS

Eros is desire; but desire for what? The problem is that Plato offers more than one answer, not just across dialogues, but even within the *Symposium* itself. Socrates isn't the only one who makes an impressive speech. Aristophanes gives a powerful alternative account of eros that will ring true to many. And even Agathon and the others give voice to features or consequences of eros that cannot be omitted from an adequate account of the phenomenon. Indeed, the real disagreement exists almost entirely among the *Symposium*'s speakers rather than between dialogues. The major treatments of eros aside from those given in the *Symposium* are given by Socrates and prove essentially consistent with one another, notwithstanding differences of emphasis and tone presumably owing to Socrates' assessments of the requirements of the respective dialogic situations. As suggested earlier, this consonance is evident even between the *Symposium* and the *Republic*, the two dialogues that speak most comprehensively to eros and its political ramifications. The different tones and emphases of these dialogues are complementary and mutually illuminating, in that each of the dialogues in some vital ways completes the other by highlighting what is only quietly present in the other. Whereas in the *Republic* Socrates generally emphasizes struggle and strife and appeals to the spiritedness of his interlocutors, his account in the explicitly eulogistic *Symposium* paints a more beautiful picture of eros, a picture designed, it seems to me, to appeal more to readers' "natural" or apolitical eros. Compare, for example, the *Republic*'s image of liberation from the Cave with Diotima's ladder of love in the *Symposium*. Each portrays an ascent. But where the Cave image emphasizes the arduous and frightening path to liberation and hence the need for courage or strength of soul, Diotima's account emphasizes the attraction of progressively greater or more substantial beauty. Whereas the *Republic* views things from a thymotic or thymoeidetic perspective, the *Symposium* looks at the world from a beautifying erotic perspective. Each perspective is partial, but less in the sense that it distorts things than that it allows one to see only part of what is. Or, rather, such distortion as each perspective generates comes from ignoring the other perspective, from overlooking its own partiality and taking its own view as the only view. Once we see past this partiality, we will be able, indeed will be inclined, to accept the two accounts as adding up to a complex (and for that reason all the more illuminating) unity.

Is it possible to discern from the *Symposium*'s disparate treatments a single coherent account of eros' essential meaning or identity? Perhaps the speakers' various answers *can* be reconciled, so that the speeches form a dialectical progress toward a final Platonic position (or at least a final position for the *Symposium*). Such a reconciliation, however, would not, because logically it could not, preserve every teaching in its given form: even if every teaching is somehow right, each cannot be simply right, insofar as it makes of its truth something too global or final. But is even such a limited reconciliation possible? Is one suggested?

The former question is the easier one to answer in the affirmative, as long as we grant ourselves the latitude to impute different "rankings" to the different teachings, so that, for example, we accept only those parts of the other symposiasts' speeches that are consistent with Socrates' speech. The real question is whether such a reading is suggested by the dialogue, for without such an indication one might just as legitimately afford pride of place to a different speech, say Aristophanes', and keep only those parts of the others' speeches that accord with *his*. Or one might forgo the attempt to reconcile the teachings altogether: after all, it is far from obvious that the complexities and contradictions of the erotic life as we experience it or as Plato depicts it lend themselves to a coherent, unified interpretation.[11] Indeed, it is not immedi-

---

11. So much does Socrates' speech conflict with those of Aristophanes and Alcibiades that Nussbaum suggests that Plato means to teach us the necessity of choosing between two irreconcilable kinds of love: "We see two kinds of value, two kinds of knowledge; and we see that we must choose. One sort of understanding blocks out the other. The pure light of the eternal form eclipses, or is eclipsed by, the flickering lightning of the . . . unstably moving body." See *The Fragility of Goodness*, p. 198.

ately evident that Socrates' speech is *self*-consistent. In the space of only a few pages he—or, rather, Diotima—first defines eros as love of the beautiful and then as love of the good's being one's own forever. Surely one of the *Symposium*'s major teachings, its chief teaching according to some, is the tension between love of the beautiful and love of the good.[12] Thus the unity of Socrates' own speech, assuming that these two phenomena can be reconciled, cannot be a simple one. At best it must be dialectical or dynamic, that is, arrived at over the course of the speech, rather than paradigmatic or structural.[13] Yet this dialectical unity is real—and is exactly what makes Socrates' speech the keystone of Plato's teaching in the *Symposium*. (This notwithstanding that Socrates places the main part of his argument in the mouth of another—a fictional other, no less[14]—and notwithstanding that his speech abstracts from eros' less than beautiful features [198c–e].) I make this claim for four reasons, each of which has to do with the speech itself and not with Socrates' special status in Plato's corpus or in the *Symposium* itself.

First, Socrates' speech—looking particularly at its characterization of eros as the desire that the good be ours forever—offers the most capacious position, the one that most allows for the inclusion of themes or insights introduced by the other speakers. Socrates' speech accommodates the truth even of Aristophanes' account, notwithstanding that Aristophanes propounds a very different *interpretation* of this truth: for Aristophanes eros is essentially love of one's own, for Socrates it is love of the good—but love of the good being one's own. The capaciousness of Socrates' account is a formal feature, but not for that reason an insignificant one.

---

12. Strauss is one who sees this teaching as central. See *On Plato's Symposium*, p. 28: "The good is not identical with the beautiful, and that is the great theme of the *Symposium*." Also see Bloom, "The Ladder of Love," pp. 127–28.

13. Regarding Platonic dialogues' use of "patterns or paradigms, on the one hand, and dynamic, on the other," and the way in which the two "are so utterly wrapped up with one another," see Burger, ed., *Encounters and Reflections*, pp. 117–44; the lines quoted are from p. 132.

14. Socrates attributes his account of eros to Diotima, whose name alone renders her a likely fiction. "The name *Diotima* means 'honored by Zeus,' and the mention of the city Mantinea, in the grammatical form it appears in here [i.e., her first mention], is identical with the word for the science of divining" (Bloom, "The Ladder of Love," p. 129). Or as Timothy Burns has put it, with only slight exaggeration, "Diotima of Mantinea" would have sounded to Plato's readers (and to Socrates' auditors) like "Prophetess from Prophetville." Much has been written regarding the question of Diotima's reality and the significance of Socrates' attributing the whole of his account to her. For present purposes it will suffice to register this matter as a warning against accepting Diotima's account as simply Socrates' view, let alone as Plato's view. For treatments of the question of Diotima and its implication for the *Symposium*, see Nussbaum, *The Fragility of*

Second, Socrates' speech tacitly responds to each of the other speeches. That the response is tacit only highlights the significance by making the correspondence Plato's own direct statement: as noted above, Socrates' speech divides into seven thematically indivisible parts that correspond, *in order*, to the teachings offered by the dialogue's seven speakers. Making the speech even more striking and suggestive in its comprehensiveness is that the seventh part corresponds to a speaker who has not yet arrived on the scene. (The seventh part presents Socrates' six-step outline of erotic education or ascent, which corresponds to Alcibiades' account of his six-step attempt to seduce Socrates.)[15] To be sure, the themes or insights from the other speakers are reinterpreted, sometimes radically, in light of Socrates' own final view. For that matter, so are the earlier parts of Socrates' own account: the love of the beautiful, having first been presented as the essence of eros, becomes a subsidiary part of the phenomenon—subsidiary, that is, to the desire for the good. But reinterpretation is still recognition—indeed, the most appropriate kind of recognition from the standpoint of dialectic.

Third, the speech's definition of eros as the desire for the sempiternal possession of the good is uniquely consistent with the presentation of eros in the *Republic*. (That presentation is made by Socrates.) The consistency between the two Socratic accounts is not perfect. Socrates never quite says in the *Republic* that eros is synonymous with desire for the good; and, as noted earlier, the *Republic* takes a relatively harsh stance toward sexual passion and the body in general. Nevertheless there is much consistency between the two accounts, concerning both the phenomenology and the nature of eros. Each dialogue depicts all who are described as erotic as dominated by an intense, determined longing for what the person believes to be good. Each dialogue suggests that what people believe to be good is usually based on a misapprehension of what is good, that is, of what would yield the satisfaction they seek. And the two dialogues make consistent if not identical suggestions, albeit rather abstractly, about what the good actually is (i.e., wherein erotic fulfillment is to be found) and about the character of the popular misapprehensions of the good (i.e., how we go so wrong). In short, both Socratic accounts of eros suggest (1) that, for all its multiplicity of objects, eros has a single ultimate aim or Object;

Goodness, p. 177; Newell, *Ruling Passion*, pp. 78–79; and Strauss, *On Plato's* Symposium, pp. 184–85.

15. Strauss outlines the six stages of Socrates' account of erotic ascent and the six stages of Alcibiades' attempted seduction in *On Plato's* Symposium, pp. 237 and 270–71, respectively.

(2) that this Object is present to varying degrees (or not present at all) in or through the innumerable objects that individuals consciously desire and seek; and (3) that the degree to which this final Object is present in or attainable through the objects we pursue is precisely the degree of the latter's goodness. Both accounts also suggest, by virtue of the choice of the term *erōs* to stand for such a multiplicity of desires, (4) that sexual desire is somehow central to or paradigmatic of the whole category.

Finally, the conception of eros advanced by Socrates' speech is most consistent with and most powerfully explains the activity of the *Symposium* itself, in the broad sense of that word ("activity") as described above (i.e., including both action within the dialogue and action associated with the various participants "offstage").

Each of these reasons is important. I would particularly like to highlight the fourth, however, partly because the other reasons have been explored elsewhere, but mostly because the appeal to activity comes closest to being an empirical argument. Indeed, it *becomes* an empirical argument when the activity referred to is actual, historical activity—as it is, in fact, in most and arguably all of the cases to be considered below. To be sure, the activity to which I refer, the erotic activity of the dialogue's "manifest lovers," represents only a portion of the wide range of erotic phenomena. That portion, though, is of signal political significance. Moreover, although I will not be able to make the argument comprehensively, I will go so far as to suggest that Socrates' speech, read correctly—that is, in light of its self-confessed selectivity and beautification of the truth and with regard to its context—plausibly explains not only the erotic activity of the "manifest lovers" but also the speeches (the *activity* of self-expression and self-justification) of everyone in the dialogue, including what is less than beautiful in the eros of those others. And if that is in fact the case, the speech may well be a plausible account of erotic phenomena as such, at least insofar as the dialogue's dramatis personae represent the full range of basic erotic stances.[16] Now to ascribe such status to Socrates'

---

16. Strauss suggests that the participants in the *Symposium* do cover the full range of basic erotic stances. "This can be [established] by a simple mathematical operation. There are three considerations which are obviously relevant: (1) the speaker may be a lover or beloved; (2) he may be old or young . . . (3) as indicated by the attitude toward wild drinking in the beginning, is he cautious or not? The incautious are subdivided into two forms: the incautious who is soft and the incautious who is manly. We have, then, three different points of view, two consisting of two alternatives and one of three—twelve alternatives altogether." Strauss then associates Phaedrus, Pausanias, Eryximachus, Agathon, Alcibiades, Aristodemus, and Aristophanes with one

speech is not to say that it conveys the entire teaching of the dialogue, that the other speeches or their truths are somehow incorporated in or discounted by Socrates' speech, so that their value lies only in helping us to understand his. Aristophanes' speech in particular illuminates much that is not addressed by Socrates: its powerful representation of lovers' experience and its central placement in the dialogue testify to its importance. But if Socrates, with his emphasis on eros' "vertical dimension," that is, the ladder of love and eros' fulfillment in philosophy, doesn't explore certain aspects of eros as extensively as does Aristophanes—and he doesn't—his account nevertheless speaks to the whole of eros. Nor, as some seem to think, does his account somehow depart from or look beyond our real experience in favor of some unreachable or even illusory end. For the end of eros as Socrates presents it is an end toward which experience itself points—an end toward which we *sense* that our experience points. Socrates' speech is as experientially or phenomenologically oriented as any other in the dialogue. (The uniqueness of Aristophanes' speech is not that it explores erotic experience—it does this, but it is not alone in doing so—but that it offers a unique *interpretation* of erotic experience.) What, then, *is* the teaching that emerges from Socrates' speech? What does eros want?

---

each of the twelve alternatives and Socrates with two ("old, manly, lover" and "old, manly, beloved"). He then explains why the remaining three alternatives might be thought to have been present at the party (there is a reference to some who were present but did not speak) and why Plato might have seen fit not to have them speak. See *On Plato's Symposium*, pp. 253–55. We should note, however, that Strauss's scheme makes no reference to female lovers, just as Plato gives us no female lovers in the *Symposium*. Does the *Symposium*, then, articulate the varieties only of *male* eros? Or do its categories cut across the divide between the sexes and apply to both male and female? In Diotima we at least encounter a woman, or are told that we do; and a wise woman ("like the perfect sophists" [208c]), at that.

3

WHAT DOES EROS WANT?

Before trying to read Socrates' speech correctly—before attempting to determine the significance of its selectivity, its beautification of the truth, and its context—indeed, *in order* to read it correctly, one would do well to read it, if not incorrectly, then naively—which, however, does not mean carelessly. Far from it. By "naively" I mean without regard for the subtleties of Plato's art whereby he calls into question what Socrates seems to be teaching. (Such naivety is not at all inconsistent with analytic rigor or indeed much of our proudest modern science and scholarship, as Nietzsche knew so well.) One must begin, that is, by putting oneself in something like the position of Socrates' more acute interlocutors, who are bound, no matter how intelligent they may be, to hear his speech without full regard for its qualifying context. Some of that context is simply unavailable to them—for example, the ways in which Socrates' seven-part speech corresponds to the seven-part procedure of the symposium. And surely Socrates' provisional warnings about his selectivity and beautification are too brief and too little stressed to dampen the effects of this selectivity and beautification. Beautiful speech about a powerful, beauty-fired passion is not much undermined by quickly spoken technical concessions, least of all when one is already enlivened if not intoxicated by eros (and wine). I will refer to the teaching that emerges from this kind of reading as Socrates' overt or explicit account of eros. In truth, though, it is not Socrates' interlocutors but rather Plato's serious but naive readers in whose position we must put ourselves, for the outlines of the overt teaching of eros are found in the combination of Socrates' accounts in the *Symposium* and the *Republic*, and no interlocutors are present at both dialogues (though Glaucon has heard both accounts). It may well be, as I have argued, that what a dialogue de-emphasizes is nevertheless present in it, so that the outlines of Socrates' overt account can be found in either the *Symposium* or the *Republic* alone. But it is also true, indeed more definitely so, that what is de-emphasized in one dialogue is not likely to be noticed without the instruction given by the other dialogue. For this reason we will consider Socrates' speech in the *Symposium* against the backdrop of the teaching he propounds in the *Republic*.

The overt account is important to know for three reasons. First, it tells us what Socrates, and even more so Plato, would teach many of those who would learn from them. (Why Plato more than Socrates? Because Socrates must already see that his interlocutors are firmly wedded to their views and will be difficult to move, whereas Plato presumably expects that readers come to him with more openness and hope for instruction than Socrates' interlocutors exhibit.) By considering the teaching that Plato presumably wishes to impart to many readers we can apprehend something of his assessment of both "ordinary" human nature and the political uses and abuses of various opinions about eros. Second, Plato's deeper teaching surely begins with this one. The depths of Platonic dialogues qualify the surfaces, often dramatically; but no such qualification, not even one that amounts to a reversal, can be comprehensible without first taking account of the surface teachings. Whatever the depths "do" they do *with* or *to* the surface. Finally, the overt account is an account of how eros typically comes to light. Indeed, its being so is precisely what makes it credible to those to whom it is offered as *the* Socratic or Platonic teaching on eros and what allows more persistent readers to make the descent to the deeper teaching(s). Herewith, then, a first reading of the Socratic teaching, a reading undertaken with an attempt at analytic rigor but without great regard for the subtler dimensions of Platonic artistry.

SOCRATES' OVERT ACCOUNT

The first elements of Socrates' overt teaching are those we encountered in Chapter 1's treatment of the *Republic*. Eros comes to light as a powerful desire or set of desires with a single aim but multiple objects. The character of this desire is acquisitive and expansionist: eros seeks fulfillment through possession, thinking increased possession to be the way to enhanced being. Eros' objects can be ranked hierarchically in accordance with whether and to what extent they yield eros' aim. The highest or truest objects of eros, because they have the most Being and are therefore most satisfying, are those pursued by the philosopher, who thereby exemplifies eros at its most highly developed and fulfilled. Each of these elements is present as well in Socrates' teaching in the *Symposium*. Each is also qualified by its treatment in the *Symposium*, however. If the *Republic* shows us eros as it most typically comes to light from a political perspective, as I claimed at the start of Chapter 1, then Socrates' overt teaching as a whole, that is, as related by the *Republic in combination with* the *Symposium*, is an account of how eros typically comes to light from a broader perspective, or rather from a combination of the *Republic*'s political perspective and the *Symposium*'s more subjective or phenomenological standpoint. The resulting teaching—Socrates' overt account of eros as it emerges from both the *Republic* and the *Symposium* (especially the latter, whose account seems longer and more complete)—can be summarized roughly as follows.

In the *Symposium* as in the *Republic* Socrates depicts erotic satisfaction in terms of objects that one might in some sense possess. But gaining possession is not the whole of the story, even if the *Republic* seems to teach that it is. In the more palpably erotic *Symposium* Socrates teaches that one pursues beautiful objects in order that he may thereby generate or give birth in them. Only through this generation can he achieve the immortality he knowingly or unknowingly seeks. (More likely *unknowingly*, especially if his eros is of the most common variety.) "And why is eros of engendering? Because engendering is born forever and is immortal as far as that can happen to a mortal being" (206e). Immortality, then, emerges on this account as the true aim of eros. It is the good as such. (True, in the next line Diotima seems to suggest that immortality is only a precondition for or an accompaniment of the good. But that suggestion is explicitly based on what she and Socrates had already agreed to and it is effectively retracted in the immediate sequel [207a–208b], wherein immortality proves to be not an accompaniment of the good but the good itself.) The "objects" one seeks are sought so that their beauty might allow for the generation of this progeny. The kind of progeny—children, works, fame—varies according to the kind of object one loves, though it would be more accurate to state this in the reverse order, since what determines the kind of object that one is drawn to (body, soul, city) is the kind of progeny with which one is already (again, unknowingly) pregnant.

The overt Socratic accounts of eros and philosophy in both the *Symposium* and the *Republic* suggest that the peak of erotic development is the philosophic life. To suggest that Plato gives us a single "philosophic life" is a bit disingenuous, for there are differences between Socrates' respective descriptions of philosophy in the two dialogues and even greater differences between the philosophic life as Socrates describes it in either dialogue and the philosophic life as Plato shows him living it.[1] Even so, each of the accounts has philosophy at the culmination of erotic development. (For that matter, as we will see in Chapter 4, the philosophic life as Socrates lives it can also—indeed, more plausibly—be interpreted as the peak of erotic life.) In the *Symposium* the philosopher is shown to exemplify not just the highest but the *truest* eros, in that the focus of his eros, the objects of his erotic desire, are surer routes to immortality.[2] The *Republic* similarly depicts philosophic eros as the truest eros by virtue of being the surest route to attaining eros' aim, though in the *Republic* the specified aim of philosophic eros is not immortality but greater *being*, to be achieved by apprehending the *eidê*. The objects of the philosopher's eros, of course, are cognitive; and at the peak, the objects reduce to—or perhaps better put, arise from and return to—one.

The overt Socratic accounts of eros and philosophy in both the *Symposium* and the *Republic* suggest that the object of the philosopher's eros and thus the final or true object of *all* eros is a kind of knowledge or insight or awareness, though not one that can be discursively represented. They suggest that there is some insight or awareness that would satisfy us comprehensively and that all souls somehow divine and hence pursue, albeit (most typically) in vain and distorted ways. The account in the *Republic* presents this insight as insight into what *is*, or sight of the *eidê*, culminating in sight (though perhaps not direct sight) of that which gives rise to the *eidê* and hence Being itself: the Good.[3] Socrates' account in the *Symposium* culminates with a focus on the beautiful rather than the Good. But it is my contention that readers will typi-

---

1. The philosopher depicted by Socrates in his speech in the *Symposium* seems complete in his quest and thus not in need of further thought or social interaction. Similarly, the philosopher-kings described in the middle books of the *Republic* are far removed from ordinary social life and possess a perfect knowledge, abiding entirely with the *eidê*, at least when philosophizing. Theirs seems a fully satisfied eros, if such could be called eros at all. Socrates, by contrast, is palpably (albeit ambiguously) erotic: intensely social, interested in all sorts of people, particularly drawn to the young and noble (or beautiful), and forever inquiring and testing.

2. To call philosophic eros both the *highest* and the *truest* eros is redundant according to the meaning of "highest" that I put forward in Chapter 1, note 24. But this usage is not necessarily common usage and thus is easy to forget. We tend to describe as "higher" those things which strike us as nobler or more refined, irrespective of whether they would bring greater satisfaction.

3. A word on usage. In accordance with the *Republic*'s presentation of the Good as unitary and transcendent, a treatment that Diotima's account does not contradict, it seems fitting to capitalize the word when what is being referred to is the Good *as such*, that is, the Good as that which is the source of both being and knowing. When I am referring to the good *for human beings*, that is, something that can in some way be possessed or incorporated or experienced, I will employ the lowercase. In accordance with this usage, one might characterize the overt Socratic teaching as follows: the good entails, or at its peak consists in, sight of the Good.

cally read the Good and the beautiful as the same thing—and that they are probably meant to do so. For one thing, although the beautiful is "only" an *eidos*,[4] it is, in effect, the *eidos* of *eidê*, the form of forms, for the *eidê* are invisible "looks" and beauty is the virtue or excellence of looks. This alone brings the beautiful close to the Good and perhaps even establishes it as identical to the Good, at least with respect to the Good as it presents itself to human beings, which is the only way we can encounter the Good in any case. The beautiful, one might say, is the face of the Good as the latter presents itself to erotic humanity. Moreover, and even more important, the beautiful stands in the same position vis-à-vis human desire in the *Symposium* that the Good holds in the *Republic*: just as in the *Republic* Socrates identifies the Good as "what every soul pursues and for the sake of which it does everything" (505d–e), so in the *Symposium* he approvingly relates Diotima's teaching that the beautiful is "the perfect end of erotics . . . that very thing . . . for whose sake alone all the prior labors were undertaken" (210e–211a).[5] Finally and most important, lovers of the beautiful, of *anything* beautiful, will tend to regard the beautiful ipso facto as good. (More on this below.)

The reader is thus led to equate—or rather is confirmed in his tendency to equate—the Good and the beautiful. Socrates offers no account of "the being" of the Good. But if he cannot show it to us—and *would* not if he could—he can point toward it. More helpfully, he can point to the path from whose end the Good will in fact be discernible. The steps of this path, at least

---

4. Although Socrates does not explicitly call the beautiful an *eidos*, he attributes to it the same characteristics he elsewhere attributes distinctively to the *eidê*: The beautiful "is, first of all, always being and neither coming to be nor perishing, nor increasing nor passing away; and secondly, not beautiful in one respect and ugly in another, nor at one time so, and at another time not—either with respect to the beautiful or the ugly—nor here beautiful and there ugly, as being beautiful to some and ugly to others; nor in turn will the beautiful be imagined by [the accomplished lover] as a kind of face or hands or anything else in which body shares, nor as any speech nor any science, and not as being somewhere in something else . . . but as it is alone by itself and with itself, always being of a single form; while all other beautiful things that share in it do so in such a way that while it neither becomes anything more or less, nor is affected at all, the rest do come to be and perish" (210e–211b).

5. Nor does this peak represent the satisfaction or redemption of eros alone. Nothing less than life itself is justified by the final erotic ascent: "'It is at this place in life, in beholding the beautiful itself, my dear Socrates,' the Mantinean stranger said, 'that it is worth living, if—for a human being—it is [worth living] at any place. Should you ever see the beautiful itself, it will be your opinion that it is not to be compared to gold and garments and the beautiful boys and youths at whose sight you are now thunderstruck'" (211c–d). If one had hesitated to accept the centrality of eros to human life, this equation of erotic satisfaction with life-justification is bound to clinch the case.

on Socrates' telling in the *Republic*, are the many studies outlined in book 7, from arithmetic to dialectic. The path in all its difficulty and peril is dramatically represented by the Cave image. The same ascent is also represented, it seems to me, in Diotima's ladder of love, with which Socrates' speech in the *Symposium* culminates.[6]

But ascent, we recall, is only part of the story. Eros seeks not simply to behold or to possess, but also to generate, to give birth, for it is through one's progeny that one lives beyond one's death and contends for immortality. Thus Socrates' Diotiman account is complete only with the progeny of this highest eros, a progeny that is superior because it stands the best chance of winning the lover immortality: "'Don't you realize,' she said, 'that only here, in seeing in the way the beautiful is seeable, will he get to engender not phantom images of virtue—because he does not lay hold of a phantom—but true, because he lays hold of the true; and that once he has given birth to and cherished true virtue, it lies within him to become dear to god and, if it is possible for any human being, to become immortal as well?'" (212a).

There is a notable qualification in what has just been quoted. The ascent of eros is said to be the means to immortality—*if* immortality is possible for a human being. For that matter, the assertion that life is worth living is subjected to the same qualification (211c). These ifs will not escape the notice of an attentive reader. Yet whether they will register as qualifications, rather than as urbane modesty of speech, is less clear, particularly amid Diotima's enchanting rhetoric. Certainly they do not seem to break her spell. It is only when we take note of other qualifications—only when we subject this account of eros to a more thoroughgoing scrutiny—that the hints embedded in these ifs will really come to mean something.

What are the practical, prescriptive implications of this account? Socrates' speech in the *Symposium* offers only the broad outlines of an answer, and

6. As noted earlier, the difference between the *Symposium*'s erotic perspective and the *Republic*'s thymoeidetic perspective is perhaps nowhere more visible than in the contrast between these two famous images of ascent. In the *Symposium*'s "ladder of love," the lover is lured upward by ever more powerful instances of beauty. In the *Republic*'s Cave image, liberation is bewildering and traumatic and ultimately life threatening, yet somehow appealing on account of that. That these contrasting images are nevertheless counterparts may be additionally indicated by their (in a sense) parallel locations. The seven parts of Socrates' speech in the *Symposium* correspond not only to seven speeches in that dialogue but also to the first seven books of the *Republic*. As Diotima's tale of ascent appears in the seventh part of Socrates' speech in the *Symposium*, so the Cave and the education toward philosophy appear in book 7 of the *Republic*.

does so only symbolically: cultivate your reason, try to determine whether you are pregnant in soul or in body, and proceed accordingly. To be sure, there are numerous subtle hints—for example, that erotic ascent entails not only new objects but also a new way of feeling toward them, a way (or ways) that will not strike the uninitiated even as erotic. (Cognates of *erōs* are used with reference to the first three rungs of the ladder of love, but not with reference to the higher rungs, where the talk is of "seeing," "beholding," or "glimpsing" beauty, not loving it.) Indeed, there is even mention of an element of compulsion in the successful erotic trek (210c), just as in the *Republic*'s Cave image (515c–516a).[7] But even assuming that these hints will be discerned, they speak less to what one needs to do to acquire a proper education than to what one will experience along the way.

The *Republic*, however, offers a more substantive reply that is compatible with Socrates' speech in the *Symposium*. The reader of the *Republic* is directed toward moral virtues and the "right" cultivation of eros and is given some idea of what these things mean. Moreover, he is taught that he must be careful to steer his eros *away from* a variety of things—from objects whose beauty is somehow false yet seductive enough to the uneducated to be addicting. More generally, the reader, having come to see his own prior education as deficient, is taught to be suspicious of the seductive appeal of the goods prized by the many. These goods, whether money, power, or prestige, promise a fulfillment, a plenitude, *a degree of being* that they cannot deliver. Ultimately the only solution is to turn to philosophy, so that one might come to recognize those objects or that way of life wherein a greater degree of being does reside. But the philosophic life is shown to be difficult and demanding of very rare gifts. And in any event it must await years of preparation. So the reader is left with a set of positive and negative opinions by which to steer his erotic life to the extent that he is able: abide with what is orderly and fair (as these terms are explained) and cease grasping unreflectively after goods whose goodness is suspect. Which goods *are* suspect? At the risk of anachronistically reading Rousseau into Plato, it seems to me that Plato, too, teaches that the surest sign of the falseness of a good is that it masters the pursuer, rendering him, like an addict, increasingly unfulfilled and dependent.[8] See, for example, book

---

7. The disappearance of the language of eros and the reference to the need for compulsion seem to support an interpretation according to which the true ascent to philosophy is an education *out* of eros. I will explain below why I do not think this view is correct.

8. Rousseau makes the point at *Emile* 445: "All passions are good when one remains their master; all are bad when one lets oneself be subjected to them."

9's account of the pursuit of pleasure by the vulgar, or "those who have no experience of prudence and virtue": "after the fashion of cattle, always looking down and with their heads bent to earth and table, they feed, fattening themselves, and copulating; and, for the sake of getting more of these things, they kick and butt with horns and hoofs of iron, killing each other *because they are insatiable*; for they are not filling the part of themselves that *is*, or can contain anything, with things that *are*" (586a–b; first emphasis added). Indeed, this addict-intensity is more than a sign; it is also a cause of deeper frustration and spiritual debilitation: one's desire for the goods one craves will intensify, to the exclusion of other goods, to the extent that one invests in their capture. (But wouldn't his capture of them finally enable him to learn that they are in fact false goods? In principle, yes; but unless one has amassed an empire, one is more likely to imagine that the promised being has eluded one only because one has not yet won enough of the desired good.) As with Rousseau, so with Socrates' overt teaching: the cruel paradox of uneducated eros, which means, for most of us, the cruel paradox of life, is that the very intensity of our desire only subverts its chances of success. Hence the rigorous regulation of the passions, eros chief among them, in the regimes of both the *Republic* and the *Laws*.[9]

Amid the pleasant precincts of Agathon's house or under Socrates' spell in Cephalus' place one might believe for a while that the peaks of eros are within one's reach. But whether they are or aren't, one still must resume living at one's current altitude. Which raises the question: Does the overt Socratic teaching on eros point readers to an understanding of why we are attracted to the goods or purported goods that attract us, the ones that call out to us now? Does it instruct readers in how to understand and judge the seeming goodness of various things? It seems to me that it does, albeit very indirectly.

People do not think much about immortality while they pursue most of the goods they pursue. If even sexual desire forgets its connection to progeny, how likely is it that one who is pursuing money or power will consider and judge the object of his eros from such a perspective? (The likely exception is the lover of fame, which is probably why that type is such an attractive candidate for philosophic education; cf. *Alcibiades I*.) Even less do they think about

---

9. Since Rousseau has entered the conversation, it is worth noting here that in this respect, as in so many others, his republicanism replicates that of the *Laws*, notwithstanding its ostensibly modern and egalitarian theoretical foundation.

eternity or about the Good, or about sight of what *is*. Which is probably just as well, given the ways in which these things are routinely conceived. What *is* in our minds as we pursue and consider the goods we erotically desire is the sense that they promise us a greater *being*. Not that one is necessarily conscious of this promise: the erotically disposed person is no more apt to be thinking about being than about immortality or the Good. Far more likely, he is thinking of beauty, or pleasure, or appetite, or honor, or simply happiness. My point, though, is that what these terms turn out to mean, what makes them attractive ends, is that they somehow promise a greater sense of being or aliveness. This is the position of Rousseau, implicit, as we shall see, in his explicit embrace of existence or the sentiment of existence as the good. But it also seems to me to be presupposed by Plato, for he frequently bases appeals to virtue or philosophy on the implicit or explicit promise that they yield more being. Consider again book 9 of the *Republic*, where the pleasures of the just man are said to entail great being while those of the tyrant and the vulgar are evanescent and lacking in being (583b–588a). See also the *Gorgias*, where both Socrates' and Callicles' arguments appeal to *greater being* as the substance and standard of pleasure. As in book 9 of the *Republic*, Socrates argues for pleasure as a filling up; his metaphor is a full wine jar. Callicles, by contrast, holds that pleasure lies in the vigorous *pursuit* of goods. But the Calliclean pursuit is so wholehearted as to constitute aliveness in and of itself. The *Symposium*, too, appeals to the desire for more being, both in the emphasis on possessing good things and in the promise of immortality. The suggestion that one can achieve erotic fulfillment and happiness by possessing good things (205a, d) will ratify the reader's likely belief that he can achieve more being through more having. And the promise of immortality through erotic ascent to philosophy will certainly seem to promise an infinite extension, and thus ipso facto a greater degree, of being. I will argue below that the deeper Platonic teaching calls for a different interpretation, according to which the pursuit of being through these avenues, indeed the pursuit of being through any avenue, is misplaced and needs to be overcome—*as long as one conceives of being in the way that people typically do.* (On my reading of Plato's deeper teaching, it does make sense to say that eros seeks more being, but the proper pursuit of being requires a certain prerequisite *non*being, i.e., self-forgetting and ultimately the dissolution or transcendence of the ordinary self. This theme is expressed by the fact that as Socrates' speech progresses, the emphasis on being is superseded by a countervailing emphasis on *non*being—self-forgetting, dissolution, etc.) But it seems unlikely to me that many readers will have come to the same conclusion. From the perspective of most readers, I would venture to say, the reason to cultivate "right eros" is to achieve more being through the possession of good things. And I believe that Plato understands this to be the case and addresses his readers accordingly.

THE SOCRATIC ACCOUNT: A SECOND LOOK

The foregoing account is, I think, a fair interpretation of the overt Socratic account of eros and some of its implications. That I have based this reading not only on Socrates' speech in the *Symposium* but also on what he says in the *Republic* ought to have helped ensure against a one-sided interpretation. His speech in the *Symposium*, we recall, is admittedly selective and beautifying and in those ways falsifying. The *Republic*, with its far more severe look at eros, acts as a corrective and, when read alongside the Socratic teaching in the *Symposium,* brings us closer to what we might plausibly suppose to be Plato's deeper teaching. But is that enough? Or, even as the two dialogues complement and complete each other in some ways, do they share any features that themselves need to be balanced or corrected? In my view there are indeed some shared features of the *Symposium* and the *Republic* that cast doubt on parts of the reading I have just offered—not doubt as to the sense of Socrates' account, but doubt as to this account being in all ways the teaching Plato intends for his more persistent readers.

I noted in the last chapter that a correct understanding of Socrates' account of eros in the *Symposium* would need to be considered in light of three things: its selectivity, its beautification of the phenomenon, and the context of the speech. The first two of these things are reasonably well "corrected for" by recourse to the *Republic*. Although itself selective, Socrates' account in the *Republic* for the most part emphasizes different and even opposing features of eros from those he emphasizes in the *Symposium*. And the account in the *Republic* certainly does not beautify eros, at least insofar as it identifies eros with the tyrant. The tyrant's life may be tempting, but it does not seem beautiful to the young men gathered at Cephalus' house under Socrates' spell. The third thing, however—that is, the context of the speech, or, more precisely, its audience—is not "corrected for" by the *Republic*. For while there certainly are major differences between the satisfied diners gathered at Agathon's house and the younger, hungry men gathered at Cephalus', the two groups have two crucial features in common, features that must surely have influenced the presentation of as sensitive and politic a speaker as the Platonic Socrates.

First, the interlocutors in both dialogues evince a deep attachment to or investment in eros. They are either erotic themselves or the knowing beneficiaries of eros.[10] Such an investment would not necessarily cause Socrates to omit inclusion of eros' darker side—he clearly doesn't do this in the *Republic*—but it would likely cause him to adjust his rhetoric, that is, (a) to narrow his critique of eros and (b) to depict as erotic and to make appealing to erotic men whatever end (i.e., whatever judgment or activity) he wanted to lead them to. Second, his interlocutors in each case are nonphilosophers, which would surely lead him to present his case in a way that is consistent with their needs and understandings and different in some measure from his own view of things. This could and almost certainly does mean many things, more than I could specify. But one thing stands out, for it is arguably the thing that most distinguishes philosophy as Plato depicts it and best accounts for the other distinctive features of the philosopher: the philosopher is one who has accepted his mortality and who thus neither dreads nor denies death and does not hope for immortality. The stances toward death among nonphilosophers vary a great deal, ranging from the calm of the pious believer to the desperate deeds of those who rage against mortality or the extravagant deeds of those who would overcome it by winning an undying name. What these have in common, though—and what all nonphilosophers have in common—is a hope for immortality. This hope would surely have been taken account of by the Platonic Socrates, who always shows respect for conventional piety and who questions its beliefs only in a very indirect way. (Indeed, the Platonic Socrates seems almost in the business of refounding popular faith in the soul's immortality.)

What, then, are the specific effects of this context on Socrates' account of eros, and how ought we to adjust our reading accordingly? There are three

---

10. Erotic themselves: from the *Symposium*, Pausanias, Eryximachus, Aristophanes, and Aristodemus (Alcibiades too, but he is not present during Socrates' speech); from the *Republic*, Glaucon, perhaps Adeimantus (though more guardedly), and probably also Polemarchus (given his eagerness for inquiry and his subsequent turn to philosophy). Knowing beneficiaries of eros: from the *Symposium*, Phaedrus (the benefited beloved) and Agathon (perhaps as a poet he is erotic, too, but mostly, as one who seeks applause through gratifying the eros of others, he seems a beneficiary of eros); from the *Republic*: Thrasymachus, who specializes in manipulating erotic passion (including thymotic passion) for political profit.

major features of Socrates' overt account that are contradicted by the broader evidence of the dialogues and that should therefore be interpreted and to some extent discounted as Socrates' politic response to the character of his interlocutors (and therefore also as Plato's response to the character of much of his readership). First, Socrates' explicit account suppresses to a considerable extent the nonidentity of the beautiful and the good and therewith the tension between love of the beautiful and love of the good. Second, Socrates' account appeals to and in the process validates the longing for immortality, seeking to render death a less terrible prospect and thereby to bank the fires that lead to all sorts of desperate and destructive behaviors, especially in politics. This concession to the popular longing for immortality accounts for the third falsehood, the misrepresentation of philosophy and philosophic eros. Some would say that Socrates misrepresents philosophy as erotic. My view is that he misrepresents *the way* in which philosophy is erotic: the philosopher does indeed love the beautiful and the good, but these terms have radically different meanings for him than they do for most of us—so much so that most of us would not recognize his beautiful as beautiful or his good as good. Indeed, the philosopher's view of the beautiful and the good requires the repudiation and transcendence of the common understandings of these things. These effects do indeed open a distance between Socrates' explicit account of eros and the teaching that Plato apparently wishes to convey to his better or more persistent readers. The question is *how great* a distance we are facing, and *how much* of Socrates' account must therefore be discounted in our effort to arrive at Plato's deeper teaching.[11]

The discrepancies I have cited between Socrates' explicit account and the deeper teaching of the dialogues concern some of the most basic as well as the peak elements of the erotic life. In an important sense, then—in an objective or theoretical sense—these discrepancies are major, and they will need to be examined. Yet before examining them I wish to suggest that in another sense—in a subjective sense or from the standpoint of the auditor's or reader's education—the distance, or at least the effect of the distance, is less great than it might appear, owing to the particular direction and effects of the explicit Socratic account. The genius of Plato's art of writing is not just to impart different teachings to different kinds of readers but to somehow align the

---

11. I do not claim to know that what I am calling Plato's "deeper teaching" is Plato's deep*est* or final teaching.

more dubious but salutary teachings with those which have a greater share in the truth. Think, in this regard, of Socrates' revised theology in the *Republic*, according to which the gods are not changeful or deceptive or cavalier toward human beings (377e–86a). Or consider the *Republic*'s "noble lie" (414b–15d). What makes it noble or nobly born (*gennaion*) is (a) that it represents symbolically some part of the truth and (b) that its effect is salutary, not just from the standpoint of the city's needs but also (though perhaps only partially) from the standpoint of the individual's good. The latter can mean more than one thing. Such a lie might serve an individual by giving him meaning and the ground for nobility. But by providing the ground for devotion to something beyond the objects of zero-sum appetite, it might also help prepare him to one day ascend from such lies to philosophy or the truth. Although the noble lie is offered as part of the civic education and not the philosophic education that is articulated later in the *Republic*, those selected for the latter education will have received the former one first: apparently some of what serves to make good and happy *citizens*, including a *lie*, can serve as a foundation for the more select education toward *human* excellence, or the philosophic love of the *truth*. Civic virtue may only be phantom virtue (443c), but a phantom is not merely a lie, even if it may need a lie in order to be inculcated. Demotic courage and moderation—the latter gained through a musical education that culminates in the habituation of eros toward "what's orderly and fine" (403a–c)—serve as the developmental foundation for true courage and moderation and, therewith, such wisdom as is available to human beings. Now the explicit Socratic account of eros, the account I outlined in the previous chapter, is precisely the theoretical underpinning or self-understanding of this subphilosophic erotic education. Thus, even as it departs from the truth or from that teaching that is nearer to the truth, the subphilosophic education serves to prepare those who receive it for an education toward that very truth. Perhaps it can similarly prepare us ourselves, who will not receive the whole education but who merely read about it, so long as we read with some care and think about its fundamental premises. If so, we will have done well to review the foundation on its own terms before seeking to go beyond it. However that may be, let us now look at each of the three discrepancies in order to move from Socrates' overt teaching toward the deeper teaching of the dialogues. The discrepancies, to repeat, arise from (a) Socrates' suppression of the nonidentity of the beautiful and the good, (b) his effective validation of the longing for immortality, and (c) his misrepresentation of philosophy and philosophic eros. Each of these features of Socrates' explicit teaching is qualified if not reversed by surrounding or underlying features of the dialogue. After examining these discrepancies, we will turn in Chapter 4 to the "manifest lovers" of the *Symposium* for a clearer idea of the practical and characterological implications of eros Platonically understood.

TOWARD PLATO'S DEEPER TEACHING

The (Non)Identity of the Good and the Beautiful

In common Greek parlance, *erōs* referred primarily to passionate desire for another person—or what most of us today call romantic love, though without the overtones of illusoriness that the word "romantic" once carried (and perhaps still does). Not mere sexual desire, no matter how intense—there were other words for that—but love: a desire to behold, to be with, and to possess a beloved not only during the sexual embrace but always. But romantic love or eros for another human being implies more than just this. One need not impute any dubious metaphysics to the phenomenon to conclude that it somehow involves, indeed is essentially constituted by, love of the beautiful: the beloved is always beautiful in the eyes of the lover; what's more, the beloved is lovable *for* his or her beauty (recalling the breadth of *kalon*). Yet even that is not the final truth of eros' phenomenology, for surely those who desire the beautiful desire it for a reason. If asked, and if able to answer (as the young Socrates was not [204d]), lovers would say that they anticipate that possession of the beautiful will somehow bring them happiness—that they desire the beautiful for the sake of happiness. And what that means, of course, is that they desire the beautiful for the sake of the good. Eros, then, proves to be nothing other than the love of the good, since the good, everyone would agree, is that which is good *for us*, that which would bring us happiness (204e, 205d). Indeed, "there is nothing that human beings love other than the good" (206a). How, then, could eros not be love of the good? Such is the logic that allows Diotima to redefine eros, from love of the beautiful to love of the good, without restructuring her argument or offering a new foundation.

That logic, however, is just a bit too eager. Perhaps we do love the beautiful for the sake of happiness, and perhaps the good is indeed that which would make us happy. But that doesn't quite mean that the happiness we seek through the beautiful is the same as that which we seek through other routes or is even compatible with it. And perhaps what we seek through possession of the beautiful is *not* happiness, at least not in any ordinary sense of the word: perhaps the young Socrates was wiser than he knew when he failed to answer Diotima's question regarding what it is that those who love the beautiful really want.[12] Moreover, whatever we seek through the beautiful, whether we call it happiness or something else, may or may not be *attainable* on these terms. Finally, even a cursory look at what normally passes for beautiful and what normally passes for good only confirms the disjunction between the two. Not that there is no overlap, but it is clearly impossible to credibly hold either that everything beautiful is good or that everything good is beautiful, at least not in the ordinary senses of those words.[13]

The nonidentity of the beautiful and the good is not all that difficult to see, and even a moderately careful reading of Diotima's account will serve to highlight this fact of life.[14] Why, then, submerge it at all? My suggestion is that Plato is here illustrating the erotic perspective, or the way that the erotic person sees things. As the *Republic* looks at things from a thymoeidetic perspective, Socrates' speech in the *Symposium* looks at things from an erotic or eros-formed perspective. And as a sensitive reading of the *Republic* reveals the character and limits of the thymoeidetic perspective, a sensitive reading of Socrates' speech in the *Symposium* reveals the character and limits of the

---

12. Diotima's question, precisely the sort of question that would be wielded to devastating effect by the mature Socrates, seems to demand that the beautiful or noble be interpreted in terms of—some would say reduced to—something more basic, that is, some single good. The charge of reductionism has been made most powerfully by Nietzsche, who accuses the mature Socrates of degrading and undermining the noble by testing it against a utilitarian and therefore *ignoble* understanding of the good (*BGE* 191; *Twilight*, "Socrates," 4–5; and *The Birth of Tragedy*, 12–15).

13. This is a very important point, but one that has been made decisively by others. See particularly Bloom, "The Ladder of Love," p. 127: "There are many things, like Locke's good bowel movement, that are good but which no sane person would call beautiful. The good is clear and reasonable: healthy, wealthy, and wise. . . . One might be inclined to say in Agathon's defense that although not all good things are beautiful, all beautiful things are good. But this is also not true. Achilles' beautiful death for his friend is, at least on Achilles' testimony, not good. The beauty of tragedy does not persuade us that we want these beauties for ourselves in the same way we want the good things."

14. The non-identity of the good and the beautiful is signaled earlier in the dialogue as well, through the casual and dubious substitution of one for the other. See the playful banter between Socrates and Aristodemus regarding the beautiful (or the good) going to the feasts of the beautiful (or the good) (174a–c). As Strauss observes in *On Plato's Symposium*, p. 28: "Socrates destroys the proverb by changing the good into the beautiful. The good is not identical with the beautiful, and that is the great theme of the *Symposium*."

erotic perspective. (We see here the likeness and complementarity of the *Symposium* and the *Republic*.) What strikes us about our beloved is his or her beauty. Whether that beauty is "real" or strictly an idiosyncratic judgment makes no difference. Whatever the source of the perception, the perception always seems to be part of erotic desire for another. The beloved's beauty, in fact, justifies the erotic experience. (This feature of erotic life becomes more clearly evident if we follow the Greek way and include within the concept of beauty [*kalon*] nobility or moral beauty.) To be called upon to justify one's love by any other standard than this—by the standard of goodness, for example—would be experienced as debasing. And yet, even while it eschews such justification, particularly if the "external" standard smacks of utilitarian calculus, eros nevertheless insists precisely on its own goodness and the goodness of the beloved. It may be offensive to have to justify one's love in terms of one's own benefit, but it is intolerable to believe that one's beloved is in no way good or that one's love is in no way good for oneself. To be sure, many people knowingly love "the wrong person," that is, someone who is bad for them in a general sense; to overcome such an erotic disposition is the focus of a veritable therapeutic industry. Yet nobody can be in love without believing that his or her love is somehow good, indeed *essentially* good—which is why the chief burden of the counselors and self-help books is precisely to convince the lovers that the goodness of their love really is somehow delusional, something that the unhappy lovers may already concede verbally but that they don't altogether believe. Eros, in other words, starts with beauty—is *of* beauty—but then imputes goodness to itself and the beloved. This is our experience, and this is what Plato helps us to see.

But if the beautiful and the good are not identical, neither are they unconnected. Diotima, after first submerging or seeming to overlook the tension between the two, in fact acknowledges the tension—but only by offering a plausible reconciliation. Her submergence is accomplished by casually shifting her focus from the beautiful to the good, thereby effectively interpreting the beautiful as an aspect of the good and love of the beautiful as a species of love of the good. Her reconciliation is accomplished by interpreting the beautiful as an instrument or means to the good. What erotic people are doing when they are pursuing *the good* is "bringing to birth *in beauty* both in terms of the body and in terms of the soul," that is, giving birth to whatever progeny they had been pregnant with beforehand (206b–d; emphasis added). From this Diotima concludes that "eros is not . . . of the beautiful," as the young Socrates had believed; rather, "[i]t is of engendering and bringing to birth in the beautiful" (206e). The beautiful makes possible the engendering and giving birth. How, though, is this a means to *the good?* It can be so only if engendering and giving birth either are themselves the good or else somehow yield the good. The latter, in fact, is the case. Or so it seems to those we call erotic: "'And why is eros of engendering? Because engendering is born forever and is immortal as far as that can happen to a mortal being'" (206e). What those who are called erotic seek as the good, then, is immortality. Immortality is what they really want and the end (the aim, or the final object) for whose sake they are drawn to beauty. Such individuals are characterized not simply by the desire to possess the good forever—*everyone* desires that—but by an intense and earnest love of the beautiful. That is what one normally means by eros. And the real meaning of that desire, by virtue not of an abstruse teleological inference but rather of the already present longing that underlies and animates the love of the beautiful, is precisely the desire for immortality, and, what's more, the hope for and the *belief* in immortality. Of course, as I have already stated, eros so constituted is a defective eros in that the pursuit of earthly immortality is both futile and based on a delusion or a distortion of something else. And so we are brought to the second discrepancy between the explicit Socratic account and the somewhat more complex teaching of the *Symposium* and *Republic.*

Immortality and Eternity

"Immortality" and "eternity" are frequently regarded as synonyms, but the negation of death is not the same thing as the negation of time. Only the first is mentioned in the *Symposium;* there is no indication of the eternal. Or is there? One of the striking images of the dialogue, yet one that does not seem to me to be adequately appreciated, is that of the solitary Socrates, standing stock-still, silent and meditative. The image precedes the festivity at Agathon's house and recurs in Alcibiades' speech (175a–b, 220c–d). What exactly Socrates is up to is impossible to say for sure. He may simply be thinking through some puzzle, as Alcibiades presumes. But the character of the occasions—that they occur apropos of no apparent external trigger or need; that they entail such stillness; and that no specific insights are said to be reported afterward—suggests that the activity involves, in whole or in part, nondiscursive contemplation. However that may be, to stand silent and still for a day and a night, awake and thoughtful, seems to imply a forgetting or a stepping out of time—a transcendence that, while not presented just so, at least seems consistent with the poetic depictions of philosophy that Socrates offers in both the *Symposium* and the *Republic*, that is, the philosopher as one who beholds the vast sea of the beautiful or who grasps true being (*Symposium* 210a–12a; *Republic* 484b). Even if we leave aside those silent spells of Socrates, the consistent Platonic depiction of philosophy suggests some kind of experience of the eternal, experience constituted by insight into what *is* and the freedom that goes with that insight. I will attempt to get closer to the heart of this matter in the next chapter. For now my purpose is to establish the distinction between the eternal and the immortal, for which it should suffice to take up, briefly, the following questions: (1) In what way does insight into what *is* constitute "experience of the eternal"? (2) What is the nature of the freedom that goes with this insight? And (3) what is the relation between the insight and the freedom?

(1) Insight into what *is*, is insight into that which does not come into being and pass away, that is, insight into the *timeless* ground of life and experience. And if we are in any way constituted by the contents of our consciousness, then such insight would itself be an experience that partakes of timelessness. What this means, practically, is seen if we consider the freedom that characterizes the one who has such insight.

(2) The Platonic philosopher, whether as described by Socrates or as exemplified by him, evinces an extraordinary and multifaceted freedom—from oppressive desire, from dependence on the opinion of others, and from dread of death. These freedoms, it seems to me—particularly the latter one—imply a kind of liberation from time itself: not necessarily an unawareness of time but an escape from the cares of the ego, cares which arise from its finitude, and thus most particularly from its mortal imprisonment in time. As indicated by this description and implicit in the words themselves, *eternity* is more basic than and subsumes *immortality*.

(3) In claiming only that this freedom "goes with" philosophic insight or "characterizes" the philosopher, I have not specified the causal relation between the philosopher's insight and his freedom. It seems to me that the relation is one of mutual or dialectical causality, consistent with my earlier discussion of the relation between demotic virtue and true virtue: demotic courage and moderation constitute a certain *freedom*, which helps make the philosophic ascent, that is, ascending *insights*, possible; and the consequence

of that ascent is the more perfect *freedom* of a Socrates. To be sure, the life of the philosopher is not explicitly described with reference to experience of the eternal. But the philosopher is explicitly linked to the immortal through his study of that which *is* and does not change, and as I have already suggested, that which *is* and does not change, though described merely as immortal, is also, and more fundamentally, eternal. And indeed, the *Symposium* offers further suggestive evidence that eternity is eros' true object. In the final section of his speech, Socrates (still ostensibly quoting Diotima) offers three descriptions of the beautiful itself.[15] In the first description, the beautiful is characterized, near the beginning of the description, as "always being" (211a). This same feature is included in the second description, though this time at the end (211b). In the third description, however, which is also the most exalted of the three, this feature is not mentioned at all (211d–e). Why not? More broadly, what is signified by the progressive de-emphasis of the beautiful's sempiternal character? A plausible answer is that it represents the change of outlook that occurs with the ascent to philosophy (the ascent being the central theme of this part of the speech). The progressive de-emphasis signifies eros's ascent from pursuit of the sempiternal to the pursuit and the experience of the eternal—an experience, if Socrates' description is to be believed, that is wondrous and life-justifying.

"Immortality," if I am right, stands in for "eternity." This is sensible usage by one who wishes to be persuasive to interlocutors (or readers) whose primary care is immortality and who would not be moved by talk of the eternal.

But why *is* immortality their primary care? Do we crave immortality strictly out of an aversion to nonbeing, or do we also somehow divine a connection to or a longing for eternity that we (mis)interpret in terms of immortality? Might the hope for immortality and, especially, the belief in immortality that the hope presupposes, be based, however tortuously or wishfully, on a divination of something real? The suggestion itself may seem to confess wishfulness. But that only takes us back to the question, since what's wanted is an explanation of the source of this wishfulness. And there is at least some reason to think that Plato answers the question in the affirmative. If the philosopher does in fact attain some experience of the eternal, then that would lend plausibility to the view that we all divine or intuit something of the eternal, for the philosopher will have arrived at his insights by way of

---

15. Strauss, *On Plato's Symposium*, pp. 238–39.

investigating and unpacking what is embedded (very deeply) in ordinary human experience. Philosophic insight on Plato's telling comes primarily not from the acquisition and analysis of more data but from a turning to see what was always already there to be seen (*Republic* 521c). And if all this is the case—if the longing for immortality is grounded in a true divination of the eternal; and if the philosopher represents the perfection of human nature by interpreting that divination and developing it correctly—then perhaps we can say that what eros *really* wants, even ordinary eros in its hidden heart of hearts, is not immortality but eternity.[16]

Eros and Philosophy

The foregoing realization allows us to resolve one of the great paradoxes of Socrates' treatment of eros. As long as one understands eros as longing for and presupposing the possibility of earthly immortality, it is difficult to see how the philosopher might be erotic. After all, the prospect of earthly immortality, not to put too fine a point on it, is delusional. Even if one grants that human beings live on in their children, in their works (poems, cities), or through fame, it is practically inconceivable upon reflection that they can live on through such progeny forever. Plato overtly suggests as much (though of course not in the *Symposium* or the *Republic*) with his notion of civilization-erasing cataclysms.[17] And he *covertly* leads the reader to the same conclusion in the *Symposium*, it seems to me, simply by inviting us to reflect on the plausibility of earthly immortality. How can it be, then, that philosophy, the endeavor characterized by rigorous intellectual integrity and fierce strength of soul, is presented in both the *Symposium* and the *Republic* as erotic—indeed, as the *perfection* of the erotic life? For that is precisely the claim of Socrates'

---

16. This is not to deny the ferocious power of the ego's aversion to non-being as a source of the desire for immortality, but only to suggest that this aversion may not be the only source of eros' power. Indeed, this aversion itself may well be grounded in the positive divination of eternity: perhaps the prospect of our own extinction offends us precisely because we have a sense, however badly misconstrued, of our real share in eternity. Plato gives a particularly elegant indication of the connection between eros and aversion to death in the *Laws*, whose very center—the end of Book 6 together with the beginning of Book 7—pairs, respectively, proposals regarding the regulation of sexual behavior with a discussion of prenatal care that culminates in a prescription for curing the terror of children—and not only children (782d–785b, 790c–791c).

17. *Timaeus* 22–23; *Critias* 108e; *Laws* 677a–b. Such an overt suggestion would not be fitting in the *Symposium* or the *Republic* for a reason already mentioned and soon to be discussed—namely, that Socrates appeals to the delusional hope for earthly immortality as a means of gaining his erotic interlocutors' attention.

explicit account of eros. Surely the philosopher ought to be the one most exempt from delusion. The answer, of course, lies in what we have just seen: the philosopher's eros is not directed by the hope of earthly immortality. He does not long for what the ordinarily erotic long for. Hence he is not erotic in an ordinary sense; far from it. Yet he longs for that of which the aim of ordinary eros is a distortion. He longs, consciously, for what the rest of us fail to divine that we long for. And for that reason he is erotic, indeed the perfection of eros.

Some who may accept the gist of my interpretation will nevertheless balk at my use of words. Eros is a word with a common meaning. That being so, why not dispense with the language of eros in connection with philosophy? If the philosopher transcends what eros usually means, why not simply say that he transcends eros altogether? Indeed, close attention to Diotima's account of erotic ascent may seem to suggest that we follow this path. As noted above, she ceases to use cognates of *erōs* once her account reaches the higher rungs of the ladder. And she even makes reference to a place for compulsion in successful erotic education (210c). These facts can be read to suggest that the journey to philosophy is not as lovely—not as erotic—as it seems at first, and that the education to philosophy entails nothing short of transcending or leaving behind eros.

Nevertheless it seems to me that it makes sense to call the philosopher erotic. The chief reason for this is what I have already argued, namely, that what the philosopher loves is what ordinary eros wants without knowing, so to speak. The philosopher's eros is directed to that toward which all eros is, but does not know itself to be, directed. To cease referring to the philosopher as erotic would submerge the important Platonic teaching that delusional eros isn't *simply* delusional but rather a distortion of a longing whose basis is not delusional and which is in fact satisfiable: for while experience of the eternal may be difficult and rare, it is possible, as demonstrated by philosophers who are able to gain insight into what *is,* that is, into the timeless (= eternal) ground and nature of things.[18]

18. *Has* the possibility of experiencing the eternal been demonstrated? Plato of course does not pronounce a definitive answer to the question—in the dialogues. As Eva Brann notes, "Plato does not reveal, indeed conceals, in the dialogues the answer to the question" of whether anyone has ever viewed or *could* view the *eidē* (*The Music of the Republic,* p. 342). Nevertheless I would argue in the affirmative, for three reasons. First, Plato's letters (if we may accept them as authentic), especially the Seventh Letter, speak of the reality of such insight. Second, Platonists and Neoplatonists such as Plotinus have claimed to have seen and embraced what I have called the eternal, including both the *eidē* and, in some cases, the One or the Good. (Plotinus speaks of

* * *

A second reason for continuing to insist on the erotic character of philosophy is that the characterizations of philosophy as erotic in the *Symposium* and the *Republic,* for all their obvious idealization, nevertheless are plausible even after one corrects for this idealization (as I have attempted to do). The philosopher is said to be moved by a keen longing for truth, born of a sense of need and of wonder. And he is rewarded, and thus further motivated, by sights that are wondrous for their clarity and beauty. The role of beauty, so essential to our ordinary experiences of eros, is plausibly present, indeed central, to philosophic eros. Seeing what *is,* precisely by virtue of its power as sight, is engagement with the beautiful, for "beauty *is* sight par excellence."[19] And in fact visible or sensual beauty itself points to—awakens in the lover an indistinct but powerful sense of—suprasensual beauty. It is not only Aristophanes who captures the experience of those who have fallen in love. Socrates does too, perhaps even more so.[20] Plato does not ordinarily *depict* philosophic activity

---

union with God, whom he understands to be identical to Plato's Good.) When contemplative practitioners who have shown themselves to be sane and rational recognize in Plato's dialogues representations of their own experience—when many such individuals do so—that should count for something. Finally, especially in light of the preceding but even on their own terms, the dialogues themselves provide strong reason to conclude that the eternal is within reach of mortal beings, for they include descriptions of philosophy to that effect. True, there is reason to consider these descriptions idealizations. But their basic elements—their stated presuppositions—are believable in light of experience available to us. Among these presuppositions are "that there are heights and there is a way to them, an ascent," and that "what is desirable is at a distance, by itself and in itself, and therefore sightlike and yet invisible, and that there must be a means for reaching it [i.e., speech]." These presuppositions are themselves undergirded by another, "that where there is a question, an answer has already been at work, and it is our human task [a task that the philosopher performs] to recollect it" (ibid.; see also, however, Brann, *The Music of the Republic,* p. 237.) None of these three reasons proves anything, for each is but a claim and interpretation of experience. But like any claims of experience, they commend themselves to us on the basis of the claimant's prior credibility and, especially, on the basis of their resonance with our own experience of the world. I will return to the question of the *eidê* in Chapter 4 and will have more to say about judging rarified experiential claims in my analysis of Nietzsche's repudiation of such things as the *eidê* in Chapter 9.

19. Brann, *The Music of the Republic,* p. 324; emphasis added. In this comment we can find an answer to those who would claim that much truth is *not* beautiful. Namely, although there is much ugliness in the world, the truth as such—the structure of what *is*—is attractive or beautiful to the philosopher by virtue of being true. Among that which is beautiful in this way for this reason is the *eidos* of the beautiful itself. In one sense, there is no reason to think that the *eidos* of the beautiful is beautiful, any more than one would consider the idea of symmetry symmetrical. But in another sense, that is, as sight par excellence, the *eidos* of the beautiful *is* beautiful.

20. Brann puts it . . . beautifully: The sensual sight of the beautiful beloved, she writes, "affects us with an exciting and utterly confounding sense of its being a mere penetrable veil, a mere representation of some divinity beyond. That is why we speak of such love as adoration. It draws us not *to* itself but *through* itself—the enchantedly attentive fascination with sensual looks

in his dialogues. The conversations are always between unequals and do not include more than one philosopher. (It seems to me that the philosophizing that goes on in or on account of the dialogues occurs not so much within them as among Plato's astute readers, at his prompting and with his inaudible direction.)[21] It is therefore difficult if not impossible to apprehend Plato's understanding of philosophy with certainty. But philosophy is *described*, and described in such a way that recourse to the vocabulary of eros does not seem too strained. Argument alone cannot definitively settle a question concerning the interpretation and naming of experience. The credibility of the portrait of philosophy as erotic will depend on one's own experience or intimations. Perhaps, though, argument can help.

Finally, as for Diotima's purported hints that philosophy is not erotic, it seems to me that one might just as easily interpret these as signifying that, as eros ascends, not only its objects but also its character changes. Eros becomes, if not less needy, then less avid and desperate, for one comes to see that eros' quarry is plentiful and "catchable" and, once caught, will be fulfilling. This would help explain how it is that Socrates might be considered erotic even while he seems to exhibit none of the intense feeling, none of the ecstasy or anxiety, that we normally associate with eros. Both the ecstasy and the anxiety of ordinary lovers arise from the separation between the lover and the beloved. Ecstasy results from the closing of that separation, either in anticipation or in fact. Anxiety results from uncertainty that the separation will be closed or remain closed. But one who loves sight of what *is*, and who *already* enjoys sight of what *is*, will not experience this same separation—certainly not in the same way. This is a point I made in Chapter 1. In addition to this, and perhaps more important, the philosopher, by virtue of facing his mortality, does not share the desperate passion for immortality that surely accounts for a good part of ordinary lovers' erotic passion.

Philosophy, as I have said, is presented by Plato as the perfection of eros.

---

goes over into something directed to the other side of that surface. Desire through distance is called love, and if what beckons is on the farther side of surface-sight, it is called philosophy." Ibid., p. 325.

21. The accuracy of my claim depends of course on what one means by "philosophizing." Brann observes that "what is called dialectic in the . . . strongest sense, thinking by and through the *eidē* [*Republic* 511c, 532], attending to their grouping, mingling, hierarchy, and 'intertwining,'" does appear once in Plato's dialogues, in the *Sophist*. See *The Music of the Republic*, pp. 337–38. (Brann also suggests that something "lower" than dialectic but still deserving of being called philosophic occurs in the *Republic*—once—when Socrates leads Glaucon into study of "the one and the two and the three" [511c]; ibid., p. 181.)

Probably the most consistent and pronounced theme of all in Plato's dialogues is the goodness of philosophy, with goodness entailing different (but not opposing) things depending on the dialogue. Philosophy proves to be the perfection of all virtues, including justice (*Republic*), courage (*Laches*), and piety (*Euthyphro*), though not quite according to the conventional understandings of these qualities. It should come as no surprise, then, that philosophy would also emerge as the perfection of the erotic life, so long as eros, too, is interpreted differently from the common understanding. This relation between philosophy and eros is elegantly if hubristically represented by the uncanny resemblance in Socrates' account between Eros and himself. But even if it is the perfection of eros in the truest sense, philosophy is at the same time utterly *unerotic* in the *ordinary* sense. Such, in fact, is the deeper argument of the *Symposium* and the *Republic*. It is the *Symposium*, as I have already indicated, that calls the careful reader's attention to the practical impossibility of earthly immortality and hence the incompatibility of the pursuit of earthly immortality with the strength and integrity of a true philosopher. And both dialogues argue the unerotic nature of philosophy through their action: in both dialogues, as in several others, Socrates seeks to disabuse his most promising interlocutors of the belief in gods who alone could make the presupposition of earthly immortality plausible. (The unerotic character of philosophy is also more directly suggested in other dialogues, such as the *Charmides* and the *Laches*.) Applying the same label to two such different categories of experience allows Plato to persuasively present and defend an activity (philosophy) that is clearly un- or even anti-erotic in one sense, the ordinary sense, as the pinnacle of eros in another, truer sense. Given the limited understanding of Socrates' interlocutors, who recognize only ordinary eros, the task can be accomplished only by blurring the difference between these two quite distinct erotes. But how better to create friends of philosophy out of erotic men?

It is not just for his own sake, however, that Socrates (or Plato) effectively eulogizes what he knows to be delusional eros. Despite its share in untruth, his praise can also benefit its hearers. As indicated by the noble lie, perhaps by *many* noble lies, Plato holds that certain false beliefs can infuse life with meaning and thereby bring order and devotion and even nobility and splendor. Ordinary eros would seem to be among such healthful delusions, certainly from the city's standpoint (it was not for nothing that Pericles asserted that every Athenian who fell for Athens would be remembered forever)[22] but not only from the city's standpoint. Cities, after all, are made of citizens, and the devotion and heroism that serve the city also serve citizens as individuals, often including the heroes themselves. Perhaps ordinary eros can even be the gateway to the very excellence that I have just described as *unerotic* (in the ordinary sense), that is, to philosophy. As I suggested earlier, in Plato's view the virtues of the citizen serve as a foundation, perhaps a necessary foundation, for the higher or truer virtue that belongs only to the philosopher. If this is so, then that which produces the virtues of the citizen, including most particularly the cultivation of eros à la the *Republic*'s civic education, might be equally useful or indispensable for true virtue. At the risk of reading too much into the *Republic*'s educational scheme, it may be that the eventual *overcoming* of ordinary or delusional eros and the attainment of true virtue (philosophy) require precisely the long-term *cultivation* of ordinary or delusional eros. It is among lovers that Socrates and Plato look for their kin.[23]

We should not be shocked that Plato would embrace the use of falsehood for a salutary effect. There is no necessary correlation between truth and social utility or even between truth and spiritual utility. But neither should we assume that the correlation is the reverse, that is, that there is always a necessary relation between good effect and lies. The nobility of the "noble lie," as I said above, consists not only in its effects but also in the fact that it has some share in the truth.

FROM TWO EROTES AND TWO TEACHINGS TO ONE

Such are the ways in which Socrates' explicit account of eros is contradicted by the deeper teaching of the dialogues in which it appears. We have seen that

---

22. Thucydides, *The Peloponnesian War*, 2.43. Thucydides also shows us, however, the grave *perils* of political eros.

23. Perhaps, though, the pool of potential candidates for philosophy is larger than this. It may be that the *Republic* and *Symposium* speak not to the development of *every* philosopher but to the development of the philosopher out of a certain *subset* of potential philosophers, that is, erotic individuals, with the possibility that other kinds of individuals may also be "eligible" for philosophy. This, perhaps, is the meaning of Socrates' claim at the end of his speech in the *Symposium* that "for this possession [i.e., true virtue] one could not *easily* get a better co-worker with human nature than Eros" (212b; emphasis added). Perhaps a better co-worker can in fact be found. In any event, whether or not those whom we call erotic are better candidates for philosophy, it still seems likely that the proper education of subphilosophic eros is necessary to

the contradictions concern fundamental questions. Yet we have also begun to see, and are now prepared to see more clearly, that in several ways the two teachings are in a certain accord.

(1) They are in accord practically, in that the apparent intended effects of the explicit account are consistent with those of the deeper account and even make the deeper account accessible: the explicit account seems intended to encourage political moderation and a regard for philosophy and, in some individuals, to serve as a kind of preparation for the philosophic life itself. This we have already seen.

(2) The two teachings are also in accord theoretically, albeit tenuously, if in fact it is true that the ultimate and therefore true object of eros is eternity. If we accept that eros' true object is eternity, then all three contradictions can be reconciled; all three of Socrates' "errors" (or what appear to be errors from the standpoint of the dialogues' deeper teaching) turn out not to be errors at all, if only they are reinterpreted in light of this premise. Socrates' first "error" was his suppression of the nonidentity of the beautiful and the good, which effectively suggested that the beautiful and the good are the same. This, however, turns out to be in some way the truth: the beautiful, insofar as it causes us to "dissolve" and give birth (206d), releases us from our time-bound selves and yields an experience of the eternal, which (on my interpretation) is the good. Socrates' second "error" was his validation of the longing for earthly immortality. This is the central error, and it is based on what can only be called a distortion or misinterpretation. But if the true meaning of the longing for immortality is in fact the longing for eternity—if what one wants via immortality is really an embrace of eternity—then the depiction of eros as desire for immortality is not altogether wrong: it represents less the wrong path than a failure to follow the right path to the end. And so too, for similar reason, is Socrates' third "error" redeemed, that is, his characterization of philosophy as erotic. If the longing for immortality somehow expresses the divination and longing for eternity, however imperfectly, then philosophy proves to be erotic after all.

(3) Finally, in consequence of the above, we can say that the two teachings are in accord with respect to their general view of what it means, or what is required, to live well. My presentation of the explicit account culminated with

---

every philosophic ascent. Only some are *called* erotic, but everyone is governed by eros: such is the implication of Socrates' repeated identification of the whole of his knowledge with knowledge of eros.

a formula to the effect that eros seeks a greater degree of being but that the grasping pursuit of more being, precisely by virtue of its grasping character, is bound to fail. The deeper teaching of the dialogue, it seems to me, does not contradict this formula, though it deepens the paradox. The best of lives, or the greatest degree of being, requires not just that one not grasp after it, but that one somehow transcend the source and agent of that grasping, the time-bound and -obsessed ego. Thus do the disparate teachings of the dialogues turn out to support and confirm one another. Thus do the words of the Platonic Socrates turn out to be consistent with the example of his life.

4

LOVE OF WISDOM VERSUS LOVE OF THE WISE: EROS IN ACTION

Having gone to some effort to break Socrates' teaching in the *Symposium* into two only to argue that two do indeed become one, let me offer a summary statement of this complex unity. Some of this has already been said, but not all of it—and not all together. I will begin with that which explains and establishes the unity, which is also where we left off—that is, with philosophy.

Philosophy may be erotic—indeed, it is himself that Socrates describes under the guise of Eros (203b–204c)—but it is not erotic in any ordinary sense of the word. Ordinary eros is love of the beautiful (or the noble: *to kalon*), a love whose meaning or source proves to be the desire for immortality (206e–208b). Eros of this sort most commonly expresses itself as romantic love, but it is also the motive force of those who seek immortality through politics or even poetry—the latter, in fact, are higher manifestations of eros, at least on the account related by Socrates and attributed to Diotima. But if philosophy isn't erotic in any ordinary sense, it is nevertheless erotic in the *truest* sense. For it understands that what we most deeply want, or what would most deeply satisfy us, is not immortality but experience of the eternal and infinite. *That* is eros' true aim, which means that what is normally called eros is a defective version of the desire for the good based on a misapprehension of what would really satisfy us. Ordinary eros, in fact, is based on two delusions: first, that immortality—*earthly* immortality—is possible, whether through children, fame, or lasting works; second, that, if attained, it would bring comprehensive satisfaction.[1] It is the first delusion that sustains the plausibility of the second: as long as one hasn't assured oneself of one's earthly immortality, one can always believe that it *would* yield the satisfaction one seeks.

---

1. Regarding the delusional nature of the belief that earthly immortality would bring happiness, see *Seventh Letter* 334e: "None of us is born immortal, nor would being so bring happiness, as most people think."

If what we most deeply want is an experience or embrace of the eternal and infinite, whence the erotic pursuit of immortality? The answer for which I have argued—an answer that explains much of the action of the *Symposium* (and other dialogues) even if it is not formally articulated in it—is that the longing for immortality represents the temporalizing of the longing for the eternal: the desire to experience that which is beyond time and beyond all limitation becomes the desire that the self or the ego be everlasting and invulnerable. The ego, already eager to survive, misinterprets its divination of the eternal as a promise of its own immortality. But doesn't everyone long for the good? And if so, isn't everyone erotic in the nondefective sense? Everyone does want the good: the good is that for whose sake we do everything (*Republic* 505d–e). But most of us are better described as erotic in the ordinary (i.e., defective) sense, in that we long primarily for immortality and seek the beautiful as a means to that end. This is certainly the case with most of those whom we *call* erotic: although everyone wants the good, only some, those who intensely pursue a beautiful beloved, are called erotic (205a–d). There is a bit of semantic confusion in all this, arising from the fact that those who are called erotic are, according to the Platonic view, defectively erotic. One could argue instead for maintaining a simpler usage, according to which we would designate as "eros" the delusional pursuit of earthly immortality and according to which philosophy would be emphatically unerotic. But such usage would submerge the important Platonic teaching that delusional eros isn't *simply* delusional but rather a distortion of a longing whose basis is not delusional and which is in fact satisfiable: for while experience of the eternal may be difficult and rare, the experience is possible, as demonstrated by philosophers who are able to gain insight into what *is*, that is, into the timeless (= eternal) ground and nature of things.

One more point needs to be made concerning the distinction I have introduced between defective or delusional eros (i.e., ordinary eros) and true or philosophic eros. The longing for immortality, as I noted above, expresses itself as love of the beautiful. That does not mean, however, that love of the beautiful is inseparable from that delusional longing. Indeed, although the beautiful and the good are not identical, beauty is still a good and love of beauty is crucial to the highest erotic development: recall that those chosen for a philosophic education in the *Republic* have first been taught an orderly love for the beautiful (403a–c). Rather than delusional, love of the beautiful might more properly be thought of as an aspect or kind of love of the good that is problematic only when fueled by the longing for immortality.[2] Nevertheless, in practice if not by nature, love of the beautiful usually *is* fueled by the delusional longing for immortality: that longing is frequently unconscious but only rarely absent in human beings.

THE POLITIC PHILOSOPHER: SOCRATES (AND PLATO)

The Platonic philosopher has come to light as a perfect lover. He loves, because he sees, that toward which we are all directed by our deepest longing. Therein lies his primary significance for humanity. This is a theoretical significance: As Plato's highest human type and the nearest thing to human perfection, he is the model and standard in light of which other types, indeed the whole panoply of subphilosophic lives, must be understood. For Plato it is always the lower that must be interpreted in light of the higher, not the reverse. But the philosopher is also practically significant to humanity—he carries an effectual truth—in at least three ways. First, he serves as an exemplar for others to emulate. True, most are not drawn to his example, and most who *are* drawn are apt to misunderstand what they are seeking to emulate. (This is a central theme of my discussions of Apollodorus, Aristodemus, and Alcibiades, below.) But, being practically wise, the philosopher can put an edifying public face on his activity and thereby encourage those who seek to emulate his example to emulate *that*. He might present himself, for example, as a model of demotic moral virtue. One sees something of this in the Platonic Socrates, even if his irony is often so evident as to give one pause in interpreting his virtue as anything ordinary. And one certainly sees something of this in Xenophon's Socrates. Second, the philosopher can exercise practical influence through education. This can take multiple forms, from Socratic conversation to Platonic lectures and writings. And third, and most expansive, the philosopher can exercise, or try to exercise, rule. Here, too, there are multiple forms, ranging dramatically in scope—and therefore, perhaps, in plausibility. At the most (politically) modest pole we find Socrates ruling over

---

2. Indeed, if love of the good involves contemplation of what *is*—and it does—then love of the beautiful has a crucial place in it. For beauty is the virtue of looks, including the invisible "looks" (the *eidē*) that occupy the mind during philosophic contemplation. See Brann, *The Music of the Republic*, p. 324; also Lachterman, "What is 'The Good' of Plato's *Republic*?"

such dialogical communities as those in the *Republic* and *Symposium*.³ Then there is the philosopher's attempt to influence political rulers or even to govern them behind the scenes. One might think here of Plato's failed Sicilian expedition or, for a more promising version, of the *Laws,* wherein a philosopher instructs a legislator, not least in the legislator's need for the philosopher. Finally, there is the prospect of philosophic rule at its grandest, wherein the philosopher legislates for a civilization by teaching it a new understanding of the gods and the good and therewith the character of the whole, including humanity's place in the whole. The idea of such grand politics will sound ludicrous to most readers, and perhaps it is. Yet the Cave image of the *Republic* at least raises the possibility, and thinkers of no less a rank than Alfarabi and Nietzsche believed not only that Plato had himself attempted such rule, but also that he had achieved it.⁴

But does the philosopher do these things—if we may stipulate for the sake of argument that he does do them—for reasons of eros? It would be hard to deny that the philosopher's erotic disposition plays *some* role in these activities, if only in making them possible and in influencing the way in which he conducts himself, since eros is so central to human life. If eros is as important a force as Plato seems to say, then we might suppose that no human activity is untouched by it altogether. The question, though, is whether eros is the motive force behind these extraphilosophic activities of the philosopher—and if so, what they in turn tell us about eros, including, by implication, eros as

---

3. Socrates' rule, and particularly his ascent to rule, over the gathering at Cephalus' house is a major and evident theme of the *Republic*. The gathering in the *Symposium* is somewhat more free-flowing, or anarchic in the strict sense, and what rule there is ostensibly follows democratic principles and procedures. Yet a close examination reveals that Socrates effectively overrides the democracy by speaking on behalf of the others; see 177d–e. Finally, the sort of rule and founding that Socrates practices in these and other dialogues may not be as narrow as I have suggested. As Brann notes of the *Republic,* Socrates founds "an educational community whose members are all the present *and future* participants in the dialogues." Among the future participants are the dialogue's readers through the ages. See *The Music of the Republic,* p. 96; emphasis added.

4. Alfarabi is characteristically more subtle in making this point than Nietzsche. Yet subtlety does not imply attenuation. Hence this from Lachterman: "Is rule of the city in any way the fulfillment of the philosopher's education or nature? Al Farabi, in *The Attainment of Happiness,* appears to have given the most systematic affirmative answer to this question." See Alfarabi, *Alfarabi's Philosophy of Plato and Aristotle,* esp. section 34. Nietzsche's view is expressed most memorably in *Beyond Good and Evil,* Preface. For extensive reflections on the subject of philosophic rule and Plato's purported seriousness about it, see Lampert, *Nietzsche and Modern Times,* pp. 127–37; and *Leo Strauss and Nietzsche,* pp. 145–65, especially p. 160: "This marriage of philosophy and politics, insight and action, *is* Platonic political philosophy" (emphasis in the original). See also Rosen, *The Question of Being,* pp. 137–75 and 187–91.

manifest in philosophy proper. (It may seem odd or somehow "unplatonic" to look for insight into eros and especially eros-in-philosophy by examining the philosopher's extra-philosophic pursuits. After all, eros as manifest in philosophy is presumably the higher and therefore the defining manifestation of eros. But providing literary access to that peak is notoriously difficult. Philosophizing doesn't lend itself to literary representation, and Plato never shows us, perhaps because it is impossible to show, a character philosophizing. [Even if the stock-still, meditative Socrates is philosophizing, the image only underscores the dramatic incommunicability of philosophizing.] We always see Socrates from outside, which means that whatever access Plato gives to the inside is provided indirectly, by pointers placed in action that *can* be represented. If indeed philosophy cannot be directly portrayed, then Plato's approach—his pointing to the truth of philosophy indirectly, including by showing us the erotic dimension of the philosopher's extraphilosophic activity—mirrors the world as it reveals itself to us. Interpreting the lower in light of the higher is Platonic, but so is apprehending the highest by way of clues provided in the somewhat less high.) To settle these questions would require a comprehensive treatment of the philosopher as a human type, which in turn would require expert knowledge of the entire Platonic corpus. Yet even on the narrow basis of what we have considered so far, each of these activities—perhaps all of the philosopher's distinctive activities—can be plausibly interpreted as erotic in some recognizable sense.

The case for the erotic basis of the philosopher's extraphilosophic activities begins with the observation that the three means of practical influence that I have mentioned can be considered species of a single genus. All three—"modeling," educating, and ruling—consist in the use of words by an unarmed thinker in order to influence others. In this they can be plausibly held to be erotic for two reasons. First, each is generative, or means to be. In fact, each generates, or at least aims at generating, a beautiful or noble progeny. The differences between the three perhaps come most keenly into sight when we ask whether in each of these cases the philosopher is giving birth *in* the beautiful. Socrates seems always to have done so, or tried to do so, to judge from the fact that he focused his attention predominantly on beautiful young men. By contrast, the philosopher whose writings are available to and are meant to influence the beautiful and nonbeautiful alike seems erotic in a different way. Yet a legislator, who perforce must work with mottled and lumpy clay, might still see in that clay what it might yet become—and therefore in a sense he, too, might be thought to bring to birth in beauty. And as we see in both tragic and comic poetry, a beautiful whole can include decidedly nonbeautiful parts. But let me be clear: If ruling can be interpreted as erotic, it is only ruling as a founder-legislator. More ordinary statesmanship, which is more like the work of a bausanic artist or artisan than of a creative artist, seems far less plausibly erotic (for the philosopher) and far more explicable in the terms stated by Socrates in book 1 of the *Republic,* where a good man's decision to rule is attributed to his desire not to be ruled by someone worse than himself (347b–c). The philosopher would not delude himself into thinking that his progeny could win him immortality. Nor can one suppose that it could gain him any communion with eternity. But I do not think it anachronistic to see in Plato what we see in Nietzsche and (arguably) Rousseau, namely, that through the philosopher's influence over others he achieves a kind of extension of himself, of his being. I have already stated my view that the pursuit of being—the pursuit of a *greater degree* of *felt* being—is an important part of the Platonic conception of erotic love. As I will argue in Chapter 10, the pursuit of being, understood correctly, is a restatement in positive terms of the pursuit of eternity.

The second reason that the philosopher's extraphilosophic activities can plausibly be considered erotic is found in the character of the experiences themselves. The key element is self-forgetting, by which I do not mean ignorance of one's own existence but rather a wholehearted absorption in and embrace of something outside oneself. This seems to me a crucial element in eros of every kind—perhaps the *chief* element from an experiential or phenomenological standpoint (i.e., the thing that most signifies or even *constitutes* the lover's enchantment and/or intoxication). Where ordinary eros is concerned, one is drawn to the beautiful so much that—and perhaps even *because*—the beautiful (i.e., the beautiful beloved) seems to promise liberation from the confines of the embattled self. As Aristophanes' speech relates and as reflection on our own experience will quickly confirm, such release into wholeness is far more present to the mind of most lovers than is any thought of progeny.[5] So, too, does true or philosophic eros involve a kind of self-

---

5. Regarding my appeal to experience: Many would say that the force of romantic attraction is supplied by a biological imperative to reproduce. Yet not even our most insistent evolutionary psychologists—nor Nietzsche, for that matter, whose Zarathustra proclaims that "Man is for woman a means: the end is always the child" (*Thus Spoke Zarathustra* I.18)—maintain that thoughts of progeny are foremost in the minds of lovers. That is not to say, however, that we can

forgetting, though to the extent that one has scaled the ladder of love the experience will not be one of escape or liberation so much as one of enhancement, since liberation will already have been accomplished. (More on all this presently.) Now what about the activities at issue? In the case of Socrates all of the activities I have listed involve his being with beautiful or promising (i.e., potentially beautiful) young men. As an exemplar of true or philosophic eros—or perhaps more instructively put, as one who has resigned himself to his own mortality, which is the definitive mark of the philosopher on Plato's account[6]—Socrates would not be seeking immortality through this pursuit. Hence his atypical conduct as lover of these beautiful young people. But neither does it seem right to interpret his interest only as a matter of seeking to generate progeny (e.g., virtue) in them, for to do so would unduly neglect Socrates' evident *pleasure* in the endeavor. Of course this pleasure may have something anticipatory about it, but Socrates knows enough to be skeptical about the end result of his educational endeavors, and in any event his pleasure seems too vivid, too immediate, to be merely anticipatory. Thus it seems more than plausible to suppose that his pleasure arises from, and hence that his activity is pursued at least partly for the sake of, a self-forgetting absorption in and embrace of beauty. And where there is such pursuit and embrace of beauty, there is pursuit and embrace of eternity, beauty being an ever-present intimation of eternity. It may be worth noting here that the sixth of the seven indivisible parts of Socrates' speech in the *Symposium*—and the only part that doesn't correspond to another of the speeches (Socrates being the sixth of the seven speakers), that is, the part that is most Socrates' own—includes a description of erotic activity that could easily be applied to Socrates' own behavior toward Alcibiades.[7]

Finally, if self-forgetting can be seen in Socrates' social activities, it can also

---

understand erotic experience without reference to the desire for progeny. Which is perhaps why Socrates, whose speech singularly thematizes progeny, attributes his teaching to a woman.

6. See especially *Phaedo* 64a.

7. "So whenever someone from youth onward is pregnant in his soul with these virtues, if he is divine and of suitable age, then he desires to give birth and produce offspring. And he goes round in search, I believe, of the beautiful in which he might generate; for he will never generate in the ugly. So it is beautiful bodies rather than ugly ones to which he cleaves because he is pregnant; and if he meets a beautiful, generous, and naturally gifted soul, he cleaves strongly to the two (body and soul) together. And to this human being he is at once fluent in speeches about virtue—of what sort the good man must be and what he must practice—and he tries to educate him" (209a–c). The sixth indivisible segment of Socrates' speech runs from the end of 208b to 209e; see Strauss, *On Plato's Symposium*, pp. 183 and 223–30.

be seen in Plato's distinctive additions to the philosophic life. Consider the extraordinary state of mind that accompanies the act of writing. Consider, too, the creator's aspiration (at least sometimes) to capture what *is* and to represent it symbolically. Socrates, of course, did not write; nor did he concern himself with rule beyond the small numbers of selected individuals with whom he conversed. Perhaps, then, these activities are not essential to the philosopher as such. Or perhaps Socrates is less than the perfect exemplar of the Platonic philosopher. (It's worth noting, though, that the Platonic Socrates is quite poetic, inventing myths and stories that work magic upon their hearers.) Whatever the case, Socrates is presented by Plato both as a philosopher and as a palpably erotic figure, both in his avid pursuit of knowledge and in his attraction to the beautiful young. He exemplifies both human excellence and erotic health (and therewith happiness). He enjoys a freedom from the cares and anxieties, most particularly those that arise from awareness of mortality, that plague almost everyone else. In the formulation offered above, he has transcended the time-bound and -obsessed ego. Which takes us more deeply into the phenomenon of self-forgetting and thus eros' character and meaning.

No passion is as self-forgetting as eros. The true lover thrives on devotion and even relishes self-sacrifice. He reaches the pinnacle of happiness when he "dissolves" into or on account of the beloved, or at least he thinks he does (206d). The beauty of the beloved is precisely that which promises this dissolution or makes it possible. Even true or philosophic eros is self-forgetting. There may be no intoxicating dissolution of the self, but one's attention is surely absorbed by the beautiful and beloved sight of what *is;* and unlike ordinary eros, one's "possession" of the beloved in this case is threatened neither by rivals nor by the beloved's rebuff, thus ensuring that the moment of self-forgetting love will not be followed by the ferocious self-concern of *thymos*.[8] Yet the very descriptions I have just employed indicate that, somehow, the self-forgetting of eros is accompanied by intense self-regard and ambition. One forgets oneself in the beloved, but only if the beloved is somehow one's own. Hence the language of possession, and hence the descent into *thymos* at the first sign that one's possession isn't absolutely secure. Even true

---

8. Regarding *thymos* as the defensive aftereffect of an eros that is either frustrated or simply not guaranteed satisfaction, see Pangle, "The Political Psychology of Religion in Plato's *Laws*."

or philosophic eros, while not subject to either extreme, is nevertheless "selfish" amid its self-forgetting. The lover of the good, after all, still loves that it be his own, that it belong to his experience, even if ownership in this case is not in principle exclusive or zero-sum.[9]

How can we resolve this paradox? Or does it need resolving at all? It is my contention that both self-forgetting and intense self-concern are evident features of erotic experience—not only sequentially but simultaneously, though one or the other feature is normally predominant in any given moment in time. This can only be true (i.e., noncontradictory) if the self that is forgotten is somehow different from the self that one continues to attend to. And so it is—or so, I contend, our experience suggests. Even the most blissfully self-forgetting lover is self-aware enough to acknowledge the experience of love and to describe it, and self-concerned enough to embrace his happiness as his own. As I noted at the outset, perhaps the first evident feature of erotic life is that lovers like to talk about their love. If love were simply or altogether self-forgetting, it would be an indifferent affair and there would be no romantic literature. Indeed, the very joy of self-forgetting stems from the fact that one is somehow aware of the experience. One writes paeans to love; one does not do the same for sleep or narcosis. A part of oneself, or perhaps better (and more Platonically) put, the self in one of its forms[10]—what we might call the egoic or Hobbesian self, that is, the self in its unwanted finitude and insecurity—dissolves or is forgotten or at any rate yields to a different form of the self, one that is not afflicted by consciousness of finitude but that does have a level of consciousness that allows for the enjoyment of (its) being. But even if this is what our experience suggests, does *Plato* suggest it? I believe he does, in the following ways.

First, it is precisely in the context of an examination of desire that Plato suggests, both in the *Republic* and in the *Phaedrus*, that the soul is a multiplicity, that it admits of multiple "forms." The most obvious meaning of this claim is that the same person may be differently disposed toward the same thing at the same time. But another meaning, one that is much easier to see when we think of the soul's multiplicity as one of forms rather than parts, is that the soul as a whole can be oriented—can conceive of itself and the world through which it navigates—in a multiplicity of ways (a hierarchical multi-

---

9. See Chapter 1, note 19.
10. See Chapter 1, note 1.

plicity, as it turns out). The vocabulary of "parts" represents this multiplicity as a matter of rule: Which part is predominant? Which part is ruling the others? The vocabulary of "forms" allows us to conceive of the soul with respect to its broad outlook or orientation. As such it allows for a more holistic and adequate portrayal of the soul—a more holistic and adequate portrayal of *particular* souls. One can easily represent the differences between human types in terms of which of the soul's parts occupies the position of rule, and there are things that this terminology is uniquely well equipped to communicate, as we saw in Chapter 1. But even if we allow for the enrichment of the tripartite model by the introduction of subparts (cf. *Republic* book 9), it seems more fully descriptive to think of the various human types in terms of what they love and, even more broadly and fundamentally, in terms of how they see the world, or how they are oriented toward it.

Second, there is the life and character of Socrates. An exemplar of true or philosophic eros, the Platonic Socrates is both self-forgetting and deeply self-concerned. His is not the self-forgetting of the romantic lover, that is, of ordinary eros. That experience, intense and intoxicating, may be foreclosed to him, depending on whether it presupposes a prior "imprisonment" (i.e., in a pinched or embattled self) from which one is liberated by eros. Yet it does still qualify as self-forgetting in that Socrates seems uniquely free from life's usual anxieties, both superficial and existential, and thus is able to be absorbed in and to *delight* in what *is*. At the same time, however, he is also aware of himself. Indeed, no one seems more competently and comfortably aware of where he is and what he wants than Socrates. And he is not only self-aware, but also self-concerned: even when benefiting others, Socrates always pursues what he supposes to be good for himself.[11] His is a highly developed but apparently not oppressive self-consciousness.

Finally, this combination of what I have called self-forgetting and self-concern is artfully underlined—and opened for exploration—by a series of subtle textual clues in the *Symposium*, all playing on the theme of something-versus-nothing or presence-versus-absence. These clues take us further into the heart of Platonic eros. What I have been calling "self-forgetting" is indeed a kind of forgetting, that is, a not-thinking-about: one ceases to be concerned

---

11. Leibowitz shows that even Socrates' ostensibly self-sacrificial civic activity, as depicted in Plato's *Apology*—that is, his public examination and refutation of the supposedly wise and his exhortation to virtue—actually serves his own interest. See "The Moral and Political Foundations of Socratic Philosophy," pp. 194–200 and 219–22.

about or to attend to oneself in one's capacity as a finite, vulnerable being. One ceases to suffer the burden of finitude and vulnerability. But another way to talk about this phenomenon, perhaps a better way, is to understand by "self" a way of seeing things and a way of being. According to this usage, the anxious or Hobbesian self is not forgotten but transcended: it yields to something else; it ceases to be. It becomes *nothing*. This, I would suggest, is the serious and literal sense of the second epigraph to Part One of this book, a line spoken by Socrates to Alcibiades years earlier and recounted by Alcibiades at the symposium, and one that appears to be simply a case of playful irony—or, to Alcibiades, maddening irony (it *is* that, but it is also more than that). Alcibiades tells the whole story (218c–219a):

Alcibiades, a very young man, has just offered to accept Socrates as his lover, on the grounds, as he puts it, that each would gain from the other's beauty. Socrates responds that if Alcibiades' assessment of their respective beauty is correct, then he, Socrates, being the one with the beautiful soul, would be getting the worst of the deal. To Alcibiades this is hubris. And it is hardly mitigated by Socrates' next remark, which Alcibiades takes as ironic but which, I am suggesting, is more serious and sincere than Alcibiades understands (and also, for just this reason, more ironic than he knows): Socrates professes to warn the young man: "But, blessed one, do consider better: Without your being aware of it—*I may be nothing*. Thought, you know, begins to have keen eyesight when the sight of the eyes starts to decline from its peak; and you are still far from that'" (219a; emphasis added). One can read this as nothing more than an urbane and deserved scolding. Having humiliated Alcibiades-the-beloved by rebuffing his offer, Socrates now mocks him as a lover. But it seems to me that the line too neatly expresses something else, something important and true about Socrates, for it to be just this. Socrates in a sense *is* nothing, and therein lies his freedom and his happiness.[12]

---

12. Newell also argues that this line ("I may be nothing") expresses something serious and sincere. In his view, however, it expresses Socrates' neediness, which differs from my reading but does not contradict it, since both readings could be true. He is worth quoting at length: "As Al Farabi remarks, Socrates is so ironic that, on occasion, he can state the truth simply and baldly because it will go unnoticed compared to the dense ambivalence that surrounds it. I think this may be one of those moments. As I interpret it, however, this nothingness is more a source of hope than despair. Socrates' suggestion that he might be 'nothing' is a further reason for thinking that Diotima's description of eros as needy and impoverished applies especially well to him. And here is where I think we can put together Socrates' self-absorption as a needy lover with the beneficence of his claim to practice politics [*Gorgias* 521d]. Socrates' description of himself as 'nothing' is the description of his need, his lack." *Ruling Passion*, p. 94.

What does it mean to be nothing? And what could be good about such a condition? To answer these questions it might be helpful to consider for a moment the Neoplatonic tradition, particularly Plotinus, who expresses more explicitly than Plato does a view that he plausibly takes to be consistent with Plato. What Plotinus claims—on the basis of personal experience—is that the self can transcend its ordinary boundaries through union with something beyond it. In the highest case the self achieves union with the One, or God, which Plotinus took to be synonymous with Plato's Good. At a lesser but still high level it achieves union with Nous, which is the realm of the *eidê*.[13] In each case the self has come to identify itself with, it has *become,* that which is beyond the realm of things; and in the highest case it has come to identify itself with that which is beyond Being itself. In both cases the self has become, the self is, more than something; it is beyond the realm of things. And if we wished to characterize such a self from the point of view of its separateness—if we were asked what a self must be that is capable of such identification—then we might best describe it as a clearing, as an emptiness—as Nothing.[14]

The story of his long-ago exchange with Alcibiades isn't the first place in the *Symposium* where Socrates comes to light in some sense as not-being. Near the start of the dialogue, Apollodorus relates the following. As Socrates and the uninvited Aristodemus were making their way to Agathon's house,

> Socrates somehow turned his attention to himself and was left behind, and when Aristodemus waited for him, he asked him to go on ahead. When Aristodemus got to Agathon's house, he found the door open, and he said something ridiculous happened to him there. Straight off, a domestic servant met him and brought him to where the others were reclining, and he found them on the point of starting dinner. So Agathon, of course, saw him at once, and said, "Aristodemus, you have come at a fine time to share a dinner. If you have come for something else, put it off for another time, as I was looking for you yesterday to invite you but could not find you. But how is it that you are not bringing our Socrates?"

---

13. *Enneads,* passim. For a succinct summary, see Wilber, *Sex, Ecology, Spirituality,* pp. 331–38 and 631–36 nn. 13–28.

14. Something like this view can be found in other Platonists and in other contemplative traditions with minimal connections or even no connections to Plato. Several of the latter employ the language of Emptiness and Nothingness to represent the exalted states of being. Wilber has treated this matter in several places; see, especially, *A Brief History of Everything,* pp. 216–24.

"And I turn around," he [Aristodemus] said, "and *do not see Socrates following anywhere*. So I said that I myself came with Socrates, on his invitation to dinner here" (174d–e; emphasis added).

Socrates has disappeared, he *is not*, precisely on account of his turn inward, a turn, as I have already suggested, that might well be taken to signify erotic contemplation. Of course his nonbeing as described here is nonbeing in the eyes of Aristodemus and the others: it is to *them* that Socrates is absent. And so striking is this to Aristodemus that he shifts into the present tense; Socrates' absence is still present to Aristodemus: "and I turn around and *do* not see Socrates."[15] In a sense, though, Socrates has ceased to be or has become absent *even for himself,* if in fact he is engaged in self-forgetting contemplation. As I have already indicated, such nonbeing is at the same time an ascent to a fuller, more expansive being, or what we may wish to call transegoic being: in forgetting himself he attends to and thus is somehow constituted by that which has *more* being than is present to the others. Otherwise put, one form of the self, the egoic form, yields to or dissolves in favor of a more exalted experience that may still, however, be called one's own experience—so that we can say that one form of the self dissolves into nothingness and in so doing yields to another, more exalted form of the self.

Lest my reading of this motif appear too strained, let me note another way in which, or another perspective from which, it makes sense to describe the height of erotic achievement—indeed, the height of human being—as "being nothing." Leave aside the self-forgetting or timeless *character* of contemplation and consider instead the *content* of contemplation as it is (admittedly, only cursorily) indicated by the dialogues we have been considering. I am referring in the first instance to the forms, or *eidê,* which are identified as such in the *Republic* and by implication in the *Symposium*. (Although the *eidê* are not mentioned *as such* in the *Symposium*, i.e., are not referred to as *eidê*, the peak of the erotic ascent in Socrates' account in the *Symposium* is sight of the beautiful as such, which is depicted in the same terms as Socrates elsewhere uses to describe the *eidê*: timeless, unmixed, etc. [211a–b].) Now the *eidê* are depicted as having *more* being than the objects that we apprehend through our senses, and the one who apprehends the *eidê* is shown to enjoy a fuller life; it does not seem too much of a stretch to say that he enjoys more

---

15. What Benardete renders as "And I turn around" is a present participle, so the phrase might as accurately read, "And, turning around." What he has rendered as "I do not see Socrates," though, is indeed in the present tense in the Greek.

being, or even that he *is* more. Yet although they have more being, the *eidê* are not *things* in any ordinary sense of the word. They are *prior* to and the source of thing-ness. A form or *eidos* is no-thing. Thus, if human beings are in any way constituted by the content of their consciousness, then he who contemplates the forms is constituted by, or simply is, nothing. And if this is true of one who contemplates the *eidê*, it is even more clearly true of one who contemplates the Good, if indeed there is such a one. As the source of Being itself, the Good is also prior to and the source of all things (and all no-things, i.e., the forms).

With the discovery of the role of nonbeing in erotic experience we are able to see more clearly the respective characters of and the relation between the *Symposium* and the *Republic*. Socrates' treatment of eros in the *Republic* emphasizes the lover's pursuit of being. His treatment in the *Symposium* begins with this same emphasis but then goes beyond it. In the second half of his speech Socrates emphasizes the side of erotic experience that involves self-forgetting, self-dissolution, and release, thereby effectively highlighting eros' share in or even pursuit of nonbeing—and thereby making of his speech in the *Symposium* a more complete account of eros.[16]

Although in the *Republic* Socrates pointedly affirms that there is something beyond and even greater than being, being is nevertheless the focus of desire and is held out as the reward for philosophic toil. In the *Republic*, eros' object is said to be sight of what *is*, and the case for the superiority of the philosopher's eros to that of the tyrant is grounded in the claim that the philosopher finds satisfaction by "filling" himself with that which has more being; whereas the tyrant, ever pursuing and consuming objects with less being, is ever hungry and dissatisfied (585b–e).[17] The same theme is emphasized in the three famous images of books 6 and 7. The effect of the Sun image is to praise the Good as the source of being: the Good is likened to the sun, whose goodness to us lies in its effects here on earth. (The Good is also praised as the source of intelligibility, but the value of intelligibility itself is that it enlarges the knower's being.) The Divided Line depicts the relations between being and

---

16. If the *Symposium* gives a fuller account of eros because it acknowledges the importance of nonbeing in eros, the *Republic* may well give a fuller account of that which eros pursues, that is, Being, for a comparable reason: Eva Brann suggests that the Cave represents Nonbeing, the "mother" who, impregnated by the Good in its role as "father" of Being (the Good is conceived as such [506e]), is also beyond and responsible for Being. See *The Music of the Republic*, pp. 211–16.

17. Also see Socrates' extended exchange with Callicles in the *Gorgias*.

becoming and between soul and Whole (i.e., knower and known), with primary emphasis on the means by which to ascend to sight of what *is:* the uppermost segment of this vertical line represents Being (the *eidê*) on one side and knowledge on the other, not the Good or the faculty by which the Good might be apprehended.[18] And the narrative of the Cave image depicts a liberation that quite literally consists in coming into (the realm of) Being. Consider, by contrast, Socrates' speech in the *Symposium*, with its emphasis on self-forgetting, self-dissolution, and release. The lover who is arrested by beauty is one who forgets himself, at least for a moment; he dissolves, or at least wants to. The one who gives birth—and recall that we are all pregnant in one way or another—can do so only by yielding, by softening—by *dissolving*. Each of these involves letting go, ceasing to grasp, even, in a sense, ceasing to be. If the *Republic*'s emphasis on eros' pursuit of being is captured by Socrates' three images, then perhaps the *Symposium*'s complementary emphasis on nonbeing is best captured, fittingly, also in an image, or perhaps I should say a nonimage: the ambiguous assertion by Socrates that he may be "nothing." As I have already argued, this ascent to nothing, and erotic self-forgetting more generally, really amount to an enhancement of being, even a greater degree of being. Still, it is well to stress that this enhancement comes about through transcendence and that transcendence always involves nonbeing or ceasing to be, even if for the sake of that greater degree of being.

Sometimes eros is self-forgetting, sometimes intensely self-concerned. When in the former condition, the experience is that of being drawn out of oneself by and toward beauty—which is the heart of the Socratic account in the *Symposium*. When in the latter condition, at least when one has not transcended egoic defensiveness by means of a conversion or "turning" (*periagoge*) to philosophy, eros has shaded into *thymos*—which is the heart of the *Republic*'s concern. In those who have not undergone this turning, the relation between eros' two poles will be inharmonious and *thymos* will appear to be at odds with eros and with eros' highest expression, philosophy—as indeed it is. Yet it would be wrong to conclude that this necessitates a permanent war within the soul. For as I suggested earlier, *thymos* might properly be understood not only as eros' opposite and antagonist but also, even more funda-

---

18. The highest things, as represented by the uppermost segment of the Divided Line, are never explicitly identified as the *eidê* but rather as the *archai*. In accordance with the usual (nearly universal) practice, I am presuming that the *eidê* are in fact the "fundamental ruling things."

mentally, as a *variant* of eros, born of eros and pointing its way back to it, however tortuously and unknowingly.

* * *

Having seen these erotic poles—being versus nothingness, which also means temporality versus eternity—makes it easier to understand eros' in-between character. Eros, Socrates teaches, is in between ugliness and beauty and in between badness and goodness. But eros is also in between being and nonbeing. This is indicated not only by the different emphases that we have just seen between the *Republic* and the *Symposium,* but also by Socrates' speech in the *Symposium* itself. (Recall that what seems to be absent or abstracted from in a Platonic dialogue often turns out to be present after all, in some way, in the shadows.) From the very start of his Diotiman account Socrates describes eros with reference to, or in the language of, being and nonbeing, or something versus nothing. Eros, we are told (as Socrates long ago was told), is of "*something*" rather than "*nothing*" (199d–e); Eros is of something that "*is not present*" or of "what he [Eros the daemon] himself *is not*" (200e); and this something is something "the need for which is *present* to him" (200e; all emphases added). Moreover, Eros periodically *dies*—just as the philosopher learns how to die (*Phaedo* 64a) and in fact *does* die (in a sense) each time he transcends egoic consciousness, each time he ascends to nothingness. Finally, as one who dies and is reborn, and as the mediator between humanity and the eternal (the gods), eros is also the mediator between being and nothingness—or perhaps I should say, between being and Nothingness. Eros' power is that of "interpreting and ferrying to gods things from human beings and to human beings things from gods: the requests and sacrifices of human beings, the orders and exchanges-for-sacrifices of gods; for it is in the middle of both and fills up the interval so that the whole itself has been bound together by it" (202e) Note the final clause. Eros as that which binds together the whole may put one in mind of the Good, as described by Socrates in the *Republic*. As the source of being and intelligibility, the Good can be understood as unity and hence, too, as that which binds together the whole. Can both claims be true? Can both eros and the Good be held to bind together the whole? I believe they can. Eros is desire for the good, a desire most fully satisfied by sight of the Good, but it is not the Good itself.[19] Yet if eros is that by which

19. As explained in Chapter 3 (see note 3), I believe it makes sense to distinguish between (1) the good as that which we seek and which would satisfy us, and (2) the Good that is identified in the *Republic* as the greatest study and the source of all being and intelligibility. The Good is

we ascend to sight of the Good, then it is *for us* that which binds together the whole. That what binds the whole together for us is desire, or *lack*, rather than knowledge, helps us see why Socrates, however much he has seen of what *is*, nevertheless continues to live by and to propound a "negative wisdom" centered on an avowal of ignorance. *Sight* of what *is* is not quite *knowledge* of what *is*. As with eyesight, what one sees with the mind's eye requires interpretation and intersubjective confirmation, without which one must remain ignorant and even with which one can never achieve absolute certainty.

What does it take to develop a healthy and therefore health*ful* eros? The sources of Socrates' extraordinary condition, the forces that guided his development, are apparently idiosyncratic—so much so, he says, as to be irrelevant to others and thus not worth mentioning (*Republic* 496c). Fortunately, a more replicable path is available—namely, the philosophic education depicted in the *Republic* and symbolically represented in the *Symposium* by Diotima's *scala amoris*.[20] Unfortunately, that path is accessible only to a few and is tread by even fewer. Nor do most people receive anything like the civic education depicted in the *Republic*—an education, we recall, aimed primarily at the "right" shaping of eros (403a–c). Hence the frequency of disordered eros and death denial, in our time as in Plato's: so many do not cease either dreading or denying or hopelessly combating their mortality. (I exempt from these categories all who confidently trust in an afterlife. But I also follow Tocqueville in surmising that a good many who profess such trust betray something less confident in their restiveness.)[21] I do not mean to suggest that, absent a Platonic education, life must be consumed either by misery or frivolity, nor that Plato saw matters thus. In this his sensibility is less grim than that which has signified "seriousness" for the better part of the past century. While eros can and often does flow in problematic directions, most erotic passion is directed precisely where the primary sense of the word suggests, and its satis-

---

the greatest study not only because of its ontic status but also because sight of it is somehow the good *for us*.

20. To be sure, the accounts in the two dialogues are not identical. But they can both be understood to represent, broadly and symbolically, the same vision of philosophic education—philosophic education, one ventures to suppose, as Plato conceived and endorsed it. For an examination of what that education might more literally have looked like, as it may have been offered at the Academy, see Nichols, "Platonic Reflections on Philosophic Education," pp. 109–20.

21. See *Democracy in America*, pp. 511–14.

faction varies considerably. But my subject is the *effectual truth* of eros, which means, primarily, the *political* effects of eros. And in politics the effects of eros are typically more troublesome than they are in private life, often disastrously so. In the *Republic* one encounters eros as the wellspring of tyranny: the tyrant is erotic and achieves power by appealing to the appetites, the eros, of the demos. This has been widely appreciated by readers. Less widely appreciated has been the political teaching of the *Symposium*, a teaching that may in a sense be more important than that of the *Republic* because it concerns a more ambiguous eros that is both harder to discern and more practically relevant to societies like our own. Our society does not seem particularly threatened by the rise of the *Republic*'s kind of tyrant. I will argue, however, that in the persons of Apollodorus, Aristodemus, and Alcibiades, and even in the "person" of Diotima, the *Symposium* points to dangerous political phenomena that are not so remote from our politics. In his treatment of these individuals Plato unfolds a part of the problem of political eros that has had particular salience in late modernity.

EROS AND POLITICS: APOLLODORUS, ARISTODEMUS, AND ALCIBIADES

Apollodorus, Aristodemus, and Alcibiades are not the only lovers in the *Symposium*. Several of the other symposiasts clearly qualify as erotic men. It would therefore seem arbitrary to single out these three as somehow exemplary of eros—were it not for two facts. First, aside from Socrates, these are the only people present to exemplify or *act* upon erotic passion in the course of the dialogue. That they and only they do so is perhaps owing to the second important fact, namely, their shared—and most extraordinary—beloved. Each of these three men is in love with Socrates and acts on the basis of this love in the dialogue proper. Apollodorus, known from more than one source as one of Socrates' most ardent lovers,[22] relishes the opportunity to "be with" Socrates by recounting the lengthy story of the long-ago symposium for the second time in days (172a). Aristodemus, utterly beholden to Socrates (he is believed by Apollodorus to have been "the one most in love with Socrates" at

---

22. See, for example, *Phaedo* 117d, where he weeps through the final scene of Socrates' life. Also see Xenophon's *Apology of Socrates*, 33, where Apollodorus is described as "an ardent lover of Socrates and otherwise a naive fellow."

the time of the symposium [173b]) and following him wherever he can, looks for all the world like Eros himself—homeless, tenacious, unprepossessing, even unshod. And so, too, Alcibiades: in the course of recounting his hopeless passion for Socrates, Alcibiades gives every sign that he has not managed to overcome it—nor even that he really wants to overcome it, which is perhaps the surest evidence of eros. A look into the lives of these three lovers reveals a third common fact as well. Each, from the standpoint of Platonic political philosophy, represents a dangerous political tendency, a tendency that is either directly or indirectly allied with tyranny. And in each case there is good reason to conclude that these dangerous political tendencies are linked to their eros for Socrates.

First, the political tendencies themselves. Apollodorus is a fanatic. A partisan of philosophy, he is full of missionary zeal, eager to convert everyone to his faith. Worse, he despises himself and everyone else except Socrates. This contempt is visceral and hard-edged and seems to be the leading feature of his character (173c–e). Properly speaking, though, "partisan of philosophy" is an oxymoron: the one whom it describes partakes of the spirit of the ideologue more than that of the philosopher and has made of philosophy something like a fighting faith or a prejudice. Perhaps Apollodorus was initially drawn to philosophy for reasons that are consistent with philosophy's true spirit (wonder, skepticism, true or philosophic eros), but in his advocacy of philosophy—and in his social existence generally—he has less in common with Socrates than with the more strident members of the eighteenth century's philosophic party.

The latter is true as well of Aristodemus, an imprudent man who shows no regard for conventional piety. Aristodemus is the public and provocative atheist, or at best a deist, ridiculing those who practice traditional rites.[23] Whether his (non)belief is itself Socratic may be open to question; whether his understanding of the theologico-political problem is Socratic is *not*, at least to judge by the practice of the Platonic Socrates. (Aristodemus's practice is that of *Aristophanes'* Socrates.) One need only compare his practice with Socrates' own—with Socrates' careful rhetoric at his trial, for example, where

---

23. See Xenophon, *Memorabilia* I.4. In answer to Socrates' challenge, Aristodemus claims not that he doesn't believe in the existence of the divine but that the gods are too magnificent to need anything from human beings and that they don't worry about human beings.

he evinces great respect for the gods of Athens even as he signals, ever so subtly, his disbelief in them.[24]

The problem of Alcibiades, finally, is both more evident and less clear than the other two. Alcibiades may or may not be reckless, and his extravagant ambition and self-regard may or may not have ensured the disaster that followed Athens' embrace of his counsel: the Sicilian expedition might well have succeeded had the Athenians not recalled its author. Incontestably, though, he is immoderate as well as subversive of the moderation of others. And the success of the Athenian expedition would have done nothing to change that; indeed, success probably would have intensified this immoderation (if that would have been possible) and its contagiousness. How, though, are these disparate dangerous tendencies linked to the three men's love? How could eros for Socrates foster such *un*socratic behavior, and what does this say about the effects, if not the truth—or perhaps I should say, about the effectual truth—of Socrates' teaching?

Socrates had more lovers than these three, and happier lovers. Plato is one, and both he and Xenophon show us others.[25] The happier lovers, though—who are also (therefore?) free of the dangerous political tendencies associated with the others—are those whose love of Socrates led them to a love of what Socrates loved. Plato loved Socrates, but he also loved wisdom.[26] To be sure, a true love of wisdom is rare. But even those who do not rise to true love of wisdom themselves might love it in a mediated way through their love of the one who does—so long as their love for him is subordinated to or at least interpreted in light of *his* love of wisdom, that is, so long as they love him for what he loves. What, then, of Apollodorus, Aristodemus, and Alcibiades? The problem is not that they aren't philosophers themselves but that they love Socrates without loving what he loves. They love the lover and not his beloved.[27] Or to put it in terms suggested by Socrates' speech, they love Love: they love Eros. For if Aristodemus looks the part of Eros, that is because he

---

24. George Anastaplo is very instructive on this point. See "Human Being and Citizen," pp. 30–31.

25. But Christopher Bruell suggests that Xenophon, too, indicates the ambiguous effects, on some, of loving Socrates. See his "Introduction" to Xenophon, *Memorabilia*, p. xiii.

26. The mature Plato also engaged in a political enterprise of his own, of course—which, though not self-evidently erotic or ill advised, at least underlines the attraction of politics even to one whose eros was directed to philosophy and who understood the dangers and delusions of political eros.

27. On Apollodorus' and Aristodemus' subphilosophic love of philosophy, see Bowery, "Responding to Socrates' Pedagogical Provocation," at http://www.bu.edu/wcp/MainAnci.htm.

imitates Socrates; it is surely *himself* that Socrates most nearly depicts under the guise of Diotima's daemonic Eros. They love Eros without loving that which Eros is *of*—which means, in essence, that they love an abstraction. They are, in short, idealists. (Perhaps the perfect emblem of this idealism is Alcibiades' shield, emblazoned not with an ancestral device or even a symbol of Athens, that is, not with the image of a "proper" beloved, but with the image of Eros wielding a thunderbolt.)[28]

But what does this mean? If eros is not beautiful or good but only *of* the beautiful or the good (199c–201c)—if Socrates is, in fact, really "nothing" in himself (219a)—what do they love in him? If they loved him *as lover*, they would love what he loves. But they do not love him as lover; they love him as Love, as Eros. They love him as daemon. Or rather, not as daemon (for then they would love him for that toward which he points) but as something more complete, more self-justifying and more *life*-justifying than a daemon, something more perfect, or divine. Socrates to them is godlike, and their love for him is somehow religious. (Like everyone else at the symposium except for Socrates, they mistake Eros for a god.) They would say, they *do* say, that he is beautiful. And the sign of that beauty, and its source or being as they behold it, is something like *power*. That is what they love in Socrates: his power over himself, and power over them.[29] Each submits to Socrates as a slave. Both Apollodorus and Alcibiades, as Seth Benardete observes, "revel in self-abasement whenever they hear the Call in Socrates' words."[30] (It is less clear that Aristodemus is affected in quite this way. Perhaps he is sufficiently humble or self-forgetting; perhaps in this he is more wholesomely erotic, more educable, than the other two.) Worshipful love in itself is not problematic (though self-despising submission may be). Socrates is no god, but it is far from clear why revering him should be troublesome. Quite the contrary: in the *Republic*, after all, Socrates prescribes public praise of good men (607a), and in the *Apology* he even suggests that he himself deserves such honor (36d). The problem,

---

28. Plutarch, "Alcibiades," section 16.
29. That men fall in love with power is taught by Thucydides. In Book 2 he shows us Pericles invoking eros by calling attention to Athens' power ("'You must yourselves realize the power of Athens, and feed your eyes upon her from day to day, till *love* of her fills your hearts'"). And his account of the Athenians' decision to launch the Sicilian expedition in Book 6 shows that Pericles knew what he was talking about: "Everyone *fell in love* with the enterprise" (2.43, 6.24; emphases added; note that in both cases the italicized word renders into English a Greek cognate of *erōs*).
30. "On Plato's *Symposium*," p. 198. To be sure, there is a difference between the two: "For Apollodorus, the Call is for philosophy; for Alcibiades, the Call is moral." I will take up some of what distinguishes the three lovers from one another below.

rather, arises from the way they interpret Socrates' greatness—or, more fundamentally, from that about these men themselves which causes them to interpret Socrates' greatness as they do.

What is most perfect and powerful in Socrates is precisely what we have already seen, namely, his acceptance of mortality and consequent transcendence of ordinary or egoic consciousness—his rise, as it were, to "nothingness." To borrow a very useful term from Rousseau, Socrates' characteristic excellence (on my reading of Plato, which may or may not be Rousseau's) is his absence of *amour-propre*.[31] (I do not mean to underestimate Socrates' sheer intellectual power and his amazing virtuosity. Nevertheless I hold that the chief source of his effect on others is something even rarer and more compelling.) But the three lovers, not being philosophers themselves and not having received anything like the Socratic civic education when young, do not see this. Not being philosophers themselves, they are creatures of *amour-propre*. Not having received the Socratic civic education, they are creatures of a disorderly *amour-propre*. They do see Socrates' greatness. Or, rather, they see *manifestations* of his greatness: they see his extraordinary and multifaceted freedom and his uncanny insight into the needs and desires of others. And they love him for the beauty and power, the strength of soul, to which these testify.[32] Unable fully to see or appreciate the source of this beauty and power,

---

31. Rousseau's treatment of *amour-propre* is extensive and complex but for present purposes can be reduced to the following three points, the first concerning what *amour-propre* is, the second concerning what it ultimately or fundamentally wants, and the third concerning its educability. (1) *Amour-propre* is the relative form of self-love; it is the desire for our own well-being that judges our well-being by our position relative to others. (2) Being relative, *amour-propre* seeks absolute primacy—which means that the person dominated by *amour-propre* seeks to be universally beloved, all-powerful, and the center of the cosmos, indeed, the whole of the cosmos himself: he is averse to "everything that by being something prevents [him] from being everything." (The latter quote appears in *Rousseau, Judge of Jean-Jacques*, p. 112; Rousseau treats *amour-propre* most extensively in *Emile* and significantly in the *Discourse on Inequality*.) (3) Finally, although civilized human beings are almost all captives of *amour-propre* (Rousseau thinks that only a very rare few can transcend it), it can be wholesomely educated, either through something like the domestic education elaborated in *Emile* or through the civic education of a well-constructed polity. The latter, Rousseau says, is exactly what Plato depicts in the *Republic*.

Some might suppose that Rousseau's *amoure-propre* is identical to Plato's *thymos*. In my view (as expressed in Chapter 1), however, *thymos* includes but also goes beyond what I have just ascribed to *amour-propre*. Socrates is without anger and is apparently free of concern for status. But he is not without courage, perseverance, and even a taste for and skill at a kind of combat.

32. Perhaps, then, they *don't* err in looking to Socrates as a god, or at least can be forgiven for the mistake—*on this occasion*: Socrates has uncharacteristically beautified himself for Agathon's party. He has even put on shoes. As Leon Craig has pointed out, it is Aristodemus alone who, à la Eros, is shoeless and who communicates the beautiful (divine?) speeches of the symposium to humanity.

however, they effectively misinterpret it as something egoic, with the consequence that their love for Socrates only inflames, even as it may in some ways "elevate," their *amour-propre*.[33]

Admittedly there is a speculative element to a portion of what I have just said: my characterization of the way the three men see or interpret Socrates's greatness is based on two inferences. But they are inferences from things we can know. Herewith the logic: We already know (a) that each loves Socrates and (b) that each engages in *un*socratic behavior that evinces a politically troublesome mentality. It is also evident, or soon will be, (c) that this unsocratic behavior arises not in spite of but because of their love for Socrates. The next point concerns the character of these behaviors or tendencies: (d) at the heart of the dangerous political tendencies of all three lovers, as we will see, is an active scorn for others, a scorn that betokens an aggressive and/or defensive self-love, or a severely inflamed *amour-propre*. Hence my inferences: first, (e) their love for Socrates has inflamed or at least given unfortunate direction to their *amour-propre*—more than likely, both. Second, and admittedly more speculative, (f) this could only have happened because they "translate" what they see and love in him into something egoic, consistent with their own egoic mentalities. The strength of the latter inference, and indeed of all of the foregoing, will be revealed by a look at each of the three cases. But irrespective of the validity of the latter inference, the three cases reveal the dangerousness, the potential *badness,* of love for the *best* of human beings.

Apollodorus

That (a) Apollodorus is in love with Socrates, and that (b) his characteristic behavior, that is, his scornful contempt for all the world apart from Socrates, is unsocratic and represents a potentially dangerous mentality, need no further demonstration. Nor is it difficult to discern that (c) this fanaticism has its source in his love for Socrates. His fanaticism is clearly born of the conviction, a *lover's* conviction, that philosophy as practiced by Socrates is the only human activity worthy of respect. And it is equally clear that (d) his anger and scorn betoken aggressive egoism, or *amour-propre* (or *thymos*—the two

---

33. If Socrates is nothing, so are these other men, albeit in a rather different sense—at least as Alcibiades sees it: "We are nothing, I tell you, and all his life he [Socrates] keeps on being ironical and playful to human beings" (216e).

are synonymous in this regard, as in others). If they don't, nothing does. Anger is prima facie evidence of this sort of self-love. And an anger as fierce and ongoing as Apollodorus's is prima facie evidence of a thymotic or aggressively egoistic form of self, a self that is dominated or primarily characterized by implacably competitive self-love. Anger can arise and be sustained only when one supposes, consciously or not, that others *willingly* injure or disrespect that which we invest with value. Someone who has not been the subject of major or irreversible injury can sustain fierce and ongoing anger only by imputing to others an ongoing, *willful* antagonism toward his hopes or designs—and precisely this tendency, the tendency to animate and personalize the sources of one's discontent, is the mark of the embattled ego. Perhaps the classical example of this tendency is the angry Achilles raging against a river: thwarted by the strong current, this paragon of *thymos* reflexively interprets it as the work or even the being of a god (*Iliad* 21.265–66). Such is the effect of the inflamed egoic self. Those who are not captives of such self-love, by contrast, are not given to such anger. Indeed, to judge from the case of the Platonic Socrates, they may be incapable of anger. Socrates does not impute malicious intent where it does not exist; moreover, even where such intent *does* seem to exist he interprets it as the product of ignorance and therefore as something less than true intent. Such is the Olympian perspective of a free mind.[34]

If one accepts that Apollodorus's fanaticism is an expression of an aggressive egoism or *amour-propre* and that its substance (i.e., its disdain for everything except philosophy) is an expression of his love for Socrates, then it is hard to resist concluding that (e) his love for Socrates has either incited or inflamed his *amour-propre* or at least given it its peculiarly unhappy direction. Prior to meeting Socrates, Apollodorus did not think ill of himself and most others; only through his association with the philosopher has he learned how pointless and miserable his life had been (173a). Socrates, in other words, is somehow the cause of Apollodorus's unsocratic behavior and discontent. He

---

34. That anger requires an aggressive form of self-love is argued by Rousseau, who observes that one who is free of *amour-propre* will lament injustice and pity its victims but not grow angry over it; see *Reveries* VIII:115–16; also see Cooper, *Rousseau, Nature, and the Problem of the Good Life*, pp. 128–29. That freedom from anger—and indeed, freedom more generally—come from seeing the falseness of free will has been argued perhaps most notably by Spinoza in the *Ethics*. (Most notably because most overtly and strenuously. The same teaching can be discerned in various other philosophers from Socrates [at least as portrayed by Plato] to Nietzsche.) Whether such freedom is altogether good for society is a separate question.

who follows Socrates—literally—is led away from Socrates. How? And why? The deepest reasons, the ones concerning his various character traits, are unknowable to us. Nor can we know whether Socrates' pedagogy hasn't been somehow faulty or irresponsible. So a full explanation is not available. What we can say, though, is that Socrates' teaching appeals to certain unsocratic dispositions and can be co-opted by them. His teaching, of course, is the goodness of philosophy as a way of life. The goodness of philosophy is manifold, but its particular appeal to *amour-propre* is undeniably its *power*. If Apollodorus simply admired Socrates and wanted to be like him, if he simply shook his head at the foolish mortals who neglect philosophy, we would have to understand philosophy's appeal to him more generously. But his angry disdain, his need to instruct nonphilosophers in the worthlessness of their lives, and perhaps, too, his particular agony at Socrates' execution—execution, not just death: what grieves him most is the injustice of Socrates' death[35]—suggest that he believes in philosophy's power and loves Socrates for that power, even while, as a nonphilosopher himself, he is angered by others' lack of respect for philosophy and appalled by the world's material power over the philosopher. Socrates surely does exemplify what we might call extraordinary power. But it is a power born of or constituted by freedom and equanimity, most particularly freedom from fear of death. Compare his equanimity in the face of his own impending execution to Apollodorus's agonized grief.[36] The difference suggests that, unlike Apollodorus, Socrates understands that the value of his being lies beyond the reach of his executioners. Apollodorus, in his anger, his anxiety, and his grief, shows that he understands Socrates' being or power differently from Socrates himself: that (f) he translates, or rather mistranslates, it into something more consistent with his own egoic frailty.

Aristodemus

As with Apollodorus, so with Aristodemus the first points are already evident: (a) Aristodemus, too, is in love with Socrates, and (b) his characteristic politi-

---

35. Xenophon, *Apology of Socrates*, 28.
36. Perhaps nothing captures the contrast so well—or captures so vividly what makes Socrates so loveable—as the exchange, related by Xenophon, following Socrates' condemnation: "But for me, Socrates," says Apollodorus, "the hardest thing to bear is that I see you dying unjustly." Socrates, stroking Apollodorus' head, replies, "Dearest Apollodorus, would you have preferred to see me dying justly?" Socrates then laughs. Ibid.

cal activity, his open ridicule of religious rites, is both inconsistent with Socrates' own practice and contrary to Socrates' advocacy of traditional religious practice, at least as Socrates is presented by Plato. (Although the Platonic Socrates reforms theology, he specifically yields to tradition with respect to religious rites [*Republic* 377b–382c, 427b–c].) Yet while his behavior is unsocratic, there is little doubt that Aristodemus understands it as consistent with or even an expression of Socratism; hence (c) there is little doubt that we may understand it as a consequence of his love for Socrates. His publicly expressed atheism is a publicly expressed rationalism, and Socrates is surely his model of rationality, even if he denudes Socratic rationalism of its respect for conventional piety. As noted earlier, Socrates hints that he does not believe in the city's gods, and it may well be that philosophy is by nature atheistic—with respect to such gods. Nevertheless Socrates seems to attribute to conventional piety a certain practical benefit. And perhaps something more: there is reason to think that Socrates sees the city's gods as representing or pointing to something real, even if they are themselves fictional. Why Aristodemus neglects what Socrates attends to so carefully (at least on Plato's telling, and on Xenophon's too) is impossible to know for certain. Perhaps he has thought things through and simply arrived at a contrary judgment. Whether or not that is the case, though, that is, whether his departure was based fundamentally on a considered political judgment or on the sensed promise of an emotional reward, the emotional reward is clearly there: (d) in mocking the sacred rites of others, Aristodemus is scorning others and asserting his own superiority in a way that gratifies egoism or *amour-propre*. And while it would be unfair to discount his conscious understanding of the theologico-political problem as rationalization in the service of *amour-propre*, the manner in which he acts on his view—that is, mockery, which by nature is harsh (note the similarity to Apollodorus's fanaticism)—does convict him of acting for reasons of aggressive self-love.

Aristodemus's ill-advised behavior seems less central to his life's activity than Apollodorus's does to his, and thus probably stems from something less central to his character. Whereas Apollodorus *is*, most essentially, a partisan or fanatic, Aristodemus, as far as we can tell, simply *does* something imprudent. His is a less troubling case; perhaps he is even happy. Nevertheless his doing is problematic and unsocratic in both its effect and its likely motive. (If Apollodorus calls to mind the eighteenth-century "party of philosophy" in its more aggressive mode, Aristodemus calls the same party to mind in its more moderate, perhaps earlier stages. For those interested in this historic parallel, it is interesting to note that Aristodemus is the earlier of the two lovers. Does the philosophic party become more extreme over time as its hopes for a reformed world fail to materialize?) Thus we may apply the same logic to Aristodemus's case as to Apollodorus's: if his behavior is motivated by an aggressive egoism or *amour-propre* and if it expresses a belief born of his love for Socrates, then it seems safe to conclude that (e) his love for Socrates has either inflamed or at least validated a politically subversive *amour-propre*.

How so? Here again, as with Apollodorus, we cannot know the whole story. We don't know enough about his character and we don't know what he was like or what he did before he attached himself to Socrates. And because of that (and for other reasons as well), we cannot know that Socrates' pedagogy isn't somehow to blame. Yet here again we can also draw the following inference, namely, that (f) Socrates' teaching appeals to certain unsocratic dispositions and can be co-opted by them. In my analysis of Apollodorus, I suggested that the likeliest element of philosophy's appeal to (some) nonphilosophers is its power. The case is harder to make on the evidence of Aristodemus—not because the evidence points toward something else, but simply because the evidence is scant altogether. But the evidence we have is at least not inconsistent with my analysis of philosophy's appeal to Apollodorus and his consequent misinterpretation and abuse of philosophy. And perhaps the evidence is not so scant after all. Aristodemus's sharp contempt for conventional piety, his disdain for that which seems most opposed to the independence and *strength* of the philosopher, suggests that he revels in a feeling of superiority that derives from his association with Socrates. His mockery of the pious, that is, his *publicly* expressed contempt, suggests that he enjoys expressing a kind of power and having it recognized. And his abject behavior toward Socrates himself expresses not just admiration or reverence but enslavement, a happy and devoted enslavement: and the happily devoted slave is one who accepts and even loves the power of his master. Thus, what is found in Apollodorus is at least plausibly found in Aristodemus. And the plausibility is only enhanced by the discovery of the same phenomenon in Alcibiades.

Alcibiades

About Alcibiades books have been written. Much has been written even about his relationship with Socrates and the question of the philosopher's influence on him. My purpose here is narrow. I only mean to show that, for all his distinctiveness vis-à-vis Apollodorus and Aristodemus, he exemplifies in the *Symposium* the same phenomena I have identified in the other two cases and thus that he, too, testifies to the danger that arises from eros for a certain kind of excellence by certain kinds of individuals. But of course Alcibiades *is* distinctive: he alone among the three lovers is a political man, and a great one at that. So his case not only confirms but also elaborates the danger.

(a) Alcibiades has loved Socrates and loves him still. That he does so, he now understands, is the consequence of a calculated effort by Socrates. As Alcibiades warns Agathon, Socrates' practice toward beautiful or noble young men is to pose as a lover only to make the ostensible beloved fall in love with him (222b). Unlike Apollodorus and Aristodemus, Alcibiades is a palpably frustrated lover. The former wish only to be with Socrates by following and beholding him, which they are permitted to do. Alcibiades, though, wants something more like what lovers ordinarily want; he wants sexual embrace. Yet he wants it for most extraordinary reasons and in an extraordinary way. Ordinarily, the lover sees the beloved as beautiful—not just bodily, but in a way that encompasses the body. Socrates, though, is a much older man and a famously ugly one at that. His beauty resides strictly in his soul (216e–217a). Still, Alcibiades wants to gratify him sexually—in order, however, that he might thereby receive something of Socrates' inner beauty and power. (By the time of the symposium there may be additional motives behind Alcibiades' desire for Socrates, arising less from Socrates' beauty than from Alcibiades' need to pay him back for his power and for the "hubris" of his rebuff.) He is now the lover, but a lover whose desire is to act the part of the beloved. Thus he seems less to want to possess Socrates than to be possessed by him.

(b) Now we turn to Alcibiades' unsocratic behavior, which is, I think, less obvious than that of Apollodorus and Aristodemus. Also unlike theirs, his is self-confessed. What is contrary to Socrates' teaching is not Alcibiades' choice of a political life but the way he conducts himself in that life and the reasons for his conduct. Alcibiades is a compelling political figure and a brilliant one. The Sicilian expedition, the product of an Athenian eros incited by the erotic Alcibiades,[37] could have succeeded in winning for Athens the first trans-Mediterranean empire and for Alcibiades personally such glory as would be won by Alexander. From the standpoint of political glory his only major mistake

---

37. Thucydides, 6.24.

was to display his personal immoderation and hubris to too great an extent, thereby sowing popular suspicion and granting his domestic enemies the chance to bring him down. Yet even though the Socratic teaching is not synonymous with the standpoint of political glory, what is problematic from the latter is also problematic according to the former. From the standpoint of the Socratic teaching, Alcibiades' great failing is that he is immoderate as well as subversive of the moderation of others, including the city as a whole. It is a failing not because it costs him glory or even because it dooms the Sicilian expedition to failure, but because it inflates his desire (his political eros) to unfulfillable proportions and thus dooms him—and the city, to the extent that it participates in his designs—to dissatisfaction. Furthermore, where erotic dissatisfaction reigns, there is bound to be increasing recklessness: here the view from the Socratic standpoint merges with that from the standpoint of glory. The immediate underlying cause of Alcibiades' unsocratic politics, we are given to understand, is an unsocratic eros for popular adulation. This is something of which Alcibiades professes, believably, to be ashamed, at least in Socrates' presence; but it is something to which he is hopelessly addicted.

(c) How, though, can all of this be attributed to Alcibiades' love for Socrates? Why not simply say that Alcibiades behaves as he does *in spite* of Socrates' efforts? Socrates, after all, counsels moderation and has tried to convince Alcibiades of his need for a real Socratic education. That education, to judge from Plato's *Alcibiades I*, would have had the effect either of directing Alcibiades away from politics or of moderating his politics: either it would have led him to see that his eros is of a nature and a magnitude that it could be fulfilled only through philosophy or it would have tamed his eros by teaching it to recognize the beauty of virtue, including moderation. (It is not clear which of the two ends Socrates hoped to accomplish. It may well be that the first of his two approaches *in Alcibiades I* represents his attempt to achieve the former end and that the second approach, in response to the failure of the first, represents his attempt to achieve the latter end.) Some have suggested that Socrates' effort to educate Alcibiades is itself to blame for the latter's errant behavior.[38] In their first serious encounter, as represented *in Alcibiades I*, Socrates attempts to convince Alcibiades of the latter's neediness by inflating his

---

38. This suggestion was of course first made—perhaps it was the most damning suggestion made—by Socrates' accusers; see Xenophon, *Memorabilia* I.2.12. The very first of the accusers, though, if we may pretend that Plato's *Symposium* is historically accurate, may have been Alcibiades himself.

political ambition. You think you want preeminence merely in Athens, says Socrates to the then very young man, but what you really want is to conquer the world—and for that you need me (119d–124e). In retrospect this may have been a risky strategy, in that Alcibiades accepts the revised assessment of his ambition without wholeheartedly accepting that he needs a Socratic education.[39] In Socrates' defense, however, it is possible that his revelation of the true scope of Alcibiades' ambition was just that, and that Alcibiades was already on his way to becoming the ambitious, immoderate statesman he later became.

However that may be, this is a question of tactics; it does not speak directly to the dangerousness of Alcibiades' erotic *love* for Socrates. Indeed, it would have been reasonable for Socrates to have supposed that Alcibiades' eros for him would have kept the young man faithful to Socrates' teaching and thus serve as a counterweight to his vaulting ambition. What proves dangerous about Alcibiades' eros for Socrates, rather, is that (d) it offends—and thus (e) it inflames—his self-regard. Feeling himself enslaved to Socrates yet unable to give up his love of popular adulation, Alcibiades experiences Socrates' existence as a rebuke. He is in thrall to someone who repudiates what he lives for. This creates an excruciating pressure: if he cannot give up his unsocratic ways, then he must overcome Socrates. How? By drowning himself in his project and pushing it to its limit, so that, by accomplishing unprecedented things or even just by the grandeur of the attempt, he will command the admiration of (nearly) all. And if even such an enterprise were to fail to win him the respect of Socrates, he would at least gain consolation through the poignancy of his failure—and through the luxurious indulgence in self-contempt: to win the admiration of the world and then admit to Socrates that his grand success is meaningless is at once to confess his debasement and to elevate himself to a level just shy of Socrates.

My suggestion with respect to Socrates' three lovers is that (f) what ultimately led them down their unfortunate or dangerous paths is that they admire and love in Socrates something that appeals to their egoic consciousness or their thymotic (aggressive, defensive) self-love. They recognize his freedom but are unable to appreciate its source in his non- or trans-egoic self. This is clearest in the case of Alcibiades. A lover and admirer of power, Alcibiades

---

39. Alcibiades abjectly admits to his ignorance and need for a Socratic education (127d). But subsequent history would show that this conviction wasn't solid, as Socrates himself feared at the time (135e).

loves Socrates, it seems to me, precisely for his power—for his power over himself, as seen in what appears to be his amazing continence, and for his ability to reveal Alcibiades to himself and to command his awe. (It is Tocqueville, hardly a political romantic, who observes that men love what holds power over them.[40]) Alcibiades' first real experience of Socrates' power set the tone for the subsequent relationship: in declining Alcibiades' sexual offer, Socrates seemed to Alcibiades to be guilty of hubris. But as important as if not more important than Socrates' power or hubris is the way these have been interpreted by Alcibiades. As important as the fact of one's love or the reason for one's love is what one *thinks* is the reason for one's love. The lover is surely affected by what he takes to be the source of the beloved's lovableness or the nature of the beloved's beauty. What then does Alcibiades see as the basis of Socrates' power? Or, perhaps better put, what does he see as the source or being of his beauty? What does he admire in Socrates? This is where he makes his crucial misinterpretation: (f) he admires Socrates for what he takes to be moral virtues, namely, his amazing endurance and moderation (219e–220b), rather than for the intellectual or spiritual qualities that are surely the deeper source of these and other extraordinary qualities.[41] It is not as a philosopher that Socrates is beloved by Alcibiades, but as an exemplar of great moral virtue, which means an exemplar of egoic power or perfection.[42]

On the basis of the foregoing, I would like to make two final, general points—one about the passions, the other about philosophy, and both about politics. In my analysis of the three lovers of Socrates I have focused on the "form" of the lover's self and on the character of his self-love. At the heart of the dangerous political tendencies that the three men represent, I have argued, is aggressive self-love. Let me now return to my earlier set of categories, that is, ordinary versus true or philosophic eros, and add that (g) this aggressive self-love, which might with perfect adequacy be called will to power, is the self-

---

40. *Democracy in America*, p. 63: "One must indeed be persuaded that men's affections are generally brought only to where there is force."

41. Whereas Alcibiades paid close attention to Socrates' endurance and moderation while on campaign, he was apparently not among those who paid attention to Socrates' daylong standing meditation (220c). Strauss, *On Plato's Symposium*, p. 277.

42. It is Rousseau, to my knowledge, who most clearly articulates the egoistic foundation (or, in his terminology, the foundation in *amour-propre*) of moral virtue. The person whose self-love is not egoistic (i.e., not relative, not *amour-propre*, but rather *amour de soi*) exercises no governance over his inclinations.

love of those who are intensely erotic *in the ordinary sense*. To view the matter this way helps explain the intensity of their eros and the consequent ferocity of their characters: those who are animated by the longing for immortality rather than eternity must always seek power and can never be content, since immortality admits of no degrees and can never be known to be guaranteed. I do not mean to say, by leaving this point for last, that the three men's ordinary or defective eros is a more basic cause of the phenomena that I have been describing than either their aggressive self-love or their egoic "form" of self. The three phenomena are in any event inextricably intertwined: where one is present, so are the others. Yet the fact that the three men's eros is defective might be the most broadly explanatory observation about them—partly because it describes desire, and desire is arguably the decisive thing about us, and partly because it alone among the three facts points beyond its limitations to a distant but real perfection.

That perfection brings us to the point about philosophy.

It is tempting to plead that the dangers represented by the three lovers have nothing to do with philosophy. The men are lovers of Socrates, not lovers of philosophy. Apollodorus and Aristodemus are groupies: they may think they love philosophy, but they have hopelessly personalized this love; they love only a philosopher, and they do not even really love him *qua* philosopher.[43] Alcibiades, meanwhile, is even less credible as a lover of philosophy. For him, too, the object of eros is a person, and for him, too, the person is loved as something other than a philosopher. But this is a temptation to be resisted. For while it is certainly true that the three lovers misunderstand Socrates and that their love for him is somehow shaped by that misunderstanding, they *believe* themselves to and in fact *do* love him for reasons that arise from his being a philosopher. They may misunderstand philosophy, but *they love philosophy as they (mis)understand it*. Perhaps this is why Socrates insists in the *Republic* that an end to human ills will come about only if rulers are overtaken by "a true erotic passion for *true* philosophy" (499b–c; emphasis added). Erotic passion for false philosophy, or for philosophy falsely understood, as he intimates there and as we have seen in the *Symposium*, spells political trouble.[44]

---

43. Also see Bowery, "Responding to Socrates' Pedagogical Provocation."

44. Sensitive readers have propounded many reasons for not taking the *Republic*'s political solution as a practical proposal: the regime of the *kallipolis* is not possible and in many ways is not desirable. The danger attaching to an "incorrect" love of philosophy is another reason to look askance at the prospect of direct rule by philosopher-kings.

THE PROBLEM OF POLITICAL EROS: DIOTIMA

The problem of political eros—more precisely, the practical problems posed *by* political eros—are hardly limited to what I have examined here. By nature a turbulent passion and typically a delusional one, eros is always a dangerous force in politics, notwithstanding its potential (so well known to Pericles)[45] to serve as a source of civic virtue. Indeed, the cases of Apollodorus, Aristodemus, and Alcibiades are only secondarily lessons about the dangerous political potential of philosophy. More deeply, they are lessons about the perils of eros. The danger posed by philosophy only exists, after all, because of a longing that precedes the discovery of philosophy. With or without a Socrates at hand, with or without sophistication or self-awareness, the attempt to achieve immortality through politics easily lends itself to tyranny and imprudence. The *Symposium*, of course, does not speak directly to the whole range of the problem. Its three exemplars of problematic eros speak to the narrower problem of the dangerous appeal and effect of philosophy on certain types of people (though the mere presence of Alcibiades, especially in light of the dramatic date of the dialogue, that is, its placement on the eve of the Sicilian expedition,[46] signifies that the dialogue speaks *indirectly* to the broader problem of political eros).[47] The *Symposium*'s only explicit treatment of political eros as such, or in a general way, occurs in Socrates' speech, where he recounts Diotima's idealistic portrayal of the phenomenon. Diotima passes over the dangers of political eros as well as its essential dubiousness (i.e., its presumption that one can win a deathless name through politics). This is fitting—not only because the occasion calls for eulogies of eros, but also because Socrates' purpose in a room full of poets and intellectuals (no politicians are present when he speaks) is less to show the problems attaching to political eros than to indicate that what it really seeks is found to an even greater degree in philosophy.

---

45. Thucydides, 2.43.
46. See Strauss, *On Plato's Symposium*, pp. 15–16.
47. Clifford Orwin demonstrates that Alcibiades' behavior in domestic politics is driven by the same principle that drives Athens' international political behavior, so that Alcibiades represents the domestication and the consistent application of Periclean principles; see *The Humanity of Thucydides*, pp. 123–26. I would add to this that Alcibiades also represents the application or working out of the *psycho*logic of Periclean principles. For as Pericles makes clear, the psychological basis of Athenian imperialism is eros, and it is in the nature of political eros to seek maximum distinction—and maximum distinction for the most ambitious individuals always involves standing beyond the city and viewing the city primarily as the vehicle for their own individual distinction.

Yet the dialogue does perhaps make one general comment on the political dangerousness of eros as such. This is found in a small detail—not from Diotima, but about her. It is part of Socrates' brief introduction to her teaching. Socrates is still talking to Agathon: "And I shall let you go for now, and turn to the speech about Eros that I once heard from a woman, Diotima of Mantineia. She was wise in these and many other things; when the Athenians once made a sacrifice before the plague, she caused the onset of the disease to be delayed ten years; and she is the very one who taught me erotics" (201d). The first thing we hear of Diotima is her name, which, in its near-implausibility,[48] would likely suggest to Greek auditors or readers that she is a fictional device of Socrates. If so, then the biographical details that follow need to be understood symbolically. It is in these next details that we encounter a comment on the political danger of eros: Diotima is wise, and she delayed the onset of the plague. The postponement of the plague is offered as testimony to her wisdom. Her wisdom, in other words, is powerful—*practically* powerful. Now consider the effects of this use of her power. Had Diotima not delayed it by ten years, the plague would have struck Athens far less severely, since, as it happened, its deadliness was multiplied by the ongoing urbanization of Athens and by the wartime decision to bring Athenian villagers and farmers inside the city's walls. (Both the urbanization and the withdrawal into the city were Pericles' doing, in the service of his erotic imperialist project.) Even more important, Athens in all likelihood would have won the Peloponnesian War; and Alcibiades would likely have been saved from exile, and Socrates from death.[49] So Diotima's "erotic wisdom"—or Athens' use of it—proved disastrous.

But if Diotima is not real, what is Socrates saying? First, the postponement of the plague symbolically represents the danger of trying to master nature. Here it is instructive to note that the story is related in the third part of Socrates' speech, which corresponds to the speech of Eryximachus,[50] whose

48. See Chapter 2, note 14.

49. Benardete, "On Plato's *Symposium*," p. 192. Perhaps, though, Socrates would have seen fit to orchestrate his "tragic" end anyway, judging from the fact that he seems to have been in a position to avoid a capital trial even after Athens' defeat. On the other hand, a victorious Athens would have been less angry at philosophy, so perhaps Socrates would have felt less need to serve philosophy by standing trial and going to his death with equanimity. Yet ironically, that might have been a *bad* outcome, at least for future ages, which would have been deprived of Socrates' most practically powerful service to philosophy.

50. Recall that Socrates' speech in the *Symposium* divides into seven thematically indivisible parts that correspond, in order, to the teachings offered by the dialogues' seven speech givers;

great emphasis was on the power of human will to master nature through *technē* (medicine). But the damage really didn't arise from the attempt to master nature so much as from an *ill-advised* attempt: the postponement of the plague was a mistake only because of its timing. The mistake was to disregard the future in favor of the present. In truth, though, "disregard" is too weak a word, for if eros disregards future consequences, that is because if *forgets* the future; and it does so because it imagines that the present moment will go on forever. *That* is the characteristic delusion of ordinary eros. Divining, dimly, the eternity that it longs for, ordinary or nonphilosophic eros tends to temporalize eternity, translating it into an ongoing or everlasting present, that is, into immortality. Such eros leads us into political trouble not only because it so avidly seeks immortality, but also, and even more fundamentally, because it *presupposes* immortality. The intoxicated lover does not really imagine that his beloved will ever grow old, and erotic statesmanship cannot quite believe that the splendor of the city could ever dim.

CONCLUSION: PROBLEMS AND SOLUTIONS

I suggested earlier that in his treatment of Apollodorus, Aristodemus, and Alcibiades—and, I may now add, with his inclusion of Diotima—Plato unfolds a good part of the problem of political eros. In the cases of Apollodorus and Aristodemus, the problem stems from the erotic appeal of philosophy and its generation of dubious political activity—though "philosophy" so used is really not philosophy at all but ideology. Neither of the two are political men, yet the behavior and especially the attitudes to which they are led are politically worrisome. Disdain and discontent that understand themselves abstractly and express themselves fanatically are inherently dangerous phenomena: in Apollodorus one sees the potential for a kind of noxious ideological politics that the modern world has come to know all too well. Attached to a less skeptical "leader" than Socrates, such an attitude could easily lead to fanatically ideological politics. Dangerous, too, are Aristodemus's harsh mockery of conventional piety and, even more so, his scorn for the needs that give rise to such piety, that is, the scorn for human neediness: here as well we sense something of the brutal utopian-rationalism of modern ideological

---

Strauss, *On Plato's Symposium,* p. 183. Eryximachus is the third of the seven. Socrates responds to Eryximachus' speech in the third part of his own speech.

politics. More generally, the lessons of these two cases concern the dangerousness of an intense eros that attaches itself to something abstract and intellectual—a philosophy, an ideology, an idea.

In the case of Alcibiades we encountered a different version of the problem of political eros. Rather than an ominous foreboding of modern ideological politics, Alcibiades is "classical" in the openness of his personal ambition and self-regard: there is nothing shamefaced about his love of power or his lust for glory. (He is to the modern ideological fanatic what Athenian imperialism is to modern empire building: no denial, no claim of beneficence or divine mandate, just a frank assertion of the rights of the more noble and powerful.[51]) Yet there is also something more than "classical" about Alcibiades' ambition. For all that he longs for glory, he cannot take his aspiration completely seriously. Whether owing to his encounter with Socrates or simply to Athenian sophistication, he is beset by a certain skepticism and ironic self-awareness. Not that this tempers his ambition. Quite the contrary, in fact: it is as if his lack of conviction unmoors his ambition from any restraining standard. If the whole thing may in the end be meaningless, then to pursue it is already to step outside the reach of any meaningful standards. Thus even simple or "classical" glory seeking is affected, at least sometimes for the worse, by sophistication generally and by philosophy specifically.

Finally, if my reading of Diotima is on the mark, we have encountered in her wisdom—or, rather, in Athens' attempt to avail itself of her "erotic wisdom"—yet another dimension of Plato's teaching. This dimension speaks not to the hazards of philosophy or personal ambition but to the perils of eros on behalf of the city—the perils of Periclean politics, we might say.

My primary purpose in this discussion has been to explore these parts of the problem of political eros as Plato sees them—and as they appear, even more frighteningly, in light of modern political history. I have emphasized the problem rather than the solution in part because the problem must be adequately understood before solutions can be prudently considered and in part because such solutions as Plato points to, if taken literally, are unrealistic, either because they violate the tenets of modern liberalism (think of the censorship and indoctrination prescribed in the *Republic*) or because the necessary resources are unavailable (we have no Socrates on hand to educate our

---

51. Regarding the character of Athenian imperialism in this regard, see Orwin, *The Humanity of Thucydides*, pp. 45–46.

most ambitious young people). Not that a solution always exists (Alcibiades did have a Socrates on hand, and still he resisted education). But the *principles* of Plato's solutions may *not* be unrealistic, and they may be all that he was earnest about in any event. Those principles are predominantly educational: inculcate a taste for harmony from the earliest age; offer as models of beauty, and hence as objects for eros, that which is truly beautiful (noble), especially virtue; inculcate devotion to the city and acceptance of one's place in it; teach appreciation for political moderation; cease telling horrifying tales about death and the afterlife (since such stories inflame spiritedness) and instead affirm the soul's immortality, a *pleasant* immortality, for those who behave justly in this life. These are the principles of erotic education for the many and even for the politically ambitious few. Their purpose is to render self-love and (ordinary) eros orderly and to prepare at least some people for an education to philosophy or true eros. Beyond these, various institutional mechanisms are called for in order to prevent the opportunity to overindulge destructive desires, though some of these restraints are incompatible with modern liberalism and others could be maintained only as customs, if that. Modern liberalism will not accept, say, sumptuary laws, nor even the informal stigmatization of the single-minded pursuit of wealth. But it can accept, and in some cases has proven adept at maintaining, publicly orchestrated patriotism, martial virtue, and strong religious institutions.

What I have not mentioned in connection with solutions is what to do about philosophy. Plato is more subtle here, since, as it seems to me, he does not want to call everyone's attention to philosophy's dangers. (The problems I have explored are only very obliquely articulated.) His goal is less to warn about than to defend philosophy and recruit capable people to its ranks. One of his means of doing this is to characterize as "false" philosophers those whose imprudence has earned philosophy its dubious reputation. Yet in his treatment of the distinction between true and false philosophy and in his exploration of how to recognize and nurture those with the requisite character for the real thing, Plato in effect instructs us to direct away from philosophy those not suited to it—and in particular those who might make ill use of it. Neither Apollodorus nor Aristodemus seems credible as a candidate for philosophy on the terms outlined by Plato (*Republic,* book 6). But who can really see to such a thing? What is one to do with individuals who are drawn to philosophy but who lack the virtue for it? What was Socrates to have done with Apollodorus and Aristodemus? Perhaps in such cases the best thing is to invite them in and to teach them, not quite philosophy, but some gentleness and skepticism—or, barring that, to deny their fanatic predisposition a dogmatic platform. Perhaps this is what Socrates tried to do with Apollodorus and Aristodemus. Perhaps he even succeeded. After all, fanatics whose ideal is Socratism are probably the least dangerous fanatics around, though, for that very reason, they may be the unhappiest ones as well.

PART TWO

Rousseau and the Expansiveness of Being

After long prosperity, after having swallowed up many treasures and desolated many men, my hero will end by ruining everything until he is the sole master of the universe. Such in brief is the moral picture, if not of human life, at least of the secret pretensions of the heart of every civilized man.

—Discourse on Inequality

O man, draw your existence up within yourself, and you will no longer be miserable.

—Emile

5

BETWEEN EROS AND WILL TO POWER: ROUSSEAU AND "THE DESIRE TO EXTEND OUR BEING"

We all want what's good. But what *is* good? Or, to begin with only slightly less ambitious a question, how can we discover the good? Classical philosophy taught that the route to knowledge of the good must begin with what is widely believed to be good: the good is the desirable, and the desirable either is, or is somehow suggested by, what we actually desire. In neither case is the inquiry an easy one, if only because we desire many mutually exclusive things. If the good is suggested by or even if it is included among what we actually already desire, we still must discover the principle by which to discern the "valid" aspect of our desires from those parts which, for reasons of accident or ignorance or misapprehension, do not point toward the truly desirable. Yet however difficult, there is a coherence and an intuitive sense to the philosophic enterprise thus conceived. The good is the desirable and the desirable is to be determined through an examination of our actual desires. Modern and postmodern philosophy have not always maintained this approach to discovering the good. Many, following Kant, have separated the moral good from considerations of desire and happiness, arguing that even if virtue does contribute to happiness, its demands must be determined and met without any regard for one's own well-being. Far from representing the fulfillment of desire, Kantian autonomy (i.e., adherence to the moral law) consists precisely in subordinating desire to duty.

Yet no one, not even those who deny that the good is somehow contained in our desires, would shrink from calling the good desirable. This is important: to call something desirable is to hold that it either satisfies or would satisfy some desire; and to call something *most* desirable (e.g., Kantian autonomy) is to hold that it would fulfill the highest or worthiest (though not necessarily the deepest or most powerful) desire (e.g., the desire for freedom and dignity). My point is simply that all serious moral and political thought, whether it would like to or not, is made by its own terms to concern itself with the factual question of desire. If even the least naturalistic, most deontological view of the good has a vital link to desire, then so does all moral and political thought.[1] The good, as the desirable, is fulfilling either of our deepest desire (Plato) or our highest desire (Kant, and also Plato). What, then, *are* our deepest and our highest desires?

Rousseau has an answer worth considering. The structure of his moral and political thought is naturalistic in several ways, and thus is more akin to Plato's than to Kant's. First, he avows that things are good only if and to the extent that they fulfill our natural desires. If men had the natures of wolves, he pointedly suggests, the man who resisted preying on his fellows would be depraved (*Emile* 287). Second, for all that his prescriptive political thought seems to eschew natural desire—Rousseau goes so far as to assert that the best political institutions are those which most *de*nature man—that departure from nature refers to the means by which society can artificially replicate something of the natural man's soul and satisfy what, at bottom, are deep natural desires (*Emile* 40); and any adequate political solution must take its bearings from natural right, knowledge of which depends on knowledge of "the nature of man," which itself includes and arguably is essentially constituted by the desires (*SD* 93). Finally, Rousseau holds that there is one good, arising from one desire, that outranks all others and indeed comprehends them, in the sense that these other goods *are* good only to the extent that they participate in or contribute to the primary good. In this, Rousseau's good is comparable to Plato's good, and his understanding of the desire for this good is comparable to Plato's eros. Yet Rousseau's good is not, in its content, presented as synonymous with Plato's, and Rousseau does not endorse or otherwise indicate that he subscribes to the Platonic conception of eros. The kinship between his thought and Plato's appears to be formal or structural more than substantive. Rather than suggest that there is some particular condition or state of being or content of consciousness that constitutes the good for human beings, he holds that the good consists in maximized existence, that is, *felt* existence, or, as he calls it, the sentiment of our being, a good whose rather formal and abstract name points to the fact that it can be gained through a number of means. Rather than suggest that we all long for or are drawn to transcendence of our finitude and mortality (which would seem to

---

1. It is worth pointing out that, even if there were no connection between the good and desire, one would still need to know what we desire, if only to know what morality is up against.

be the core meaning of eros), he seems to hold that our desire for the good, that is, our desire to exist, a desire whose name is self-love, is more a push than a pull and an intrinsically directionless, nonteleological push at that.[2] Self-love is inherently expansive: it seeks to extend one's very being or self—though not, apparently, toward any particular end.

Whether Rousseau's divergence from Plato is as considerable as it appears is debatable, for Rousseau's chosen standpoint, his determination to examine phenomena in strictly empirical and phenomenological ways, arguably would lead him to eschew Plato's more "metaphysical" language even if he believed in something like Plato's Good and Platonic eros. Yet precisely because he adopts this more modern-scientific perspective, his thought commends itself to those inclined to the Platonic view, for this perspective allows Rousseau to offer a supplementary articulation, an articulation "from below," as it were, of the same phenomena treated by Plato. Interestingly, it does something comparable for the Kantian view of the good (though here, I think, there is definite disagreement regarding the status of that good), for Rousseau's good allows for *and explains the goodness of* virtue and autonomy (or, in Rousseau's terminology, moral freedom). For these reasons, Rousseau's notion that existence is the good and his notion that, as creatures of self-love, we all desire the maximization of this good, are worthy of our serious consideration. There are other reasons as well, not least among which are the surface plausibility and the explanatory power of these ideas. Indeed, Rousseau offers a credible basis for a comprehensive interpretation of the human problem. His thought on these matters is not in the least metaphysical but it is metapsychological, and as such it speaks to the wellsprings of all sorts of behavior, including political behavior, and to the question of moral and political standards and their basis in nature.

The focus of the following inquiry will be less existence itself (i.e., less the sentiment of existence) than the desire for existence, that is, the desire to maintain and extend our being. This emphasis matches Rousseau's own: perhaps because his perspective is phenomenological, concentrating more on our inner experience than on that toward which our experience seems to point,

---

2. Self-love of course goes by *two* names in Rousseau, *amour de soi* and *amour-propre*. As will be discussed below, though, each of these versions of self-love is fundamentally constituted by the desire to maintain and extend existence, or the sentiment of existence. In the rest of this discussion the words "being" and "existence" will always refer to the feeling or sentiment of existence.

and perhaps, too, because he sees that this desire attaches itself to myriad objects, he says more about the desire than the thing desired.[3] Nevertheless Rousseau does speak about existence, both directly and by implication. Indeed, it is not clear that one can speak coherently about a desire without at least a brief preliminary look at the object, even if that object is a kind of metaobject that is rarely experienced as the focus of longing. Let us then look briefly at what existence means to Rousseau and why we may conclude that he considers it the good for human beings.[4]

BEING

To experience the sentiment of existence seems to mean nothing other than simply to feel alive, and to experience the sentiment of existence to a great extent means to feel intensely alive. Rousseau nowhere addresses the matter systematically, and it is not clear that one *could* capture such a thing systematically. He neither catalogs the modes of existence or its dimensions nor states the relation between existence and lesser or more proximate goods. Fortunately, though—so, at least, it seems to me—he doesn't need to. For we all have some sense of what it is to feel alive, to feel *particularly* alive, and of the variability of the degree or extent to which we feel alive; and we would probably all agree that some people, in some basic way, seem "larger" than others, seem to experience life more intensely and act with greater verve than others. The way to convey this phenomenon is indirectly, either through poetic representation of inner experience or through descriptions of behavior that are

---

3. If this single desire can attach itself to various objects, why call it a single desire? The answer is that these various objects are pursued for the sake of a single, unvarying aim or "metaobject," namely, maximized existence. This expansive use of the word "desire" is consistent with Rousseau's usage: it is he who speaks of "the desire to extend our being" (*Emile* 168). Compare to Aristotle's coinage of the relatively expansive *orexis*, or "reaching out," usually rendered as "desire." Aristotle, *De Anima* 433a–b; Larry Arnhart, *Darwinian Natural Right*, p. 19.

4. The meaning and significance of existence, or the sentiment of existence, in Rousseau's thought has been addressed by a number of interpreters, among whom I would cite two as particularly worthy of note: Melzer, in *The Natural Goodness of Man*, pp. 39–46, 64–69, and 103–5; and Grace, in "Conscience: The Ambiguous Science of 'Simple Souls'" as well as in her "The Restlessness of 'Being,'" 133–51. (For brief surveys of other interpreters, see Melzer, p. 40n20, and Grace, "Conscience," p. 37n38.) I explored these issues myself in Chapter 1 of *Rousseau, Nature, and the Problem of the Good Life*. In its investigation of "the desire to extend our being" the present investigation goes beyond my earlier discussion, but the following brief survey is based on that longer account.

novelistic enough to convey the inner life behind the behavior. Rousseau offers examples of both—the former in various autobiographical passages (to be considered below), the latter in his portrayals of certain literary characters (Emile chief among them) and in the occasional general statement such as this one: "To be something, to be oneself and always one, a man must act as he speaks; he must always be decisive in making his choice, make it in a lofty style, and always stick to it" (*Emile* 40). Immediately prior to this explanation of what it means to "be *something*" (note the existential language) Rousseau had described "the men of our days," the bourgeois, as "*nothing*."

We learn more about the sentiment of existence from Rousseau's discussions of what does and does not contribute to or enable us to feel it. "To live is not to breathe," he writes, "it is to act; it is to make use of all our organs, our senses, our faculties, of all the parts of ourselves which give us the sentiment of existence" (*Emile* 42). Rousseau's various depictions of impressive and/or strong-souled individuals, from the savage to Emile to the exemplary citizen to the legislator to himself, serve to confirm this statement and to articulate its various permutations.[5] As this range of personalities suggests, these permutations are many. The faculties chiefly employed by, say, Rousseau himself are far removed from those of the savage (and each of the others, for that matter), and so, presumably, is the manner in which he experiences the sentiment of existence: through reverie and meditation Rousseau experiences a pure version of the sentiment of existence, "stripped of any other emotion" and apparently all the more intense for that, whereas others seem to enjoy a less pure experience of existence through the exercise of more ordinary physical, social, and mental faculties (*Reveries* 69; *Lettre à Voltaire, OC* IV, 1063–64). One experiences being through *doing*, though the modes of doing are innumerable.

That Rousseau considers existence good in and of itself is incontrovertible. In the passage just cited from the *Reveries of the Solitary Walker*, he speaks of the peace and contentment and sweetness of the sentiment of existence; and in the letter to Voltaire he famously proclaims that, "for anyone who feels his existence, it is better to exist than not to exist" (*OC* IV, 1070).[6] That existence

---

5. Rousseau's pantheon of impressive human types includes some who are strong of soul, strength of soul being the foundation of virtue; and others (most notably himself) who lack strength of soul but who are impressive for some gifts or for their goodness.

6. Rousseau's belief in the goodness of "enlarged" existence and his disdain for smallness of soul (or being) are perhaps most strikingly displayed in his famous comparison between religious fanaticism and the "philosophic indifference" of "the allegedly wise man." The former,

is the highest good, indeed *the* good or the comprehensive good for Rousseau (in that it is the source or standard by which other goods are good), is less obvious but no less true. That existence holds this status can be established by examining how Rousseau describes, and that for which he praises or recommends, other goods. Virtue, for example (which various neo-Kantian interpreters mistakenly consider Rousseau's highest good),[7] is treated as praiseworthy because it in some way satisfies the desire for more being. (In *what* way will be addressed below.) Even happiness, the only other plausible contender for highest good, proves to be second to existence in two senses. First, the content of happiness consists in feeling, which always means in enjoying, one's existence. This is true at the highest reaches, of the happiness, described in the *Reveries* and cited above, which consists in the sweet sentiment of existence "stripped of any other emotion"; but it is equally true of more commonly available kinds of happiness. The latter is implied both in Rousseau's various depictions of happiness and in his argument that happiness depends not so much on pleasure or any other positive thing but on the relative absence of pain and psychic conflict: that the mere absence of pain yields happiness can only mean that the positive element of happiness is already present by virtue of one's being and feeling alive. The second important sense in which existence is a good prior to happiness is that it can be attained, and can thereby give meaning and quality to life, apart from happiness. Happiness, as Rousseau uses the term (*bonheur*), depends partly on our own conduct and internal state but also on external conditions beyond our control (*Reveries* 137). Sadly, external conditions are often worst for those whose character is most admirable. Too often the best among us have been made to suffer precisely for what is best about them. Yet those individuals are not foolish or without earthly compensation, for, though obviously not happy, their contentment with themselves and their intensity of experience yields them a magnificent share of existence and renders their lives exemplary. To be sure, happiness is a great good. Probably we ought to think of it as the crowning good, since true happiness does not entail the compromise of any

---

though destructive, at least manifests "a prodigious energy that need only be better directed to produce the most sublime virtues." The latter, by contrast, is irredeemably contemptible for exemplifying and encouraging an existentially constricting egoism. See *Emile* 312n.

7. For the neo-Kantian interpretation, see Cassirer, *The Question of Jean-Jacques Rousseau* and *Rousseau, Kant, and Goethe*; Gurvitch, *L'idée du droit social;* and Levine, *The Politics of Autonomy*. Derathé offers a related interpretation in *Le Rationalisme de Jean-Jacques Rousseau*.

other good. Nevertheless I call existence the greatest good since it is the *source* or substance of other goods.

The means and conditions required for attaining a "large" existence are many and complex and in some ways ultimately mysterious. It is possible to say something now about the "shape" of the endeavor, however; and it will be possible to say something more once we have examined Rousseau's treatment of the "*desire* to extend our being." In brief, an examination of the various character types admired or endorsed by Rousseau reveals that, for all their (enormous) differences, they all share two basic features, or metafeatures.[8] First, they all approximate the "negative" perfection of the first man, whose soul was troubled neither by inner conflict nor by a painful excess of desire. None of them, it should be noted, quite attains that ideal. Yet the means by which they approximate it more than compensate them for that imperfection, for these means themselves derive from the second, and "positive," shared feature of all good human types—namely, the harmonious development and employment of faculties that in and of themselves constitute extended or enlarged being. This is seen most clearly in Emile, whose imagination and passion keep him from quite attaining the savage's equality between desire and faculty but whose *will* is kept from outpacing his power. The part of his desire that exceeds his faculties is mastered by virtue, which, being both a kind of rationalized passion and a faculty (will), yields a certain satisfaction and an extension of being (*Emile* 80).

Existence, then—which, we recall, means *felt* existence—requires, first, a sufficient freedom from inner division and distraction that one's being may be felt; and, second, that there be something to be felt. The extent of one's existence depends on the degree to which these requirements are met. The second requirement is the one that admits of greater variability: the faculties that can contribute to the enlargement of existence are numerous and diverse. To the extent that most of us fail to achieve a desirable level of existence, though—and it is quite clear that Rousseau would find the vast majority of us wanting, just as he found the vast majority of his contemporaries want-

---

8. The character types to which I refer include the virtuous citizen; "the natural man living in the state of society [i.e., Emile]"; the contemplative Rousseau as he portrays himself in his autobiographical writings; and even the tribal savage, the denizen of "nascent society" (*SD* 150–51). These four hardly exhaust the list of types approved of by Rousseau. But they do seem to me to occupy the "pure" positions and thereby to constitute the "markers" by which to understand all other worthy individuals.

ing—the primary locus of the failure would seem to lie in the first or "negative" part of the project. Our smallness is first and foremost a product of inner conflict and excessive, unfulfillable desire; it is these things, along with the consequent tendency to obsess over the past and to fret over the future, that keep us from living with whole hearts in the present moment. The ultimate source of this evil is society. By making us dependent on one another, society puts our most urgently felt needs and interests, themselves the product of socialization, into contradiction with the requirements of our desire—our *need*—to enhance the degree of our existence.[9] (We see now why liberal or bourgeois society comes in for particular scorn from Rousseau: it deliberately intensifies personal dependence.) Society's existence-diminishing effects are not inevitable, however. In principle, they can be checked either by the construction of a regime based on the principles of political right as articulated in the *Social Contract* or by isolated individuals, through education or moral reform. Rousseau sees the former as highly unlikely for reasons explained in the *Social Contract* (70–75). What about the latter?

Whether in the case of the naturally exceptional individual as exemplified by Rousseau himself or that of an ordinary person as exemplified by Emile, the key to a high level of existence is the proper ordering of self-love. (Note that both men were raised amid an unregenerate society.) Neither case seems very encouraging from a practical standpoint. The exceptional individual by definition is not a model for most, and Emile, *practically*, is no proof at all, for Emile was not only conceived by a philosophic genius, he was raised by one as well. Nevertheless, improvement *is* possible, as is indicated by Rousseau's various efforts to stimulate social and moral reform. One of these efforts is the *Lettres morales*, whose rhetoric is designed to persuade individuals to self-reform and whose prescriptive content is designed to yield a more natural life and hence a greater degree of existence (*OC* IV). Yet even this more modest but accessible possibility is remote for most people. Most of us, Rousseau would say, fail to understand—in fact, resist understanding—that we might increase our happiness and existence by shedding illusory hopes and false attachments. Here we arrive at a key cause of our diminished existence and return to the primary focus of our inquiry. For it turns out that the proximate cause of this tragic blindness—and, indeed, the cause of much of

---

9. For an illuminating discussion of the "contradiction of society," see Melzer, *The Natural Goodness of Man*, pp. 69–85. Regarding the connection between this contradiction and the sentiment of existence specifically, see Grace, "Conscience," pp. 22–24.

our existential diminishment in the first place—is precisely the desire to *extend* our being.

"THE DESIRE TO EXTEND OUR BEING"

It is a peculiar ethical naturalism that identifies our greatest good with the object of our deepest desire but then identifies that desire as the source of our diversion from the good. Yet that is Rousseau's view—in part. In any number of forceful passages he warns us against the desire to be more than we already are. This is one of the more pronounced strains in *Emile*, from the rather Stoical discourse on happiness at the start of book 2 ("O man, draw your existence up within yourself, and you will no longer be miserable" [83]) to the account of the young man's study of history in book 4 ("He will be afflicted at seeing his brothers . . . turn into ferocious animals because they do not know how to be satisfied with being men" [242]) to the tutor's counsel near the end of the book: "I have only one precept to give you, and it comprehends all the others. Be a man. Restrain your heart within the limits of your condition. Study and know these limits. However narrow they may be, a man is not unhappy as long as he closes himself up within them. He is unhappy only when he wants to go out beyond them" (446). To be sure, the latter two of these admonitions concern not the desire to extend our being in toto but only the desire to be more than human. Yet the latter, inherently dangerous desire is arguably the logical endpoint of the desire to extend our being and in fact is the hidden desire of "every civilized man" (*SD* 195).[10] Therefore Rousseau's counsel against wanting to elevate our being above the realm of the human effectively comes down to counsel against, or at the very least an urgent plea for caution regarding, the desire to extend our being as such; and often the counsel he gives is directly concerned with extension as such.

Yet if Rousseau counsels against the desire to extend our being—and if he would leave his readers above all with a sense of the danger of that desire—that doesn't mean that he views this desire in an altogether negative light. I wish to argue, in fact, that Rousseau views the desire to extend our being as a

---

10. "After long prosperity, after having swallowed up many treasures and desolated many men, my hero will end by ruining everything until he is the *sole master of the universe*. Such in brief is the moral picture, if not of human life, at least of the secret pretensions of the heart of every civilized man" (emphasis added).

highly ambiguous thing. Belonging to the essence of self-love, the desire to extend our being is natural in its origins and potentially good even for civilized human beings, even if that potential is rarely realized. Indeed, it is the motive force directing us to the *greatest* good, just as, as we have just seen, it also directs us to the greatest evils. In this the desire to extend our being resembles Platonic eros, which is the motive force of both the best and the worst of men.[11] One of my hopes in this chapter is to distinguish between these divergent potentials, that is, to ascertain the defining criteria of what, for lack of more elegant terms, I will simply call "good" and "bad" versions of the desire to extend our being. But before considering versions or species we would do well to look into the genus. What *is* the desire to extend our being?

I remarked above that this desire belongs to the essence of self-love. That statement requires elaboration and qualification. Rousseau famously divides self-love into two types, *amour de soi* and *amour-propre*, the latter being the unnatural but inevitable outgrowth of the former in civilized human beings.[12] It is not difficult to discern the centrality of the desire to extend one's being to *amour-propre*, which, being a relative passion, always seeks preeminence over others and typically wishes for mastery over others. (Recall "the secret pretensions of the heart of every civilized man" [*SD* 195].) Preeminence and mastery bring, and are surely sought for the sake of, recognition by others; and for social man this recognition is the very stuff of being (179). Although born in response to the frustration of desire, *amour-propre*, much like Plato's *thymos*, soon grows beyond the proportions demanded by its initiating provocation and takes on a very large (indeed, a typically tyrannical) life of its own.[13] Rather than seek merely to overcome a particular obstacle to a particu-

---

11. The ambiguous potential of eros is one of the great themes of the *Republic*, in which the philosopher, the most self-sufficient and just of men, and the tyrant, the most avidly insatiable and unjust of men, are identified as erotic beings. See, respectively, 475e, 485a–b, 501d, and 573b–579d. Also see 491d–492a, where Socrates links these two extremes by suggesting that those with highly erotic natures are destined for one or the other, with little likelihood of a middle position.

12. Rousseau's most succinct articulation of the distinction between the two types of self-love appears in note "o" of the *Second Discourse* (221–22). When I use the English term "self-love" I will be speaking of both *amour de soi* (or *amour de soi-même*) and *amour-propre*.

13. Rousseau gives several accounts of the genesis of *amour-propre* out of *amour de soi*. The one that most highlights the triggering role of obstacles or frustration appears at *Dialogues* 9. Regarding Plato's account of the birth of *thymos*, see Newell, *Ruling Passion*, pp. 3–4 et passim; and Pangle, "The Political Psychology of Religion in Plato's *Laws*." Also see Chapter 1 of the present study.

lar desire, it comes to see the world as full of obstacles and to view everything outside itself, including, especially, other people, as little else than obstructions or threats or objects of conquest:

> As soon as th[e] absolute love [of oneself] degenerates into amour-propre and comparative love . . . as soon as one adopts the habit of measuring oneself against others and moving outside oneself in order to assign oneself the first and best place, it is impossible not to develop an aversion for everything that surpasses us, everything that lowers our standing, everything that diminishes us, everything that by being something prevents us from *being everything*." (*Dialogues* 112; emphasis added)

Whatever the initiating provocation, then, *amour-propre* comes to experience it as merely the edge or "presenting symptom" of the *real* provocation, namely, the fact that we are limited or finite beings, the fact that we are not "everything." How far we have traveled from the benign self-love of the indolent natural man.

Yet *amour-propre* is not injected into the soul by an alien force. It is born when self-consciousness, the awareness of one's separateness and relatedness to others, triggers the transformation, the relativization, of *amour de soi*. That self-consciousness should relativize self-love, making self-esteem problematic and giving it a moral dimension, seems logical enough. (One would like to say, "seems *natural*" enough, but that would be to settle an important question without first asking it.) But that self-consciousness should ignite infinite passion where before there had been only contentment with one's level of being is baffling—so much so, in fact, that we might question our premise and wonder whether the longing for infinity was not in fact *already* present in *amour de soi*, either in latency or in some live but benign way. For it would be much easier to make sense of the birth of *amour-propre*, of the sudden rebellion against finitude, if the *amour de soi* out of which it is born were already expansive. And so it is. We might recall that Rousseau's single explicit reference to "the desire to extend our being" occurs in connection with the preadolescent Emile, in whom *amour-propre* had yet to be born (*Emile* 168). In Rousseau's view self-love, by its very principle, is expansive—which is to say that human beings, who, after all, are motivated exclusively by one kind of self-love or another, seek to be all that they can be. Human being as such is expansive.[14]

To register the precise meaning of this expansiveness it would help to take note of what it does *not* mean. That self-love and human being are expansive does not mean that the longing to be everything belongs to *amour de soi*. "Everything" is a relative term and as such can be the object only of the relative form of self-love. Nor does it mean that the desire to extend our being is an essential or universal feature of *amour de soi*. In the strict sense, at least, the desire to extend one's being would seem to require that one be capable of desiring more than just the satisfaction of physical needs, a condition that excludes men and women in the pure state of nature as well as (perhaps) very small children amid civilization. (True, I just said that self-love, by its very principle, is expansive; but this principle can be operative only where a certain level of cognitive development has taken place; more on this below.) Nor does it mean that every person, at every moment, somehow or other seeks to be more than he or she already is. Those who are weak or weakening seek only to preserve the being they already enjoy. For them, seeking to be all they can be is more in the nature of a defensive enterprise than an expansive one. Yet even this defensive posture testifies to the positive inclination of self-love and human being, that is, testifies to the reach for maximum existence. Let us then examine this inclination and let me specify what I think it *does* mean.

Stated positively, my interpretation of Rousseau's view of self-love and the expansiveness of human being consists in the following points, the first of which has already been stated. (1) Self-love of every variety, and human beings in whatever condition, seek the maximum possible degree of existence. (2) In those who are capable—those who are sufficiently energetic and sufficiently advanced cognitively—the pursuit of maximized existence manifests itself as the desire to extend their being. This desire for extension appears both (a) in *amour-propre*, in which case it manifests itself as the desire to be everything, and (b) in *amour de soi*, in which case it manifests itself as a more benign reach for extension. (I am assuming that *amour-propre* and *amour de soi* are in principle distinguishable in the soul of civilized human beings and that they can, and do, coexist in the same soul.) (3) In those who are weak, the

---

14. Regarding self-love as the source of all human action, consider that passion is the source of all action and that self-love is the source of all passion (*Dialogues* 9; *Emile* 183 and 212–13). For more on the expansiveness of *amour de soi* and the closeness between *amour de soi* and *amour-propre*, see Grace, "The Restlessness of 'Being.'"

pursuit of maximized existence manifests itself in the desire only for preservation, not expansion. (4) In those who may be sufficiently strong but who lack the requisite cognitive capacity to conceive and desire things that are superfluous to their physical well-being (i.e., human beings in the pure state of nature and the very young amid civilization), the inclination to maximize existence manifests itself not as the desire to extend being but simply as a love of being that expresses itself as exuberance or overflowing activity and that, being love—indeed, being a passion (*Emile* 213)—would seek extension if it knew enough to be able to do so. Perhaps one could say that this primitive self-love is latently expansive. Finally, (5) what transforms the not-yet-expansive self-love and being of the savage or the infant into one or more versions of the desire for extension is the advent of self-consciousness, or the awareness of oneself as a separate self related to other selves. With self-consciousness comes the capacity to desire more than what would satisfy one's physical needs, and the principle of self-love (the fact that it *is* love) dictates that this capacity will be employed.

(1) The first and most basic point is nowhere categorically stated by Rousseau, but it is suggested, definitively I think, by the principle of self-love. Self-love, we recall, is not only the source of passions but a passion itself, whether in the form of *amour de soi* or as *amour-propre* (*Emile* 213; *SD* 195 and 221–22). Passion implies desire. When one loves something one desires either to obtain it (or to obtain more of it) or to maintain possession of it, or both. When the object of love is something as unending as being itself, one never stops wanting *more* of it, at least not until one feels oneself somehow in possession of it (or more likely, union with it—about which more below). That most people do not *consciously* seek or desire extended being does not count against my interpretation. It does indicate, though, that most of us are ignorant of what we most deeply want. Now this analysis by itself is hardly proof of anything. It does, however, represent a key premise of Rousseau's moral and political philosophy, which will become apparent as we consider some of the particulars of Rousseau's treatment of the expansiveness of self-love and the desire for extended being. Let us therefore proceed to those particulars, beginning with what I take to be Rousseau's most complete summary statement of the nature and sources of human action (and hence human being). Besides testifying to Rousseau's belief in a universal tendency of self-love to maximize existence, this passage from the *Dialogues* also lays out the distinction between the two basic versions of the desire for extended being:

> Sensitivity is the principle of all action.... There is a purely passive physical and organic sensitivity which seems to have as its end only the preservation of our bodies and of our species through the direction of pleasure and pain. There is another sensitivity that I call active and moral which is nothing other than the faculty of attaching our affections to beings who are foreign to us. This type, about which study of nerve pairs teaches nothing, seems to offer a fairly clear analogy for souls to the magnetic faculty of bodies. Its strength is in proportion to the relationships we feel between ourselves and other beings, and depending on the nature of these relationships it sometimes acts positively by attraction, sometimes negatively by repulsion, like the poles of a magnet. The positive or attracting action is the simple work of nature, which *seeks to extend and reinforce the feeling of our being;* the negative or repelling action, which compresses and diminishes the being of another, is a combination produced by reflection. From the former arise all the loving and gentle passions, and from the latter all the hateful and cruel passions.... Positive sensitivity is directly derived from *amour de soi.* It is very natural that a person who loves himself should seek to extend his being and his enjoyments and to appropriate for himself through attachment what he feels should be a good thing for him. This is a pure matter of feeling in which reflection plays no part. But as soon as this absolute love degenerates into amour-propre and comparative love, it produces negative sensitivity, because as soon as one adopts the habit of measuring oneself against others and moving outside oneself in order to assign oneself the first and best place, it is impossible not to develop an aversion for everything that surpasses us, everything that lowers our standing, everything that diminishes us, everything that by being something prevents us from being everything. (112; emphasis added)

Prior to and cutting across the distinction between *amour de soi* and *amour-propre* is the distinction between the (passive, physical) sensitivity that tends to the preservation of our being and the (active, moral) sensitivity that tends to the extension of our being. The point of immediate relevance is that the expansive tendency belongs to self-love as such—that it is expressed, however differently, by both *amour de soi* and *amour-propre*—and that, belonging to the *nature* of self-love, it does not arise only in response to some threat. (See also *OC* III, 1324–25, and *Emile* 79.)

(2, 3) I noted above that expansiveness, or the desire for extended being, requires sufficient force; absent such force, self-love or the desire for maximized existence manifests itself defensively, as the desire for preservation only. "In the state of weakness and insufficiency concern for our preservation concentrates us within ourselves. In the state of power and strength the desire to extend our being takes us out of ourselves and causes us to leap as far as is possible for us" (*Emile* 168).[15] Although in this line from *Emile* Rousseau seems to speak of a singular "state of power and strength," the more comprehensive analysis in the *Dialogues* indicates that the force requisite for the desire to extend one's being can come in either of two variants—either strength of soul, in which case the result is a "positive" expansiveness, or the energy of those not strong of soul but nevertheless full of desire, in which case the expansive tendency is "negative," seeking its own fullness only by diminishing others.[16] Examples of the former include the adolescent Emile and, indeed, all adolescents who have not fallen into dissipation: "a superabundance of life seeks to extend itself outward" and brings about friendship, compassion, and romantic love (*Emile* 220). Of the newly compassionate Emile, Rousseau observes that "he feels himself to be in that condition of strength which extends us beyond ourselves and leads us to take elsewhere activity superfluous to our well-being" (229).[17] Examples of the expansiveness born of the desire or energy of those who are not strong of soul are found throughout Rousseau's corpus, from the "agitated" sociable man of the *Second Discourse* to the assiduous conspirators persecuting Rousseau (*SD* 179; *Dialogues,* passim).

15. Compare to Nietzsche *GS* 349: "The wish to preserve oneself is the symptom of a condition of distress, of a limitation of the really fundamental instinct of life which aims at *the expansion of power* and, wishing for that, frequently risks and even sacrifices self-preservation" (emphasis in the original).

16. In absolute terms, one who expands his being only by diminishing others (even assuming such a thing is possible) is not expanding his being at all. But that is just the point: such a person is entirely relative in his being; caring only about his standing vis-à-vis others, he only cares about proportions and thus feels himself more for their being less. People who live in this way may be active and even energetic, but they are weak. (This is a different kind of weakness from that which constitutes a lack of energy.) This we may conclude from Rousseau's dictum that "all wickedness comes from weakness" (*Emile* 67). Here, too, Rousseau anticipates Nietzsche, who plumbed the depths of this phenomenon in his analysis of the spirit of revenge.

17. Rousseau does not claim that strength of soul and healthy expansiveness belong only to the young. But it is a bit discouraging that his most compelling portrait of adult strength of soul and healthy expansiveness is found in his fantastic depiction of an "ideal world" (Rousseau, *Dialogues,* 9–12).

(3) Just as there is a distinction among those with the psychic force to desire extended existence, so there is a distinction to be made among the weak, that is, those with little physical and psychic energy. Those who are weak from old age, husbanding what they understand to be waning resources, typically seek only calm, whereas those who are weak because they are still too young to provide for themselves are active and rambunctious in anticipation of greater power (and perhaps, too, because unlike the old they are confident that their preservation needs will continue to be met by others). See, in this regard, Rousseau's comparison of the child, whose strength is not great but whose "activity . . . is superabundant and extends outward," to the similarly (but of course not similarly) weak "old man," whose "failing activity" is "concentrated in [his] heart" (*Emile* 67).[18] Also note Rousseau's observation that it belongs to every age but especially to childhood "to want to create, imitate, produce, give signs of power and activity," a propensity that can be seen in children as a harbinger or even direct evidence of the desire to extend their being (*Emile* 98). Though weak in an absolute sense, children typically have the energy and confidence to let them take preservation for granted and seek extended being according to their own lights and capacities.

(4, 5) I suggested above that the discovery of *amour de soi*'s expansiveness makes the birth of *amour-propre*, with its aggressive expansiveness, somewhat less baffling. What occurs with the birth of *amour-propre* is not the creation but rather the transformation, the relativization, of a pre-existing tendency. *Amour-propre* and *amour de soi* prove to have more in common than is initially apparent. Yet precisely by grasping this link we come to see a different disjunction and are faced with another baffling evolutionary step: How are we to understand the development of an expansive self-love (i.e., self-love as it appears in civilized human beings, whether in the form of *amour de soi* or *amour-propre*) out of the apparently *non*expansive self-love of the savage? Why did contentment give way to infinite and usually insatiable longing?

Rousseau famously describes the savage as idle and lazy (*SD* 118 and 208; *Last Reply* 266n.)—and not only lazy, but also content: what little he wanted was in his power to procure (*SD* 116). Rousseau does not even hint that the soul of the savage harbored any deep-seated agitation or any impulse to overflow itself. The extent of the savage's expansiveness was his repugnance at

---

18. For more on how the desire for being varies according to the the stages of life, see Grace, "The Restlessness of 'Being,'" pp. 138–40.

seeing sensible beings perish or suffer, a phenomenon that does denote a kind of extensive impulse but one whose smallness Rousseau underscores by attributing it to horses as well as to men (*SD* 95 and 130). Yet the savage was a creature of self-love, and self-love, as noted earlier, is a passion that carries a desire for maximized existence. This desire is the principle of self-love as such, as applicable to the savage as to civilized humanity. (It is important to recall Rousseau's insistence that the inhabitant of the pure state of nature was indeed a human being.) Because of his limited cognitive development, the savage was not able to conceive or desire more than he needed, and what he needed was normally available to him—hence the contentment. With the appearance of incipient self-consciousness, however, he became capable of conceiving new objects of desire and began to be aware of his finitude and vulnerability. That is to say, he began to feel, however inarticulately, both that his existence *could* be extended and that, if he was to be happy, his existence *needed* to be extended. Self-consciousness is what triggered the desire to extend one's being.

This logic, though nowhere simply stated by Rousseau, is borne out by his depictions of the various human types. While the savage is depicted as uninterested in, because not able to conceive, things that would extend his being, *all* sufficiently energetic self-conscious or civilized human beings are depicted as desiring extended existence. Those who are dominated by unruly *amour-propre*—think here of "the secret pretensions of the heart of every civilized man"—are depicted as insatiable in their desire to outstrip others, to dominate everyone, to *be everything*. Those governed by an orderly *amour-propre*—citizens of a well-constituted republic, for example—while well disposed toward fellow citizens, still seek preeminence both for themselves and for the nation. Finally, those in whom *amour-propre* is not predominant, such as the young Emile and the older Rousseau, also evince a desire to extend their being. Emile's case has already been discussed: his education in compassion is explicitly said to consist in the channeling of an overflowing or expansive strength, and it is in connection with Emile's scientific education that Rousseau speaks of "the desire to extend our being" (*Emile* 167–68). But what about the dreamily contemplative and self-describedly idle Rousseau (*Confessions* 537; *Reveries* 64)? Can one really maintain that *he* exemplifies a desire to extend his being? Yes, in fact. And with this we come to the next part of our discussion.

HOW, AND HOW NOT, TO "EXTEND OUR BEING"

No one but a philosopher would speak of "the desire to extend our being," and most philosophers have preferred to speak of some other goal—power, or pleasure, or preservation, for example—when postulating the ruling desire of human beings.[19] Even Rousseau agrees that extended being is not the immediate object but rather the ultimate object—or, to use again the psychoanalytic distinction, the aim—of many other desires. (Undoubtedly this is one reason for the infrequency of the language of "being" in his work: one who wishes to reform judgment, as Rousseau clearly does, needs to speak to people's desires in more familiar terms.) These other desires are many indeed, their foci ranging from material possessions, prestige, and mastery over others and over oneself, to compassion (the desire that others not suffer), friendship, patriotism, familial and romantic love, and knowledge and understanding.[20] In many, probably most, of these cases, it is intuitively plausible that the desired object is desired for the sake of extended being (this is especially true where and to the extent that *amour-propre* is seen to be at work), though to say that things are pursued for the sake of extended being is not to say that they necessarily bring extended being when they are attained. Material possessions, for example, are typically experienced as extensions of oneself, even if many would follow Hobbes and Locke in holding that this extension is sought as a fence of our preservation and not as an end in itself. The desire for prestige, though again thought by many to serve some other end, can also rather easily be interpreted as an expression or manifestation of the desire to

---

19. The examples are too numerous to analyze, but the mention of such names as Machiavelli, Nietzsche, Epicurus, Hobbes, and Spinoza should make the point. Plato immediately comes to mind as one who does seem to say that human beings desire more being. Their shared emphasis on being constitutes an important affinity and perhaps an instance of influence between Plato and Rousseau.

20. This list is incomplete, and the explanations that follow will be more so (with the important exception of my treatment of the last item). I am permitting myself this incompleteness partly because some of the points are obvious enough to require minimal explanation; partly because some of them, especially those belonging to the category of moral phenomena, have been treated well by other scholars; but also because the full meaning of the desire for extended being will be illuminated less by a necessarily superficial survey of its many manifestations or subsidiary desires than by a detailed examination of that activity which best succeeds at *attaining* extended existence—hence the more extended treatment of the last item on the list. Finally, let me stress that I am not proposing that the "mechanisms" whereby extended being is sought or found are the same in each case, or that Rousseau thinks they are. Indeed, quite the contrary: while positing existence as the comprehensive good for human beings, Rousseau, it seems, allows for as many modes of existence and thus of extending existence as there are faculties.

extend one's being, for one who is recognized and admired by others sees himself reflected in them and knows himself to exist somehow in and through their consciousness. Perhaps mastery over others is the clearest case of those cited. Mastery over others consists in the extension of the effective range of one's will, an extension believed by the lover of such power to constitute an extension of his existence, since he views his will as the essential part of himself or the thing he most *is*.

The desire for self-mastery can be interpreted in this vein as well. The most remarked-upon kind of self-mastery in Rousseau, and certainly the most important, is virtue. Virtue, which by definition entails a kind of self-overcoming, is pursued for the sake of satisfaction with oneself, a satisfaction born of the very fact of overcoming, that is, born of the exercise of strength by one part of oneself—presumably the truer part of oneself, the part one considers the core of one's identity—against another part. This mastery of one part of oneself by another part can be seen as rule by, and therefore as *the extension of the being* of, the active, rational, moral part of the self, the part one considers one's true self. (How else to explain why, when the will successfully governs appetite, we say that we have won a victory over ourselves? Why not say we have been defeated by ourselves, or that, as always, we have both won and lost?)[21]

Not only virtue, but the other key element of the moral life, compassion, can also (and more easily) be seen to entail the extension of one's being. Compassion, according to Rousseau, consists in the extension of our being to, and consequently our suffering in, others (*Emile* 221, 223; *Last Reply* 261).[22] And if compassion entails extension, so must that whose source is compassion—friendship, most notably (*SD* 131–32). Patriotism, too, can be interpreted along these lines. Citizens who identify with one another are in some sense extending their being to one another, and of course the imperialism that is frequently born of this collectivization of *amour-propre* is self-evidently a case of attempting to extend being. If citizens identify with one another, so do members of a family, which in fact serves as both the prototype for and the training ground of civic identification and devotion (*Emile* 363). Thus family

---

21. Cf. *Republic* 430e–431b. For more on the satisfactions of virtue, see Melzer, *The Natural Goodness of Man*, pp. 100–104.

22. A whole range of moral phenomena beyond virtue and compassion can also be seen as expressions of expansive self-love, including benevolence, generosity, gratitude, and promise keeping; see Grace, "Conscience."

love, too, qualifies as a manifestation of the desire for extended being. The next item on our list is romantic love, which, with its intense mixture of (a) the desire to possess the beloved and (b) sympathetic devotion to him or her, seems to me to qualify on two grounds, the former exemplifying the desire for extended being as expressed through *amour-propre,* the latter through *amour de soi.* Finally, the desire for extended being can often be discerned as the source of the desire for knowledge and understanding. After all, it is in connection with the young Emile's new education in science that Rousseau actually speaks of "the desire to extend our being" (168), and it is easy enough to see that knowledge of the way the world works grants some power, some extension of oneself, over and in the world.

Now science as Emile learns it is not the science (the botany) of the older Rousseau, and it is certainly not the same as Rousseau's philosophizing and reverie. Emile's study, at least in its origin, is undertaken in the service of his immediate and palpable interest, that is, for the sake of some end beyond itself. Yet I wish to suggest that not only his but also Rousseau's intellectual activity is pursued for the sake of extended being. Indeed, I would suggest that Rousseau's activity is a more direct means of extending being than that of Emile—and not only more direct, but truer: I propose that the intellectual activity recounted in and exemplified by Rousseau's autobiographical writings, and especially the *Reveries,* is the truest manifestation of the desire for extended being of all those which appear in Rousseau's work in that it seeks—and therefore gains—maximized existence where it is most amply available. It—or, rather, Rousseau himself, Rousseau the dreamer/thinker/artist—recognizes what would best satisfy the desire for extended being, just as the Platonic philosopher recognizes what alone would satisfy the deepest human longing. Rousseau's intellectual activity thus demands our attention, if only because a desire cannot be truly understood without some grasp of the thing that would best satisfy it.

In taking up the case of Rousseau himself I must begin by responding to an obvious objection. Like the savage, Rousseau leads an idle life (*Confessions* 537; *Reveries* 64 et passim.) How then can he be seen as pursuing and gaining extended existence? Would it not be more accurate to see him as having shed the desire for extended being along with, or as a part of, his having (for the most part) shed *amour-propre* (*Reveries* 117–18)?

The force of this objection dissipates when we take note of the peculiar character of Rousseau's idleness. Idleness, as Rousseau conceives of it, is not all of a piece. Some varieties are active and even involve much thinking: "The idleness I love is not that of a do-nothing who stays there with his arms crossed in total inactivity and thinks no more than he acts. It is both that of a child who is ceaselessly in motion while doing nothing and, at the same time, that of a dotard who strays when his arms are at rest" (*Confessions* 537). The reference to thinking is not insignificant. In the very next paragraph Rousseau recounts his forays into botany, which he describes as "precisely an idle study," yet one that consists in "analysis" and eventuates in written documents of considerable sophistication (*Confessions* 537; also see the "Seventh Walk" of the *Reveries*).[23] "Idleness," it would seem, means nothing more than that the activity is pursued for its own sake, or for the sake of immediate enjoyment.

Yet, as even so empirically oriented a thinker as Aristotle teaches, things that we choose for their own sake or for the sake of our immediate enjoyment are also chosen for the sake of that one thing that we seek only for its own sake: for him, *eudaimonia*;[24] for Rousseau, the maximization of being. Indeed, Rousseau seems to teach that we want everything we want *exclusively* for the sake of this one, ultimate good. However that may be, it seems to me quite clear that Rousseau's intellectual activity as recounted in and exemplified by his autobiographical writings, however "idle," is pursued precisely and even consciously for the sake of extended being, and that its success indicates that it is propelled by the most enlightened version of the desire for extended being.[25]

At their peaks, the *Reveries* and even the *Confessions* recount episodes in

---

23. For more on the character of Rousseau's botanizing, see Paul A. Cantor, "The Metaphysics of Botany," 362–80. Also see Davis, *The Autobiography of Philosophy*, for a provocative discussion of the philosophic significance of botany in Rousseau's work. Rousseau's botanical writings include *Dictionnaire des termes d'usage en botanique* and *Lettres elementaires sur la botanique à Madame de Lessert*; each of these appears in *OC IV*.

24. *Nicomachean Ethics* 1097a–b.

25. The reader will have observed that my initial references to the desire for knowledge and understanding have given way to the more vague term "intellectual activity," as the discussion has moved from the "ordinary" or interested pursuit of science (e.g., that of the young Emile) to the extraordinary practice of Rousseau himself. Precisely what constitutes the latter is not easy to say, for Rousseau does more than depart from ordinary science; he also departs, or at least seems to depart, from the traditional modes of philosophy. For now I would simply point out that what I have been calling "Rousseau's intellectual activity as described and exemplified in the autobiographical writings" consists in at least four distinct activities—namely, botany, reverie, philosophic meditation on the reveries (and on other things besides), and the artistic rendering of the preceding three.

which Rousseau overcomes "civilized self-consciousness" and thereby enlarges or extends his existence to extraordinary proportions.[26] (For the sake of economy I am passing over Rousseau's botanizing and will focus instead on the reveries. Not that botany is unimportant—indeed, its accessibility to people of ordinary intelligence makes it particularly important from a practical standpoint—but as a lesser peak than the reveries, botanizing reveals less about the desire for and possibility of extended being and is thus less theoretically significant than the reveries.) That his being is enlarged or extended is not an interpretation I have imposed but Rousseau's own explicit claim. It is presented as the immediate source of the pleasure and therefore (I would argue) the deliberate goal of the activities he describes.

Rousseau depicts at least two types of extraordinary existence-enlarging reveries. Sometimes the enlargement of existence occurs through the identification of the self with the whole of nature in its beautiful harmony of diverse parts: "I never meditate, I never dream more deliciously than when I forget myself. I feel ecstasies and inexpressible raptures in blending, so to speak, into the system of beings and in making myself one with the whole of nature" (*Reveries* 95). Although the raptures of which Rousseau speaks are not rational experiences, his use of the word "system" suggests that they may somehow include or otherwise entail rational awareness. Yet if they include rationality they also supersede it, thus rendering them suprarational rather than irrational;[27] and the result is something beyond discursive knowledge: "The more

---

26. "Civilized self-consciousness" is Kelly's term; see his *Rousseau's Exemplary Life*, p. 243.

27. To supersede, as Hegel famously put it, is at once to negate and to preserve (*The Phenomenology of Spirit*, p. 68). But *do* the reveries include rationality? Many interpreters, fastening onto Rousseau's talk of intoxication and not-thinking, conclude that the reveries are non- or even sub-rational experiences; and such remarks as Rousseau's proclamation of his preference for "stupefying ecstasy" over philosophic clarity in "Letters to Malesherbes" (*CW* 5:579) only strengthen the case for this reading. (See Grace, "The Restlessness of 'Being,'" pp. 148–51; also see Sorenson, "Natural Inequality and Rousseau's Political Philosophy," 763–88.) Yet as Kelly notes, even amid his ecstatic reveries Rousseau sometimes engages in a kind of philosophic contemplation (*Rousseau as Author*, p. 181). Even more important—and this is the decisive consideration in my view—however one would characterize the reveries, it seems impossible that such experiences would be available to any but a rational being: merging with a whole presupposes *seeing* that whole, that is, seeing it for a whole. What, then, to make of Rousseau's talk of intoxication, stupefaction, and confusion, which is surely the stuff of subrationality or irrationality rather than suprarationality? One possibility is that it is part of his general rhetorical strategy of dissociating himself from reflection and philosophy. This strategy and its grounds are addressed further in the concluding section of Chapter 6, below. Yet I don't want to overstate the case. It is also possible that Rousseau's reveries are admixtures of the subrational and the suprarational, as was the case with so much of nineteenth-century Romanticism. Finally, it is worth noting that even if Rousseau's experiences do have a subrational element, their suprarational

sensitive soul a contemplator has, the more he gives himself up to the ecstasies this harmony arouses in him. A sweet and deep reverie takes possession of his senses then, and through a delicious intoxication he loses himself in the immensity of this beautiful system with which he feels himself one. Then, all particular objects elude him; he sees and feels nothing except in the whole" (*Reveries* 92). From the standpoint of ordinary or civilized consciousness, there is a paradoxical quality to these experiences. On the one hand, the self seems to expand, to incorporate something far greater than its original content. This is reflected in Rousseau's continued use of personal pronouns to describe the experience: it is always "I" or "he" who feels himself one with nature. On the other hand, though, he refers in both passages to a forgetting or submergence of the self ("I forget myself," "he loses himself").

The second kind of existence-enlarging experience described in the *Reveries* seems on its face to contain neither side of this paradox. Rather than expand its boundaries, the self seems to narrow: it identifies itself not with nature but only with its own innermost core. And far from being forgotten or submerged in something larger, the self, even in its now narrow form, occupies the whole of consciousness:

> If there is a state in which the soul finds a solid enough base to rest itself on entirely and to *gather its whole being* into, without needing to recall the past or encroach upon the future; in which time is nothing for it; in which the present lasts forever without, however, making its duration noticed and without any trace of time's passage; without any other sentiment of deprivation or of enjoyment, pleasure or pain, desire or fear, except that alone of our existence, and having this sentiment alone fill it completely; as long as this state lasts, he who finds himself in it can call himself happy, not with an imperfect, poor, and relative happiness such as one finds in the pleasures of life, but with a sufficient, perfect and full happiness which leaves in the soul no emptiness it might feel a need to fill. Such is the state in which I often found myself during my solitary reveries on the île de Saint-Pierre, either lying in my boat as I let it drift with the

---

elements point to a realm of possibility that has been articulated by a number of contemplative traditions. Those traditions may or may not illuminate Rousseau, but they may help illuminate that which Rousseau does so much to illuminate.

water or seated on the banks of the tossing lake; or elsewhere, at the edge of a beautiful river or of a brook murmuring over pebbles.

What do we enjoy in such a situation? Nothing external to ourselves, nothing if not ourselves and our own existence. As long as this state lasts, we are sufficient unto ourselves, like God. (*Reveries* 68–69; emphases added)

Yet if this second experience does not partake of the paradox of the first experience, it nevertheless shares much with it: in each of the experiences, civilized self-consciousness and the separate-self sense have given way to a kind of thoughtless but not unconscious feeling of existence.[28] In fact, the two experiences even share the greater paradox of which the *other* paradox, the one found only in the first experience, is an effect. Namely, in each of the two experiences we find both an enhancement of the self ("we are sufficient unto ourselves, like God") and a simultaneous letting go of or disinvestment from all that belongs to the self in its separateness. In fact, though, this will seem a paradox only to those who believe that the road to enlarged existence is through the enhancement or aggrandizement of the separate self. To Rousseau, by contrast, it is no paradox at all, for he teaches through the *Reveries* (and other texts) that the transcendence of the separate self along with its possessions and encumbrances is a legitimate way, probably the *best* way, to enlarge one's being.[29] What I described as the narrowing of the self in the second experience is a narrowing only with respect to space and time. The self narrows until it includes nothing but the sentiment of its own existence, yet this sentiment (as experienced by the cultivated Rousseau), with its perfect and conscious satisfaction, seems to me to constitute a great enlargement of existence. Whereas *amour-propre,* at least in its typical form, inevitably fails to win the satisfaction it seeks (it's not easy to achieve preeminence, much less to "be everything"), the desire for extended being that arises from *amour*

---

28. Far from unconsciousness or regression, these experiences are presented as being above and beyond ordinary consciousness. Although they partake of the savage's inner balance and harmony, Rousseau all the while retains *and employs* a level of awareness, an aesthetic sensibility, and a scientific expertise that outstrip those belonging to the typical civilized person, let alone the savage.

29. By "transcendence of the separate self" I mean that the self ceases to be mindful of its separateness. Objectively speaking, of course, the existence the self enjoys is still its own.

de soi can win greater existence for the self by liberating it from identification with the ego.[30] That, it seems to me, is the lesson of the reveries.[31]

The lesson of the *Reveries* (the *book,* not just the activity recounted therein) is far more complex and multifaceted than this one part. As noted above, the book recounts and/or exemplifies at least four distinct activities. Aside from the reveries themselves (and botany) we also encounter Rousseau's meditation on them and his artistic (re)presentation of both the reveries and the meditation. It seems to me that all four activities contribute to the enlargement of being, and even that the latter two—the reporting, as it were—may be *more* important than the experiences reported. Why else would Rousseau "waste" his time in meditation and writing? This suggestion has important

---

30. As the comparison to God may indicate, Rousseau thinks that this means of enlarging one's being lies beyond the power of most people. It would seem to require a highly improbable combination of natural genius and a difficult-to-choose solitude. Here, as elsewhere, though, some may question Rousseau's pessimism while embracing his basic theoretical insight. An interesting and very important question is whether *amour-propre* can in any way serve the cause of its own reform or overcoming: one can imagine people reading Rousseau, concluding that the greatest happiness entails a transcendence of *amour-propre,* and then seeking that happiness . . . *for reasons of amour-propre* ("why shouldn't I have what *he* has?"). The question is whether such an egoistically propelled attempt to overcome egoism could ever succeed. There are perhaps some grounds for thinking it might.

31. For an opposing interpretation of the reveries, see Grace, "The Restlessness of 'Being,'" pp. 148–51. Grace holds that the reveries can best be understood not as a great expansion of being but as the enjoyment of being by one who, nearing death and diminished in his powers, has little being left to enjoy. That reading is consistent with what Rousseau says about the old. I resist this reading, however, for the following reasons. First, Rousseau speaks of ecstasies, not just peace; and ecstasy, particularly when rendered in Rousseau's vivid and evocative prose, seems to me to require some energy or capacity—some more being—than Grace's interpretation allows. (Grace concludes, as does Davis in *The Autobiography of Philosophy,* that Rousseau's talk of ecstasy and rapture is fiction, and that this is indicated by Rousseau at the end of the Fifth Walk. But even faking ecstasy, even in print, requires energy, at least if one's act is creditable; and it's not clear that he is in fact fictionalizing, or why he would do so.) Second, we find an overcoming of ordinary or civilized consciousness not only in *Reveries* but also in the *Confessions,* notwithstanding that the latter's description of life on the île de Saint-Pierre differs from that of the former. Finally, many who are neither old nor weak will recognize in Rousseau's reveries something like their *own experience.* If this weren't the case, there would have been no sense to Rousseau's fictionalizing these experiences, if in fact he did fictionalize them. This kind of fiction can only pass for fact if readers have some sense of the plausibility of such experience, and they will not have that sense unless their own experience shares something with what Rousseau is describing. Now one could say that the experiences of his readers that make Rousseau's accounts believable are experiences of essentially weak people, people who are weary of life's struggles and who long for peace. But it seems to me that one recognizes in Rousseau's reveries a clarity of perception and an enjoyment of life possible only for a mind that is very much awake, and that this wakefulness needs to be seen as something positive, something other than mere escape.

implications for the status of philosophy in Rousseau's thought. We have already seen Rousseau teach that reflection diminishes existence by deflecting passion (*Dialogues* 112), and we may recall his famous near-suggestion ("I almost dare affirm") "that the state of reflection is a state contrary to nature and that the man who meditates is a depraved animal" (*SD* 110). Moreover, Rousseau routinely portrays philosophers as creatures of an engorged if refined vanity, and he pointedly resists calling himself or even allowing himself to be called a philosopher.[32] In light of these statements philosophy seems to emerge as at best a necessary evil—necessary, that is, for those who are guided by the philosopher (*Emile* 219), but an evil for the one chosen by fate and a sense of responsibility to do the guiding. And of course the best case is rare. Yet the *Reveries*, with its philosophic portrait and analysis of Rousseau's happiness (and unhappiness), may well point to the pleasure, the enlarged existence, of a certain kind of philosopher—not only in his reveries but also in his rigorous, directed thinking.

How might rigorous thinking and writing extend one's being? Rousseau does not say; and given the corrupt state of most self-described philosophy and philosophers (as he sees it), he has good reason not to say.[33] Nor has the matter been much appreciated, let alone well understood, by scholars.[34] But on the basis of Rousseau's characterizations of his intellectual life and, even more so, on the basis of the character of his philosophic activity as revealed in his writings, it seems reasonable to surmise that philosophic thinking and writing directly extend the philosopher's existence in at least three ways.[35] First and more simply, thinking and writing exercise major capacities of the

---

32. See Kelly, *Rousseau as Author*, pp. 172–73.

33. As long as what calls itself philosophy is corrupt, Rousseau would not wish to lend philosophy any further allure. For more on the rhetorical stance demanded by Rousseau's dim assessment of most philosophy and philosophers, see the concluding section of Chapter 6, below.

34. An important exception is Kelly's "Postscript" to *Rousseau as Author*, pp. 172–82. Though brief and tentative in its conclusions, Kelly's treatment makes good on its claim to have set "the question of Rousseau and philosophy . . . on its proper footing" (p. 182). The issue has also been thoughtfully addressed by Sorenson, "Natural Inequality and Rousseau's Political Philosophy."

35. As indicated, what follow are ways in which philosophy might *directly* extend the philosopher's being. Philosophy can also extend the philosopher's being *indirectly*—by serving as a cure for such existence-diminishing phenomena as vanity and unreasonable hopes and fears, by making possible a variety of artistic activities, and by constituting a part of the sorts of reveries discussed above; see Kelly, *Rousseau as Author*, p. 181. What I am calling indirect ways in which philosophy contributes to the philosopher's well-being are for Kelly *all* the ways in which philosophy contributes to the philosopher's happiness.

soul, just as running and climbing exercise the body. The capacities with which one thinks and writes may or may not be natural, depending on how one sees fit to define "nature" in Rousseau's thought (which is not an easy matter to get right),[36] but they certainly belong to what Rousseau calls "the present nature of man" (*SD* 93). And they belong all the more, and all the more prominently and insistently, to the philosopher's nature. Not to think much would be to leave some faculties underemployed and hence to exist to a lesser extent than one otherwise would. For most people, including most intellectuals and self-described philosophers, such underemployment would be a net gain, since they are led by reflection into existence-diminishing pathologies such as vanity and excessive desire. But for some few, including Rousseau himself—for those who, for whatever reason, are given to thought and who, either from wisdom or strength of soul or happily preserved natural goodness, resist the corrupting influences of *amour-propre*—philosophic thinking and writing can extend being.

"For whatever reason"—for *what* reason? Why are genuine philosophers drawn to philosophy? Rousseau does not speak of anything like an eros for truth (though he does speak of "an ardent desire to know" in the likes of Plato, Thales, and Pythagoras [*SD* 211]).[37] Yet implicit in what I have been saying is the possibility, perhaps even the likelihood, that genuine philosophers are drawn to the life of thought because they divine that therein lies an expanded being—partly through the full development and exercise of cognitive capacities but also through the liberation of the self from narrow egoism (i.e., from the dread, anxiety and defensiveness that keep one from living wholeheartedly in the present), a liberation that occurs on gaining sight of certain truths—truths that one has perhaps come upon through reverie. Liberation from narrow egoism means overcoming the dread, anxiety, and defensiveness that so typically attend it. This transcendence or liberation is the second way in which philosophy might extend one's being. By using the rever-

---

36. I have argued for the naturalness of various "higher" capacities or, more precisely, capacities that were not present or active in the denizen of the pure state of nature, in *Rousseau, Nature, and the Problem of the Good Life*, Chapter 3. By the logic of that argument, philosophic activity might well qualify as natural, if it were to meet certain criteria. Sorenson, too, has argued for the naturalness, and hence the goodness—indeed, the greatest goodness—of philosophy in Rousseau's thought.

37. Rousseau also speaks of an "ardor to know" in *Emile* (167). In Emile's case this passion arises from curiosity connected to interest, when it doesn't arise from the desire to be esteemed learned. But I will try to show in Chapter 6 that it can develop into something more like the "ardent desire" to know for its own sake associated with Plato, Thales, and Pythagoras.

ies as a starting point for philosophic thinking—by reflecting on them—one can not only relive them but also come to understand them. Or rather, come to see, more clearly and securely, what the reveries have first revealed—that is, the possibility of transcending ordinary or civilized self-consciousness in favor of a more satisfying mode of self. Such seeing amounts to a new way of being—and *more* being. Thus what one would have first glimpsed or experienced in reverie comes to be a more general possibility: one who has achieved a degree of liberation through philosophy would presumably enjoy that liberation and its benefits in all of life's pursuits. To understand the expansiveness of the reveries, to recognize that the extension of being arises from a transcendence of ordinary or egoic consciousness, is arguably to have transcended civilized self-consciousness generally. This is the thinking behind various traditions of mindfulness practice, and it seems to me plausibly implicit in Rousseau. Consider, for example, that the Rousseau of the *Reveries* seems to enjoy deeply everything that he chooses to do—not only his reveries but all of his various projects, including, I would say, the project of writing the book.

The idea that the philosopher's insights, drawn perhaps from reflection on reverie, lead to a transcendence of narrow egoism and a consequently freer mode of self in all of life's pursuits is akin to Socrates' suggestion in the *Republic* that the philosopher, who is characterized by the development of and rule by a particular "part" of the soul, also gets more satisfaction than anyone else from the other parts of the soul (586e). Perhaps, then, the distance between Rousseau's understanding of philosophy and the classical view is not as great as it appears. Indeed, there is additional reason for thinking so. I suggested above that, on Rousseau's account, philosophy's attraction to genuine philosophers is the sensed promise of enlarged being. This sounds worlds apart from accounts that emphasize eros for truth. Eros, after all, suggests a forgetting of self and absorption in a beautiful beloved. Yet as I argued in Part One, the attraction of the beautiful beloved—the pull of eros—may well lie in the promise of enlarged being. Erotic life is remarkable for its combination of self-forgetting and intense self-concern. And at the peak of erotic attainment, the self rises or grows into a nothingness that proves to be an *enhancement* of being. Philosophy for both Rousseau and Plato is essentially connected to the pursuit of more being.

To be sure, there are significant differences between Rousseau's and Plato's respective accounts of the process whereby one achieves liberation from ordinary consciousness and attains more being. The classical account emphasizes the objects of contemplation, the *eidê*, which lie beyond the self and "beckon" to it. Rousseau, by contrast, seems to suggest that the phenomena that draw our contemplative interest do so not because they are beautiful or intrinsically worthy but because they somehow reflect our own deep feelings. As Christopher Kelly puts it, "Rousseau's peculiar form of confronting being is to see his own restless longing reflected in the universe itself. In contemplating the universe, he identifies with his own feelings. The universe becomes a metaphor for himself."[38] Even that which seems to draw us because of its beauty does so not because of intrinsic beauty but because it permits us to experience beauty, that is, because it provides the occasion whereby we express something that already exists within us. Beauty lies not in the object but in our experience, which is why one can experience as beautiful things that are so different from one another—not only the intricate structural harmonies of plants but also the wild disorder of a tempest.[39] Philosophic contemplation for Rousseau is thus an engagement with the self, a return to the self. This return is the third way in which philosophy can extend our being.

Now "engagement" or "return" may seem to contradict my claim of a moment ago that philosophy enlarges our being by bringing about a transcendence of ordinary, egoic consciousness. In truth, though, the engagement or return that occurs with philosophic contemplation is an engagement of or return to longings or intimations that are trans- or at any rate nonegoic, longings that are themselves expansive: one who contemplates the harmonious structures of plants or the awesome power and *dis*order of a raging storm loses himself in them. Or rather, identifies with them, as they fill his awareness

---

38. Kelly, *Rousseau as Author*, p. 181. Unlike Kelly, I regard this kind of contemplation as part of philosophy (both in Rousseau's view and in reality).

39. Ibid., p. 180. In *Rousseau, Nature, and the Problem of the Good Life* I suggested that the love of beauty is for Rousseau an expression of the love of order, which I found to be the basic principle of conscience (based on Rousseau's definition of conscience as "the love of order . . . made active"). On the basis of the current analysis that claim needs to be qualified—or rather, bracketed: what I offered as an explanation of the love of beauty applies only to those beauties that are orderly (e.g., the harmonious structures of plants or certain music). When we love orderly things we love them because they satisfy our love of order. But we also sometimes find and love as beautiful things that are disorderly. When this is the case, some other part of ourselves than the love of order has found expression. The love of order is intrinsic to our nature and the basic principle of conscience, as I argued; but it isn't the only principle within us or the only one that leads us to judge something beautiful. An interesting question is whether the love of order is deeper or more powerful than these other features of ourselves that account for our experience of beauty, if not in human beings generally, then in the healthier ones. If it is, then Rousseau's view would be even closer to the view of the fully developed soul expressed in the *Republic* and the *Symposium*.

and inspire his thoughts and thus in a crucial sense constitute his consciousness or simply his self. But then if that is the case, perhaps even in this Rousseau is not as far from Plato as we had thought. For one could say that for Plato, too, philosophic contemplation involves, and its goodness consists in, the engagement of and return to some "part(s)" of the self. Why do the *eidê* draw us and satisfy us on Plato's account? Is it not because the deepest and truest part of ourselves is akin to them? Isn't this the meaning of philosophy as recollection?[40] If so, then at least some of the apparent difference between Rousseau and Plato on this innermost meaning of philosophy is a difference of perspective. Plato attends primarily to the object of awareness, Rousseau to the underlying truth of the one attracted. (It might seem that Plato's perspective is objective and Rousseau's subjective, but that isn't so. Plato's perspective is more truly subjective than Rousseau's, in the sense that it starts where the lover himself starts: lovers may speak the language of eternity and seek infinite being, but the focus of their thoughts and awareness is the beloved. Rousseau's perspective, by contrast, is that of depth psychology.) How much difference remains between Rousseau and Plato depends on their respective assessments of the parts or passions or principles of the soul: What passions or principles do seek expression? What are their respective ranks and strengths? Is there a certain organization of the soul that stands above all others as the healthiest and even the most natural? It seems to me that, notwithstanding the differences in the ways that Rousseau and Plato characterize the soul and even the differences in the ways they characterize philosophy, each propounds as an exemplar of health and (thereby) naturalness one who engages in philosophic contemplation—one who loses himself in contemplation but who also takes it upon himself to give artful expression to his thought, whether orally (Socrates) or in writing (Plato, Rousseau), and even in practical politics (Plato regarding Sicily, Rousseau regarding Poland and Corsica). Rousseau shows us in himself a philosopher who, by returning to some deep part of himself, transcends ordinary, egoic consciousness. Plato shows us contemplation that, by removing the self from the realm of ordinary concerns, returns the self to its own core or innermost truth.[41]

40. Even if one doesn't take the notion of philosophy as recollection literally, it reminds us that Plato posits a correspondence between the mind of the knower and the being of the known.
41. At the risk of an anachronistically Nietzschean reading of Rousseau (having already taken the same risk vis-à-vis Plato), we might consider whether philosophy extends one's being in yet another way: by legislating. Rousseau does not speak of philosopher-kings or commanders in the manner of Plato or Nietzsche, but it is no accident that some of his readers, including major

Rousseau depicts himself in the *Reveries* as having largely overcome *amour-propre*. Or, more precisely (since *amour-propre* continues to afflict him during the quarter of the time that he is forced to engage society), Rousseau *as philosopher* is free of *amour-propre*. Have we then arrived at the decisive distinction between good and bad versions of the desire to extend our being? Shall we simply conclude that, in Rousseau's view, the desire for extended existence is good, because successful, when born of *amour de soi*, and bad, because unsuccessful (and destructive of others), when born of *amour-propre*? Not quite—which is good news, given the overwhelming and inevitable predominance of *amour-propre* in the souls of civilized men and women. It does seem to be true that the most perfect expansion of existence comes from a state of mind born of *amour de soi* and that the most ill-fated and tyrannical attempts at extended existence arise from *amour-propre*. More broadly, Rousseau undoubtedly sees a strong correlation between *amour de soi* and good desire for extended existence on the one hand and *amour-propre* and bad desire for extended existence on the other hand, a correlation that makes sense in light of the respective origins of these desires: recall that the expansiveness of *amour de soi* arises from overflowing strength while that of *amour-propre* arises from weakness and aversion. Recall, too, the passage from the *Dialogues* quoted above (*Dialogues* 112), in which "all the loving and gentle passions" are said to arise from the "positive sensitivity" born of *amour de soi*, and "all the hateful and cruel passions" are attributed to the "negative sensitivity" produced by *amour-propre*. Nevertheless the correlation is not perfect. *Amour de soi*, though "a good and absolute feeling," can lead people into conflict.[42] Conversely, *amour-propre*, though rivalrous and irascible, is educable and can be made to serve both civic well-being and one's own happiness (one's own enlarged existence). All the hateful and cruel passions come from *amour-propre*, but *amour-propre* does not produce *only* hateful and cruel passions: one need only recall my earlier list of phenomena that arise from the longing

---

Romantic poets, saw him as one who taught the practical potency of writing. Such a route to extended being may seem too much an expression of *amour-propre* to belong to Rousseau's conception of the genuine philosopher. But Rousseau's claim that "It belongs to *every* age . . . to want to create, imitate, produce, give signs of power and activity" suggests that wanting to exert oneself over or upon things outside oneself has a more natural and wholesome basis than the association with *amour-propre* might suggest (*Emile* 98; emphasis added).

42. At its peak, however, that is, as it appears in the highly cultivated Rousseau, *amour de soi* seeks extended being through the kind of inward or spiritual activity discussed above and so does *not* risk conflict with others.

for extended being and then notice the involvement of *amour-propre* in some of the best among them, including virtue, compassion, romantic love, and patriotism.[43]

Certainly the relative proportions of *amour de soi* and *amour-propre* in one's soul will deeply influence the way one pursues extended existence: the person governed by *amour de soi* lives within him- or herself and will therefore presumably seek extension differently from, more inwardly and/or directly than, the person governed by *amour-propre*, who, already "liv[ing] only in the opinion of others," will likely seek extension through rule or recognition (*SD* 179). To determine how Rousseau thinks one *should* or might *best* extend one's existence, however—to determine the criteria of good and bad versions of the desire to extend our being—one needs to look beyond the crisp distinction between the two kinds of self-love to Rousseau's many particular judgments of specific instances of the desire. Such a survey yields the following results.

We begin with two qualifications. First, with the possible exception of the sort of reverie discussed above, no particular activity aimed at extended existence can be called good in an unqualified sense: social or political considerations might well argue against this or that activity at this or that time. Even Rousseau's kind of reveries might prove inconsistent with social well-being if too many people were drawn to them. Second, how one might best pursue extended existence surely depends on who one is—on one's station in life as well as one's abilities and inclinations. That having been said, it is possible to discern in Rousseau's thought some general themes regarding good and bad, or better and worse, ways of pursuing extended existence. The most prominent of these, perhaps, involves the distinction between having and doing. By "having" I mean to refer (more or less) to the pursuit of what Aristotle calls "external goods";[44] by "doing," I mean activity undertaken for its own sake or for the sake of the experience itself. Being, Rousseau teaches, is attained or realized through doing: "To live is not to breathe, it is to act; it is to make use of all our organs, our senses, our faculties, of all the parts of ourselves which give us the sentiment of existence" (*Emile* 42). This dictum effectively suggests that, in general, the best way to pursue maximized existence is to develop and exercise our faculties to the maximum possible extent. This advice is hardly

---

43. I have addressed the role of *amour-propre* in these and other human goods in *Rousseau, Nature, and the Problem of the Good Life*, pp. 122–30.

44. *Nicomachean Ethics* 1098b, 1099a–b.

without peril. The development of the various faculties, both in the species at large and in innumerable individuals, has more often than not resulted in a *diminishment* of existence and happiness, for the growth of one's faculties has typically stimulated even greater growth of one's desires (*SD* 147; *Emile* 80–81). Yet consider wherein this peril consists. The danger is that the pursuit of more capacity for *doing* will lead (for reasons that are complex but familiar to Rousseau's readers) to an even greater pursuit of *having*. Having—or, rather, excessive desire for having—is the problem. It would be simplistic but not altogether wrong to ascribe to Rousseau the Marxian view that having is the enemy of being.

When is the desire to possess excessive? One could say that it becomes excessive simply when it outstrips our power to satisfy it, which is true enough. This, however, occurs when we lose control over it—when *it* gains control over us (*Emile* 445).[45] And *that* happens, I would argue, precisely when and to the extent that these things become the primary vessels through which we seek extended existence. Wanting external goods—wanting wealth, or prestige, or rule, or any other possession—is not inherently problematic, either for ourselves or for others. Making these things one's primary route to extended being, however—pursuing the soul's deepest longing through having rather than through doing—*is* problematic, for it invests these desires with more weight than they can bear. The consequences of this ill-fated investment include the incitement of ever new and unfulfillable desire; ever greater vulnerability, anxiety, and dependence as one's possessions expand (the rich fear losing their wealth, the powerful are dependent on those they rule [*Emile* 83–84]); and, in consequence of this vulnerability, anxiety, and need, an increasing inability to live in the here and now, which is a kind of vacating of the self, and an inability to act with a whole heart. Each of these consequences significantly diminishes existence.

A comparison of (a) the doomed enterprise of seeking extension through possessions with (b) the successful attempt at extension recounted in the *Reveries* suggests an even more fundamental distinction than the one between having and doing: In Rousseau's view, the attempt to extend our being is doomed when it consists in the attempt to aggrandize or empower the self as it already is, that is, to dress up or equip the current self, the social self so

---

45. "All passions are good when one remains their master; all are bad when one lets oneself be subjected to them."

famously depicted at the conclusion of the *Second Discourse*, with more things. By contrast, the attempt to extend one's being stands some chance of success when it involves certain kinds of inner transformation, whether the further cultivation of existing faculties or the development of new abilities, provided that such cultivation or development does not incite excessive new desires. It is in this proviso that the difficulty and the enormity of the challenge come to light. Typically, the cultivation of our faculties *does* incite excessive desire; indeed, it typically leads to all the unfortunate consequences outlined above (not only excessive desire but also vulnerability, anxiety, dependence, and a consequent emptying of the self). It does so because the self, governed predominantly by an unruly *amour-propre*, sees itself as an embattled entity whose very substance consists in its external goods or possessions.

I pointed out above that the pursuit of being through *doing* often fails because it degenerates into the pursuit of being through *having*. We see now that the source of this degeneration lies in the way one experiences and conceives the essence or ground of the self. The self whose desire for extension manifests itself in the futile pursuit of being through having is the self that believes itself or its being to be constituted by external goods; this is the fearful self, the self governed by disorderly *amour-propre*—in a word, the Hobbesian self; in another word, one that helps illuminate Rousseau's political program, the bourgeois self. Thus a healthful desire for extended being would seem to require either that *amour-propre* be transcended (à la Rousseau himself) or that it be educated in such a way that one looks to a larger community as the source of one's identity and ground of one's being. The latter course, which would lead the individual to seek extended existence in a context of devotion to others, is available through participation in a well-constructed polity. In such a polity law and education would reform *amour-propre* by generalizing or collectivizing it: much of its self-seeking character would manifest itself on behalf of the community, and the personal ambition of citizens would lead them to pursue honor through civic service. Such a polity, Rousseau believes, is difficult to the point of implausibility in the modern age. Nevertheless some degree of reform does seem to be possible and worth attempting, as witness his efforts in *Considerations on the Government of Poland* and *Constitutional Project for Corsica*.

A third course is available as well, a kind of middle course between the rare transcendence of *amour-propre* and its radical reform through politics. That course is the life of devoted domesticity of the sort for which Emile is educated and which, to varying degrees, we find elsewhere in Rousseau's work (e.g., the idyllic life at Clarens in *Julie* and the rustic life of the free peasantry referred to in various writings). This life would be characterized by a *moderation* of *amour-propre*, both quantitatively and qualitatively: *amour-propre* would become less "large" and powerful a force in the soul, and would be generalized or extended to the family as a whole, so that relations within the family would be free of fractious self-seeking. In the best of circumstances, wherein the individual feels him- or herself relatively well off, *amour-propre* would be "humane and gentle" (*Emile* 235). Like the political solution (though to a lesser extent), this course has the weight of modern sensibilities against it, in Rousseau's view. But it is still attainable for those so inclined, and it can be encouraged, or at least protected where it already exists, through political means.[46]

BETWEEN EROS AND WILL TO POWER

On the basis of the analysis I have presented, it is possible to offer a few reflections on Rousseau's thought from a broader, comparative perspective. Early in this chapter I suggested that, in positing the existence of a single, comprehensive good and a multiply expressed desire for that good, Rousseau is similar to Plato. We have now encountered an additional affinity between the two philosophers, for in holding that there are good and bad and better and worse ways of trying to extend our being, Rousseau effectively attests to something like a natural hierarchy of ends and desires. In neither thinker's case is the hierarchy easily known or simply expressed, yet each appeals to nature as the ground of judgment regarding the human good. Plato teaches nothing if not the difficulty of apprehending human nature, a difficulty which stems from the fact that, as part of the whole, the human being cannot be

---

46. My sketch of Rousseau's three solutions is just that. But one further point is too important to go unmentioned: each of three specified routes to a new self-understanding entails, at its core, a new stance toward death, that is, an overcoming of the desperate desire to resist the inevitable, this desire being the chief incitement if not the animating nerve of *amour-propre*. As Kelly has noted, Rousseau seems to present three different ways of dealing with the problem of death: an acceptance of necessity, à la the savage; a forgetting of death, such as we see in Rousseau's reveries; or an equanimous acceptance of death arising from so great a fulfillment of our being that we ask nothing more from life and are ready to die. Perhaps the list is even longer than this, for the citizen arguably "escapes" death by imagining that the nation will live forever.

fully known without knowledge of the whole. Nevertheless Plato points to nature as the appropriate standard for a sound philosophic anthropology.[47]

Rousseau's appeal to nature is even more complex. How can I suggest that Rousseau appeals to nature at all when he endorses several different and even opposing versions of the good life, one of which in fact is characterized by its being *denatured* (*Emile* 39–40)—and when, consequently, we can specify the features or requirements of the good life as Rousseau sees it (i.e., the good life as such, including all versions) only in the most formal language? (Those features or requirements, we recall, are psychic unity and absence of inner conflict, which together constitute what I have called the "negative" side of the project of the good life, along with the development and employment of the various faculties of body and soul, so long as these do not come at the cost of the first two features.) Substantively, the various versions of the good life entail the development and employment of different faculties in pursuit of different ends. These differences, however, are not the whole of the story, and they should not blind us to the common elements. There is in fact a substantive common ground between these lives, consisting, for example, in wholesome sociability.[48] Moreover, and more important for the present argument, the formal requirements themselves have definite and unalterable substantive implications. Even if one must speak largely in formal terms when speaking generically of Rousseau's multiple versions of the good life, the requirements of living well, of enlarging one's being, whether for the citizen or for the person trying to lead a more natural life, are definite and substantive, so that a Rousseauan therapist, as it were, taking account of one's aspirations and current condition, could in principle advise each of us in a nonarbitrary way regarding the best way to live. True, the therapist's advice would vary according to which type of good life one is attempting to approximate, and would in effect appeal to a few (though only a few) different hierarchies of ends; but these ends are subsidiary to and derive from universal and nonnego-

---

47. Plato's presumption of the existence and (in principle) the knowability of nature is implied by the entirety of his corpus, which would be rendered incoherent without the presumed *possibility* of apprehending nature. For instances in which nature is overtly appealed to in ways that speak both to its necessity and to its opacity, or at least to the misuses to which the concept is put, see *Republic* 369c–72b and 451c–66d and *Gorgias* 499e–500a. As we will see in Part Three, what I have just identified as common ground between Rousseau and Plato is also shared by Nietzsche.

48. See Marks, *Perfection and Disharmony*, pp. 54–88, for a very fine elaboration of this point.

tiable requirements of human well-being.⁴⁹ What should one call this if not a normatively prescriptive human nature, however indirect the prescribing?⁵⁰

Nevertheless Rousseau still seems to differ from Plato—from the "standard" reading of Plato, at any rate—in two decisive regards, one concerning (a) the character or content of the good and its "location" vis-à-vis the self, the other concerning (b) the consequent character or phenomenology of the desire for the good. With respect to both of these matters, Rousseau seems to occupy a position somewhere between Plato and Nietzsche, who as well suggests that human activity is driven by a single, comprehensive, multiply expressed desire or will (*Zarathustra* II, "On Self-Overcoming"; *BGE* 13 and 36) but who depicts both the character of the desired object and the character of the will itself in terms that he understands to be radically opposed to Plato's public teaching.

(a) Rousseau's "existence," attainable as it is through numerous means and signifying a feature of experience rather than something independent of the self, is more subjective a thing than what Plato's good is typically understood to mean. Few readers claim with confidence, let alone with credibility, to have understood the nature of the good as treated by Plato; but most would agree that, as the source of both being and intelligibility (*Republic* 504d–508b), Plato's good has a power and relation to human life, and thus a claim to human regard, that Rousseau's "existence" does not have. By the same token, the fact that existence can be enlarged only through a finite range of lives or ways of being, such that some of the most popular means through which it is sought only serve to diminish it, renders it in some ways *less* subjective, or more beholden to the stubborn demands of a prescriptive nature, than Nietzschean power is typically understood to be.

(b) Precisely because it is a feature of experience rather than an objective (even if mysterious) thing that lies beyond ourselves, enlarged existence cannot be thought to pull or attract us. In this, too, Rousseau seems decisively different from Plato. Whereas Plato seems to suggest that the good exerts an erotic attraction, a pull, Rousseau seems to portray the desire for extended

---

49. Compare to Aristotle's likening of the legislative art to that of the sports trainer at *Politics* 1288b10–20.

50. That nature's prescriptions are indirect does not prove that nature is incoherent or only a fiction, but only that philosophy is necessary. I have elsewhere offered an extended argument contending that each of Rousseau's versions of the good life is grounded in nature and that his conception of nature is not merely formal (*Rousseau, Nature, and the Problem of the Good Life*, pp. 37–65). For an even stronger claim, see Marks, *Perfection and Disharmony*.

being and the self-love of which it is an expression as an intrinsically directionless, nonteleological *push,* a kind of inchoate expansiveness or overflowing. Rousseau may well hold with Plato's suggestion that the good is that for which we do all that we do, but the subjective way in which he conceives the good necessarily results in—or perhaps follows from, but in any case "goes with"—a very different understanding of the phenomenology of the desire for the good. Platonic eros admits of innumerable forms, but common to all of them is the experience of attraction to something beautiful outside the self. Indeed, the experience of intense eros is marked by self-forgetting. The lover loses him- or herself in the beloved. Rousseau, by contrast, while he does acknowledge that the desire for extended existence manifests itself in various kinds of attraction and even employs the metaphor of magnetism (see the extended quote from the *Dialogues* above), nevertheless does not portray the desire for extended being as *essentially* a self-forgetting attraction to a beautiful object. The magnet metaphor, with its absence of beauty and with its essentially "horizontal" character—there is no sense of uplift or transcendence—is instructive in this regard. Here, too, as he distinguishes himself from Plato, Rousseau seems to land somewhere on the way to Nietzsche, whose account of will to power and of the origin of human action emphasizes the psychophysics of the actor, that is, his need to discharge energy, over and against the particular attraction or meaning of any given object (*GS* 360).[51]

Then again, if we put aside the passage from the *Dialogues*—a passage which, as an attempt to divide the whole of human motivation into a few categories, is necessarily highly abstract—and consider instead Rousseau's accounts of the *experience* of healthy souls, we remember that Rousseau does allow both for the attraction of beauty and for self-forgetting. Emile's love for Sophie comes immediately to mind: explicable in terms of the desire for extended being, it is even more easily explicable in terms of eros. Rousseau's asocial reveries, with their sweet self-forgetting, also come to mind, even if the self-forgetting wasn't the result of attraction to a beautiful beloved; and the self-forgetting *may* have been the result of absorption in the beauty of nature or the whole, in which case it seems not so very different from the purportedly erotic experience of philosophy as Plato presents it (*Republic*

---

51. Nietzsche's will to power is characterized precisely as an eruption rather than a drawing out or up. The eruption always takes some direction or other and can even be sublimated or spiritualized, but nature does not direct our inclinations toward any such end, let alone toward the Good.

484a–90b; *Symposium* 210a–12a). This is not to say that the distance between Rousseau and Plato disappears. There is still the sticking point of the status or "location" of the good, that is, whether it lies beyond the self or somehow within it. It does seem to suggest, though, that the distance is smaller than has so far seemed to be the case.

The distance is perhaps even smaller yet: for if Rousseau emerges from close scrutiny as somewhat more of a Platonist than he had appeared, Plato arguably closes some of the distance from the other side. As we saw in Part One and as I noted in the discussion of the *Reveries* above, a reading of the phenomenology of eros as depicted by Plato, that is, an investigation of what, on Plato's treatment, eros actually seeks, reveals something not so different from Rousseau's desire for extended being. For that matter, the same may well be true of Nietzsche and will to power if one considers that, despite ostensibly eschewing Nature or any other source of value or valuation beyond the human will, he somehow lands at the side of Plato—and Rousseau—both in his ranking of the philosophic life and, at least somewhat, in his explanation of the goodness of that best of lives. The nature of a desire is most clearly revealed in that which would most satisfy it. If what would most deeply satisfy eros (Plato), the desire to extend our being (Rousseau), and will to power (Nietzsche) is the activity of the philosopher, then, however differently one might understand that activity, an important similarity would seem to be indicated.[52]

CONCLUSION: ROUSSEAUAN DESIRE AND ROUSSEAUAN RHETORIC

Before ending this investigation let us take note of one other general distinction between Rousseau's "good" and "bad" ways of pursuing extended existence—a distinction so sharp it might seem to challenge my premise that for Rousseau there *is* such a thing as a good (meaning healthful and pro-social) desire for extended existence. I have suggested throughout this chapter that Rousseau imputes "the desire to extend our being" to all sufficiently strong or energetic human beings, not only to those who pursue property or power or reputation but also to those (such as himself) who have detached themselves from these passions. There can be no question about the former. In

---

52. This theme will be pursued more fully in Chapter 10.

his heart of hearts, as we have seen, the pursuer of property or power or reputation—the "civilized man"—wants to be "the sole master of the universe"; he resents "everything that by being something prevents [him] from being everything" (*SD* 195; *Dialogues* 112). Yet we see no such avidity and agitation in Rousseau. He never, to my knowledge, voices a felt need to be more than he is; and neither, for that matter, does Emile. On the contrary, Rousseau demonstrates contentment and equanimity (at least during the three-quarters of the time that he is not overtaken by *amour-propre*), and of himself and Emile he states, "No one knows better than we do how to keep in our place, and no one has less desire to leave it" (*Emile* 467). Might it not be the case that Rousseau's extraordinary expansion of his being occurs without being preceded by—even *because* it is not preceded by—a desire for expansion? And might that be another reason for the overwhelmingly negative thrust of his rhetoric on the subject of wanting to be more than we are?

The answer to both questions, it seems to me, is no, albeit a qualified no. That Rousseau chooses to cultivate certain experiences, that he devotes himself to botany and reverie, is sufficient to establish that he desires the content of those experiences, and there can be no denying that that content consists, in the ways in which we have seen, in an expansion of being. That he undertakes this activity without avid desire or agitation does not prove that no desire is operative. What it suggests, simply, is that the desire for an experience that is gotten by doing something that is within one's power has a different character, a calmer and more assured character, than the desire to acquire something external to the self. Nevertheless the questions have a real basis, and they point to an important truth. For while it may be true that, like everyone else, Rousseau is moved exclusively by passion or desire, his success is as much a result of what he does *not* desire as of what he does desire. Declining to pursue extended being through the acquisition of external goods is perhaps *the* crucial step in the progress toward expanding one's being, more crucial even than the positive step of conceiving one's identity in more healthful terms. This is so not because the positive step is less important but because it may well follow the negative step as a natural consequence. If self-love and human being really are by nature expansive, then closing down the external route may well force the self's expansive energies inward (using that term loosely, to refer to the cultivation and exercise of one's faculties for their own sake), where they could succeed in enlarging one's being. This, arguably, is the shared source of both Rousseau's and Emile's happiness.

Thus the first question points to a truth: it would be incorrect to say that Rousseau's extraordinary expansion occurs because it is not preceded by a desire for expansion (it *is* preceded by a desire for expansion), but it is fair to say that the expansion occurs because it is not preceded by a certain *kind*, the most common kind, of desire for expansion. And (to take up the matter of the second question) that *would* be reason for the harsh rhetoric Rousseau aims against the desire to be more than we are. Rousseau's teaching about the good is not always good to hear. Most of us, "always outside of [ourselves]" and believing our being to consist in external goods, would probably respond to a promise of extended being only by intensifying our ill-directed pursuits. More needful than the truth about being—and the proper preparation for the safe use of that truth—would be a program of moral reform that reshapes people's self-understanding and aspirations. Such a program is precisely the legislative agenda of Rousseau's political philosophy.

6

EMILE, OR ON PHILOSOPHY?

> Let us call your future beloved Sophie. The name Sophie augurs well.
>
> —*Emile* 329

Rousseau's treatments of the expansiveness of being are both brief and prosaic. To speak evocatively of extended being would likely prod those who have not been properly educated or otherwise prepared toward pursuits that would *diminish* being rather than enhance it. Such is the sad paradox of the human condition, as we have already seen. And the crown of that paradox is seen in Rousseau's stance toward philosophy. Most who have called themselves or been known as philosophers have been creatures of vanity. Most who have studied philosophy have been corrupted by it—not just as social beings but in the depths of their souls—though it would be more precise to say that they have had their corruption deepened, since the ill effects of philosophy consist largely in deepening already-present unwholesome dispositions that drew them to philosophy in the first place (vanity, petty egoism, dependence on the good opinion of not very good people). Yet in its genuine form, as we might say—or in the rare cases of "celestial intelligences" or "friends of the truth," as Rousseau says[1]—philosophy yields an expansion of being that may well outstrip that which is yielded by any other sustained activity or way of life. This expansion, moreover, can be good not only for oneself but for other people as well, through the propagation of new teachings on fundamental matters. But how can this better case be realized? How can individuals be led toward genuine philosophy? And is it only the gifted few, or, in principle at least, are ordinary human beings capable of the ascent to philosophy? These are educational questions, though as questions concerning the extraordinary

---

1. *Last Reply* 66; *Emile* 110, 260; etc. Also see Kelly, *Rousseau as Author,* pp. 173–74.

capabilities of extraordinary human beings they would not seem to have any place in Rousseau's educational novel—which, masterful though it may be, limits itself to the already massive task of explicating human nature and human possibility as revealed by an ordinary man (*Emile* 52, 245, 393).

There is nothing paltry about *Emile*'s depiction of the moral and spiritual heights attainable by a man of ordinary gifts. Through a natural education, Rousseau brings the book's eponymous hero to a clarity of vision, a purity of sentiment, and a wholeness of heart that we cannot but greatly admire. Doubtless this revelation of the extraordinary potential of ordinary men is among Rousseau's reasons for calling *Emile* "his greatest and best book" (*Dialogues* 23). Still, for all his attainments, Emile does not abide on the *very* highest peaks, the peaks constituted by the most expansive and hence most enviable experience of existence. The most exalted life to be found in Rousseau's corpus is not Emile's but rather his own, that is, the life of a philosopher, as depicted in the late autobiographical writings. It is not Emile but the solitary walker of the *Reveries* whose experience of life is godlike (68–69) and who thus occupies the peak of human attainment. His compelling portrait of Emile and his democratic political theory notwithstanding, Rousseau takes his place alongside Plato and others who, by proffering the philosopher as the highest human type, propound an aristocratic view of the life of the mind and therewith of human possibilities as such.[2] That he treats this peak in works other than *Emile* does not count against the greatness of that work. Even in limiting itself to the realm of ordinary possibility, *Emile* still addresses the greatest questions as they pertain to the greatest part of humankind. Indeed, it would be unjust to expect Rousseau to follow Plato's *Republic* and successfully outline both philosophic and nonphilosophic education in *Emile*. The *Republic*, after all, depicts a discussion that moves freely from one of the city's classes and one set of human possibilities to another, whereas *Emile*, a bildungsroman, depicts the education of only one person.

Or perhaps such an expectation would not be unjust after all; in any case it would not be unrealistic. For it turns out that *this is exactly what Rousseau*

---

2. Nonphilosophers are certainly capable of expansive peak experience through the ecstasies of romantic love. This is one of the memorable teachings of book 5 of *Emile*. But the duration of this experience is necessarily limited, the charming delirium of romance giving way (in the best case) to the enviable but less than ecstatic sweetness of domestic life. Ordinary men are also capable of achieving the estimable satisfaction of citizenship—or would be, were citizenship possible in the Christian or post-Christian modern world.

has done. What I contend is that *Emile* speaks at one and the same time to both nonphilosophic and philosophic education. In this it follows the *Republic.* More specifically, *Emile*'s book 5 follows book 5 of the *Republic*, its three primary teachings, like Socrates' "three waves" of paradox, indicating by analogy three key attributes of the philosophic soul. And in doing so it brings to light two important features of philosophy and extended being that we have not yet seen.

The first feature concerns accessibility. The veiled inclusion in *Emile* of a teaching on philosophy qualifies what I described above as Rousseau's aristocratic view of human possibilities, for it turns out that a kind of philosophic life is possible for an ordinary man, even if only in principle, and that Rousseau's effort to discourage the popularization of philosophy is rooted more in prudential concerns than in the basic principles of his philosophic anthropology. Emile does not have the capacity to become a great philosopher. Nor could anyone become a great philosopher by virtue of the education he receives: the great ones are always and necessarily self-educated (*FD* 62–63, *Emile* 52). Neither does Emile appear likely to devote his life to philosophy in the comprehensive manner of a Socrates or even a Rousseau. Nevertheless he emerges from his tutelage with qualities that, in combination, constitute a philosophic character. We will take up these qualities below. For now it suffices simply to state them: the mature Emile evinces (1) the ability to think clearly, (2) an extraordinary freedom from prejudice and delusion, (3) a love of truth, and (4) an ardent desire for knowledge and understanding for their own sake. These qualities don't guarantee greatness, but they do constitute the desire and ability to see the truth about great things. Ordinary human beings can have some share in the most exalted—the largest—of lives.

The second feature of philosophy and extended being that comes to light with the discovery of *Emile*'s teaching on philosophic education is less sociological than the first and concerns the natures of the things themselves. In light of the previous chapter's analysis, we will not be surprised to find that *Emile*'s philosophic education, like much of the rest of his education, appeals to and shapes the desire for extended being. What may surprise us, though, is that *Emile*'s philosophic education also appeals to and shapes *eros*, understanding by that term an ardent desire for comprehensive satisfaction, a desire whose most frequent and basic expression is sexual love and all of whose objects are regarded by the lover as beautiful, indeed are loved *for* their perceived beauty. Allan Bloom has brilliantly shown how Emile's education in taste and morals and even politics is an essentially erotic education.³ In the course of what follows I will show that eros is central to *Emile*'s philosophic education as well. Eros is both the source of the philosophic education (i.e., the student's motive force) and its "matter" (i.e., philosophic education consists in and aims at the refinement or sublimation of eros). This discovery leads to a deeper one: if *Emile*'s philosophic education can in fact be interpreted as an erotic education, we will have found cause to regard philosophic eros as an expression of the desire for extended being and to regard eros as such as, if not quite synonymous with the desire for extended being, then arguably its primary expression.

Can one really learn about the desire for extended being, not only as it manifests itself in an ordinary person, but also even as it appears in the most extraordinary people, from a book that tells the story of an ordinary man? Yes, and not merely because the possibilities open to an ordinary man are, by historic standards, quite extraordinary. *Emile* is more than the story of its hero. Like the *Republic*, it speaks to the whole range of human being and human possibility, including the highest. Throughout the narrative we encounter a number of set-piece treatments of various important topics—happiness, desire, strength versus weakness, and so on—sometimes as spoken by the tutor to Emile, sometimes by Rousseau to us. And "underlying" the narrative in book 5 is a teaching on philosophy, just as a teaching on philosophy underlies the main narrative (the "three waves of paradox") in book 5 of the *Republic*.

EMILE AND THE REPUBLIC

Emile's connection to the *Republic* is apparent from the start. Early in book 1 Rousseau cites the *Republic* as *the* book on public education (in the process correcting those who take it to be a book about politics) and seems to offer his own work as a counterpart that treats "domestic education or the education of nature" rather than public education—that is, the education of a man rather than a citizen (40–41). In fact, though, *Emile* might better be seen less as a counterpart than as a rival or even a companion, for immediately after identifying its topic as domestic or natural education, Rousseau speaks of

---

3. This is a major theme of Bloom's extensive commentary on books 4 and 5 of *Emile* in Chapter 1 of *Love and Friendship*.

achieving "the *double* object we set for ourselves (emphasis added)," by which he means educating a man to be both natural and social–which is to say that Emile's natural education is also, though admittedly less so than Plato's, a public education. And even before book 1, in the Preface, the *Republic* is called to mind, though not by name. "In every sort of project there are two things to consider: first, the absolute goodness of the project; in the second place, the facility of execution (34)." These are the same two criteria established by Socrates in connection with the three waves in book 5 of the *Republic* (450c–d) and systematically employed by him and his interlocutors throughout their consideration of those radical proposals.

Or, rather, they are *nearly* the same. Where Rousseau speaks of facility of execution, Socrates had asked whether "the things said are *possible*"; and where Rousseau speaks of absolute goodness, Socrates had asked whether they "would be what is *best*" (emphases added). The similarity of the two sets of standards surely links the respective projects of the two works, or at least it links *Emile* with the *kallipolis* of the *Republic*'s middle books and especially book 5. But Rousseau's slight modification of the Socratic standards is as important as the similarity. In each case, Rousseau's revision shows his project to be less utopian than Plato's. "Facility of execution" presupposes possibility; and "absolute goodness" constitutes a more expansive and therefore a less difficult standard to meet than whether a thing is best (since a thing can be good without being best). Indeed, Rousseau's relative realism is seen in the extraordinary detail in which he outlines Emile's education. Whereas Aristotle could charge the Platonic Socrates with failing to consider what his proposals would produce in actuality,[4] Rousseau undertakes to do just that: "I have hence chosen to give myself an imaginary pupil.... This method appears to me useful to prevent an author who distrusts himself from getting lost in visions; for when he deviates from ordinary practice, he has only to make a test of his own practice on his pupil" (50–51). This is not to say that Rousseau intended this project to be adopted in practice: in the *Lettres écrites de la montagne* Rousseau characterizes *Emile* as "a new system of education the plan of which I present for the study of the wise and not a method for fathers and mothers" (*OC* III, 783). But it does suggest that Rousseau is in earnest when he claims that his project is in fact good and possible, if only in principle, and that it is so because it accords with nature—which is something that

---

4. *Politics* 1264a5–7.

we cannot say with any confidence of Plato and the *Republic*'s city in speech.[5] In the person of Emile, Rousseau means to show us the extraordinary possibility open to an ordinary mind.[6]

By invoking Socrates' standards in his own Preface, Rousseau may be signaling the special significance for *Emile* of the three proposals for whose sake the standards were introduced. But no such signal is necessary to establish this significance: Book 5 of *Emile* treats the same three themes, in the same order, as book 5 of the *Republic,* and for this reason alone can be seen as a response to it. The response appears at first to be wholly negative. Whereas Plato has Socrates argue for equal treatment and education of the sexes, Rousseau strenuously insists on differences. Whereas Socrates seems to advocate abolition of the family in favor of communism of women and children, Rousseau stresses the importance of romantic love and family to a good life. Whereas Socrates argues that the only solution to human ills would be rule by philosopher-kings, Rousseau suggests that a king who is wise would abdicate his throne (467). And rather than a philosopher-king, it is a private woman of ordinary gifts who is to govern Emile (even as he commands her) and who stands as the greatest guarantor of his happiness. In each case Rousseau's opposition to Plato involves the governance and employment of eros.

Yet despite initial appearances, Rousseau's response to Plato's three waves of paradox is not simply negative—and in several ways it is not at all negative. In fact, even as it opposes the *Republic*'s teaching on one level, book 5 of *Emile* is in important ways consistent with and actually a development of the Platonic argument. Amid—or beneath—opposition one finds agreement. And the underlying agreement, like the opposition, concerns eros. The disagreements arise chiefly from the divergent goals of the two works, that is, from the fact that Plato concerns himself with the pursuit of justice in a city whereas Rousseau concerns himself with the domestic grounds of a largely

---

5. This is no place to get into the debate over Plato's earnestness regarding the *kallipolis.* Suffice it to say that he has Socrates himself raise serious doubts as to the possibility and goodness of the city, and that these doubts are not all answered very convincingly.

6. Interestingly, after moderating Socrates' standards in the ways indicated above, Rousseau returns to the Socratic standard at the conclusion of his Preface. Yet he does so in a way that does not undercut the plausibility of his program. Just the opposite, in fact: "It is enough for me that wherever men are born, what I propose can be done with them; and that, having done with them what I propose, what is best both for themselves and for others will have been done" (35). By speaking of possibility rather than facility of execution he implicitly allows for the extreme difficulty of executing his project. By claiming that it is "best" he underscores its goodness and thus puts it in direct competition with the *Republic.*

apolitical good life. My supposition, though, is that both works—indeed, both books 5—are multilayered and address *other* themes than these, and that while they do indeed differ greatly on the surface, they also turn out to be in surprising accord with each other at a deeper level. To be specific, the *Republic* is about justice in the city, but it is also about justice in the soul, or philosophy. *Emile* is about the education of "a savage made to inhabit cities" (205), but it is also about (or so I will argue) philosophic education, or philosophy. And in its treatment of philosophy, the teaching of book 5 of *Emile* is remarkably akin to that of book 5 of the *Republic*.[7]

THE THREE WAVES

It would be nice to know how Rousseau read Plato—whether, for example, he shared Montaigne's view (with which he must certainly have been familiar) that Plato propounded doctrines and proposals in which he did not believe.[8] The difficulty of knowing how Rousseau read Plato is increased by Rousseau's own art of writing: if he did share Montaigne's skepticism about Plato, prudence might well have kept him from saying so.[9] But we do at least know that

---

7. The correspondence between the respective books 5 was originally observed by Masters, *The Political Philosophy of Rousseau*, amid a larger and worthwhile discussion of "The *Emile* as Rousseau's Answer to Plato's *Republic*." See pp. 98–105, esp. 99–100. Masters, however, does not identify anything like the sympathy I see between the two books 5. One commentator who has argued for a sympathetic relation between the two books 5 is Ellis in *Rousseau's Socratic Aemilian Myths*. Ellis interprets not only book 5 but the whole of *Emile* as a response to the *Republic* and as a response to other ancient sources as well, especially the Bible; she even sees the "architecture" of *Emile* as a representation of an ancient Greek temple. Ellis reads book 5 as a dual-level story whose hidden level concerns philosophy à la the *Republic*, as I do, though the particulars of her interpretation are quite different from mine. In her more allegorical reading, Sophie stands for her namesake (as well as for the beautiful and the good) and Emile for humanity or human nature.

8. Montaigne, an avowed skeptic who believed that in skepticism lay the grounds of a more humane politics, viewed Plato as a skeptic who hid his skepticism behind what was intended as a salutary dogmatism. Montaigne writes of Plato that "where he writes on his own, he makes no certain prescriptions. When he plays the lawyer, he borrows a domineering and assertive style, and yet mixes in boldly the most fantastic of his inventions, which are as useful for persuading the common herd as they are ridiculous for persuading himself; knowing how apt we are to accept any impressions, and most of all the wildest and most monstrous." See *The Complete Essays of Montaigne*, pp. 879. Also see pages 370–80, which are part of his "Apology for Raymond Sebond." Rousseau's frequent references to the *Essays* show that he knew the book well.

9. For illuminating treatments of Rousseau's respect for salutary belief and consequent opposition to the espousal of skepticism, see Kelly, *Rousseau as Author*; and Orwin, "Rousseau's Socratism."

Rousseau read Plato unconventionally, as seen in his correction, cited above, of those who read the *Republic* as a political work (*Emile* 40). And we certainly know that he read Plato carefully; a close reading of almost any of Rousseau's major works demonstrates that.[10] So whatever he thought of Plato's seriousness regarding equal treatment and education of the sexes (the first wave), communism of women and children (the second wave), and rule by philosophers (the third wave) in a real city, he also knew that the city in speech was created as a sort of soul writ large and that what is said about the city is supposed to be true in some sense of the soul—indeed, that at least some of what is said of the city may be true *only* of the soul.[11] And it is here, where what is said of the city is applied to the soul, that we discover significant affinities between *Emile*'s book 5 and that of the *Republic*.

The facility with which we can extract a teaching regarding the soul varies among Plato's three waves, but there can be little doubt that each of the waves carries such a teaching: the city in speech, after all, is said in the end to be a pattern for the soul (592b), and so what is ostensibly said to be necessary for the noble and fair city has some bearing on what is necessary for the noble and fair soul. More specifically, each wave says something about the constitution and orientation of what emerges from the dialogue as the *most* noble and fair of souls, that is, the philosopher's soul. And in each case the teaching speaks to the philosopher's eros, either directly (the second wave) or indirectly (the first and third).

The analogue of the first wave in the soul is a kind of spiritual bisexuality: the equal treatment and education of the sexes, applied by analogy to the soul, comes to mean equal development and nurture of what are considered masculine and feminine elements or characteristics or capacities.[12] Plato doesn't catalogue masculine and feminine traits as Rousseau does. But the Greek world had definite views on the matter, from whose standpoint Plato's hero Socrates most certainly does exemplify a peculiar hybrid of masculine

---

10. Those who desire more concrete evidence of Rousseau's rigor in reading Plato may consult Siverthorne, "Rousseau's Plato." And of course one may consult any of a number of scholarly analyses of Plato's influence on Rousseau; for a list of some of the more important of these, see Melzer, *The Natural Goodness of Man*, p. 24.

11. The city–soul analogy is launched at 368d–369b, where the (first) city is created expressly for the purpose of considering the relative merits of justice and injustice in and for the soul. Among the things postulated of the (noble and fair) city that may be true only of the (noble and fair) soul is the very possibility of its existence (592b).

12. See Bloom, "Interpretive Essay," pp. 383–84; Hyland, "Plato's Three Waves and the Question of Utopia"; and Craig, *The War Lover*, pp. 235–36.

and feminine characteristics. And not only exemplify, but *propound*. Socrates undermines his interlocutors' understanding of and attachment to manliness and teaches instead a *human* excellence that includes qualities associated with both sexes.[13] The philosopher's "bisexuality" manifests itself not only in his observable behavior—not only in his preference for private talk over political action—but also, presumably, in his soul and even his eros. What this might mean is suggested by Socrates' teaching in the *Symposium*, according to which eros involves not only the manly pursuit of the beloved but also the archetypically female phenomena of pregnancy, softening, and giving birth. To be sure, this teaching is said to pertain to all eros, not just the philosopher's. But the philosopher is uniquely aware of this side of eros and thus is unique in giving proper expression to it.

The second wave would seem to express the necessity of generalizing and elevating one's eros. Although there is no obvious analogue in the soul to the city's communism of women and children, the need to overcome a narrow and exclusive love of one's own and attach one's eros to something more elevated and nonexclusive than a particular corporeal being is decisive among the requirements for the philosophic soul as it is presented in the *Republic*.

The third wave, finally, is the easiest to apply: for the rule of philosophers over the city we need only read rule by the philosophic part over the rest of the soul. This wave, too, has erotic implications, since (1) the philosophic part of the soul, like the other parts, turns out to be characterized essentially by what it *loves* (580d), and since (2) rule by the philosophic part, in ensuring that the other parts will receive maximum satisfaction, is tending to the erotes of those parts as well. Perhaps, too, (3) rule is erotically satisfying to the philosophic part in the ways explored in Part One of the current study. This summary doesn't begin to do justice to the *Republic*'s three waves, but it will suffice for the purpose of permitting insight into *Emile*, which embraces all three of these teachings and indicates as much in appropriately placed passages.

Before turning to *Emile*'s specific responses, though, let's take note of a suggestive feature that appears just before book 5 and that may be read as a preparation for its erotic-philosophic education—a feature that is itself an affirmative response to the *Republic*'s teaching on eros and philosophy. Late

---

13. In *Gender and Rhetoric in Plato's Political Thought*, Michael S. Kochin lays out the leading Greek conceptions of manliness (one "civic," the other "heroic") and shows how Socrates argues against both of them for failing to deliver the fulfillment they seem to promise.

in book 4, immediately prior to the speech of disclosure that launches Emile's search for his beloved, Rousseau sets Emile to the one occupation that could distract him from thoughts about love and sex: hunting (320–21). Hunting is presented as ostensibly an- or even anti-erotic. One wonders, though, whether it is introduced not just to distract Emile but also to prepare him for the dual erotic pursuits of book 5, that is, for the hunt—or pursuit (the French is *la chasse*)—of both Sophie and Sophia. Regarding the latter, it is instructive to remember that the *Republic*, in addition to likening philosophy to a beautiful beloved (496b *et passim*), also likens the philosophic quest to the hunt (432b *et passim*), a comparison that Rousseau knew and echoed elsewhere (*SD* 98).

The First Wave

Rousseau certainly identifies various mental capacities as belonging more to one sex than to the other (357–87). The question then arises: Does he believe that the full development of one's humanity depends on developing equally elements associated with both sexes? One is tempted to say no, for he counts on the uneven development within man and woman as the very ground of their spiritual complementarity: men and women in whom the psychic strengths of each sex were fully developed would have less need for one another and hence a weaker bond. One might say that for Rousseau, full humanity is achievable not by the individual (or at least not by the ordinary individual) but rather by the "moral person" that is created by the union of separate and incomplete individuals (377). In fact, though, Rousseau does suggest that the full development of one's humanity requires the cultivation of both male and female characteristics. This becomes clear when we consider just what, or who, constitutes full humanity for Rousseau.

As suggested above, the person who most represents full humanity in Rousseau's works is Rousseau himself, at least as described in his final autobiographical writings, and especially the *Reveries of the Solitary Walker*. There Rousseau presents himself as one who exercises the highest or most distinctively human capacities largely unimpeded by the intellectually and psychologically crippling *amour-propre* that taints almost everyone and everything human. And he also presents himself there, as in all his autobiographical writings, as spiritually bisexual, as one who has the strengths of both sexes—as a *person* more than just a man. To explore the full meaning of Rousseau's bisexuality would take us too far afield from *Emile;* and in any case the issue has been well treated elsewhere.[14] But the point of greatest relevance to the present inquiry is that his bisexuality is essential to his activity as a philosopher.[15] If Rousseau seems to assign philosophy to the male brain, so to speak, that is hardly a compliment to men: more often than not, "philosophy" refers to abstruse and arid speculation or else simple sophistry. Indeed, to my knowledge "philosophy" for Rousseau *never* signifies something that is simply praiseworthy unless it is preceded by a modifier such as "true." And even then it refers to moral integrity and awareness of the limits of human possibility, not to any kind of theoretical activity. See, in particular, the concluding paragraph of the *First Discourse,* where "true philosophy" refers to "listen[-ing] to the voice of one's conscience in the silence of the passions" (64).[16] This is not what most of us, or what Plato, means by philosophy. And it is not what I mean when I refer to philosophy in this study. When I speak of "philosophy" in these pages I mean to refer to high-level theoretical inquiry conducted with passion and marked by intellectual integrity. This is consistent with ordinary common usage, and no adequate substitute comes to mind. Rousseau's idiosyncratic usage seems a part of his larger campaign to promote moral integrity and to safeguard it against what he sees as the inevitably demoralizing effects of popularized philosophy. (We will explore this theme below, at which time we will also look into the relation—the necessary relation, as Rousseau sees it—between what he means by "true philosophy" and sound theoretical activity.) Those who are considered by common consent to be great philosophers are generally identified by Rousseau not as philosophers but as "sublime geniuses" (*Preface* 107) or "celestial intellects" (*Last Reply* 66) or "preceptors of the human race" (*FD* 63)—and even these terms are used

---

14. Schwartz, *The Sexual Politics of Jean-Jacques Rousseau,* pp. 7, 107–8, and 171–72.

15. As we have seen, Rousseau's self-depiction in his final autobiographical writings (the *Reveries, Dialogues,* and the latter part of the *Confessions*) is unlike any traditional notion of the philosopher. As Kelly puts it, "he paints a picture of himself as a dreamer rather than a thinker." *Rousseau's Exemplary Life,* p. 73. But he is a dreamer who also thinks. The *Reveries,* for example, contain sophisticated and subtle discourses, such as the Fourth Walk's examination of truth and lying. And even when Rousseau paints himself as a dreamer, it is only the subject of the picture who dreams; Rousseau *as painter* manifestly thinks.

16. Rousseau's distinction between (the disparagingly used) "philosophy" and "philosopher" on the one hand and "true philosophy" or "true philosopher" on the other is maintained throughout all his major works, including *Emile.* (See, for example, *Emile* 243: "Philosophy is the station with the most prejudices.") The distinction is most emphatically pronounced in the *First Discourse* and pages 104–7 of the *Preface to Narcissus.* As admirable as this might be, it is not what we, or what Plato, normally mean by "philosophy."

only so long as he is not speaking of their deleterious moral or political influence.

So when Rousseau says that "men will philosophize about the human heart better than she ["woman"] does" (387), we know better than to take that as a statement of the sufficiency of masculine mental characteristics for an adequate philosophic understanding of things. And indeed, the lines that immediately follow, including the remainder of the sentence of which the line just quoted is only a part, assert quite clearly that understanding the human heart—that the practice of what one might call *Rousseauan* philosophy—requires a marriage of what Rousseau considers masculine and feminine strengths. The passage, which best expresses Rousseau's view of the philosophic mind as a bisexual mind, appears in the first of book 5's three sections, the section that corresponds structurally to the *Republic*'s presentation of the first wave:

> Men will philosophize about the human heart better than she does; but she will read in men's hearts better than they do. It is for women to discover experimental morality, so to speak, and for us to reduce it to a system. Woman has more wit, man more genius; woman observes, and man reasons. *From this conjunction results the clearest insight and the most complete science regarding itself that the human mind can acquire—in a word, the surest knowledge of oneself and others available to our species.* And this is how art can constantly tend to the perfection of the instrument given by nature. (emphasis added)

It is not lost on the attentive reader that *Emile* itself means to provide just this "clearest insight and . . . most complete science regarding . . . the human mind."[17] Which is to say that its author relies on the combined mental strengths of both men and women.[18]

But enough about the author; what about the hero?[19] Does Emile himself,

---

17. Schwartz makes the same point; see *The Sexual Politics of Jean-Jacques Rousseau*, p. 172.
18. Another "feminine characteristic" needed by the philosopher, or at least by a philosopher (such as Rousseau) who seeks to change beliefs and attitudes, is the ability to tell the truth (but not only the truth) in a way that is pleasing. For Rousseau's association of this characteristic with women, see *Emile* 376.
19. Not that the author is of secondary importance. I have been arguing that Emile is educated to a kind of philosophic life. Those who remain skeptical of this claim might still agree that in *Emile* Rousseau speaks to philosophy and philosophic education.

who represents the fullest humanity attainable by a man of ordinary gifts, attain anything like the bisexuality of his creator and governor? It seems probable that to a degree, at least, he does. Undoubtedly the "conjunction" of which Rousseau speaks consists in the first instance is the conjunction, the marriage, of Sophie and Emile, and does not refer to anything internal to Emile; and the mention of "art" in the closing line refers to the social artifice of marriage. But it is also possible that the art referred to is the art of pedagogy, and it seems probable that something of this conjunction does take place within Emile—as indeed it must, if and to the extent that he ever successfully philosophizes.

Does Emile philosophize? Certainly he is no Rousseau. His "ordinary mind" (245) presumably precludes his joining the ranks of great philosophers. But he does receive something like a philosophic education. His final journey with his governor, which might seem to be only a political education, begins with a trip "back to the state of nature" in order to examine such questions as whether men are born enslaved or free and whether they are naturally social (459); and it involves an effort "to know men in general" (451) and the discovery (discovery, not mere receipt) of the principles of political right. (Nor should we forget his earlier study of history, which Rousseau likens to "a course in practical philosophy" [242].) These principles can be discovered only by *philosophic* inquiry.[20] That Emile's explorations are indeed philosophic is perhaps obscured by the fact that we recognize this section as a rehearsal of the *Social Contract*, a book that, though available to us, is not available to Emile—which is to say that where we need only to receive passively, Emile needs to explore actively. The philosophic nature of his explorations is also indicated by the title of this section of the book ("Des Voyages") and by Rousseau's two comparisons of his and Emile's traveling to that of Plato and Pythagoras (412 and 454; Thales is also included in the first reference). Also note that Emile's journeying and his active pursuit of the truth (he has a guide but no preceptor) are consistent with the principles of Platonic philosophic education (*Republic* 518d, "Seventh Letter" 341b–d).

Indeed, the entirety of Emile's education preserves or inculcates such extraordinary qualities as to suggest that he will be, if not a great philosopher, then a true one—even according to the conventional sense of that term (i.e., one who engages in high-level theoretical activity). Four of these qualities

---

20. See Sorenson, "Natural Inequality and Rousseau's Political Philosophy," pp. 780–81.

seem to me to form the core of a philosophic mind. First, his education teaches him how to think—how to reason on his own from facts that he himself has observed. Second, it preserves him from distorting prejudice so that his observation and reasoning will be true. Third, it inculcates a love of truth. And fourth, and probably least widely noticed, it encourages his natural curiosity until it grows into an ardor to know.[21] These four characteristics, combined with the goodness that is preserved in Emile and the virtue that he acquires, cover most, and arguably all, of the traits said in the *Republic* to constitute the elements of a philosophic nature.[22] Surely Emile remains less bisexual, more strictly masculine in his mental profile, than Rousseau. And surely he is meant to: there is no reason to suppose that Rousseau is not in earnest in his celebration of complementary emotional differences between the sexes. But needing or loving a woman does not indicate that a man lacks the mental endowment to be a philosopher. Rousseau himself, after all, fell in love with his own Sophie (d'Houdetot) while at the peak of his powers. And Wolmar, a true philosopher particularly notable for his powers and love of observation, traits identified as feminine by Rousseau, came to be dependent on Julie.[23] Whatever the extent of Emile's philosophic activity as an adult, the education he has received is an education that opens the door to philosophy and that encourages the capable student to walk through it.

This last point is crucial and deserves development. That Rousseau's pedagogy purports to teach the pupil how to think for himself and that it purports to keep him free of prejudice and to love the truth is obvious. Emile has never really inhabited the *Republic*'s famous cave (514a–517c). However much his tutor has employed artifice and prejudice—creating the appearance of a beneficent nature and hiding all evidence that anyone's will (aside from Emile's own) has shaped his life—Emile emerges from his tutelage uncommonly free of corrupting and distorting prejudice. Yet not even this extraordinary clarity

---

21. The first three of these qualities are readily apparent in such capsule descriptions of Emile's education as this one: "My object is not to give him science but to teach him how to acquire science when needed, to make him estimate it for exactly what it is worth, and to make him love the truth above all (207)."

22. These elements are laid out three times in book 6. The first of the lists, which is also the most expansive, appears at 485a–486d. Its nine elements are as follows: love of knowledge of everything that *is*, dislike of falsehood, moderation, magnificence, fearlessness regarding death, justice (and gentleness), skill at learning, good memory, and measure and charm (or love of proportions and gracefulness).

23. For the characterization of Wolmar as philosopher and passionate observer, see *Julie* 402–4.

is sufficient for Emile to qualify as a philosopher in the conventional or the Platonic understanding of that term[24]—which is also the sense in which Rousseau himself qualifies as a philosopher—even if it *would* qualify as "true philosophy" in Rousseau's peculiar, moralized usage.[25] To be a philosopher requires, additionally, philosophic eros or an ardent desire for the truth. If we find that Emile's education instills or encourages this final element we will have established that it is an education toward, and perhaps even *in*, philosophy, and we will thus have exposed the core of the kinship between *Emile* and the *Republic*.

THE SECOND WAVE

The most obvious interpretation of Plato's second wave as applied to the soul is that it signifies the need to detach one's eros from the private and exclusive and redirect it "upward" toward that which is common or general—toward knowledge of the *eidê*. So directed, this eros will issue in offspring, that is, in ideas or insights, that are similarly common or general. Does the education outlined in *Emile* aim at something comparable? In fact it does.[26] The second

---

24. I do not mean to equate the conventional and the Platonic understandings of philosophy and the philosopher. By the "conventional understanding" I mean, simply, high-level theoretical activity, whereas the "Platonic understanding" means a whole way of life. But that way of life—a life of questioning based on an awareness of the impossibility of final knowledge (and hence the necessity of philosophy) and of the wondrousness of being (and hence the joy of philosophy)—is a life devoted to high-level theoretical activity, and so stands alongside the conventional understanding for our purposes (as its perfection) and apart from what Rousseau means by "true philosophy."

25. As noted above, "true philosophy" as Rousseau uses that term does not presuppose theoretical desire or expertise. Rousseau's true philosopher is one who loves a wisdom that consists in knowing and remaining within the limits of the possible rather than knowing or seeking to know the character of the whole; he is one who lives by the original, pre-Socratic understanding of the inscription on the temple of Delphi. The two conceptions of philosophy are hardly unrelated, however. Rousseau implies that to be a true philosopher in the *conventional* sense requires that one first be a true philosopher in *Rousseau's* sense; without that foundation, vanity will cause one to move further from the truth even as one purports to pursue it (204). Despite the different vocabulary, Rousseau on this point is close to Plato, who suggests that the proper exercise of the highest mental capacities requires that the vicious part of one's nature be "trimmed in earliest childhood" (519a). The relation between true philosophy in the conventional sense and true philosophy in Rousseau's sense will be further addressed below.

26. The second wave may well have additional meanings for the soul—for example, that only the better drives or desires ought to be permitted to propagate, and how this might be ensured—but the meaning I have cited seems to be the primary meaning and in any event the one that is most clearly replicated in *Emile*. My thanks to Kanishka Marasinghe for suggesting the additional reading of Socrates' second wave.

part of book 5 of *Emile* depicts, in turn, the tutor's instructions regarding what the young man should be seeking in a woman; the search for such a woman; Emile's discovery of Sophie; their courtship, featuring both passion and delicacy, obstacles and overcomings, and perhaps most notably, the "charming delirium" of the lovers; and, finally, the tutor's command that Emile leave Sophie for two years for the sake of their long-term happiness upon his return. All of this must be primarily understood as what it is: a great romance, an erotic story about a man and a woman. Each element can also be read, though, as, if not quite representing, then at least as speaking to the elements of an erotic teaching about the love of wisdom: the need to determine what it is that we really want; the need for patience and persistence in our pursuit of what's wanted; the need to court wisdom, and the exquisite pleasures thereof; and the need to ensure that one's desire for wisdom doesn't undermine one's integrity.

To be sure, the sublimation of eros adumbrated in *Emile* is not as comprehensive as that which Socrates depicts in the *Republic* and *Symposium*— Emile's eros does not become *exclusively* philosophic (neither did Rousseau's, as mentioned above)—but it does become at least partly philosophic. Emile develops an "ardor to know" that, though born of a natural and utilitarian concern for his own well-being (167), ultimately incorporates objects of philosophic inquiry unrelated to any personal interest other than the pleasure of knowing. He becomes curious about all he sees (and doesn't see). Even before reaching adolescence his curiosity has become general, as seen, for example, when he dines at an opulent home (190–91). Amid a potentially intoxicating "apparatus of pleasure and festivity" the tutor puts a question to the pupil: "'Through how many hands would you estimate that all you see on this table has passed before getting here?'" Whereupon Emile instantly plunges into meditation, a meditation driven by an intense and self-forgetting curiosity; he even forgets to eat and drink. This particular meditation may not rise to the level of philosophy. But in its character and motive it is perhaps on the way to philosophy: Emile "burns" to know something that is not connected to any personal interest. (Nor is this example unique. We are told that Emile's education is designed to give him "the taste for reflection and meditation" [202], and by the time he reaches adolescence he has become, at least compared to others his age, "a contemplative, a philosopher, a veritable theologian" [315].) And so it is with some justice that Rousseau says of his no longer hungry (for food) pupil that "he is all alone philosophizing for himself in his corner."[27]

The process whereby an originally utilitarian curiosity evolves into a more disinterested ardor to know is complex. The key ingredient, however, is surely the "desire to extend our being," which is introduced and named as such only in connection with man's natural curiosity and ardor to know (168). This is what "takes us outside of ourselves and causes us to leap," *in thought and in exploration,* "as far as is possible for us." The desire to extend our being, as we know, doesn't always express itself in this intellectual way. But the desire is always within us—it belongs to "the present nature of man"—which is why Rousseau counts on our being able to make our own students curious, despite their not having had the extraordinary upbringing of Emile: "Make your pupil attentive to the phenomena of nature. Soon you will make him curious" (168).[28]

But curiosity, no matter how intense, does not in itself constitute philosophic eros—at least not as Plato presents it, and not as Rousseau presents it either. Philosophic eros, being eros, longs for the beautiful. This is illustrated most clearly in the *Symposium,* but it is discernable in the *Republic* as well, where true philosophers, in contradistinction to "the lovers of hearing and the lovers of sight," are described as "those who are able to approach the beautiful itself and see it by itself" (476b). For the education depicted in *Emile* to be (à la Plato) an education in or toward philosophy it must sublimate the pupil's eros: it must lead him to philosophy for the sake of satisfying his longing for beauty. And so it does. Upon reaching adolescence Emile becomes curious about beautiful things. He is curious about them *because* they are beautiful (316). But his governor is not content to leave the matter rest at curiosity. He "teach[es] him to feel and to *love* the beautiful of all sorts" (344; emphasis added). Given that this line appears almost immediately after mention of the *Symposium,* it is not unlikely that among "all sorts" of the

---

27. Rousseau speaks of "an ardent desire to know" in another context: in the *Second Discourse,* in connection with the travels and inquiries of Plato, Thales, and Pythagoras (211).

28. Whether a disinterested ardor to know, especially when it is philosophic, is natural, is as complicated a question as the naturalness of the desire to extend our being, which is its material cause, so to speak. Clearly this ardor to know is not natural in the sense employed in the *Second Discourse,* where "natural" equals "original" or "prehistoric": the savage attended only to that which had a palpable connection to his own interest (*SD* 137). But in another sense one could argue in the affirmative: however alien to the original natural man, the disinterested ardor to know is an ardor to know things *as they are,* that is, to know them *naturally.*

beautiful Rousseau means to include objects of philosophic inquiry.[29] Now all that I have just recounted about Emile's desire to know—its birth prior to adolescence, its originally utilitarian (i.e., subphilosophic) character, its subsequent turn toward the beautiful—is recounted prior to the section of *Emile* that corresponds to the *Republic*'s second wave—and appropriately so. These developments must all have occurred prior to the conversion of this desire into something philosophic. Only that conversion—only the education and transformation of what had already become eros for knowledge into *philosophic* eros—corresponds to Plato's second wave and thus belongs in the second section of book 5. And indeed, that section, whose main action is Emile's and Sophie's romance, culminates in this perfect—and perfectly Platonic—expression of philosophic eros: "'Do you want, then, to live happily and wisely? Attach your heart only to imperishable beauty'" (446). Reasonable people might disagree as to what Rousseau means by "imperishable beauty." The immediate context might suggest that it refers to virtue; and indeed, Rousseau does speak elsewhere of the beauty of virtue (397). But there is also reason to think that the reference is to something comparable to Plato's *eidos* of beauty: only a page after the injunction to love only imperishable beauty, Rousseau tells Emile that "except for the single Being existing by itself, there is nothing beautiful except that which is not" (447). Thus does he attempt to direct at least some of Emile's eros beyond the realm of sensual objects—thus does he endorse the second wave—and in the most appropriate of places.

The situation is not quite so neat, however. For a closer consideration of Rousseau's statement (just quoted) indicates that he doesn't wholly affirm Socrates' teaching about philosophic eros. Rousseau's statement indicates a kinship to Plato but also the limits of this kinship, or perhaps better put, his modification of Platonism. Like Plato, he suggests that the greatest beauty is not to be found before our eyes. But unlike Plato, who presents the *eidê* as having *more* being than the objects of the visible world, Rousseau indicates that that which is most beautiful "*is not*": for the *eidê* he substitutes ideals.

THE THIRD WAVE

Much of what has already been said should suffice to demonstrate that Rousseau is in agreement with, and that Emile's education aims at accomplishing,

---

29. It should be noted that Rousseau at this point voices a fear that the *Symposium* (along

the third wave's teaching when applied to the soul. There can be no doubt that Emile's education leads him to be governed by wisdom and the love of wisdom. True, there is no distinct "wisdom-loving" part of the soul to be accorded rule, as there is in the *Republic* (581b), but Rousseau does present the healthy soul as an internally harmonious soul, which puts him in accord with the corresponding Platonic portrait. And late in book 5—in a place corresponding to Socrates' pronouncement of the need for philosophic rule—Rousseau proclaims that "the wise man" is governed by "the eternal laws of nature and order," which "are written in the depth of his heart by conscience and reason" (473). For that matter the *Republic*'s assertion of a wisdom-loving part may be nothing more than a translation into structural or political language of the love of wisdom, as noted in Chapter 1. But if the third wave is where Rousseau's agreement with Plato is most obvious, it is also where his departure from Plato is most discernable. Whereas for Plato there seems to be no true wisdom or even love of wisdom short of that which belongs to the philosopher (understanding by that term one who lives the theoretical life), for Rousseau, as noted above, a kind of wisdom and "true philosophy" is available to those who never philosophize; nor does one need extraordinary natural gifts to ascend to what Plato calls philosophy (to be a *great* philosopher, yes; but to be simply a philosopher, no).

In practice Rousseau tends to be something of an elitist. This is evident in his politics, where his advocacy of popular sovereignty is tempered by his equally firm insistence that the people need to be led by an excellent few (at first by a legislator and later by wise ministers). And it is evident in his effort to discourage the many from pursuing science and philosophy. In this Rousseau is close to Plato. But *in principle* Rousseau is democratic in important ways. Even though Emile is not capable of attaining the heights of a Bacon or Descartes—Rousseau is not so democratic as to deny widely variable innate capacities or their significance—he *is* capable of a kind of wisdom and philosophy. In fact, as we have seen, he is capable of *two* kinds of wisdom and philosophy. First, by virtue of an education that teaches him how to think and that prevents the growth of corrupt *amour-propre*, Emile attains a wisdom

---

with the fourth book of the *Aeneid* and Tibullus) will prove too moving for his young student and thus lead him astray. But rather than an indication that he means to steer Emile away from philosophy, this is more likely a reflection of Emile's tender age. The passage appears in book 4, whereas it is not until book 5 that Emile's education becomes oriented toward philosophy.

or "true philosophy" that consists in listening to his conscience, viewing the world without prejudice, and respecting the limits of the human condition. No such scenario appears in Plato, where the possibility of avoiding the cave is never raised and the possibility of escaping the cave is limited to the most exceptional human beings. (Rousseau, too, sees escape as exceedingly difficult and rare.) And second, the latter parts of his education, the parts recounted in book 5, lead him toward what even Plato would call wisdom and philosophy. As I have shown, Emile's education encourages him (successfully, I think) to philosophize and, through his philosophizing, to know "men in general" and to discover the principles of political right.

What is the relation between these two kinds of wisdom or philosophy? (To ask this question is also to inquire into the relation between book 5's two levels.) We noted above that, in Rousseau's view, to become a true philosopher in the conventional sense requires that one first be a true philosopher in Rousseau's own peculiar sense of that term. Another way of expressing this would be to say that to reach the highest intellectual peaks one must first have occupied the firmest moral ground. This dependence of the intellectual on the moral is clearly seen in the following characterization of the highest intellectual attainments; the lines appear in the *Preface to Narcissus:* "I acknowledge that there are a few sublime geniuses capable of piercing the veils in which truth wraps itself, a few privileged souls able to withstand the folly of vanity, base jealousy, and the other passions to which a taste for letters gives rise" (107; also see *Observations* 34). Note that the obstacles to truth are moral phenomena: vanity, jealousy, and "other passions." Intellectual virtue is implicitly but clearly attributed to moral strength.[30]

But that which I have called moral is not *simply* moral, nor is it simply negative: the wisdom or true philosophy that consists in heeding conscience, viewing the world without prejudice, and knowing and remaining within the limits of the possible entails such extraordinary knowledge and understanding as to qualify as wisdom (even if not philosophy) by virtually any imaginable standard. It would be hard to deny the mantle of wisdom—indeed, of comprehensive human wisdom—to one who enjoys the deep understanding of things that Emile has acquired even before he has been given the education

---

30. Similarly, in response to those who believe that people can be taught the truth and thereby led to wisdom and virtue, Rousseau argues that "on the contrary, it is necessary first to make men wise/virtuous [*sage*] in order to make them love the truth." See Melzer, *The Natural Goodness of Man*, p. 137.

depicted in book 5. Consider the following mental portrait of the adolescent Emile: "The true principles of the just, the true models of the beautiful, all the moral relations of beings, all the ideas of order are imprinted on his understanding. He sees the place of each thing and the cause which removes it from its place; he sees what can do good and what stands in its way. Without having experienced the human passions, he knows their illusions and their effects" (253).

Is such attainment really plausible—for an adolescent, no less? It is hard to think so, and thus hard to suppose that Rousseau believes so. Indeed, the fact that Emile's education doesn't end here, the fact that he must undertake study of things he is said here already to know, confirms this judgment. But if Rousseau is exaggerating (and one can imagine why he might wish to do so), it *is* plausible to suppose that he is *only* exaggerating, that is, that there is a basis to what he says. If indeed Emile has never inhabited the Platonic cave, if his understanding is uncorrupted, then he is well positioned to acquire the knowledge to which the passage refers. Even those who prefer to reserve the label "philosophy" for theoretical inquiry would not deny that the prephilosophic Emile has acquired, if not an understanding, then the basis of an understanding of things that few philosophers have credibly claimed. Nor would they deny that this prephilosophic understanding might well be the best preparation for philosophic inquiry. Thus the two kinds of wisdom—and the two levels of book 5—prove to be not so far from each other as they might have seemed, and the idea that book 5 of *Emile* speaks to philosophic education becomes less surprising and more credible. One in whom "all the ideas of order are imprinted" is perhaps uniquely prepared to philosophize, and so we should not be surprised that his tutor leads him toward philosophy, however ordinary his innate mental endowment.[31]

POSSIBILITY AND PRACTICABILITY

Why, though, if my interpretation is even partly correct, would Rousseau so submerge Emile's philosophic education as to make it barely discernable?

---

31. The closeness between the prephilosophic and philosophic educations of *Emile* is also seen in their shared pedagogical principles. We noted above that Emile's philosophic education is consistent with the principles of Platonic philosophic education in its promotion of active learning and discovery as opposed to learning by precepts. It ought to be noted now, if indeed it

Rousseau fairly trumpets the extraordinary potential of ordinary minds, so much so as to demonstrate the theoretical possibility of what by historic standards could only be called universal aristocracy. And he does not shrink from publishing views that would feed or even ignite others' revolutionary fervor, even if he himself eschews revolution. Why then bury this one part of his teaching? The answer is entirely prudential. To argue for the possibility of the popularization of philosophy could only feed the corruption of the age (and of philosophy), notwithstanding that the possibility is only theoretical and that the philosophy Rousseau is teaching is worlds away from most of what calls itself philosophy. We have encountered this concern already. But perhaps we can go a bit further, not only into Rousseau's prudence but into its basis and some of its consequences. To do so, we need only think back to the most conspicuously prudential of Rousseau's major works—which is also, paradoxically, the writing that made Rousseau infamous. (Such was the imprudence—or was it the noble sacrifice?—of this most prudentially minded of modern philosophers.)

In the *First Discourse* Rousseau disparages the popularization of the arts and sciences, especially philosophy. He illuminates the dangers, both moral and intellectual and therefore also political, of the pursuit of learning by those who have not been fitted with the kind of moral foundation that makes the pursuit safe and rewarding for Emile. These dangers are intensified by the unfortunate fact that philosophic learning—or, rather, the pretense of philosophic learning—is especially appealing to our vanity. One of Rousseau's tasks in the *Discourse* is thus to diminish the appeal of higher learning in order to keep those who are unprepared—which in Rousseau's view means the vast majority of readers—from giving themselves over to it.[32]

The question, of course, is whether these overt concerns of the *First Discourse* played a role as well in the construction of *Emile*. The answer is that they almost certainly did. Rousseau maintains that all his works are based on the same systematic set of principles (*Dialogues* 211–14), and he considers *Emile* and the *First Discourse* to be parts of a single whole whose three parts (the other part being the *Second Discourse*) are "inseparable" (*Confessions* 575). If the *First Discourse* articulates the dangers of the arts and sciences and

---

needs noting at all, that these same principles govern the whole of Emile's education, from (prephilosophic) start to (philosophic) finish. It is not in book 5 but in book 1 that these principles are first pronounced (51–52).

32. See Orwin, "Rousseau's Socratism."

especially philosophy, and if one of its primary purposes is to steer the unprepared away from them, then it is not surprising—indeed, it would be surprising if it were otherwise—that philosophy is disparaged and that philosophic education is only barely visible in *Emile*.[33] At the very least Rousseau does not want to burnish philosophy's natural appeal to vanity.[34] Rousseau's democratic project is not a practical one. *Emile* is a work that explores human nature by discovering the limits of the possible, not the practicable. The success of Emile's education has depended on the full-time devotion of a great philosopher over more than twenty years, not to mention the cooperation of many others, from Robert the gardener to Sophie's parents. And so what is possible for Emile—what is possible for an ordinary man *in principle*—remains out of reach in practice. And not only out of reach, but also, and consequently, dangerous to reach for.

This gap between possibility and practicability is sad and even tragic. Such a gap is of course evident in Plato as well. The institutions proposed in book 5 of the *Republic* are seen as laughable when not infuriating and thus prove utterly impracticable (451a, 473c). Rule by philosophers, for example, barring "some divine chance" (592a), would be acceptable only to those who had already been the beneficiaries of such rule—which is to say that from a practical standpoint the founding of the noble and fair city presupposes its own prior existence.[35] Yet one hesitates to call Plato tragic, for if it is unlikely that philosophy will ever rule the city and bring justice to it, it is at least possible

---

33. Not only does Rousseau veil philosophic education in *Emile*, but he effectively veils it—by ignoring it—in the *Republic* as well. As we have seen, he refers to the *Republic* as a book about public education, which it undeniably is (40); but he neglects to mention that a substantial portion of the dialogue (books 6 and 7) quite specifically outlines philosophic education.

34. Those inclined to doubt my interpretation of book 5 of *Emile* on the grounds that, if it is correct, Rousseau ought to have proceeded to outline philosophic education as openly as Plato does in books 6 and 7 of the *Republic*, have now had their objection answered. Rousseau's career-long effort to diminish philosophy's public appeal is in precise opposition to Plato's apparent effort to argue for philosophy's, or at least the philosopher's, public value. Indeed, it is fitting that *Emile* ends with book 5—and not only because it is already a very long work. In the *Republic* philosophy represents the peak of human attainment; and since the larger context is a political one, and since philosophy is considered in its political aspect, this peak is placed at the center of the book. In *Emile*, too, philosophy represents the peak of human attainment; but since the larger context is a bildungsroman, in which the higher always comes after the lower, this peak—barely discernable through the clouds, as it were—naturally comes in the final sections of the book.

35. There may well be another layer to Plato's teaching, according to which philosophic rule is possible, albeit in an indirect fashion. Nietzsche certainly understood Plato in this way, and others have too. (See the opening section of Chapter 7, below.) But that does not in any way reverse the implausiblity of the kallipolis sketched by Socrates in the *Republic*.

for capable individuals to live a life of philosophy and thus cultivate justice in their own souls. Political salvation is foreclosed, but individual salvation is not (592b). But precisely this possibility, this saving element, appears to be practically foreclosed in *Emile*. As a practical matter it would seem that philosophy is *not* available to us, since it requires that we be educated in the extraordinarily improbable manner in which Emile is educated. (And not only philosophy but also the nonphilosophic aspects of Emile's development are impracticable, for the same reason.[36])

But perhaps, in this as in the other ways we've seen, Rousseau is not quite as far from Plato as he at first seems. True, the enterprise outlined in *Emile* is impracticable, the nonphilosophic parts as much as the philosophic ones—or, rather, the nonphilosophic parts *more than* the philosophic ones. It is the nonphilosophic education that depends on the perfect execution of innumerable plans under virtually unrealizable conditions: Rousseau frequently observes of particular moments of Emile's education that if things go wrong here, all is lost. As for philosophic education, on the other hand, does Rousseau not presuppose its practicability and in fact engage in it by virtue of writing *Emile*? I suggested earlier that one can say of the *Republic*, indeed of all of Plato's dialogues, that the philosophizing that goes on in or on account of them occurs less within the dialogues' action and speeches than among the dialogues' capable readers, at Plato's prompting and with his inaudible direction. Can one not say the same of *Emile*? Those who read *Emile* well do not just read *about* (philosophic) education, they receive the beginning of one, too. Yet if this is true, one might wonder, hasn't Rousseau violated his own prudential principle by encouraging unprepared readers to take up philosophy? Not necessarily. For one can argue that the book is written in such a way as to appeal to, and encourage to philosophy, only those who *are* prepared, or at least only those who are already given to philosophic inquiry. Indeed, there is even reason to think that Rousseau means to *create* prepared

---

36. A comparable distance between possibility and practicability also exists with respect to the political theory of the *Social Contract*, where Rousseau ignites political passion in his readers only to tell them that the singularly just regime he has articulated is beyond the reach of virtually all modern peoples (*SC* 74–75). Perhaps this helps explain why Rousseau's readers have so often disregarded his teaching on practicability and eluded his attempt to moderate their aspirations and expectations, that is, why the works of this avowed pessimist should have inspired romantic and revolutionary fervor. Plato chastens one's political idealism but redirects one's passion to philosophy. Rousseau ignites idealism and then tells it there is no place for it to go. We should not be surprised that idealism that is given no new direction would refuse to be chastened.

readers. After all, it is difficult to dispute that he uses his poetic and rhetorical power in an attempt to reform the taste and the moral judgment of his readers. Why not, then, understand this effort at moral reform as an effort to prepare at least some readers for the philosophic education the book offers? On the basis of the foregoing interpretation of book 5 this would be a thoroughly reasonable supposition, and one that constitutes yet another affinity between Rousseau's enterprise and Plato's.

And Nietzsche's, too.

PART THREE

Nietzsche's New Eternity

"What? Doesn't this mean, to speak with the vulgar: God is refuted, but the devil is not?" On the contrary! On the contrary, my friends. And, the devil—who forces you to speak with the vulgar?

—*Beyond Good and Evil*

7

NIETZSCHE'S POLITEIA, I

The mature Nietzsche was never quite sure about Plato. About Plato*nism*, yes: a catastrophic idealism based on two great falsehoods, the pure mind and the good in itself (*BGE* Preface)—catastrophic because it undermined the glorious civilization of classical antiquity. But Plato himself, "the most beautiful growth of antiquity," remained elusive. At times Nietzsche seems to absolve Plato of any sincere Platonism—for example, in book 5 of *The Gay Science*, where the invention of Platonism is attributed to prudence, or to fear on behalf of others (372). According to this account, Plato was not himself a vengeful idealist. Though gravely mistaken in doing what he did, he wished only to provide new warrant for morality in an era that was suffering its own death of gods. At other times Nietzsche looks at Plato with a less charitable eye, ascribing something of the -ism to the man. Yet even when he takes this view, as he does in *Beyond Good and Evil*, Nietzsche pointedly does not convict Plato of the weakness or vengefulness of the typical idealist. At worst Plato was seduced by the desire "to prove to himself that reason and instinct of themselves tend toward one goal, the good, 'God'" (191), a seduction to which he was rendered vulnerable less from vengefulness or weakness than from innocence. Indeed, Plato's innocence was the innocence of nobility in the face of plebeian (read: Socratic) cleverness; and as for power, his was "the greatest strength any philosopher so far has had at his disposal" (ibid.). In the end—perhaps because Nietzsche met *his* end so early and unexpectedly—we are left with a Nietzsche who is not quite certain which Plato to believe in.[1]

---

1. There are some grounds for concluding that the more exculpatory view was Nietzsche's final view, for the works in which it finds expression, most notably book 5 of *The Gay Science* (quoted above) and *Twilight of the Idols*, came after *Beyond Good and Evil*, if only by a short while. Lampert supports this view in *Nietzsche's Task*, pp. 160–61, though in his earlier work, *Nietzsche's Teaching*, p. 269, he makes the case that "Nietzsche the philologist was not deflected into the perhaps interminable philological inquiry into what Plato really believed." The reason I stop short of embracing the view that Nietzsche finally settled on the more exculpatory position and hold instead with the claim that Nietzsche never settled the question is that he seems to reiterate the more severe judgment of *Beyond Good and Evil* in the *Genealogy of Morals*, which appeared later than book 5 of *The Gay Science* (though not later than *Twilight*); see *GM* III 25,

But however tantalizing the question of Nietzsche's Plato—and it only becomes more tantalizing as we come to see the extent to which Nietzsche means to rival and contend with Plato—it is less important than a question that Nietzsche did settle. Whatever his uncertainty about what precisely Plato *was*, Nietzsche did claim to know what Plato *did*, what Plato *undertook* to do. (And therewith, given the world-historic scale of Plato's task and the nobility with which he undertook it, Nietzsche also claimed some certain knowledge about Plato himself, namely, his extraordinary strength and "monstrous" pride [*GS* 351]. Not everything about such a soul could remain mysterious.) This knowledge is more important because, as an exercise in "monumental history," it showed Nietzsche what a powerful thinker could do (*UD* 2). Plato's task, as Nietzsche had begun to understand it as early as the writing of *Daybreak*, had been nothing less than to create and rule over a civilization. Plato aimed to become "the lawgiver of new customs;" he intended "to take in hand the direction of mankind" (*Daybreak* 496; also see *WP* 141). And he succeeded (*BGE* Preface). Plato's legislating was the task of a lifetime, accomplished by means of dozens of writings and the establishment of an Academy. An account of the task, though—a laying out of its grounds and an intimation of its means and ends—is largely available in a single writing, the *Republic*.

If Plato was the one who put all philosophy and theology on the same track (*BGE* 191), and therewith all culture and hence all politics (for the political is shaped by the horizon formed by philosophy and theology),[2] it is in the *Republic* that he shows how, why, and to what end he means to accomplish all this. It is there that Plato teaches (sometimes openly, sometimes not) about the natural divisions among human beings; about the wisdom and necessity of rule by philosophers; about the being and the coming-into-being of philosophers; about the substance of the philosophers' legislation; and even about

---

where he refers to Plato as "the sincerest advocate of the 'beyond,' the great slanderer of life." One possibility that would support Lampert's view is that Nietzsche wanted the *Genealogy* to be consistent with *Beyond Good and Evil*, since he presents the *Genealogy* as a polemic and as a series of elaborations on teachings of *Beyond Good and Evil*. For a detailed account of Nietzsche's evolving but probably never settled view of Plato (along with a general interpretation of Nietzsche's relation to Plato), see Zuckert, *Postmodern Platos*, pp. 10–32.

2. The primacy of philosophy and theology for politics is indicated by the order of both the *Republic* and *Beyond Good and Evil*. In the *Republic* the transformation of the feverish city into a beautiful and just city begins with the propagation of new teachings about the gods and the soul. In *Beyond Good and Evil* the investigation of morality and politics and the propagation of new moral and political principles (parts 5–9) follow investigations of philosophy and theology (parts 1–3).

the means by which philosophers could achieve and exercise rule. (These means, the only means possible to those armed only with speech, are new teachings about humanity, the Good, and the character of the Whole, and the recruitment of readers to propagate these teachings through cultural revolution or reformation.) The *Republic* is not the only dialogue in which these themes are addressed, though it may be the only one in which they are all addressed. Moreover, given that Plato's political project was to proceed by instructing and recruiting readers who would then become cultural warriors and leaders, the *Republic* is not only a political discourse but also a decisive political *act,* the primary and perhaps the most important act of Plato's "great politics." For these reasons it enjoys a special status among the dialogues. And any book meant to rival the *Republic* by a later thinker who understood the dialogue in this way might justly be considered to aspire to a comparable character and status. My primary purpose in this and the next chapter will be to show that *Beyond Good and Evil* meets that description.[3] *Beyond Good and Evil,* as we shall see, emerges as a part by part and often a subpart by subpart reply and rival to the *Republic.* As such it comes to light effectively as Nietzsche's own *Politeia.*[4]

---

3. *Did* Nietzsche understand the *Republic* as I've described it? The fact that Nietzsche does not comment on the dialogue by name in any of his published books might seem to argue for hesitancy in saying so. Nietzsche did, however, describe Plato as a would-be, indeed a successful, ruler, as we have seen. And it is almost inconceivable that one who reads Plato in such a way would fail to read the *Republic* in the way I have outlined. The strongest evidence, though—overwhelming evidence, in my view—is the extensive set of parallels between *Beyond Good and Evil* and the *Republic,* which will be the focus of the next and longest part of this inquiry. Once one sees the relationship between the two books, their formal and substantive parallels, one need only attend to the obvious political character of Nietzsche's book in order to surmise that Nietzsche saw the *Republic* as an equally political book.

4. For all the attention that has been paid to the Nietzsche–Plato relation, no one to my knowledge has come close to fully developing the relation between *Beyond Good and Evil* and the *Republic,* and I am only aware of two scholars who have even suggested it. (1) Craig made the suggestion in the course of an unpublished conference paper, "Strange Images"; see pp. 69–70, note 21. Craig also illuminates some of *Beyond Good and Evil*'s many references and responses to Platonic dialogues other than the *Republic.* (2) McGuire has developed the theme further, though still very sketchily, in a short paper devoted to the task; see his "Beyond Good and Evil." McGuire appends to his study the further suggestion that, with the seven books that followed or were meant to follow *Beyond Good and Evil,* Nietzsche meant to equal or surpass Plato's seven "late" (i.e., post-*Republic*) dialogues. Lomax has also suggested a kinship between *Beyond Good and Evil* (along with *Zarathustra*) and the *Republic*—not, however, because each attempts to legislate but because each shows the impossibility of successful philosophic legislation of this magnitude. See *The Paradox of Philosophical Education,* pp. 7–8. Dannhauser offers a revealing account of the many ways in which "the wisdom of the ancients is recaptured by this most modern of thinkers," though he doesn't speak extensively about the relation between *Beyond Good and Evil* and the *Republic.* See *Nietzsche's View of Socrates,* pp. 269–74.

To establish the relation between these two books, as I mean to do, is to open the way to a new understanding of many elements of Nietzsche's thought. (It is also to lend support to some of the better interpretations of Nietzsche.[5]) My project in these chapters is to address just one of those elements, and only from the standpoint from which it is addressed in *Beyond Good and Evil*, though it is the most basic element of Nietzsche's mature thought and constitutes the matter, as it were, to which Nietzsche's political project in *Beyond Good and Evil* is a giving of form. That matter, if it is permissible to speak in such terms of something that is essentially energic, is will to power. The standpoint from which it is addressed in *Beyond Good and Evil* is the standpoint of politics, understanding that word in the broadest possible sense. Like the *Republic*, *Beyond Good and Evil* addresses a great number of topics and often revises or even overturns earlier formulations. Nevertheless Nietzsche's book, like Plato's, is unified by an overarching theme and structure—a dynamic or developmental structure, which is what allows for unity in the face of revisions and reformulations. Indeed, in the broadest sense *Beyond Good and Evil* and the *Republic* have identical themes and structures. The organizing theme is nothing other than what Plato's title suggests. His dialogue, and Nietzsche's book, are fundamentally concerned with the question of the best *regime*—the best regime for the city and the best regime for the individual human being. (Notwithstanding early appearances to the contrary, it is for the sake of the latter that the former is addressed [*Republic*

---

5. There is an enormous literature on Nietzsche and a growing literature on Nietzsche as a political thinker. But comparatively few interpreters are prepared to acknowledge that Nietzsche is anywhere near as serious and comprehensive a political thinker as Plato. *Very* few would agree that he attempts as grand a constructive or legislative enterprise as Plato. For most, Nietzsche is at best an incisive critic. For a summary of this "standard reading of Nietzsche," a list of its leading expositors, and its possible source in the influential interpretation of Martin Heidegger, see Conway, *Nietzsche and the Political*, pp. 119–23. One interpreter who *has* recognized the Platonic dimensions of Nietzsche as a political thinker is Lampert, whose commentaries establish that Nietzsche meant to be what he took Plato to be, namely, "a genuine philosopher," a "*commander*" and "*legislator*" who "determine[s] the Whither and For What of man" (*BGE* 211). See especially *Nietzsche's Teaching*, esp. pp. 263–86 ("Nietzsche's Founding"), and the entirety of *Nietzsche's Task*, Lampert's commentary on *Beyond Good and Evil*, to which my own reading is significantly indebted. Lampert does not read *Beyond Good and Evil* as a specific reply to the *Republic*, however. Another interpreter who recognizes Nietzsche's grand political ambition is Eden, in *Political Leadership and Nihilism: A Study of Weber and Nietzsche*, esp. chap. 4, though where Lampert sees Nietzsche's project as grounded in loyalty to nature, Eden sees it as nihilistic. My own reading should, among other things, confirm that Nietzsche did indeed aspire to be a philosopher in his sense of the word and that his commanding and legislating took their bearings from what he took to be nature.

592b].) My ultimate purpose in this comparative textual analysis, then, is to explore the relation between *Beyond Good and Evil* and the *Republic* in order to consider will to power as it is revealed in the former, that is, from the standpoint of the question of the best regime. At best this can only yield a very partial account of will to power, given that Nietzsche examined will to power from multiple standpoints and came to see it as the fundamental fact not only of politics but also of human life, indeed all life and even all that exists. Yet as partial perspectives go this isn't a bad one, for it is precisely by studying the psychic regime of the highest humans in the way that Nietzsche does in *Beyond Good and Evil* that one can learn most about the Whole (36). This methodological principle is not the least of Nietzsche's affinities with Plato.[6]

"Will to power," of course, is Nietzsche's own coinage, and nothing like it appears in the *Republic*. Or, rather, nothing like it is sustained as a plausible Platonic teaching. (Arguably the "defeated" positions of Thrasymachus in book 1 and of Glaucon and Adeimantus in book 2 are positions based on something like will to power. Positions even closer to Nietzsche are advanced in other dialogues—though, again, never by Socrates: see Callicles in the *Gorgias* and Aristophanes in the *Symposium*.) Yet the relation between Nietzsche's book and Plato's can still teach us about will to power, for will to power is to and in *Beyond Good and Evil* what eros is to and in the *Republic*.[7] This will become clear, or at least as clear as I can make it, as we address the two texts. But since the examination to come is comparative and concerns Plato less than Nietzsche, or rather Plato *for the sake of* Nietzsche, it would be well to preface the comparative analysis with a statement on eros in the *Republic*.[8]

Namely, (1) insofar as it offers a teaching on individual and political health; (2) insofar as it depicts the education of Socrates' interlocutors; and (3) insofar as it thereby seeks to educate its readers, both consciously (via persuasion)

---

6. Like Plato, Nietzsche can draw inferences about the character of the Whole from its highest parts because, like Plato, he sees the Whole *as* a whole, that is, as continuous—at *WP* 272 he notes "the absolute homogeneity of all events"—and because he sees it as hierarchical. See Lampert, *Nietzsche's Teaching*, p. 254.

7. We may also say that will to power *is not* to and in *Beyond Good and Evil* what eros *is not* to and in the *Republic*. In each text psychological inquiry is ostensibly undertaken for the sake and from the standpoint of a political question. Plato offers a more direct, perhaps a more erotic, inquiry into eros in the *Symposium*. Nietzsche's corresponding treatment of will to power was to have been the focus of his incomplete *Hauptwerk, The Will to Power*.

8. The following two paragraphs summarize Chapter 1's more extensive treatment of the *Republic*'s teaching on eros' primacy in the soul and in politics.

and unconsciously (via subtler forms of soulcraft), the *Republic* focuses predominantly on eros. (1) Eros proves to be the source of both the greatest health (or justice) and the greatest sickness (or injustice) in human beings. This is seen in the fact that the philosopher and the tyrant, the most just and the most unjust of men, respectively, are uniquely defined by their "large" and concentrated eros. (2) Eros is clearly the leading passion of Glaucon, to whom Socrates especially attends throughout the dialogue and in the action prior to the dialogue: Glaucon is described by Socrates and depicted by Plato as erotic or full of longing (474d, 468b, 468c), and furthermore, eros proves to be the source of his attraction both to injustice (at the start of book 2) and to justice (thereafter). And if we recognize spiritedness (*thymos*) as a version of eros and great spiritedness as an indicator of erotic character, as indeed we should, then the primacy of eros in Glaucon's psychic economy only looms larger—and the education of Glaucon emerges as an erotic education. (3) Finally, while it is not possible to speak definitively of Plato's intentions or expectations with respect to his readers, it seems reasonable to suppose that readers who are "hearing" speech that is both about eros and that engages and educates the eros of Socrates' interlocutors are meant to be erotically engaged and educated themselves.

To state the matter even more briefly, on the evidence of both Socrates' explicit teaching and the way he teaches, eros comes to light as the most consequential force in the soul and, as such, the most consequential of all political phenomena. A good regime, whether psychic or political, will be one in which eros is well governed, and the way toward such a regime will be through the education of eros. What good governance of eros means, and how it ought to be educated, is of course another matter—the essential matter, really, since it resolves into the question of eros' nature—and I don't mean to suggest that Nietzsche is altogether in accord with Plato on *that*. There is a reason Nietzsche chooses to speak the language of will rather than desire, and power rather than beauty. But let us not get to divergences until we have first apprehended the illustrative parallels.

TWIN PEAKS

The parallels between *Beyond Good and Evil* and the *Republic* are both general (i.e., transcending any single division of the books) and specific. A skeptical reader might at least be won to interpretive openness, and all of us might better prepare ourselves to make sense of the more specific parallels, by considering the general ones first, which primarily concern the question of human types and the question of rule. Herewith, then, a catalogue of some of the more striking general similarities:[9]

- Each book propounds a natural articulation of human types. Each, in fact, propounds a tripartition of humanity, with a pyramidal distribution and a hierarchical structure—all, to say it again, as part of the nature of things.
- In each book the highest and naturally ruling class consists of philosophers, who are to be assisted by an instrumental warrior class. (I include under the latter heading those whose war is spiritual or cultural.) Each book presupposes the realistic possibility of philosophic rule. Indeed, Nietzsche presupposes its actuality and even inevitability. In each book, moreover, the highest class is distinguished and selected from what had initially appeared to be the highest class but turns out not to be: In the *Republic,* the "complete guardians" are drawn and distinguished from those who had earlier been called guardians but who are renamed "auxiliaries" (414b). In *Beyond Good and Evil* the philosopher of the future is drawn and distinguished from those called "free minds" (or "free spirits": *freien Geister*).
- In each book what turns out to be the middle class is distinguished from the lower class by a pronounced and refined spiritedness, and the highest class is marked (among other things) by a further enlargement and refinement of this very quality.
- In each book, however, the highest type is defined *essentially* in terms of the psychic dynamic whose centrality I have already commented on: eros for Plato, will to power for Nietzsche. Plato's philosopher is a knower and a lover, but a lover first, since it is by dint of loving knowledge that he pursues and gains it. Nietzsche's philosopher is the one with the most spiritual and, more to the point, simply the greatest will to power (though he is also a knower and a lover, like Plato's and for the same reasons as Plato's).
- In each book—in each body of thought—the psychic force whose peak development distinguishes the highest human type is also the deepest and most powerful psychic force in all human beings, the soul of the soul. Not

---

9. Most of the following observations will be familiar, even if the parallels between them are not. Evidence for those which are apt to be less familiar will appear in the part-by-part analysis below.

only the healthy but also the sick and everyone in between are propelled by this force. What distinguishes high or healthy from low or sick are the ways in which this force manifests itself in them. Moreover, goods are determined and ranked according to their relation to this force; and for both Nietzsche and Plato the force points to a single, overarching good. (This is not to say that the good for Plato is the same as the good for Nietzsche, though, as we will see, there is an extraordinary and perhaps surprising affinity between them.)

- In each book, rule by philosophers consists of foundational or architectonic legislation that is accomplished by new teachings about the soul, the gods, and the character of the Whole. These teachings are not only pointed at but sketched in the books themselves. Both the *Republic* and *Beyond Good and Evil* contain much that does not strike the reader as obviously political. Yet as we have already seen with respect to the *Republic,* even that which seems nonpolitical is looked at from a political standpoint (and some things that *seem* nonpolitical turn out not to be, as we will also see). Nietzsche's and Plato's metaphysical and theological teachings are presented in connection with and even in the language of the political question of the best regime. (Even Plato's choice of the term "the good," where he might have opted to speak, say, of "God" or "the One," may reflect this perspective.) The means by which these teachings are advanced include an array of poetic and rhetorical devices. *Hidden* devices: philosophic rule does not mean philosophizing publicly.

- In each case the philosophers rule, or would rule, philanthropically. The philanthropic thrust of the philosophers' activity is widely recognized in Plato's case, but Nietzsche, too, insists that philosophers work for the "enhancement" of man (212). Philanthropy does not mean self-sacrifice, however. The Nietzschean philosopher is moved by his nature to rule and presumably to want to rule. The Platonic philosopher is less clear in this regard, but a strong case can be made that he, too, is compelled by his nature. (Certainly the Platonic philosopher would have to be compelled by others, or by a sense of responsibility, i.e., not by the prospect of enjoyment, were he to rule in any ordinary sense. But philosophic rule is no ordinary rule. It is rule by means of propounding new teachings; it does not involve the drudgery of everyday governance or a public life in the usual sense. Indeed, if Nietzsche is right about Plato's success as ruler over subsequent generations, the philosopher-ruler need not be recognized as a ruler by

more than a few.) In any case, it is worth noting that the legislation of both the Nietzschean and the Platonic philosopher provides first and foremost for the nurture and protection of ones like themselves.
- Finally, each book examines morality from the demanding standpoint of personal happiness. Why be just? In Nietzsche's words, "the whole morality of self-denial must be questioned mercilessly" (33). He does just this in *Beyond Good and Evil*, as Plato's Socrates has done at Glaucon's and Adeimantus' urging in the *Republic*. Each book is in this sense an exercise in moral and political naturalism: the good is prior to the right.
- Beyond these discrete features, I would also submit that each book aims to do the things I mentioned earlier. Each aims to educate its readers to a new outlook. Each aims to do so by educating or redirecting—or better, sublimating—readers' eros or will to power. And in so doing each means to lead readers closer to the very health that it discovers and displays.

These general features only tell the beginning of the story of the relation between the two books. But in so doing they tell readers of *Beyond Good and Evil* that they are reading a political work. This will be particularly the case among readers who have learned from the *Republic* just how much that seems to lie beyond politics, or above politics, or below politics, in fact bears on or belongs to or even constitutes the political. Something else one might have learned from the *Republic* is that a grand political endeavor must begin negatively, with critique. The old must be undermined or cleared away before the new can take its place. The conversation depicted in the dialogue begins in earnest with the critique of leading contemporary conceptions of justice. And the *kallipolis* itself grows out of the reform, based on the critique, of an imagined feverish city whose unwholesome ways and beliefs, come to think of it, were not so imaginary after all but rather quite typical of the surrounding reality. Similarly, Nietzsche describes *Beyond Good and Evil* as a "critique of modernity" and of "what lies nearest," and as the first step in conjuring "the great war" against the values of the age, a war on behalf of a new nobility that can only take root if the critique succeeds (*EH*, Books, "BGE" 2, 1). Finally, if one learns anything from the *Republic* it is the momentous political significance of education. Here, too, Nietzsche's description of his book accords with Platonic teaching: as the *Republic* devotes enormous space to the educations of the auxiliaries and guardians and as the entire dialogue depicts the education of Glaucon et al. and thereby educates its readers similarly, so *Beyond Good and Evil* is "a school for the *gentilhomme*" (*EH*, Books, "BGE" 2).

Less obvious but perhaps even more striking than the foregoing similarities are those that emerge when one attends to matters of structure, to which we turn now, beginning with the question of how to relate Nietzsche's work of nine discrete parts (*Hauptstücke*, literally "chief parts") plus a preface and "Aftersong" (*Nachgesang*) to the ten books of the *Republic*. The evidence suggests that the nine numbered parts ought to be seen as corresponding to their similarly numbered Platonic counterparts; the Aftersong as Nietzsche's counterpart to Plato's book 10; and the preface as something apart from the book proper. What evidence? Two kinds. First and more powerful are the extensive structural and thematic parallels between Nietzsche's numbered parts and Plato's books of the same number—from Nietzsche's part 1 to Plato's book 1, and so on. To give just one example in advance of the more extensive survey to come, notice that the sixth chapter of each book concerns itself primarily with identifying the true philosopher, distinguishing him from other types, and laying out the conditions that favor or undermine his proper development. There is no such parallelism between Nietzsche's preface and the beginning of the *Republic*, though I will suggest a different—and, if accurate, more appropriate—parallelism below. The second source of this judgment is the physical layout of *Beyond Good and Evil*, which we know to have been planned by Nietzsche. In accordance with Nietzsche's dictate, the preface is separated from the rest of the book by the contents page, while the Aftersong is treated exactly like the nine numbered parts, receiving its own title page—a fairly striking feature, given the brevity of the poem. Thus *Beyond Good and Evil*, like the *Republic*, may be read as a book of ten parts.

The relation between *Beyond Good and Evil* and the *Republic*—in any event, that there *is* a special relation—is first indicated by a number of numerical anomalies and coincidences, beginning with the number and enumeration of Nietzsche's sections.[10] (The reader will recall that *Beyond Good and*

---

10. As Lampert documents, Nietzsche routinely "played with numbers"—for example, in *Zarathustra*, whose chapter division recalls the Bible, and the *Genealogy*, "in which section 13 in all three treatises begins 'Let us return,' all three section 12's having dealt with fundamental matters somewhat tangential to the themes of the three treatises." See, respectively, Lampert's *Nietzsche's Teaching*, pp. 240–41, and his *Nietzsche's Task*, p. 140n6. In all of the ways that follow, Nietzsche indicates that *Beyond Good and Evil* both follows the *Republic* and opposes it.

Evil's enumeration of sections is continuous from the beginning of part 1 through to the end of part 9: the count does not begin anew with each new chapter.)[11] The final numbered section of the book is 296. As a sum, however, this final number is misleading, since there are three instances where Nietzsche repeats a section number: in the form in which Nietzsche submitted the book to his printer there are two each of sections 65, 73, and 237.[12] It is hard to know what to make of these repetitions. Does Nietzsche mean to say that the two sections numbered 65, for example, are somehow equivalent? or complementary? or specially connected in some other way? Perhaps one or another or all of these things is true, but no interpreter that I am aware of has settled the matter. I will offer my own suggestion about these repetitions shortly. But first let me draw attention to one *consequence* of the repetition, which, among other things, may help us make sense of the specific repetitions themselves. The effect of the numerical repetition is that a book of 299 sections looks like, is *deliberately made* to look like, a book of 296 sections: Nietzsche exercised particular care over the details of this book, which he published himself;[13] we therefore have every reason to suppose that these anomalies were intentional and that he saw fit to present Beyond Good and Evil as (apparently) a book of 296 sections. Consider next that the final enumeration was the result of a last-minute change, at Nietzsche's own behest. What is now the ultimate aphorism of the book (section 296) was originally to have appeared, unnumbered and set off by little stars, at the start of part 4. Only very late in the production process did Nietzsche change his mind and direct his printer to move the aphorism to the end of part nine and give it its own number.

---

11. Each section is an aphorism and thus to some extent seems to stand on its own. Many readers have drawn the mistaken conclusion that Nietzsche's use of aphorisms reflects a lack of order or continuity. That Beyond Good and Evil does not lack order or continuity should become obvious over the course of what follows. (It has been shown even more extensively by Lampert in *Nietzsche's Task* and, albeit more cursorily, by Strauss in "Note on the Plan of Beyond Good and Evil," in *Studies in Platonic Political Philosophy*.) For useful discussions of the meaning of Nietzsche's aphoristic style and its appropriateness to his antidogmatic thought, see Löwith, *Nietzsche's Philosophy of the Eternal Recurrence of the Same*, pp. 11–20, and Dannhauser, *Nietzsche's View of Socrates*, pp. 195–207. Löwith writes: "Nietzsche's philosophy is neither a unified, closed system nor a variety of disintegrating aphorisms, but a system in aphorisms" (p. 11). Also see Lampert's commentary on aphorism 381 of *The Gay Science* in *Nietzsche and Modern Times*, pp. 306–10.

12. In his translation Kaufmann has appended a superscript "a" to the second occurrence of each of these numbers. Hollingdale has done the same in the cases of 65 and 73 but has simply assimilated the content of the second 237 to the first 237, thereby burying the fact that there ever was a second 237. See Kaufmann's explanatory footnotes.

13. Lampert, *Nietzsche's Task*, pp. 140, 141–42.

What that means is that Nietzsche's original, well-considered, and in fact completed plan was to have a book whose enumeration stopped with 295. What of it? Perhaps nothing. But at the risk of losing the reader's indulgence I will point out that 295 is also the number of pages in the standard, Stephanus edition of the *Republic*.[14] This could all be a meaningless coincidence, but the improbability of Nietzsche accidentally arriving at this particular number, combined with the repetition of the three section numbers (whose result, and thus perhaps whose *purpose,* is to preserve the desired count), suggests that the coincidence may well be meaningful, that is, a playful and subtle nod to the *Republic,* especially in light of the extraordinary structural parallels between the two books.

But then what about the late decision to add a section 296? Two not incompatible possibilities suggest themselves. First, if 295 is significant for being the number of pages in the *Republic,* 296 is significant for being the number of pages in the *Republic* plus one (particularly if it is known that the final section was a late addition). What better way to one-up Plato than to one-up Plato? The second possibility is more polite and is suggested by the content of section 296. Section 295, one will recall, reads as a true culmination of the entire book. The appearance of the philosophizing god Dionysus and the celebration of his union with Ariadne mark the apotheosis of Nietzschean humanity (assuming that human beings, too, can philosophize) and the birth or foretelling of a religion under which humanity, led by a new nobility, might overcome itself and its history of vengefulness.[15] Section 296, by contrast, is a beautifully wistful denouement in which the philosopher speaks evocatively of the limits of language vis-à-vis his young and "wicked" thoughts—evocatively because he still recalls these thoughts in their youth and wickedness:

> What things do we copy, writing and painting, we mandarins with Chinese brushes, we eternalizers of things that *can* be written—what are the only things we are able to paint? Alas, always only what is on the verge of withering and losing its fragrance! ... it is only your

---

14. Nietzsche surely knew and used Stephanus pagination, which has been the standard way of citing Plato's works since its development by Henri Estienne (for whom it is named) in the sixteenth century.

15. It is also worth noting that section 295 recalls the "musical Socrates" named Nietzsche and, therewith, the original Socrates, too. The section refers to Dionysus as a "genius of the heart" and "pied piper," the latter of which Nietzsche elsewhere applies both to himself (*TI* Preface) and to Socrates (*GS* 340).

afternoon, you, my written and painted thoughts, for which alone I have colors, many colors perhaps, many motley caresses and fifty yellows and browns and greens and reds: but nobody will guess from that how you looked in your morning, you sudden sparks and wonders of my solitude, you my old beloved—wicked thoughts![16]

Notice, though, that the matter is more general than just *Nietzsche's* language vis-à-vis *Nietzsche's* thoughts. There may not be many such writers and painters, but the plural pronoun (*"we* mandarins") suggests that Nietzsche is not alone. The greatest thoughts, at least the greatest among "wicked" thoughts, are too maliciously shy and sly to admit capture in words by the greatest thinkers. Surely this encompasses not only Nietzsche but also other thinkers of the highest rank—of whom Plato is surely the very highest, at least if measured in "strength" (*BGE* 191). If so, then section 296 is and means to be a proper denouement not only to *Beyond Good and Evil* (let alone just part 9) but also to *all* genuine philosophy, the *Republic* certainly included. Nietzsche sighs with and for Plato as well as for himself. He even acknowledges that, like Plato, he sees philosophy as an embrace of eternity ("we eternalizers"), even if the meaning he attaches to eternity is emphatically non-Platonic.[17] *Beyond Good and Evil's* final lines of prose are an act of courtesy toward Nietzsche's kin, an act befitting noblemen of the highest rank. (As an act of courtesy among gentlemen, section 296 is also an appropriate denouement to part 9, "What is *Noble?*")[18]

As Nietzsche ends the prose portion of his book with a beautiful philo-

---

16. Italics here and elsewhere are always Nietzsche's unless otherwise noted. Ellipses are normally my own, signifying gaps in my quotations. (Kaufmann replaces Nietzsche's ellipses with dashes. I have maintained this adjustment except where the ellipse ends a numbered section.)

17. Both Kaufmann and Hollingdale mistranslate *Vereweiger* ("eternalizers") as "immortalizers" and *verewigen* ("eternalize") as "immortalize," thereby masking what may well be Nietzsche's innermost affinity with (and divergence from) Plato. That Nietzsche also uses *unsterblich* ("immortal") in this section only makes the mistranslation worse. Nietzsche's non-Platonic conception of "eternity" will be addressed extensively in Chapter 9.

18. It might seem odd or even implausible that Nietzsche would base so much on a system of pagination that could very well have become obsolete in the future—especially since Nietzsche is writing with an eye to the future. But obsolescence was not in the offing when Nietzsche wrote (nor is it today), and *Beyond Good and Evil*, while tending to the future, is a book for its time (*EH* "BGE") and a book for scholars. So Nietzsche's use of Stephanus pagination is fitting. But in any event the real case for my interpretive claims lies in the evidence we've just examined and that which we will soon encounter. Is it more reasonable to attribute the numerical coincidences between Nietzsche's and Plato's books to accident or to design?

sophic denouement, let me conclude this section with a scholarly denouement that is not beautiful though it may be comical (which would be entirely fitting: surely Nietzsche knows that scholars are the *true* mandarins among writers). We return as promised to the question of the three repeated section numbers. I have already confessed my inability to explain how the members of the equivalently numbered section-pairs relate to each other. Perhaps, though, an answer—at least part of one—lies not just in the contents of the sections but also in the numbers themselves. Perhaps Nietzsche's numerical anomalies, like his final enumeration (295/296), were designed with the *Republic* in mind. How so? Numerically speaking, there are three elements to Nietzsche's repetitions: first, that there are three of them; second, that the numerical values of the sections are what they are, that is, 65, 73, and 237; and finally, that the sum of these three values is 375. Each of these features has a plausible and suggestive link to the *Republic*.

(1) The first element is the simplest and least suggestive of the three and would not merit notice were it not for the broader context provided by the second and third elements. In connection with the fact that Nietzsche repeats section numbers three times I will offer only the observation that the *Republic* is, notably and in ways both obvious and subtle, a book of threes: that there are three classes of human beings corresponding to three "parts" of the soul is among the most famous teachings of this book, which itself is tripartite (the central division being the lengthy digression on philosophers and philosophy that consumes books 5–7).[19]

(2) But why *these* three? Why 65, 73, and 237? The answer emerges when we recall that these are ordinal numbers: There are thematic correspondences between sections 65, 73, and 237 of *Beyond Good and Evil* and the 65th, 73rd, and 237th pages of the *Republic*, respectively. In each case Nietzsche's text parallels and effectively criticizes or disputes Plato's. Though not an attempt

---

19. For a reading of the *Republic* that interprets the dialogue as a three-step dialectic, see Roochnik, *Beautiful City*. Craig suggests that the triadic character of the *Republic* is merely superficial and covers a deeper *quadratic* structure, which would give the *Republic* yet another affinity to Nietzsche's penchant for fourfold analyses. Consider, for example, that the working class is divided into an iron and a bronze class, thus making a total of four classes; also consider that the Divided Line has four segments and that Socrates gives us four actual or "real world" political regimes. In this light it may be worth noting that although Nietzsche repeats section numbers only three times in *Beyond Good and Evil*, the book does contain a fourth numerical anomaly, namely, his numbering 247a what should have been simply section 247. For a plausible interpretation of that substitution, see Lampert, *Nietzsche's Task*, pp. 250–51.

at a comprehensive analysis, the following should suffice to establish the point:

- The 65th page of the *Republic*, or 391, is where Socrates inveighs against the "current lies" that portray gods and children of gods as susceptible to the worst of human passions and vices. Gods, Socrates instructs, do not and must not be thought to do evil. Compare this to the second section 65 of *Beyond Good and Evil*, which reads, in its entirety: "One is most dishonest to one's god: he is not *allowed* to sin."
- The 73rd page of the *Republic*, or 399, gives us Socrates legislating the harmonic modes and instruments proper to the reformed city that he is constructing with Glaucon. He concludes at 399e as follows: "'It's nothing new we're doing, my friend,' I said, 'in choosing Apollo and Apollo's instruments ahead of Marsyas and his instruments.'" The reference is apparently to a fabled contest. The satyr Marsyas, proud of his musical skill, challenges the god to a contest: his flute-playing against Apollo on the cither. The Muses deem Apollo superior, whereupon the god flays the satyr. Marsyas' pride costs him his skin. The lesson of the story, at least on one reading, is that he would have done better to have hidden his pride, and to have taken pride in *that* (to use one's cunning to escape divine retribution is indeed something to be proud of). This is exactly the phenomenon addressed—critically, it seems—by the second section 73 of *Beyond Good and Evil*, which reads in its entirety: "Many a peacock hides his peacock tail from all eyes—and calls that his pride." Nietzsche stands with the prideful Marsyas over and against the prudence taught by Socrates.
- The 237th page of the *Republic*, or 563, concerns the outrages of democratic freedom and anarchy and the ways in which they "prepare a need for tyranny" (562c). Under democratic regimes, as Socrates depicts them, hierarchies are upended as authority figures effectively abdicate their positions for fear of unpopularity. After enumerating several instances, several "small things," Socrates' indictment reaches its peak. Here is his statement, along with Adeimantus' reply:

> "And *the ultimate* in the freedom of the multitude, my friend," I said, "occurs in such a city when the purchased slaves, male and female, are no less free than those who have bought them. And we

almost forgot to mention the extent of the law of equality and of freedom in the relations of women with men and men with women."

"Won't we," he said, "with Aeschylus, 'say whatever just came to our lips'?"

At the peak of Socrates' indictment we find equality between masters and slaves and between men and women.

Now consider Nietzsche's second section 237, which falls amid a several-page discourse about women (roughly at the mid-point, not numerically but absolutely). Having devoted the preceding several sections to "a few truths about 'woman as such'" (231), Nietzsche turns in the second 237 to the relations between the sexes. In a discussion that continues through the end of part 7, he details the dispiriting effects—the unsexing and "uglifying" effects—of the democratic denial of "the most abysmal antagonism" between man and woman in favor of women's ostensible liberation and equality between the sexes (238). Like Socrates, Nietzsche laments the democratic distaste for possession of some human beings by others and for different roles and rights for the sexes. Both of these themes, that is, possession and sexual (in)-equality, are treated in the second 237. In fact the two themes are treated as one. Here is the section in its entirety: "Men have so far treated women like birds who had strayed to them from some height: as something more refined and vulnerable, wilder, stranger, sweeter, and more soulful—but as something one has to lock up lest it fly away." Among other things, this brief aphorism calls attention to the subtler forms of and motivations for possession. Even more, it seems to state the *naturalness* of the male propensity to try to possess women and the grounds of that propensity. The section also points to the (happy) impossibility of complete possession: birds that are caged do not cease thereby to be wilder, stranger, sweeter, and more soulful—and hence elusive.

Apropos of Adeimantus' invocation of Aeschylus, we might wonder whether Nietzsche's lament over the demystification of women isn't itself a reply to the *Republic*, for in Nietzsche's work Aeschylus is associated primarily with demystification. Aeschylus was tried for divulging the secrets of the Mysteries—the line quoted by Adeimantus may have been spoken by Aeschylus in his defense against this charge[20]—and the work of Aeschylus on which

---

20. See Bloom, *The Republic of Plato*, p. 469n24.

Nietzsche comments most extensively is itself centrally concerned with mystery and violation. (The action of *Prometheus Bound* centers not around Prometheus' theft of fire, which precedes the action of the play, but around his refusal in the face of horrific punishment to divulge to Zeus the secret of the god's doom—a secret that centers around a *woman* whose name he refuses to reveal.) Perhaps, too, it is worth noting that Prometheus (and thus indirectly Aeschylus himself) is a central character in Aristophanes' *Birds*, a significantly titled comedy by "that transfiguring, complementary spirit for whose sake one *forgives* everything Hellenic [read: *Platonic*] for having existed."

Nietzsche's section 237 does not criticize or challenge the corresponding passage of the *Republic* as much as sections 65 and 73 criticize theirs. Nietzsche shares Socrates' seeming antipathy to democratic attitudes concerning relations between masters and slaves and between men and women. Or is Socrates' professed antipathy only a sop to Adeimantus, in which case Nietzsche *is* opposing the ironic and plebian Socrates. In either case Nietzsche opposes the professed grounds of Socrates' concern—namely, Socrates' fear of tyranny—as well as Socrates' evidently crude understanding of desirable male-female relations and his understanding of tyranny. Unlike Socrates and Adeimantus, Nietzsche celebrates women's power and beauty. He blames democracy for a debasing equality whose effect is to lower women with respect to both beauty and power.

(3) Finally, we turn to the sum of the three section numbers, 375, which is as significant and suggestive as the thematic correspondences we have just examined. It so happens that page 375 of the *Republic* is where both spiritedness (*thymos*) and philosophy are first mentioned (375a–e and 375e respectively).[21] That philosophy and spiritedness are mentioned together is no accident. As noted earlier, in the *Republic* as in *Beyond Good and Evil* the philosophers emerge from a larger (though still small) class characterized by its spiritedness. And philosophy itself—in Nietzsche's view and in the view of Nietzsche's Plato as well—proves to be an expression of the highest spiritedness. Nowhere else in the *Republic* are philosophy and spiritedness so clearly and notably linked as they are at 375. Nowhere else does Plato say something

---

21. Unlike the numbers we have just been considering, 375 is an "absolute" page number, a Stephanus number, and not, say the 375th page of the text. From a certain standpoint this might seem a troubling inconsistency on Nietzsche's part or, more likely, an argument against my interpretation. But it makes sense for Nietzsche, who means to be comprehensive in his philosophic project, to be comprehensive in his artistic playfulness as well.

so Nietzschean and so consistent with and important to the teaching of *Beyond Good and Evil*. At the risk of abusing interpretive hindsight I would suggest that no other number from the *Republic*, aside from the number of pages, could be more significant to Nietzsche than 375.[22]

Next let us attend to the specific parts of *Beyond Good and Evil* and their relations to the corresponding books of the *Republic*. In what follows I make no claim to exhausting the subject: the point of my broad and selective survey is to demonstrate parallelism for the sake of a narrower analysis of will to power in Chapter 9, though I also hope that it will prove useful to other scholarly explorations of Nietzsche's thought. Nor do I contend that the parallelism is complete. There is much in *Beyond Good and Evil* that is not in direct response to the *Republic* and much in the *Republic* that is not answered by *Beyond Good and Evil*. I do hold, though, that the parallels are so many and striking as to render *Beyond Good and Evil* a response to the *Republic in significant part*. Some parallels are sweeping and easy to see. Consider again, for example, the parallels between the two books' respective sixth chapters, each of which is devoted to identifying the true philosopher, distinguishing him from other types, and laying out the conditions that favor or undermine his proper development. Other parallels are subtler or ambiguous and necessarily less certain. At the risk of undermining the stronger evidence but with the hope that acknowledging the risk will diminish it, I will include some of the latter class so that readers may consider them for themselves.

We begin with the one part of Nietzsche's book that does not correspond to any discrete part of Plato's: the preface. Insofar as *Beyond Good and Evil* is Nietzsche's own *Politeia*, the preface (*Vorrede*) introduces but is not part of

---

22. Those who wish to pursue the significance of all four of *Beyond Good and Evil*'s numerical anomalies (not only the three repeated section numbers but also section 247a) might wish to consider that the sum of all four numbers, 65, 73, 237, and 247a, is 622 or 622a. Whether this is meaningful I'm not certain. But it may be worth noting that Stephanus page 622 (and there is only one such page number among the three volumes of dialogues) is the page that immediately follows the *Republic*, which ends on page 621. It is therefore a blank page—or, in light of Nietzsche's section 247a, perhaps we should say, a *silent* page. In section 247a Nietzsche contrasts German writing style, which takes little account of the ear or how writing *sounds*, with the style of antiquity, which most definitely did take the ear into account. He particularly dwells on the "*period*," which, "in the classical sense is above all a physiological unit, insofar as it is held together with a single breath." "*We*," Nietzsche says, "really have no right to the *great* period, we who are modern and in every sense short of breath" (emphases in the original). Might it also be worth considering that the silence of Stephanus page 622 is Plato's *greatest* period, the pause or breath between his two longest dialogues? For on page 624 begins the *Laws*.

the book. That it stands apart in this way makes it not just a starting point or a way into the book but a general statement. How telling, then, that Plato—and the *Republic* in particular—figure so prominently in the preface, even if Nietzsche never mentions the *Republic* (or any other dialogue) by name in *Beyond Good and Evil*. Barely a page into the preface Nietzsche attributes to Plato "the worst, most durable, and most dangerous of all errors so far . . . [the] invention of the pure mind and the good as such." Readers will recognize these "errors" as belonging to the *Republic* and will thus recognize that Nietzsche identifies the *Republic* as the chief or at least the most notable vehicle by which Plato set the West upon its painfully dubious course of two millennia. Nietzsche's indictment of Plato begins early.[23]

In fact, though, Plato and the *Republic* are invoked even earlier, in the opening line of the preface: "Supposing truth is a woman—what then?" What is this but an invocation of philosophic eros, a theme that figures so prominently in the *Republic*? Yet unlike the other reference to the *Republic*, this one—this most important reference, if indeed "the beginning is the most important part of every work" (*Republic* 377a–b)—expresses *agreement* with Plato, both in positing the philosopher as a lover[24] and in indicating the primacy of a single psychic force. (But shouldn't Nietzsche have opened not with eros but with will to power—unless, perhaps, eros somehow *is* will to power . . . ?) Prior to the indictment of Plato by name comes this anonymous embrace of Plato. How instructive that both stances appear in the preface, and in the different ways they do (name provided, name withheld)—and in the *order* they do. The visible face of Plato is dogmatic Platonism, which Nietzsche repudiates—or *would* repudiate if it weren't already dying. The hidden Plato, however, is Nietzsche's kin, not only with respect to ambition but also even with respect to the highest theme.[25]

---

23. In *Beyond Good and Evil* "proper," that is, not counting the Preface, Plato is referred to in seven sections—six times by name (7, 14, 28, 190, 191, 204), and once, in section 105, by uniquely clear implication: in 105 Nietzsche comments on the offensiveness to the free mind of the *pia fraus*. How interesting that the latter is the central reference of the seven: the central fact about Plato for Nietzsche is not what he was (the name "Plato" does not appear) but what he did, and what he did was lie. The name "Plato" appears seventeen times—four times in section 7, twice in 14, twice in 28, six times in 190 (including two mentions in Greek), twice in 191, and once in 204. As with the reference in section 105, the central of *these* is also a comment separating Plato from Platonism: it concerns Plato's secret love of Aristophanes.

24. Others have recognized this erotic and thus in some way Platonic character of Nietzsche's opening line. See Pippin, *Idealism as Modernism*, p. 360.

25. Platonic eros may be invoked even earlier than I have said, in the title of the book itself. What *is* "beyond good and evil"? The phrase appears several times in the body of the text, but

But wait . . . If Platonism is dying, and if Nietzsche's primary task is, as he says, to defeat the soul-sapping "democratic enlightenment," which is the movement that helped kill off Platonism (i.e., Christianity, or "Platonism for the people"), then *is* Plato really so central to Nietzsche's project? Indeed he is, for two reasons: First, Plato is Nietzsche's model. Whatever enemy he needs to overcome, Nietzsche means to legislate as grandly and as comprehensively as he thinks Plato legislated. And second, Nietzsche's enemy, the democratic enlightenment, is itself a species of Platonism, appearances notwithstanding. Or so he contends. Although it has waged war against "Platonism for 'the people,'" the democratic enlightenment proves to be but a different version of Platonism insofar as it seeks to overcome what it sees as a defective world by means of rational understanding and scientific-technological mastery.[26] The democratic enlightenment tends toward materialism rather than idealism, and in this it seems un- or anti-Platonic; but the source of its utopianism is the same spirit of revenge that gives rise to the idealism it opposes.[27]

It is with part 1, "On the Prejudices of Philosophers," that the textual parallels begin. Nietzsche's first chapter, like Plato's, is essentially destructive. Where Plato has Socrates finding fault with prevailing conceptions of justice and thereby paving the way for a fresh consideration, Nietzsche finds fault with past and present modes of philosophy and science and thereby paves the way

---

only once, in section 153, does Nietzsche speak in his own name of activity that is "beyond good and evil" (the other uses of the phrase appear in sections 4, 44, 56, 212, and 260): "Whatever is done from love [read: *eros*] always occurs beyond good and evil."

26. Among the chief defects of the natural world that the democratic enlightenment seeks to correct are inequality between human beings, differences between the sexes, suffering, and even mortality. The belief that the world can be known and even corrected by knowledge, along with the belief in the moral governance of the world, are in Nietzsche's view the legacy not only of Platonism but also, first, of Socratism. On the Socratic basis of both Platonism and the democratic enlightenment, see Dannhauser, *Nietzsche's View of Socrates*, pp. 85–86.

27. A final thought about the preface. The *Republic* has a sort of preface of its own, at least according to a traditional reading: namely, the *Cleitophon*, a short dialogue in which the title character, after praising Socrates for a number of his teachings, criticizes him for not revealing what justice is. Cleitophon wants answers, not questions. Nietzsche's preface, with its repudiation of dogmatism, reads almost as a precise response, as a Socratic countercharge, faulting philosophers as it were for giving *too much* in the way of answers. With dogmatism lying dead or dying and with strength acquired from the long fight against dogmatism, Nietzsche excitedly anticipates new and higher possibilities, possibilities that surely would have excited Socrates and Plato, too, notwithstanding their reservations about public philosophizing. Note also that *wakefulness* is cited as an effect of philosophy in both the brief *Cleitophon* (408c) and Nietzsche's brief preface, indeed, very nearly at the precise center of both writings. It is not mentioned again in either the *Cleitophon* or the whole of *Beyond Good and Evil*.

for the philosophy of the future. Indeed, it is possible to read Nietzsche as performing three such critiques in answer to Socrates' three critiques. (In each case the first critique begins a few pages into the chapter.) Where Socrates takes on the positions of Cephalus, Polemarchus, and Thrasymachus, Nietzsche deals specifically with ancient philosophy (sections 7–9), modern philosophy (10–11), and modern science (12–23). Even the order seems right: ancient philosophy corresponding to the ancient Cephalus; modern philosophy to Polemarchus, son of Cephalus just as modern philosophy is the heir of Platonism (heir, not just successor); and aggressive, materialistic, and proudly frank science to the aggressive and proudly frank sophist Thrasymachus. In both cases the third critique is longest and is aimed at the rising or newly ascendant power in the world. I am including as part of Nietzsche's discourse on modern science his deconstruction of the "'immediate certainties'" of modernity, false "certainties" that arise from grammatical habit and from the failure to doubt as deeply as one should—such beliefs as the unity of the self, the unity of willing, free will (and unfree will for that matter), and reified conceptions of cause and effect (16–21). While these beliefs are hardly unique to modern science—indeed, they are the ancient legacy of the evolution of consciousness and language—they are particularly important to modern science because they compromise its claim to be truly scientific. Modern science, like the "modern" Thrasymachus, believes itself to be far more honest and self-aware than it really is.

In fact, parallels are evident prior to these three critiques. Each book opens with a tableau that sets the problem of the entire text. The tableau in each case depicts a kind of arrest. Plato gives us Socrates caught and detained by Polemarchus. Nietzsche gives us a different Greek hero of knowing—Oedipus, a hero who, unlike the prudent Platonic Socrates, owned up to the ambition to rule—arrested by the Sphinx. Socrates, caught from behind by Polemarchus' slave, "*turned around* and asked him where his master was" (327b); Nietzsche, caught by "strange wicked, questionable questions," asks if it is any wonder that "we" should finally become suspicious, lose patience, and *turn around* impatiently" (emphases added).[28] Each scene depicts what Nietzsche calls "a rendezvous . . . of questions and question marks." The problem that each scene raises has to do with wisdom and power. For Plato,

---

28. Both Kaufmann and Hollingdale give us Nietzsche "turning *away*" rather than turning around. The German, however, is *umdrehn*.

the problem is how to overcome the (political) powerlessness of wisdom: "Could you really persuade [us not to detain you]," Polemarchus asks Socrates, "if we don't listen?" For Nietzsche, the problem is how to overcome the destructive power of wisdom or truth, or how to reconcile the passion for truth with life itself. In fact, though, Nietzsche's solution, entailing as it does a reinvigoration of philosophy (a reinvigoration and then some), also solves Plato's problem. By dint of finding or developing the strength to withstand the destructive power of truth, the strength to affirm all that is, Nietzsche's philosopher acquires the strength and the ambition to be a ruler—which suggests that in an important sense the problem of *Beyond Good and Evil* is the *same* problem as that of the *Republic,* that is, the problem of establishing philosophic rule. Nietzsche's solution, of course, differs from Plato's in a number of ways, chief among which, in Nietzsche's own estimation, concerns how much truthfulness can be publicly dared. Yet if Plato was not willing to take on what Nietzsche admits is a very grave risk, Nietzsche hints in section 1 that Plato understood the problem: it "*almost* seems to us," Nietzsche writes, "as if the problem [of the value of truth] had never even been put so far" (emphasis added). *Almost*. Plato did understand the problem. As Lampert points out, "*Beyond Good and Evil* itself suggests that Plato faced the question of the value of truth," even if he responded more cautiously than Nietzsche.[29] Finally, in light of the fact that Socrates was in the process of coming up from the Piraeus, having gotten there in the first place by going down (327a), and that his arrest was therefore the thwarting of an ascent, it may be worth noting that Nietzsche concludes his section 2 by declaring "in all seriousness" that he sees new philosophers—philosophers whose ascent can no longer be thwarted—"coming up."

There are three further parallels of note between the respective first chapters: First, it is amid his critique of ancient philosophy that Nietzsche pronounces that nature is without purpose, indifferent to its creatures, and without mercy or justice (9). This of course is a direct rejection of Cephalus' view, and it appears just where it ought to. This mention of justice is the first in *Beyond Good and Evil,* just as Socrates' exchange with Cephalus includes the *Republic*'s first mention of justice (330d). Note, too, that its being without mercy and justice is listed fourth, or centrally, among the seven characteristics that Nietzsche here ascribes to nature. And in the subsequent line, where

---

29. *Nietzsche's Task*, p. 21.

Nietzsche lists five characteristics of "living," "being unjust" falls third. In Plato, central placement normally indicates *thematic* centrality. This is certainly the case in the *Republic*. Is the same true in *Beyond Good and Evil*?

Second, and similarly, the first mention of will to power occurs in this same section, corresponding to the fact that sexual desire (which I am taking to be a representative, indeed the primary incarnation, of eros) is first mentioned and discussed by Cephalus.

And finally, just as Socrates ends book 1 of the *Republic* by admitting that his refutations of others haven't gotten him anywhere, so Nietzsche observes in the final section of part 1 of *Beyond Good and Evil* that "nobody has yet come close" to a proper understanding of psychology, that is, an understanding of psychology as "morphology and *the doctrine of the development of the will to power*" (23)—whereupon he dares those who can't resist to join him in undertaking just this kind of inquiry. (Socrates, too, entices his interlocutors by an appeal to a kind of hunger: he compares his foregoing inquiry, before a company of *hungry* young men, to the experience of a *banqueter* who has failed to enjoy the courses set before him.) The work of destruction having been accomplished, the time has come to build.[30]

Building is in fact the major theme of both Plato's and Nietzsche's second chapters. It is in book 2 of the *Republic* that Socrates begins to build the city in speech—and this only after first reflecting on the difficulty of the challenge and then justifying and explaining the construction procedure.[31] Similarly, Nietzsche's part 2, "The Free Mind" (or "Free Spirit"), not only builds toward some powerful and global claims, but also is primarily concerned with estab-

---

30. A final possible parallel between the respective first chapters is noted by McGuire in "Beyond Good and Evil." Book 1 of the *Republic* introduces us to a gathering with eleven guests, and "this is the only time in the *Republic* so many thinkers and philosophers are assembled." Correspondingly, in part 1 "Nietzsche 'gathers' eleven philosophers and thinkers together, who, while not talking to each other directly, engage in a sort of conversation with Nietzsche. These thinkers are: Schelling, Descartes, the Stoics, Kant, Copernicus, Boscovitch, Spinoza, Locke, Schopenhauer, Plato, and Epicurus."

31. See 368c–369a: "'Since we're not clever men,' I said, 'in my opinion we should make this kind of investigation of it: if someone had, for example, ordered men who don't see very sharply to read little letters from afar and then someone had the thought that the same letters are somewhere else also, but bigger and in a bigger place, I suppose it would look like a godsend ... if, of course, they do happen to be the same.... So then, perhaps there would be more justice in the bigger and it would be easier to observe closely. If you want, first we'll investigate what justice is like in the cities. Then, we'll also go on to consider it in individuals, considering the likeness of the bigger in the *idea* of the littler?'"

lishing the *possibility* of such construction. As well it might be, given part 1's demonstration of the near-impossibility of knowledge.[32] See, especially, section 36, in which Nietzsche proposes a thought experiment that aims at nothing short of knowledge about the world as a whole.[33] No such knowledge—indeed, no knowledge at all—can be absolute or beyond question, nor can it ever be entirely sure of its ground, for there is always a ground beneath the ground upon which one has rested. Nor does Nietzsche perform the experiment here. But one can infer from the book and from his mature work as a whole that he has performed the experiment to his own satisfaction, at least to a considerable extent, and that in doing so he has taken account of all the difficulties and limitations he identified in part 1 and has respected all of his consequent methodological rules (e.g., no superfluous teleology).[34] Looking beyond section 36 to the whole of part 2, one can say that Nietzsche teaches the principles of method and the character attributes necessary for construction, for what deserves to be called knowledge.

Three further parallels between the two second chapters stand out—two from the early sections of the chapters, one from the latter sections.

32. Some readers would dispute the *near-* in my formulation. Notwithstanding all that stands in the way of knowledge, though, Nietzsche proceeds as if he does know things; and it seems to me that he does so because he considers himself really to have knowledge—not absolute knowledge, perhaps not knowledge by older standards, but something nonarbitrary and based on the rigorous evaluation and interpretation of empirical phenomena and thus deserving to be called knowledge. For the argument that part 1 does not render knowledge impossible and that part 2 in fact aims to establish the possibility of knowledge, see Lampert, *Nietzsche's Task*, chap. 2. For a powerful alternative account that sees Nietzsche seriously but inconclusively wrestling with the implications of the supposed impossibility of objective truth—including the truth about will to power—see Dannhauser, *Nietzsche's View of Socrates*, pp. 259–69.

33. As a set of scientific instructions, this aphorism demands to be read in its entirety. The following excerpts, however, assuming one can recall something more of the passage as a whole, can at least establish the point I am trying to make: "Suppose nothing else were 'given' as real except our world of desires and passions, and we could not get down, or up, to any other 'reality' besides the reality of our drives—is it not permitted to make the experiment and to ask the question whether this 'given' would not be *sufficient* for also understanding on the basis of this kind of thing the so-called mechanistic (or 'material') world? I mean . . . as a more primitive form of the world of affects in which everything still lies contained in a powerful unity . . .—as a *pre-form* of life. . . . In the end not only is it permitted to make this experiment; the conscience of *method* demands it. Not to assume several kinds of causality until the experiment of making do with a single one has been pushed to its utmost limit. . . . Suppose, finally, we succeeded in explaining our entire instinctive life as the development and ramification of *one* basic form of the will—namely, of the will to power . . . then one would have gained the right to determine *all* efficient force univocally as—*will to power*. The world viewed from inside, the world defined and determined according to its 'intelligible character'—it would be 'will to power' and nothing else.—"

34. Lampert points out that Nietzsche meant to perform the experiment publicly in the *Hauptwerk* that he was planning but did not live to finish. See *Nietzsche's Task*, pp. 85–88.

Book 2 of the *Republic* begins with the "always most courageous" Glaucon pressing Socrates for a better defense of justice than he has yet given (357a). Assuming the ostensibly antagonistic stance abandoned by Thrasymachus (abandoned too easily, according to Glaucon), the young man levels his famous challenge: Socrates must explain why it is better to be just though one be martyred for it than to be unjust and rewarded. Similarly Nietzsche, after opening part 2 with a comment on the pleasantness of ignorance and simplification (a pleasantness that is justification enough for those who are not as adventurous and demanding as a Glaucon), turns in the second section (25) to a more serious message—a warning: "Take care, philosophers and friends, of knowledge, and beware of *martyrdom*" (my italics). The martyrdom of which he speaks is internal and spiritual, not political or physical. Yet it is martyrdom for being what the *Republic* itself eventually designates as the just man. In accepting that the philosopher risks martyrdom, Nietzsche effectively takes on the burden assigned by Glaucon to Socrates, to vindicate philosophy even in spite of martyrdom. Nietzsche's point may even be implicit in Plato: it is not inconceivable that Plato attaches to Glaucon's challenge an overtone unknown to the young man. For in Plato's view, as in Nietzsche's, philosophizing poses the danger of spiritual martyrdom: such is the implication of the great caution with which philosophy is treated (e.g., that dialectic be studied only at a mature age after years of moral and intellectual preparation). That Socrates is palpably happy does not contradict philosophy's potential to lead others to spiritual destruction.

Glaucon's challenge to Socrates is followed immediately by Adeimantus' addition, the focus of which is conventional opinion. Listen to those who praise justice, Adeimantus says—listen to "the speech of both the many and the eminent" (366b)—and you will find that men praise justice only for its extrinsic rewards. The implication of such praise is that in itself, justice is worthless—or worse. There is no indication that these lauders of justice really appreciate this implication. Thus Plato reveals for his readers the real meaning of conventional opinion and in the process indicates the need for philosophic inquiry to begin by investigating common opinion. Similarly, Nietzsche devotes his next section (26) to the need for exceptional or "choice" human beings to learn from "the crowd, the many, the great majority." Echoing perhaps the most famous language and imagery of the *Republic*, he proclaims of the exceptional human being, the one who seeks knowledge: "And he would go *down*, and above all, he would go 'inside.' The long and serious study of the *average* man . . . constitutes a necessary part of the life-history of every philosopher." Characteristically, though, and *un*like Plato's Socrates, Nietzsche signals his intense distaste for such investigation. Plato's cave is dark but not necessarily off-putting; Nietzsche's is dank.

Finally, just as it is late in book 2 of the *Republic* that Socrates introduces a guardian class into the city (374d), so it is in the final four sections of his own second chapter that Nietzsche introduces *his* highest class (41–44). In each case, moreover, the new class consists of philosophers. Socrates says the members of the highest class must be philosophers; as mentioned earlier, this is the dialogue's first mention of philosophy (375). Nietzsche, who has said much about philosophers already, says the members of the highest class must be *new* philosophers; this is the book's first mention of new philosophers: "A new species of philosophers is coming up: I venture to baptize them with a name that is not free of danger . . . *attempters* [*Versucher:* also *tempters* or *experimenters* or *essayists*]" (42). To be sure, Socrates' guardians are philosophers only as dogs are philosophers; but there turns out to be more earnestness in Socrates' playfulness than is apparent at that moment, in that the guardians will later prove to be true philosophers. Neither Socrates nor Nietzsche tells us here more than a small fraction of what we will ultimately learn about the philosopher's being and coming-into-being. But that only makes what *is* revealed even more striking. What we learn from these introductions to the philosopher as the highest human type is the crucial place and play of spiritedness in the philosophic nature. Plato reveals this by connecting Socrates' first mention of philosophy with his first mention of spiritedness (375), as we have already noted. Nietzsche reveals it with his reference to the danger and adventurousness of the new philosopher (42) and with his summary characterization of the new philosophers in the final aphorism of part 2: "Need I still say expressly after all this that they, too, will be free, *very* free minds [spirits], these philosophers of the future" (44).

Book 3 of the *Republic* divides thematically into three discourses of unequal length. So does part 3 of *Beyond Good and Evil,* "The Religious Essence" (*Das religiöse Wesen*).[35] The first and longest portion of *Republic* 3 is essentially a critique of prevailing modes of musical and gymnastic education (386a–410b).

---

35. Kaufmann renders this title as "What is Religious" for reasons given in a footnote (page 57). Hollingdale opts for "The Religious Nature."

The second consists in a brief, positive account of what a properly conceived musical and gymnastic education could accomplish, and how this right practice grows out of the balanced integration of two otherwise problematic (because imbalanced) things (410c–412a). The third portion is more narrowly political: having laid out the uses and abuses of various practices, Socrates and his interlocutors take up the question of who should rule, some of the devices the rulers should use, and some of the practices that must be adopted to keep the rulers from becoming corrupt (412b–417b). Each of these divisions is paralleled by Nietzsche.

(1) Where Plato gives us a critique of music and gymnastics, with special emphasis on purging poetry of unwholesome teachings, particularly about death and the afterlife, Nietzsche presents a critical analysis of the history of Western religion (45–55). (Is religion really comparable to music and *gymnastics?* Yes: both musical and gymnastic education turn out to be established "chiefly for the soul" [410c]. They constitute what moderns would call a religious education.) After a prefatory word about what's needed to reach the truth in such matters (45), Nietzsche proceeds to an analysis of actual religions of the past, not only Christianity but also ancient Greek religiosity and ancient Judaism (46–52); he then turns to contemporary atheism, interpreting it as the outcome of the internal logic of Christianity, modern philosophy, and the psychology of self-denial (53–55). Like Socrates, Nietzsche is essentially negative or critical here. To be sure, a critical analysis of *historical* moments is different from the Socratic critical analysis of Greek poetry and educational practice. But not so different, at least not functionally: each philosopher is analyzing the predominant given or pre-given reality in the interest of coming up with a new way that avoids the problems of the old. For Nietzsche, writing with an extensive historical knowledge and writing for readers who understand themselves as legatees of a long history, the reality with which one must deal is a historically formed reality.

(2) As Socrates' critique gives way to a brief statement of the good that a properly constituted musical and gymnastic program could produce, Nietzsche's historical critique gives way to a brief disclosure of "the ideal of the most high-spirited, alive, and world-affirming human being," the human being whose response to life is to "shout[] insatiably *da capo*" (56). (This brief glimpse of Nietzsche's ideal is followed by a brief sketch of how the world looks to the one who has embraced the ideal [57].) In each case, moreover, the way to the desired end entails the embrace of moments that are potentially

or actually undesirable. Socrates' recommended practice is combination of elements that, if not conjoined, would lead to undesirable outcomes: music without gymnastics would make the soul "softer than it ought to be"; gymnastics without music would yield cruelty and harshness. Nietzsche's ideal comes into sight only by "think[ing] pessimism through to its depths" and "look[ing] into, down into the most world-denying of all possible ways of thinking." These respective embraces of the potentially or actually undesirable may or may not be a parallel: there is a great difference between charting a middle or integrative course (Socrates' path) and finding one's way through and then out of the deepest abyss (Nietzsche's path). But the very difference is instructive and in a sense confirms the claim of parallelism: where Socrates teaches balance and moderation, not only here but elsewhere, Nietzsche celebrates singularity and extremism. Neither Socrates nor Nietzsche says very much about the desired end.

(3) It is in the final, most narrowly political, portion of the chapters that the parallels are most pronounced. The question at hand is who should rule. After (a) some brief discussion of methodological matters (concerning how to determine who should rule), and (b) a discussion that amounts to a celebration of civic piety (since the chief criterion for ruling is steadfast love of the city), (c) Socrates introduces a new social distinction and therewith a new ruling class, the true guardians, who are no longer to be assimilated with those who will now be called auxiliaries (414b),[36] whereupon (d) he teaches the need for a noble lie whose evident purposes are to inspire civic devotion and acceptance of one's place in the city. Then (e) he takes up questions pertaining to the ruling class, that is, who should be chosen for membership, on what basis (by what tests) they should be chosen, and in what way the rulers should live. A peculiar way of life is required for the highest class, since ordinary ways would be corrupting for these exceptional men. Apart from one instance of reordering within category (e) (which I will address below), Nietzsche proceeds in parallel fashion.

Nietzsche begins with (a) his own brief methodological discussion (concerning what's required to understand and appreciate religion) (58) and then (b) pays extraordinary tribute to the benefits of piety even among adherents of otherworldly religion: "It may be that until now there has been no more

---

36. The guardians are drawn from the ranks of the spirited. The same is true for Nietzsche's highest class, as we have seen: "Need I still say expressly after all this that they, too, will be free, *very* free minds [spirits], these philosophers of the future."

potent means for beautifying man himself than piety: it can turn man into so much art, surface, play of colors, graciousness that his sight no longer makes one suffer" (59).[37] At the start of section 61 (c) Nietzsche speaks of philosophers as rulers for the first time since the preface. Indeed, this is the first time since the preface that Nietzsche has spoken of any kind of rulers: "The philosopher as *we* understand him, we free minds [spirits]—as the man of the most comprehensive responsibility who has the conscience for the overall development of man—this philosopher will make use of religions for his project of cultivation and education, just as he will make use of whatever political and economic states are at hand." And just as Socrates introduces the noble lie immediately after designating his own ruling class, (d) Nietzsche turns immediately to the benefits of religion that are used by the philosopher "for his project of cultivation and education" (61)—benefits that are uncannily similar to the benefits Socrates attributes to his noble lie. This life-affirming religion, like the religion of gratitude of the ancient Greeks (49) or the religion of justice of early Judaism (52), would presumably also be more truthful than otherworldly religion. Even so, no religion can be simply truthful. A relatively truthful religion will still make up stories, though these stories need be no more false than the myth of the metals, the second part of Socrates' noble lie (414c). (Can one really doubt that Socrates holds the myth of the metals to be *essentially* true?)

Nietzsche divides the benefits of this affirmative religion—the benefits of *his* noble lie—into three categories, one each for three kinds of human beings. For the higher ranks of humanity, "for the strong and independent who are predestined to command, religion is one more means for overcoming resistances, for the ability to rule—as a bond that unites rulers and subjects and betrays and delivers the consciences of the latter . . . to the former." To those of a middle rank, religion offers preparation for future ruling through the refining and ennobling discipline of asceticism and puritanism. And to "ordinary human beings" "religion gives an inestimable contentment with their situation and type, manifold peace of the heart, an ennobling of obedience, one further happiness and sorrow with their peers and something transfigur-

---

37. Also see section 60, where Nietzsche pays the following extraordinary tribute to a religious tradition that he otherwise opposes: "To love man *for God's sake*—that has so far been the noblest and most remote feeling attained among men. . . . Whoever the human being may have been who first felt and 'experienced' this, . . . let him remain holy and venerable for us for all time as the human being who has flown highest yet and gone astray most beautifully!"

ing and beautifying, something of a justification for the whole everyday character, the whole lowliness, the whole half-brutish poverty of their souls." I am not aware of a better gloss on Socrates' noble lie than this.[38] Note, by the way, that Nietzsche's tripartite treatment of the different benefits of religion to the different classes of people corresponds perfectly to Socrates' class tripartition. Note, too, that this is the first time in either book that this class tripartition appears.[39]

As book 3 of the *Republic* concludes with a brief depiction of the guardians' way of life that is really about the dangers that threaten exceptional men (415d–417b)—consider that the justification for common property and living arrangements is entirely negative, that is, based on the dangers of private property and private attachments—so (e) Nietzsche devotes the final section of part 3 (62) to the dangers posed by "sovereign religions," that is, religions devoted above all to the happiness of ordinary human beings, to the best of men. Such religions, including Christianity, "gave comfort and courage to the oppressed and despairing," and other goods to other kinds of human beings. But they did this, indeed could only do this, by undermining the better –turned-out: "Stand all valuations *on their head—that* is what they had to do. And break the strong, sickly o'er great hopes, cast suspicion on the joy in beauty, bend everything haughty, manly, conquering, domineering, all the instincts characteristic of the highest and best-turned-out type of 'man,' into unsureness, agony of conscience, self-destruction—indeed, invert all love of the earthly and of dominion over the earth into hatred of the earth and the earthly—*that* is the task the church posed for itself and had to pose." In the same way that Socrates' guardians need to be protected against ordinary ways of life, Nietzsche's highest human beings must be protected against rule by or on behalf of the ordinary.

---

38. A final observation related to the noble lie, provided by McGuire: Socrates introduces his noble lie as "a Phoenician thing" (414c). At an earlier point in his own chapter, Nietzsche speaks of "the cruelty and religious Phoenicianism" of the Christian faith. For Nietzsche the Phoenician thing is Christianity (a *pia fraus*), not the religion he means to propound (a noble lie). (McGuire misidentifies the placement of Nietzsche's "Phoenicianism," inaccurately claiming correspondence with Socrates' "Phoenician thing.") Both the *Republic* and *Beyond Good and Evil* mention the Phoenicians only one other time (436a, 229).

39. Nietzsche had effectively presented another tripartite classification scheme earlier, in section 27, where he distinguished between three kinds of minds marked by three different tempos: *gaṅgāsrotagati, kūrmagati,* and *maṇḍūkagati* (as the Ganges moves, as the tortoise moves, and the way frogs walk, respectively; see Kaufmann's notes). This earlier tripartite classification may or may not correspond to the one I have been discussing, but Nietzsche does not present it as a basis for any political distinction, nor does he state that the categories are exhaustive.

It is only at the conclusion of part 3's final aphorism that we encounter anything comparable to Socrates' articulation of the criteria for membership in the guardian class. The criteria are implicit, but clearly so, in Nietzsche's summary indictment of Christianity's rule over Europe: "Christianity has been the most calamitous kind of arrogance yet. Men, [1] not high and hard enough to have any right to try to form *man* as artists; men, [2] not strong and far-sighted enough to *let* the foreground law of thousandfold failure and ruin prevail, though it cost them sublime self-conquest; men, [3] not noble enough to see the abysmally different order of rank, chasm of rank, between man and man—*such* men have so far held sway over the fate of Europe." From this condemnation we may infer Nietzsche's criteria for rule: the highness and hardness requisite to the great artist, the strength and far-sightedness to let fail and perish what must fail,[40] and the nobility to recognize and embrace hierarchy. As I noted above, these criteria are slightly "misplaced" vis-à-vis the *Republic*, appearing at the very end of part 3 whereas Socrates' corresponding discourse occurs a bit earlier. Perhaps this "inapt" placement means that the passage does *not* correspond to Socrates' discussion of the best means by which to determine which men deserve to become guardians (412e–413e). But an alternative explanation suggests itself. Perhaps Nietzsche has put his passage as close to Socrates' as he could. Socrates' means of determining which men deserve to rule consist "only" of finding men with an unshakable devotion to the city. Thus Socrates could adduce his methods early. Nietzsche, though, must wait, for he is testing for something far more exclusive and difficult to see. He could not lay out the tests for identifying philosophers until he had first given some indication of his extraordinary notion of what a philosopher is ("the man of the most comprehensive responsibility who has the conscience for the over-all development of man" [61]).

If there is any place that the parallelism between *Beyond Good and Evil* and the *Republic* would seem to break down, it is in their respective fourth chap-

---

40. In advocating that that which ought to perish be allowed to perish, Nietzsche is applying the principle proposed by Socrates near the culmination of his treatment of the guardians' musical and gymnastic education—which immediately precedes the sequence we have been examining (how to find the right men to rule, the complete guardians distinguished from the auxiliaries, the noble lie, etc.). Socrates poses the matter as a question to Adeimantus: Having provided the city with a medical and a judging art "which will care for those of your citizens who have good natures in body and soul," won't they "let die the ones whose bodies are [bad], and the ones whose souls have bad natures and are incurable, they themselves will kill?" (409e–410a).

ters. Book 4 of the *Republic* continues the thread of the preceding discussion. Indeed, book 4 marks the culmination of the inquiry, or seems to. Socrates reveals the definition of justice (not to mention the other three cardinal virtues) and, after determining that the soul is multiformed in a way that corresponds to the city, applies the definition to both soul and city and thereby establishes the goodness of justice in and to each. Nietzsche's part 4, by contrast, is just what its title promises: "Epigrams and Interludes," though it's worth noting that the apparent randomness of the aphorisms is mitigated by the fact that the great majority of them concern the soul. And while it is always safe to assume that any writing of Nietzsche's is constructed according to a literary and/or philosophic logic, part 4 is certainly not continuous with the preceding parts in the way that book 4 of Plato's book is with *its* preceding parts. What, then, are we to make of this anomalous part?

The character of part 4 is problematic only with respect to the kind of *Republic*-based interpretation I am offering here. If we forget about the *Republic* and concentrate only on the internal workings of *Beyond Good and Evil*, it makes sense that Nietzsche would proceed as he does, for part 4 can be seen as an interlude between two great divisions. Parts 1–3 concern what Nietzsche sees as the highest things, philosophy and religion. Parts 5–9 "descend" to the moral and political realms, exploring them in light of the discoveries of the first and "higher" part. In between, marking the separation, is part 4, a series of provocative brief aphorisms that connect with and illuminate various themes from elsewhere in the book.[41] But of course I *am* propounding a *Republic*-based interpretation. And while I do not think that my claim that Nietzsche's book is a response to Plato's hangs on a perfect parallelism—indeed, none of Nietzsche's parts matches up *perfectly* with its corresponding Platonic book—it is at least incumbent on me to consider part 4 in that light. So let me begin by offering for consideration the suggestion that part 4 of *Beyond Good and Evil* replies to book 4 of the *Republic* precisely by being so different, precisely by *not* responding through the use of parallel constructions. (Such a suggestion would be scandalous were it not for the fact

---

41. See Strauss, *Studies in Platonic Political Philosophy*, p. 176. The quotation marks above do not signify direct quotes from Strauss. An alternative interpretation of the relation between the two great divisions of the book is offered by Lomax, who sees the turn from philosophy and religion to morality and politics as an *ascent*: "In the light of Nietzsche's assertion that morality is the alpha and omega for philosophers, the earlier chapters can appear [rightly] to serve as handmaidens clearing the way for the later ones." *The Paradox of Philosophical Education*, p. 6.

that the other nine parts, including the Aftersong, do respond via parallelism.) As we have seen in connection with the earlier chapters, where Nietzsche holds a view that parallels Plato's (remember that "parallels" does not mean "agrees with"), he reflects this with a parallel construction. However, *and accordingly*, where Socrates propounds a formula or grounds an argument on a presupposition to which Nietzsche has no parallel—when Socrates offers a teaching that Nietzsche not only rejects but to which he also has no counterformula—he might well be responding advisedly by breaking form, that is, by abandoning parallelism. It so happens that the three most important elements of the teaching of *Republic* 4 meet that description.

The first of these elements is the definition of justice and indeed the definition of each of the other cardinal virtues—wisdom, courage, and moderation. Now Nietzsche certainly does have a teaching about the virtues. Part 7 of *Beyond Good and Evil* is true to its title, "Our Virtues." Interestingly, that part does correspond to the *Republic,* for Socrates can reveal what true virtue is only after he has explored the being and coming-into-being of the philosopher. But then what is it that Socrates is doing with his definitions of the virtues in book 4? It turns out that those definitions are, and could only be, definitions of *demotic* virtues, which is to say incomplete or not quite true virtues. This may be a key to understanding Nietzsche's part 4. Unlike Plato, whose prudence leads him to teach and defend as virtue that which is not true virtue, Nietzsche will have no part of such a thing. Where Plato has Socrates offer an edifying but untrue teaching, Nietzsche is silent. Or, rather, not silent, but, one might say, *musical.* For what is part 4 if not a musical interlude?[42]

The second element that finds no counterpart in *Beyond Good and Evil* is Socrates' demonstration of a "structural" likeness between the city and the soul. This presupposition, introduced as a hypothetical assumption in book

---

42. As Michael Gillespie has demonstrated, several of Nietzsche's later works are constructed according to plans borrowed from standard musical forms. *Twilight of the Idols,* for example, is a sonata in prose. See "Nietzsche's Musical Politics," pp. 117–49, esp. 117–21. Lomax interprets the whole of *Beyond Good and Evil* as a musical composition, though he does not claim that the book is constructed according to any standard musical *form*. And Eden finds part 9 of *Beyond Good and Evil* to be "a series of speeches ordered within a sonata-like form." See Lomax, *The Paradox of Philosophical Education,* p. 3, and Eden, *Political Leadership and Nihilism,* p. 286n173. To my (very limited) knowledge part 4 is not constructed according to any standard musical form. If it is music, it is perhaps a pastiche (my thanks to Joel Schlosser for the suggestion)—which, come to think of it, seems the most appropriate choice in any event, given its function in the work and its substantive relation to *Republic* 4.

2, is of course what allows book 4's conclusions about the meaning and goodness of justice in the individual. That Nietzsche rejects this likeness is evident from a comparison of his separate comments on societies and on the soul. Societies are indeed, or by nature ought to be, tripartite, as we have seen. The soul, though, has many more "parts" than three. The soul is a "social structure of the drives and affects" (12), each of which wants to rule (6), but these drives and affects do not sort naturally into anything like a tripartite set of categories. So even if Nietzsche were in a position to respond here to Socrates' teachings on justice and the other virtues, his rejection of the city-soul analogy would still keep him from doing so in a parallel fashion.[43]

The structure of the soul—the question of tripartition versus (let us call it) supermultiplicity—is the third matter on which Nietzsche's teaching does not parallel that of book 4 of the *Republic*. It is worth noting that, just as Socrates' treatment of the virtues in book 4 turns out to be provisional and is corrected in book 7, so, too, his treatment of the soul in book 4 is provisional and is corrected in book 9, where, among other things, he "complicates" the soul's structure by effectively allowing for numerous subparts and endless variety of inner conflict and strife. This, too, keeps Nietzsche from anything comparable to the discussion in *Republic* 4, for there is little in what Socrates teaches that is not based on the tripartite soul. Moreover, Nietzsche's alternative hypothesis, that is, the soul as supermultiplicity, may help explain not only why his fourth chapter doesn't parallel Plato's but also why it is structured as it is. For, to repeat, however opaque the order of any of Nietzsche's writings, it would be very unwise to suppose that an order is lacking. If the soul is a multiplicity, as Nietzsche proclaims in the central section of part 1 (12); if the soul is the overarching, structuring concern of *Beyond Good and Evil*; and if Nietzsche's book really is a reply to Plato's; then it would be most appropriate to construct the part of his book that corresponds to the part of the *Republic* that proclaims the tripartite soul in a way that represents *his own* conception of the soul. More simply put, as the soul for Nietzsche is a supermultiplicity of competing drives, part 4 of *Beyond Good and Evil* is constructed as a supermultiplicity of competing thoughts. If this is true, then in a sense Nietzsche *does* follow Plato. Like Plato, he mirrors the soul's structure in another structure. The other structure for him is not a city, but a text.

43. But even if he rejects the city–soul analogy, couldn't Nietzsche have treated the relation between the city and the soul here, thereby paralleling Plato in an appropriate way? He could have—and arguably he does, as I will suggest presently.

8

NIETZSCHE'S POLITEIA, II

Book 5 of the *Republic* marks the beginning of a digression. But it's a "digression" that continues for three full books, and rather than some sort of side trip it takes us to the defining peaks of the dialogue. For these reasons book 5 constitutes a new beginning of the entire dialogue. This is confirmed at the start of the chapter, with a scene that reprises Socrates' "arrest" at the start of book 1. Similarly, part 5 of *Beyond Good and Evil* marks a new beginning. Having first explored philosophy's limits and then its possibilities (parts 1 and 2, respectively); having then established the possibility of philosophy as rule, that is, as rule via religion (part 3); and after a refreshing interlude (part 4); Nietzsche turns to the many questions, implications, and *possibilities* that flow from what he has already done. Each of the remaining parts sets out to reveal what must be known for the sake of Nietzschean philosophic legislation.[1] Part 5 inquires scientifically into the history, nature, and varieties of morality for the sake of developing a new morality that accords with nature instead of denying it. Just as Socrates is interrupted only a paragraph or so into book 5 with the demand that he provide wanted information ("'a whole section of the argument, and that not the least'" [449c]), so Nietzsche only several lines into part 5 makes his own demand for information (a demand that, like Socrates, he will now begin to satisfy): "One should own up in all strictness to what is still necessary here for a long time to come . . . : to collect material, to conceptualize and arrange a vast realm of subtle feelings of value and differences of value . . . all to prepare a *typology* of morals" (186). Nietzsche then goes on, in the same aphorism, to suggest that the knowledge that is still wanting requires that the inquirer overcome parochialism. This, too, echoes book 5 of the *Republic*, with its shockingly antiparochial proposals.

Book 5 of the *Republic* is most notable—certainly it is best known—for

---

1. Lampert makes a similar claim about parts 5 to 9, though with different particulars in some cases. See *Nietzsche's Task*, pp. 146–47: "The final five chapters of *Beyond Good and Evil* present a reasoned case for a new morality served by a new politics."

Socrates' three waves of paradox: equal nurture and treatment of the sexes, communism of women and children among the guardians, and, most controversially and most seriously, rule by philosophers. If part 5 of *Beyond Good and Evil* is any kind of reply to Plato, we should expect to find some kind of parallel to the three waves. And so we do.

Before turning to the waves themselves, let us take note of something common to each of them—or more precisely, something common to Socrates' arguments for each of them. Namely, the waves are justified and advocated on the grounds of their supposed naturalness. This, too, marks a new beginning. Nature (*physis*) had been mentioned numerous times in the prior four books of the *Republic*. But it is only in book 5 that nature is actually and explicitly adduced, however questionably, as the standard by which to settle such important questions. Similarly, nature becomes a standard, and is investigated as such, only in part 5 of *Beyond Good and Evil*. The word "nature" and its cognates appear many times in parts 1 through 4, but never in this new, deeper way. One finds in the earlier parts many references to the "nature" of this or that person or type, as well as references in which "nature" seems to refer to "what is," so that, for example, Nietzsche can praise ancient Greek religion for its stance toward nature or criticize other religions as "anti-natural" (49, 51). One even finds Nietzsche addressing those who claim to have understood nature (21–22) and to have adopted it as their standard (9). Yet his response to these claims is so negative as to make one wonder whether nature properly understood *could* serve as a standard. Consider his mockery of the Stoics: "Imagine a being like nature, wasteful beyond measure, indifferent beyond measure, without purposes and consideration . . . how *could* you live according to this indifference?" (9). In part 5, by contrast, nature is investigated as a standard and finally, if subtly, embraced as such. The key moment is in section 188, where, after referring to "nature" or the "natural" six times, each time in quotation marks, Nietzsche drops the quotation marks in the seventh and final instance, which happens to be a statement about "the moral imperative of nature." The placement of this passage with respect to the whole of part 5 also happens to correspond to the point in book 5 of the *Republic* where Socrates introduces nature as the standard by which to judge the goodness and possibility of the three waves (453a–456d).

Now to the waves themselves. The "biggest and most difficult, the third wave" (472a), is also the clearest, so let us begin there and work backward. No reader of the *Republic* and *Beyond Good and Evil* will need to be reminded that each book embraces rule by philosophers. What readers may not have noticed, though, is that it is not until the latter sections of part 5 that Nietzsche actually advocates and makes a case for rule by philosophers. In part 3, as we have seen, he had spoken of the philosopher as the cultivator and educator of humanity whose tools include religions as well as "whatever political and economic states are at hand" (61)—just as Socrates had used religion and the rest in fashioning his city in speech in book 3 of the *Republic*. But just as Socrates doesn't explicitly pronounce the need for philosophic rule until late in book 5, contending that there will be no end to human ills until this need is met (473d–e), so Nietzsche waits until the same moment to explicitly proclaim philosophers the answer to the grave problems of the age: "Where, then, must we reach with our hopes? Toward *new philosophers*; there is no choice" (203). There are also two interesting and revealing differences between the two texts—differences that do not compromise the parallelism, however. One of these is "local" or time-specific, the other global if not cosmic in scope. First, whereas Socrates presents philosopher-rulers as the only solution to what are presumably age-old ills, Nietzsche presents them as the only way to stop and reverse a situation that is worsening. The philosopher's task is to halt the *"over-all degeneration of man,"* his diminution into "the perfect herd animal." Hence the particular urgency of Nietzsche's task. Second, whereas Socrates speaks of the philosopher as the solution to the ills besetting a particular society, albeit any society, Nietzsche looks to philosophers for nothing less than redemption for all humankind. By "teach[ing] man the future of man as his *will*" and "prepar[ing] great ventures" the new philosophers will "put an end to that gruesome dominion of nonsense and accident that has so far been called 'history.'" As different from each other as these two distinctive features are, they are alike in raising the stakes and creating a great sense of urgency.

Socrates' second wave concerns private attachment and possession (i.e., love as possession) and advocates a new way. As the second of the three waves that occupy the whole of book 5 this can be thought of as the center of book 5. Accordingly, Nietzsche takes up the same theme and arguably advocates his own new way at the center of his own fifth chapter. Part 5 contains eighteen sections. Its precise numerical center therefore falls between the ninth and tenth sections (194 and 195). Section 194 is an extended discourse on the meaning and varieties of possession and wanting to possess (*Habenwollen*). Nietzsche opens with this assertion: "The difference among men becomes manifest not only in the difference between their tablets of goods" but "even more in what they take for really *having* and *possessing* something good." He then provides examples of ways of possessing, exemplifying varying degrees of refinement, from four realms, beginning with the possession of *women* by men and ending with the possession of *children* first by parents and then by "teachers, classes, priests, and princes." The range of examples becomes progressively truncated. In the case of possessing women, Nietzsche articulates three different degrees of refinement. Least refined are those men who "consider the mere use of the body and sexual gratification a sufficient and satisfying sign of 'having,' of possession." A second type, "with a more suspicious and demanding thirst for possession . . . wants subtler tests, above all in order to know whether the woman does not only give herself to him but also gives up for his sake what she has or would like to have." Finally, there is a third type, who "does not reach the end of his mistrust and desire for having even so . . . He wants to be known deep down . . . He feels that his beloved is fully in his possession only when she no longer deceives herself about him, when she loves him just as much for his devilry and hidden insatiability as for his graciousness, patience, and spirituality." By the time Nietzsche gets to possession of children, he mentions only one degree of refinement, and only the least refined, leaving the discourse incomplete. As he sometimes does, Nietzsche ends the section by breaking off his discourse: "So it follows . . ." The "it" that follows is the unspoken but precise center of part 5. What follows, then? A reasonable conclusion is that what follows is what was missing from the preceding, that is, that there are other, more refined ways of possessing children than the ways explicitly cited, and what these more refined ways are.[2]

The likelihood of this interpretation is heightened by what next appears in the text. Section 195 seems to mark a new turn in the chapter. Its subject is announced in its opening words: "The Jews—." Nietzsche's ostensible focus in 195 is the Jews' significance as the initiators of "the slave rebellion in morals." Yet Nietzsche's view of the Jews is a tangled and complicated business with many themes. One of these is that the Jews (for Nietzsche) are a people whose characteristic virtue—indeed, the source of their strength (a strength greater than that of any other "race now living in Europe" [251])—is loyalty

---

2. I owe this reading to Lampert. See *Nietzsche's Task*, pp. 163–67.

to one's fathers.³ The Jews, in other words, stand out in Nietzsche's view for their emphasis on and skill at possessing children; and in this they can teach humanity a source of great strength. But when one considers the ideal Nietzsche is teaching in *Beyond Good and Evil*—that is, freedom of mind as laid out in part 2—one must conclude that Nietzsche regards the way of the Jews with respect to possession, however admirable, as nevertheless contravening his ideal by fettering the mind in accordance with the dictates of tradition. In light of this, one must also conclude that in silently pointing to new, more refined ways of possessing children, Nietzsche is also effectively *advocating* a new way of possessing children, just like Socrates.⁴

And not only children: applied by analogy to the soul, Socrates' second wave advocates a more refined possession and, even more so, a more refined *seeking of* or *wanting* possession. The second wave, at whatever level one interprets it, teaches an overcoming of crude egoism and a new, more refined love of one's own. (It is important to appreciate that the communism of the *Republic* does not entail overcoming love of one's own but rather expanding and refining one's conception of what *is* one's own and what it means for something to be one's own.) Whether Nietzsche also means to speak to this subtler, more interior form of possession in this section is unclear. He refers explicitly only to "external" possessions (women, peoples, children). Then again, so does Socrates. Of course, by propounding the city–soul analogy, Socrates virtually instructs us to interpret the waves with reference to the soul. Nietzsche, on the other hand, seems to reject that analogy. Nevertheless there is good reason to suppose that Nietzsche, too, speaks to the soul even as he appears to be speaking only to social phenomena. However little he credits the city–soul analogy, he still locates the same forces in both city and soul; he still concedes that the shape and character of the city will have a decisive, even formative and mimetic impact on the soul; and he consequently still applies the same basic principles to the construction of all regimes, political or psychic. Like

---

3. See *Zarathustra* I, "On the Thousand and One Goals": "'To honor father and mother and to follow their will to the root of one's soul'—this was the tablet of overcoming that another people hung up over themselves and became powerful and eternal thereby."

4. How extensive the new way would be is an open question: Nietzsche does not suppose, as so many of his liberal and Left admirers do, that freedom of mind is a universal possibility. But in this, too, he is consistent with Socrates, whose communism is prescribed only for the guardian class. (Socrates doesn't speak to the living arrangements of the other classes.) Under Nietzsche's scheme the example of the Jews may thus remain instructive for the majority of humanity.

the *Republic*, *Beyond Good and Evil* is about the best regime, the best regime *as such*, which is to say the best regime at every level.

Of the three waves, the first is probably the one that is least obviously paralleled in *Beyond Good and Evil*. It is not until part 7 that Nietzsche addresses the question of male and female nature in any sustained way. Yet what he does offer in the sections of part 5 that roughly correspond to Socrates' first wave can nevertheless be reasonably understood as a response to Socrates' teachings—or perhaps I should say, to *Plato*'s teachings, since Nietzsche's text in this case parallels the *form* of Socrates' case more than its specific substance. Socrates' first wave, equal treatment of men and women, ostensibly propounds the oneness of human nature in the face of its apparent twoness. Correspondingly, the early sections of Nietzsche's part 5 effectively propound the oneness of morality in the face of its apparent multiplicity. Having issued his call for a truly scientific investigation of morality in section 186, Nietzsche takes the first step himself in 187, listing in no apparent order some ten different unconscious purposes for which different moralities have been created. (This multiplicity of purposes surely indicates a corresponding multiplicity of moralities, for Nietzsche teaches that it is in such purposes that the real essence of philosophies and worldviews lie.) Yet no sooner has he established the multiplicity of moralities—going far beyond what others have understood—than he turns to what all moralities have in common. "*Every morality is*"—these are the first words of section 188 (emphasis added). And what every morality *is* is not just some set of formal features, for example, "every morality is a set of rules according to which . . ." Rather, what every morality *is* is something emphatically substantive, something with a distinctive character. "Every morality is, as opposed to *laisser aller*, a bit of tyranny against 'nature'; also against 'reason.'" That this interpretation of morality is not merely formal is indicated by the fact that it is at odds with various other understandings, among which, and the one Nietzsche cites, is utilitarianism. This, too, has some relevance to the *Republic*, for the reasons Socrates adduces on behalf of the first wave are nothing if not utilitarian. (To look upon men and women only with respect to what jobs they can perform, with no regard for their different propensities or for the complexities of their attraction to each other, seems the very stuff of Nietzsche's "utilitarian dolts" [188].) To be sure, Nietzsche's reduction of a multiplicity of moralities isn't substantively similar to Socrates' ostensible reduction of the sexes. Except, perhaps, that what Nietzsche's moralities reduce *to*—namely, "a bit of tyranny against 'nature,' also against 'reason'"—is a fine description of Socrates' reduction of the sexes in the name of a kind of morality. Which makes Nietzsche's discourse an apt comment on Socrates'.

Finally, having just argued that Nietzsche parallels Socrates in reducing apparent multiplicity to oneness, I must add that he also, in a different sense, reduces the same multiplicity to a two-ness. Such at least is one reading of his list of ten purposes for which moralities have been created. For beneath that multiplicity arguably lies a polarity that is expressed explicitly in the last pair[5]: "Some moralists want to vent their power and creative whims on humanity; some others, perhaps including Kant, suggest with their morality: 'What deserves respect in me is that I can obey—and you *ought* not to be different from me'" (187). There are moralities of command and moralities of obedience. This twoness is consistent with, indeed a reflection of, the central theme of Nietzsche's thought: will to power. On the one hand, Nietzsche sees will to power as the unitary driving force of all life. This is reflected in his "reduction" of every morality to tyranny. On the other hand, his readers will also know that will to power is expressed differently among different kinds of people, and that while at one level these expressions are endlessly various, at a deeper level they can be understood in terms of a pair of opposing poles: strength versus weakness, or command versus obedience. But does this twoness have any positive relation to the *Republic*? It may well. For Socrates' argument for the sameness of the sexes, that is, the oneness of human nature, is so simplistic and abstracts so obviously from common experience as to point the reader's awareness to the *differences* between the sexes; and there is more than a slight correlation in Nietzsche's work between command-versus-obedience on the one hand and man-versus-woman on the other.

Nowhere are the parallels between *Beyond Good and Evil* and the *Republic* more evident than in part 6. In each case the main thrust of the discourse is to establish the possibility and reality of true philosophers. This requires that true philosophers be distinguished from pretenders; that explanations be given for the low repute in which philosophers are held and for the too frequent corruption of those who might have become philosophers; and that the conditions be laid out for the philosopher's successful coming-to-be.

Book 5 of the *Republic* ended with a discourse on the philosopher that

---

5. Lampert, *Nietzsche's Task*, p. 151.

might have seemed adequate. The philosopher was defined as a lover of learning (and was thereby distinguished from lovers of sights and hearing) and as a knower (and was thereby distinguished from mere opiners). Yet Socrates begins book 6 by acknowledging that there are still "many things left to treat for one who is going to see what the difference is between the just life and the unjust one" (484a). The guardians must not be *blind*, or, which amounts to the same thing, must not lack knowledge. Moreover, they must also not lack *experience* or fall short in any part of virtue (484c–d). Next comes an account of the qualities that constitute "philosophic natures," followed by an expression of skepticism by Adeimantus to the effect that "of all those who start out on philosophy . . . most become quite queer, not to say completely vicious," while the few decent ones become useless (487c–d). Socrates agrees with Adeimantus but distinguishes between those who are falsely thought to be philosophers and the few who truly are philosophers. Each of these elements is repeated in the first aphorism of part 6 of *Beyond Good and Evil* (204). Nietzsche opens the question of "the respective ranks of science and philosophy" by asserting "that only *experience* . . . can entitle us to participate in the discussion of such higher questions of rank, lest we talk like *blind* men about colors" (first emphasis in the original, the second added). There then follows an explanation for the "current" low standing of philosophy; and just as Socrates acknowledged that Adeimantus was right to disdain most who are called philosophers, so Nietzsche acknowledges that scientific men are right to disdain philosophy: he attests to "the wretchedness of the most recent philosophy itself that most thoroughly damaged respect for philosophy." He concludes not by citing the existence of philosophers worthy of the name (in this he paints a more dire picture than did Socrates) but by effectively insisting on the *possibility* of true philosophers. Whatever the current state of philosophy, philosophy nevertheless deserves—and by its nature is directed—to rule.

Socrates turns next to the perils facing those who have the requisite nature to become philosophers—and so does Nietzsche. Socrates: "'Now consider how many great sources of ruin there are for these few'" (491b). Nietzsche: "The dangers for a philosopher's development are indeed so manifold today that one may doubt whether this fruit can still ripen at all" (205). And Nietzsche, like Socrates, locates several of these dangers among the potential philosopher's virtues.

Socrates then goes on to explain what happens to philosophy when "she" is abandoned by the best men. Under these circumstances "unworthy men" will come "and disgrace her" (495c); and these will be followed by other men who are unworthy though merely small rather than corrupt. The latter, whom Socrates refers to as "manikins," are characterized by the smallness of the issue of their "consummation" with philosophy: "When men unworthy of education come near her and keep her company in an unworthy way, what sort of notions and opinions will we say they *beget*? Won't they be truly fit to be called sophisms, connected with nothing genuine or worthy of true prudence?'" (496a; emphasis added). Both these types are paralleled in Nietzsche: the first in his reference to the "philosophical Cagliostro and pied piper" (205), the second in his discussion of "the scientific man"—a man who is honorable but still not worthy of philosophy, a man who is revealed by his inability to *"beget"* or "give birth" (206).

Having gone through all this, Socrates accounts for the "very small group" who engage in philosophy worthily (496a–497a), that is, those who have somehow avoided or withstood the dangers he has already cited, and then lays out the conditions required for the protection and nurture of such people (497a–498d). I find no clear parallel to these in Nietzsche's part 6, at least not in discrete ways in the "appropriate" sections. Perhaps this is because for Nietzsche the true philosopher is so rare a phenomenon that there can be no such sociological analysis. Socrates says that his own case is so rare as not to be worth mentioning. For Nietzsche, it seems to me, *every* case of a true philosopher is that rare. Or perhaps Nietzsche's silence here reflects the fact that the new philosophers whom he heralds are yet to come.

Socrates' next major step is to restate the need for philosopher-rulers (499b). Nietzsche does the same. He does so by clear implication in section 207, where the philosopher is shown to be not only a grand ruler—"the *philosopher* . . . the Caesarian cultivator and cultural dynamo" who employs the scientist or scholar as "an instrument" and slave—but a *needed* ruler: he is not only a director, a means, but also a "goal . . . conclusion and sunrise," a "complementary man in whom the *rest* of existence is justified" (207).

After restating the need for philosopher-rulers, Socrates suggests that it would be difficult but not impossible for philosophy to gain respect among the currently hostile many (499d–500b). Nietzsche effectively does the same. It would be difficult because true philosophy would be *assertive* philosophy, and assertiveness is just what the current age cannot accept: "When a philosopher suggests these days that he is not a skeptic . . . everyone is annoyed" (208). This annoyance is itself an expression of something deeper, "the European sickness," an exhaustion and paralysis of the will. Yet this sickness can be, in fact will be, cured—which means that Nietzsche, too, outlines the way in which the many can be disabused of their dislike of philosophy. The way out begins with politics: Nietzsche looks forward to a burgeoning Russian menace that would force Europe "to resolve to become menacing, too." With this would begin an era of "great politics" and a "new warlike age," the effect of which would be, or at least could be, the development of "another and stronger type of skepticism," "the skepticism of audacious manliness," a skepticism more favorable to a philosopher who claims to pronounce truths.

Next, Socrates speaks of the philosopher as one who models himself after the divine (500b–d). He concludes that " 'it's the philosopher, keeping company with the divine and the orderly who becomes orderly and divine, to the extent that is possible for a human being.' " Corresponding to this is Nietzsche's lengthier disquisition in sections 210 and 211, where various traits are cited that add up to a final portrait of philosophers as those who "determine the Whither and For What of man": "With a creative hand they reach for the future, and all that is and has been becomes a means for them, an instrument, a hammer." As Socrates likens the philosopher to his conception of the divine, so Nietzsche does to *his*. (And to ours: Nietzsche's philosophers are assigned the work of the Biblical God.)

Socrates next declares that philosophic rule would require a "wip[ing] clean" of the social landscape (501a). He goes on to explain what philosophers must look to in "produc[ing] the image of man" (501b). This is paralleled by Nietzsche's argument in section 212 that the philosopher, "being *of necessity* a man of tomorrow and the day after tomorrow," must oppose "the ideal of today," must apply the knife vivisectionally to the chest of the virtues of his time and discover a *new* greatness, determining what constitutes greatness by looking to society and its weakness. Philosophers have always had to act against their times. What that means today, though, is something unprecedented. Today's world is a world of specialities; therefore "a philosopher—if today there could be philosophers—would be compelled to find the greatness of man . . . precisely in his range and multiplicity. . . . Today the taste of the time and the virtue of the time weakens and thins down the will. . . . In the philosopher's ideal, therefore, precisely strength of the will, hardness, and the capacity for long-range decision must belong to the concept of 'greatness.' " Finally, today "only the herd animal receives and dispenses honors in Europe" and one makes war on the rare and high; therefore "today the concept of greatness entails being noble, wanting to be by oneself, being able to be different, standing alone and having to live independently."

Finally, Socrates launches a discourse that will take him through the remainder of book 6 and all the way through book 7. The subject is philosophic education, or cultivation, and those fit for it: "'Now that this discussion has after considerable effort reached an end, mustn't we next speak about what remains—in what way and as a result of what studies and practices the saviors will take their place within our regime for us and at what ages each will take up each study?'" (502c–d). It turns out that among the tests given to identify potential true philosophers is one that has not yet been mentioned. In addition to all that has already been specified, the person must "be able to bear the greatest studies" (503e); above all, he must be tenacious enough to labor at "the greatest study," "the *idea* of the good" (505a). The good lies beyond the reach of Socrates' interlocutors—even his *opinion* of the good lies beyond their reach ("'it looks to me as though it's out of the range of our present thrust to attain the opinions I now hold about it'" [506e])—but Socrates is willing to tell about it indirectly. He concludes book 6 with two of his famous images, the Sun and the Divided Line. Here we know not to expect too obvious a parallel from Nietzsche. Nietzsche virtually began *Beyond Good and Evil,* after all, by referring to "the good in itself" as "the worst, most durable, and most dangerous of all errors so far." But if Nietzsche rejects the good in itself, he does not reject the existence of a hierarchy of studies. Where Socrates speaks of "the greatest studies," Nietzsche talks of "the highest problems" (213). And where Socrates locates the greatest of these studies beyond the reach of his companions, Nietzsche asserts that "the highest problems repulse everyone mercilessly who dares approach them without being predestined for their solution by the height and power of his spirituality." Nietzsche doesn't name the highest problems here. Yet if they do not include the good in itself, they still warrant being compared to "the 'court of courts,'" a phrase that isn't dissimilar in spirit from the way that Socrates talks about the good.

Or perhaps Nietzsche *does* name, or at least point to, the highest problems. And in so doing perhaps he does offer a kind of response to the two images. According to the demands of a strict parallelism Nietzsche should respond to the Sun image, if he does at all, toward the end of part 6. Now it turns out that Nietzsche does make what can be understood as a reference to the sun in part 6. This appears not in section 212 or 213, however (213 being the final section of part 6), but in section 207, as part of his restatement of the need for philosopher-rulers (see above). We have already taken note of some of Nietzsche's language, particularly his more "redemptive" claims (the philosopher as *goal* and as *justifier* of the rest of existence). Another phrase he uses to describe the philosopher is "*Ausgang und Aufgang*"—which Kaufmann translates as "conclusion and sunrise." (The literal translation is, "going out and going up.") And in the next line he refers to the philosopher as "a begetting and first cause." Now, to repeat, this is in section 207, not 213. But consider the following. Nietzsche begins section 213 with the words, "What a philosopher is." What *is* a philosopher? He is a sunrise. He is a begetting and first cause, a creator of the world in which humanity lives.[6] He is other things too, of course. But in all that he is—as goal, as justifier, as complementary man and as creator of worlds—he is both beyond the reach of ordinary understanding and beyond—indeed the source—of the world he created. Or to put it in the language Socrates uses at the conclusion of the Sun image, he is "beyond being, exceeding it in dignity and power" (508b).

Nietzsche stands no less opposed to Socrates' claims about the possibility of "pure" knowledge (i.e., knowledge that is unmediated, disinterested, and complete) than he does to his teaching about the good in itself. Thus the Divided Line, at least insofar as it suggests the possibility of such knowledge, should be as problematic for him as the Sun. (Virtually the whole of part 1 of *Beyond Good and Evil* can be read as Nietzsche's repudiation of this possibility and virtually the whole of part 2 as Nietzsche's presentation of his counterteaching, i.e., the kind of knowledge that *is* possible, and how.) Yet the Divided Line does more than *represent* thinking. Precisely by doing that it also *promotes* and *teaches* thinking: by representing the full range of thinking and the relations among the kinds of thinking, it *cultivates* the mind of one who reflects on it. (In this it is like the Cave image, which is its immediate sequel.) Recall that the Divided Line and the Cave are offered in the service of a larger project. They belong to Socrates' effort to lay out "in what way" and through "what studies and practices the saviors will take their place within our regime." Now consider the last part of the last section of Nietzsche's part 6, beginning with the following: "For every high world one must be born; or to speak more clearly, one must be *cultivated* for it" (213). Nietzsche then goes on to reflect on how this cultivation is to have been accomplished and then,

---

6. Regarding the philosopher as creator of worlds, see the final line of Nietzsche's account of *Beyond Good and Evil* in *Ecce Homo*.

finally, on what virtues need to have been cultivated if one is to have a right to philosophy. The number of virtues he lists is eight, which is the same number of items depicted by the Divided Line[7]—one more reason to suspect that Nietzsche's discourse on the cultivation of the philosopher be read as his response to the Divided Line as an image *of,* and an image that *promotes,* the cultivation of the philosopher.

A final observation from part 6. Readers of the *Republic* do not doubt that Socrates is portrayed by Plato as a philosopher. Readers of *Beyond Good and Evil,* by contrast, often believe that Nietzsche considers himself to be what he seems to tell us he is: a free mind or spirit, perhaps a very free spirit and herald of new philosophers, but not a philosopher himself. The title of part 6 is "We Scholars," not "We Philosophers." Yet it seems to me that Nietzsche *is,* and understands himself to be, a philosopher—and that he says as much at the start of section 213. "What a philosopher is, that is hard to learn because it cannot be taught: one must 'know' it, from experience." Yet Nietzsche *does* know what a philosopher is. Thus he tells us, implicitly but clearly, that he knows it from experience—that he is a philosopher. (Notice, too, that among many descriptions of the philosophers of the future in section 210, almost all of which is written in the future tense, two observations are made in the present tense.) Just as Zarathustra stops talking about preparing for the superman and effectively takes up the superman's task himself, so does Nietzsche reveal himself as a philosopher in the book that "says the same things as *Thus Spoke Zarathustra* but differently, very differently."[8] But it is not only Zarathustra that Nietzsche emulates in this way. There is also a connection here between the Nietzsche of *Beyond Good and Evil* and the Socrates of the *Republic.* For both Nietzsche and Socrates present themselves as something less than true philosophers—Nietzsche because he diminishes himself, Socra-

---

7. The Divided Line has only four segments, but each segment refers to two things, that is, a level of being and the corresponding mental faculty. Here are Nietzsche's eight virtues: "Many generations must have labored to prepare the origin of the philosopher; every one of his virtues must have been acquired, nurtured, inherited, and digested singly, and not only [1] the bold, light, delicate gait and course of his thoughts but above all [2] the readiness for great responsibilities, [3] the loftiness of glances that dominate and look down, feeling separated from the crowd and its duties and virtues, [4] the affable protection and defense of whatever is misunderstood and slandered, whether it be god or devil, [5] the pleasure and exercise of the great justice, [6] the art of command, [7] the width of the will, [8] the slow eye that rarely admires, rarely looks up, rarely loves."

8. From a letter to Burckhardt, September 22, 1886, quoted in Kaufmann's "Translator's Preface," p. x, and Lampert, *Nietzsche's Task,* p. 2.

tes because he idealizes the philosopher. Each is ironic in his self-presentation. Nietzsche's irony, however, has been less widely seen than Socrates'. Perhaps this makes him the truer Socratic. However that may be, we have encountered another parallel of sorts.

Book 7 of the *Republic* is the culmination of the dialogue's long digressive inquiry into philosophy. Virtually the entire chapter treats the education of those intended for philosophy. Under this heading fall the Cave image, a course of studies, and a program specifying what those being bred to philosophy ought to be doing at what age. Even the final comment of the book, prescribing the rustication of everyone over the age of ten (541a), can be understood as an educational measure in the sense that those who have not begun the proper educational program early in life have been rendered ineducable in the way that is wanted. There is much in all this programmatic detail that has no specific counterpart in part 7 of *Beyond Good and Evil*. And there is much in Nietzsche's part 7 that does not obviously answer Plato. But these unanswered and "de novo" details are secondary to, indeed required by,[9] the two books' *shared intention* to teach what is most needful for philosophic education. In fulfilling this intention each book also gives its clearest portrayal yet of what philosophy is—not the philosopher and his nature (which was the particular focus of the sixth chapters), but philosophic activity itself: what drives it and in what it consists. So at the most important level Nietzsche's seventh chapter does respond to Plato's. Nor is the response "merely" general or thematic. Nietzsche may not offer anything that parallels Socrates' program of learning, but he does nod to and echo other details—too many, again, to dismiss as accidental coincidence.

Looked at with respect to book 7 of the *Republic*, part 7 of *Beyond Good and Evil* can be divided into three main subparts. Sections 214 to 226 parallel or otherwise respond to the Cave image. In these thirteen sections Nietzsche addresses the distinctive character of what one might think of as the modern cave and comments, like Socrates, on the hostility of cave dwellers toward higher spirits and the relation between true and demotic virtue. Sections 227 to 231 address the actuality of philosophy, eyeing it with severity even while maintaining Nietzsche's extraordinary elevation of philosophy. This severity

---

9. Another feature I would assign to both Plato and Nietzsche is "logographic necessity" (*Phaedrus* 264b): the shape, form, and details of a discourse are dictated by the larger intention.

corresponds to and rebuts Socrates' idealization of philosophy, an idealization that reaches its apex in Plato's book 7. Nietzsche doesn't only take a severe look, he specifically rejects—and signals his grounds for rejecting—precisely such idealization. And whereas in part 1 he exposed the prejudices of *other* philosophers, that is, defective philosophers, here he takes a hard look at his own, or genuine, philosophy. Finally, sections 232 to 239 present what Nietzsche announces as "a few truths about 'woman as such' . . .—*my* truths" (231). These last sections are most anomalous with respect to the *Republic*. Socrates offers no corresponding discourse on women. Yet it is possible to connect Nietzsche's discourse to that of Socrates in light of its location in the text.

We begin with sections 214 to 226. Nietzsche makes no reference in these sections to a cave or any other kind of dark place or prison, unless it is his mention in section 214 of "our labyrinths." After announcing that "it is probable that we, too, still have our virtues" (214), albeit different ones from those of "our grandfathers," Nietzsche devotes the next dozen sections to the virtues of the modern world. The virtues of the present day are neither the virtues of "our grandfathers" nor the virtues of those among whom Nietzsche numbers himself in 214, that is, "We Europeans of the day after tomorrow, we first-born of the twentieth century." It is in the course of his investigation of the modern moral consciousness—of the modern *cave*—that Nietzsche makes the observations that echo Socrates' presentation of the Cave image. In sections 218 and 219 Nietzsche explores the hostility felt by "good, fat, solid, mediocre spirits" toward "higher spirits and their tasks" (218) and the dangerous consequences of that hostility, namely, the "moral judgments and condemnation" of "the spiritually limited against those less limited" (219). This echoes—resoundingly—Socrates' depiction of the deadly hostility of the cave dwellers toward the one who had escaped and then returned wanting to liberate them: if they were able, Socrates asks, "wouldn't they kill him?" (517a).

Also in section 219 we encounter Nietzsche's "proposition" pertaining to the relation between what one might call the higher virtues and the lower ones: namely, "that high spirituality itself exists only as the ultimate product of moral qualities; that it is a synthesis of all those states which are attributed to 'merely moral' men, after they have been acquired singly through long discipline and exercise, perhaps through whole chains of generations." Our concern here is not this higher spirituality itself (whose content Nietzsche goes on to describe) but its relation to "merely moral" qualities. High spirituality, presumably including the highest spirituality, the spirituality of the philosopher, though decidedly "beyond" merely moral virtue, has nevertheless grown out of it—which means, among other things, that moral virtue would seem to be a developmental prerequisite for the highest, supramoral virtue. In this Nietzsche perfectly echoes the teaching of the *Republic*. According to Socrates it is in the philosopher alone that one finds the virtues in their true form, yet the virtues have developed so only because they were preceded by moral virtues. True virtue is knowledge, whereas demotic or moral virtue is based on opinion. And such knowledge will only be possible, says Socrates *amid his presentation of the Cave image*, if the vicious parts of one's nature "were trimmed in earliest childhood" (519a–b), that is, if the person has received an education in moral virtue—presumably the musical education that he outlined in books 2 and 3. (Recall that those chosen for an education in philosophy were drawn from the ranks of those who had already received the education of books 2 and 3.) Note, too, that by assigning true virtue to the philosopher alone, leaving others only with demotic or moral virtue, Socrates effectively asserts that different kinds of people are suited to and should be taught different kinds of virtue—something that Nietzsche teaches in more than one place but that he especially stresses here in part 7: "Moralities must be forced to bow first of all before the *order of rank;* their presumption must be brought home to their conscience—until they finally reach agreement that it is *immoral* to say: 'what is right for one is fair for the other'" (221).

Insofar as Socrates' Cave symbolizes the all-too-human love of comforting illusion and consequent aversion to the higher reaches of knowledge and spirituality, Nietzsche emphatically subscribes to its teaching. Its pretensions to the contrary notwithstanding, modern civilization is no less cavebound than any of its predecessors. Yet modern civilization enjoys (though that may not be the word for it) an important distinction vis-à-vis its predecessors. It knows about the Cave. Its historical and anthropological science has discovered that the multitude of past civilizations were governed by a multitude of moral teachings, each of which claimed for itself and thus claimed for that civilization a special place in the scheme of things. (This scientific discovery may itself have been promoted by modern civilization's multiple sources of morality. Men who "are determined . . . by *different* moralities" will more easily recognize the contingency of their morality; they are like planets whose orbits are "determined by two suns" [215].) Thus, if modern man still resides in a cave in the sense described above, in another sense he has indeed left the cave: no longer enclosed within a particular horizon, he no longer believes his society's place and values to be divinely sanctioned.[10] (With this he has lost a source of ennoblement.) This loss at the hands of science was the climactic theme of Nietzsche's early essay on "The Uses and Disadvantages of History for Life." It is also addressed in *Beyond Good and Evil*—at just the right place.

Having made the parallel points regarding the hostility of the many toward the "higher spirits" and the relation between moral virtue and high spirituality, Nietzsche makes a series of observations regarding what seem to me to be consequences of modernity's discovery of and partial escape from the cave. (Partial escape, but also a deeper imprisonment, insofar as modernity falsely believes its discovery of the cave to constitute, ipso facto, liberation.) In section 222 Nietzsche speaks of modern man's self-contempt. Such contempt would seem to be a natural consequence of the loss of self-esteem that comes with the de-divinization of one's own civilization. In section 223 he addresses nineteenth-century homelessness, the fickleness of nineteenth-century man, and his "moments of despair over the fact that 'nothing is becoming'": "again and again a new piece of prehistory or a foreign country is tried on, put on, taken off, packed away, and above all *studied*." What is this, too, if not the result of the same de-divinization or decentering? It is only a civilization that has understood the contingency of its own ways that dabbles in and experiments so with other ways. And in section 224 Nietzsche examines—and names—the quality that lies at the heart of these phenomena, and other phenomena besides: "The *historical sense*" to which Europeans lay claim as their specialty has brought it about that "the past of every form and way of life, of cultures that formerly lay right next to each other or one on top of the other, now flows into us 'modern souls,' thanks to this mixture." The historical sense is nothing *but* the awareness of one's civilization as just another civilization and one's membership in it as an utterly contingent affair. My purpose here is not to explore these features of modern life but to link Nietzsche's treatment of them to the corresponding part of the *Republic*. Yet one further point needs to be made, for it conditions Nietzsche's political project: unlike in the treatment in the essay on history, Nietzsche now sees that the loss brought about by scientific history and the discovery of the cave is also an opportunity: "'the spirit' sees its advantage in this." Nietzsche as sculptor

---

10. I have capitalized "Cave" when referring to Plato's image and its meaning. When "cave" is not capitalized, it refers to the reality to which Plato's image points, that is, dependence on meaning-giving myths.

(62) has more variegated stone at his disposal than Plato did and thus enjoys a greater range of artistic possibility.

Nietzsche concludes his response to the Cave in section 226,[11] where, like Socrates, he speaks of himself and those like him as "men of duty," even while, *un*like Socrates, he labels himself and his fellows "immoralists." Even this dissimilarity belies a deeper similarity, though: for Socrates certainly was seen as an immoralist by Athens—and rightly so, from the Athenian standpoint: every philosopher is an immoralist, for every philosopher stands free of the reigning moral consciousness and propounds something new (212). Nietzsche simply pronounces what Socrates had not quite successfully hidden and what, according to Nietzsche, Plato had succeeded in hiding. What *is* the duty of these immoralists? An explicit answer isn't given. But an explicit answer isn't needed. The "world that concerns *us,* in which we fear and love," Nietzsche says, is a "world of subtle *commanding* and subtle *obeying*" (final two emphases added). Surely the duty, at least a part of the duty, is to rule, just as Socrates' philosopher is obliged to "go down." It is not clear what other duty men like Nietzsche could be called to in a world of commanding and obeying. It isn't clear why else he would say, "Occasionally . . . we dance in our '*chains*'" (emphasis added).

In sections 227–31 Nietzsche turns to philosophic activity proper. The philosopher is both a *knower* and a *maker*. Nietzsche has already spoken powerfully of the philosopher as maker, that is, as a creator of values. (It is by means of this value creation that he commands and legislates.) The philosopher's making follows necessarily from his knowing, though the necessity lies in *his* nature rather than in the nature of knowing.[12] Here in part 7 he turns to the business of knowing, to the roots of the desire to know. In this Nietzsche responds directly to Socrates, who provides in book 7 of the *Republic his* most complete account of the philosopher's activity and coming-to-be. Yet whereas Socrates gives an idealized account, ascribing to the philosopher a power and

---

11. What about section 225? Those seeking a Platonic parallel in every section of *Beyond Good and Evil* might want to consider whether that section's contrast of "*our* pity" with the pity of the prevailing modern morality—"it is pity *versus* pity"—responds to the pity that Socrates' enlightened one would feel for his former fellow prisoners back in the cave (516c, 518b).

12. Whether the philosopher's making is part of philosophy per se or, rather, is something distinct from philosophic activity proper is hard to say. Not everything a philosopher does, even if it is unique to him and clearly follows from his philosophizing, necessarily qualifies as philosophic activity. Consider, for example, Socrates' unique behavior as a citizen, that is, his moralizing and exposing the pretensions of the allegedly wise, as recounted in the *Apology.*

transperspectival purity that he himself evidently does not have,[13] Nietzsche goes as far as he can in the other direction: mindful of the dangers of idealization, he explicitly repudiates it in favor of a severe analysis that, while not denying the divine/devilish heights of philosophy, locates its roots in bestial depths.

In section 227, the central section of part 7,[14] Nietzsche identifies *Redlichkeit*—usually rendered as "honesty," it also includes overtones of probity or integrity—as the singular virtue of free minds. Philosophers, we recall, are free minds, *very* free minds, even if they are also more than that. So in addressing the knowing of free minds or in speaking of "all desire to know" (229) Nietzsche is speaking, indeed speaking particularly, of the philosopher as knower. No sooner has he identified this virtue, though, than he attends to the possibility of its growing weary. The answer to this danger is to "remain *hard*" and to "dispatch to her assistance whatever we have in us of devilry," by which is meant such resources as disgust with clumsiness, choosy curiosity, spiritual will to power, and, at the center of Nietzsche's list (just as it appeared at the center of two of Socrates' lists), "our adventurous courage." This call for hardness and "devilry" is part of Nietzsche's effort to "see to it that it [honesty] does not become our vanity, our finery and pomp, our limit, our stupidity." The danger is real and ever-present, for "every virtue inclines toward stupidity; every stupidity, toward virtue." After addressing what he sees as an example of such stupidity, English utilitarianism (228), Nietzsche takes up cruelty, identifying its spiritualization as the source of "almost everything we call 'higher culture'" and particularly philosophic inquiry: "even the seeker after knowledge forces his spirit to recognize things against the inclination of the spirit, and often enough also against the wishes of his heart—by way of saying No where he would like to say Yes, love, and adore—and thus acts as an artist and transfigurer of cruelty" (229). This cruelty is not merely incidental to philosophy or an attendant cost. Cruelty accounts for the will to know. The pleasure of cruelty, cruelty exercised against oneself, accounts for—it *is*—the pleasure of philosophic inquiry: "Indeed, any insistence on profundity and thoroughness is a violation, a *desire to hurt* the basic will of the spirit which unceasingly strives for the apparent and superficial—in all

---

13. As noted in Chapter 1, there is a significant distance between what Socrates *says* about the philosopher and what he himself evidently *is*.

14. With its two sections numbered 237 (or 237 and 237a in Kaufmann's translation), part 7 has twenty-seven sections, of which 227 is the fourteenth.

desire to know there is a drop of cruelty" (emphasis added). (This is not to say that the whole of the philosopher's pleasure can be understood as the pleasure of cruelty: presumably the philosopher is pleased in various ways by the results of some of his inquiries and by his conquest of various mysteries. But the pleasure of *the philosophic inquiring itself*—that *does* seem on Nietzsche's account a case of the pleasure of cruelty, cruelty turned against oneself.)

Having made this case (229) and after offering further clarification (230, first part), Nietzsche returns to the dangers of euphemism or idealization. Such words as "love of truth, love of wisdom," and the like belong to "the old mendacious pomp, junk, and gold dust of unconscious human vanity," a vanity that obscures what "must again be recognized." What must be recognized is "the terrible basic text of *homo natura*" (230),[15] and the reason it *must* be recognized is that recognition of this text is the precondition of man's translation "back into nature." To perform this translation is the task, the "strange and insane task," that Nietzsche has assigned to himself. Thus Nietzsche's eschewing "mendacious pomp," that is, his repudiation of Socrates' idealization of philosophy, is far more than a matter of taste or pride. It is necessary to the naturalization of humanity. Perhaps this is why Nietzsche does not speak of himself and his kind as philosophers in this part of the book: the word itself might come too close to being the gold dust of vanity. Notice that "love of wisdom" (*Liebe zur Weisheit*) is included among the examples of such, is in fact the central example. Indeed, unlike "philosophy," which at least has some subversive overtones out of which Nietzsche is able to spin a new definition, "love of wisdom" would seem to be hopelessly compromised by vanity. The phrase appears at only two other places in *Beyond Good and Evil*: section 295, where, as praise of Dionysus, it is nevertheless scorned by the god as "venerable junk and pomp"; and section 5, in connection with Spinoza, where a different but even more devastating critique is made: "consider the hocus-pocus of mathematical form with which Spinoza clad his philosophy—really 'the love of *his* wisdom,' to render that word fairly and squarely."

In the passage just cited Nietzsche convicts Spinoza of dishonesty. The dishonesty lay not in the interested motives that gave rise to his philosophy but in his denial of such motives. Thus it is not a self-indictment when Nietz-

---

15. "Terrible" (*schreckliche*) is omitted from Kaufmann's translation. It does appear in Colli and Montinari, *Nietzsche Werke*, and in Hollingdale's translation.

sche launches his discourse on women, which concludes part 7, by announcing that what follows "are after all only—*my* truths" (231). But what is this discourse even doing here? I have already made one suggestion, regarding the significance of section 237, though that can hardly suffice to explain the whole of sections 232 to 239. Two additional explanations suggest themselves, neither of which precludes the other. First, it seems likely that in speaking about women Nietzsche is also speaking about truth, that is, about truth as it presents itself and, more significantly, as it eludes those who court it. He began the book by hypothesizing that truth is a woman and states the matter definitively—in part 7 in fact: "In the end she [truth] is a woman: she should not be violated" (220). Socrates, we should recall, speaks of philosophy in just such a way in books 6 and 7 of the *Republic*. Insofar as this discourse on women is in fact about truth and how it must be courted, it makes good sense for Nietzsche to place it in the latter sections of part 7.

But even if Nietzsche is *also* speaking about truth, he is *primarily* speaking about women—or, more precisely, how women appear to him ("*my* truths"). Why? And why here? An answer is suggested in section 230, where Nietzsche announces his self-appointed—no, his fated—task, the recovery of nature. This task belongs to philosophy, which alone has the power to uncover and then to affirm nature. Recall that to translate man back into nature requires in the first instance that the philosopher uncover the eternal basic text of *homo natura*. The text of *homo natura* is undoubtedly a very big book. But one of its most important parts—its central chapter, I would suggest[16]—is the fact of human bisexuality, of differences between the sexes, and all that follows therefrom.

There is no need to go into too much detail here, other than to say that Nietzsche clearly credits sexual attraction and sexual energy with being the source of enormous aspiration and creativity—indeed, an *indispensable* source of aspiration and creativity, for it is in this realm that one's will to power is most deeply and resoundingly stimulated. Eros, if you like, is the

---

16. Sexuality appears more than once at the center of Nietzsche's writings. The central section of part 4 of *Beyond Good and Evil* concerns marriage and concubinage (123). The central section of part 8 asserts that "there are two types of genius: one which above all begets and wants to beget, and another which prefers being fertilized and giving birth.... These two types of genius [which are evident among peoples as much as among individuals] seek each other, like man and woman; but they also misunderstand each other—like man and woman" (248). And the central section of book 5 of *The Gay Science* (363), written the same year as *Beyond Good and Evil*, is titled, "How Each Sex Has Its Own Prejudice About Love."

primary instance of will to power and hence a necessary stimulus of a broader and more variegated will to power. (This echoes what we discovered about eros' relation to Rousseau's desire for extended being.) Indeed, eros is paradigmatic of will to power insofar as man's will to power and feeling of power "fall with the ugly and rise with the beautiful" (*Twilight,* Skirmishes, 20). But eros isn't so lovely. The reason that sexual attraction is so necessary and powerful a stimulant to will to power is that between man and woman there exists an "abysmal antagonism," "an eternally hostile tension" (238)—at least where man is still man and woman still woman, that is, where something of the basic text of *homo natura* has been preserved or uncovered. Which is precisely why the differences between the sexes must not be denied. Sexual energy, which owes so much to the differences between the sexes, originates in the depths of the soul but animates and informs the heights of the soul: "The degree and kind of a man's sexuality reach up into the ultimate pinnacle of his spirit" (75). Heat rises. So Nietzsche's placement of a man's discourse on women here, in the latter sections of part 7, makes sense after all. Part 7 as a whole, like book 7 of the *Republic,* treats the coming-to-be of philosophy. For Nietzsche, philosophy, as the most spiritual expression of will to power, requires that will to power be enlivened by sexual tension, which in turn requires that the differences between the sexes be maintained. There can be no spiritualization if there is nothing to spiritualize. Knowing this, Nietzsche tends to the survival and perpetuation of philosophy by defending its wellspring. Nor is it only philosophy that would be served. Sexual difference and tension would also regenerate more ordinary men and women (239) and would help reverse "the general *uglification* of Europe" (232).[17]

17. That the discourse on women appears in part 7 instead of part 5, where it would correspond to the first wave, suggests that Nietzsche cares more about the philosophic than the civic effects of sexual differentiation. Plato's first wave, of course, can be read allegorically as a teaching about the soul, that is, that the fully developed soul must develop and employ and integrate both "masculine" and "feminine" virtues and capacities. Nietzsche, by addressing moralities instead of the sexes in the first third of part 5, cannot respond to this teaching. Perhaps, though, by addressing moralities and exposing the willful or tyrannical nature of all moralities, Nietzsche *is* doing something comparable to what Socrates was doing. Socrates was seeking to overcome a "masculinism" that inhibited the development of potential philosophers. (By "masculinism" I mean the contempt for dialectic as "womanish" mere talk.) For Nietzsche, presumably as a result of democracy or Christianity, the danger of masculinism has been replaced by the danger of squeamishness toward the kind of spirited command exemplified by the notion of morality as tyranny.

As book 8 of the *Republic* descends from the peaks of philosophy to the lowlands of politics—*defective* politics—so part 8 of *Beyond Good and Evil* takes account of the all too imperfect "Peoples and Fatherlands" that figure most importantly in the European present and (hoped for) future. Socrates treats four regime types, in descending order of decency: timocracy (or timarchy), oligarchy, democracy, and tyranny, though the latter isn't addressed in earnest until book 9. Nietzsche treats four peoples: the Germans, the Jews, the French, and the English. It is not clear that any order of decency is implied by this order, nor would such an order really make sense. Unlike Socrates, who judges the four defective regimes in light of their closeness to the *kallipolis* from which they have descended (in both senses of the word), Nietzsche looks toward the *future*. The four peoples are treated entirely from the point of view of what might be made of Europe in the years to come. Nietzsche seeks European unification—on a ground of new nobility—as the beginning of the creation of a new global humanity. The sculptor works with the materials at hand, and these four peoples are the most important of Nietzsche's materials in his role as would-be founder and legislator.[18]

If Nietzsche focuses primarily on peoples and fatherlands, however, he also speaks, perhaps even more powerfully, to regime types. His critical analysis of contemporary Europe is by necessity an analysis of burgeoning *democracy*. And his analysis of the prospects for a nobler future takes its bearings from the possibilities and limits imposed by a democratic reality. In light of book 8 of the *Republic,* Nietzsche's treatment of democracy and the future that might succeed it is notable for two features. First, just as Socrates sees democracy as peculiarly susceptible to tyranny (564a), so Nietzsche observes a growing tendency toward tyranny in modern Europe (242). His reasons are the same as Socrates', namely, democracy's permissiveness and variety. Second, just as Socrates observes that the kind of philosophic enterprise he and his interlocutors have been engaging in is probably only possible in a democracy, owing to democracy's motleyness and diversity of human types—democracy, says Socrates, uniquely offers the philosopher a "general store" of regimes (557d)—so Nietzsche makes his own similar acknowledgment. He, too, suggests that democracy, at least *modern* democracy, offers conditions uniquely

---

18. Lampert provides a persuasive account of Nietzsche's political project, his project for a new Europe as the leading edge of a new global civilization, and the specific significance of the Germans, the Jews, the French, and the English in the requisite founding. See *Nietzsche's Task,* chap. 8.

favorable to genuine philosophy. The suggestion is not explicit but is clearly implied by democracy's susceptibility to tyranny. Tyranny for Nietzsche can mean many things, including rule by a philosophic aristocracy. And he insists on just this breadth of applicability in the present case: "The democratization of Europe is at the same time an involuntary arrangement for the cultivation of *tyrants*—taking that word in every sense, including the most spiritual." The most spiritual tyrant, of course, is the philosopher (9). So even as he makes the same point that Socrates makes, that is, the susceptibility of democracy to brutish tyranny, he also (like Socrates?) speaks to the prospect of democracy's giving way to aristocratic philosophic rule. Nietzsche finds on the shelves of late modern Europe the materials with which to build his own (cosmo)polis.

In book 9 of the *Republic* Socrates continues to investigate the tyranny that succeeds democracy and at last makes good on his promise to compare the lives of the most unjust and just of men, who turn out of course to be the tyrant and the philosopher. In part 9 of *Beyond Good and Evil* Nietzsche argues for what would appear to modern eyes as tyranny and then addresses the characteristic experiences of the philosopher—*only* the philosopher, though the philosopher, as we have noted, is also ipso facto a tyrant. Nietzsche has already addressed the philosopher's nature, his virtues, his development, and his task. What remains to discuss is the philosopher's characteristic experience—the experience, as Nietzsche has it, of the highest nobility (*Vornehmheit*). (Nietzsche's substitution of nobility for justice as the highest rung of human attainment is itself worthy of note and will be discussed in Chapter 9.) Appropriately, the inquiry ends with the highest and most personal of its revelations.

In the first half of part 9 Nietzsche gives the culmination of his political teaching: an argument for aristocracy. That the political argument precedes the revelatory discourse on the nobility of the highest human type suggests architecturally what Nietzsche also states explicitly: that the political argument is made for the sake of something suprapolitical. The "enhancement of the type 'man'" has always required an aristocratic political and social structure (257), and a healthy aristocracy must believe itself—correctly—to be the end for which the rest of society ought to exist (258). For Nietzsche as for Plato, the highest purpose of politics and even the highest purpose of their respective political discourses is to promote the excellence of the most potentially excellent. (Characteristically, the point is made more subtly and more gently by

Plato than by Nietzsche. It is implied by Socrates' effectively ignoring the education and way of life of ordinary people in the *kallipolis* as well as by the closing lines of book 9 of the *Republic*, where the foregoing long night's construction of a city in speech is justified by its serving as a model by which the individual—the *aristocratic* individual—may order his soul [592a–b].)

Although it makes perfect sense for Nietzsche to proceed as he does in part 9, his procedure at first seems anomalous from the standpoint of the parallelism between *Beyond Good and Evil* and the *Republic*. If he were simply replying to Plato, he should have made the political argument that occupies the first half of part 9 earlier. Or maybe not. For although Socrates certainly does construct his city in earlier books of the *Republic*, his true constitutional principles arguably don't become clear until book 9. I say this for two reasons. First, there is ample reason to believe that Socrates understands the regime sketched in the earlier books, the regime marked by communism of women and children among the ruling class, to be impracticable and even undesirable.[19] Second, as the various names of regime types imply, what most fundamentally determines a regime is the identity of those who rule. Thus if Socrates favors aristocracy, that is, rule by the wise, then the full meaning of that regime—its constitutional principles—will not begin to emerge until the aristocracy itself is examined and understood. And in addressing the philosopher and the tyrant in book 9 Socrates is doing just that. The examination and comparison of the philosopher and the tyrant is on its face something apolitical, an inquiry into *individuals*. But the character of these individuals makes this inquiry the culmination of the *Republic*'s political teaching. The difference between Nietzsche and Plato here is that whereas Plato has Socrates consider the cases of the two most powerful claimants to aristocracy, Nietzsche, living amid the apparent entrenchment of democracy, must take up the matter at a more basic level and argue for aristocracy in the first place.

Parallels or echoes of book 9 of the *Republic* are scattered throughout part 9 of *Beyond Good and Evil*. These textual indications are, as the earlier ones were, mostly small and unremarkable when looked at singly. Yet as was also the case in the earlier parts, they are significant when considered in their totality.

19. This is not the place to make the case, but it is difficult not to conclude that Socrates argues insincerely with respect to the first and second waves. The strength of his arguments depends on the neglect of things that should have been very hard to neglect and that, indeed, he elsewhere does not neglect, that is, the body and all the psychological, sexual, and social consequences thereof.

In the opening sections of part 9 we find some subtle nods to the *Republic*. Let us consider three of them. First, very early in book 9 Socrates returns to the tripartite soul (introduced in book 4) and introduces further divisions. What had earlier appeared to be a single desiring part of the soul is now divided into three subparts, the lowest of which, "the beastly and wild part" (571c), being the ruling element in the tyrant's soul. In the first section of part 9 Nietzsche insists on the "hard" truth about the origins of aristocratic society. Those who became aristocrats did so because they were strong and predatory enough to conquer, strong and predatory at the deepest level: "their predominance did not lie mainly in physical strength but in strength of the soul—they were more *whole* human beings (which also means, at every level, 'more whole *beasts*'" (257; final emphasis added). What is striking here is not so much the corresponding mentions of beasts as the corresponding assertions that beastliness belongs to the tyrant and even to the philosopher. Socrates, of course, suggests that the philosopher has learned to tame the beast within and thus seems to depict the philosopher as a philosopher in spite of his beastliness. One might wonder, however, especially in light of various comments indicating a kinship between the philosopher and the tyrant, particularly with regard to eros, whether Plato doesn't in fact join Nietzsche in conceiving of the philosopher as depending on or even as constituted by the sublimation of beastliness.[20]

Second, after subdividing the desiring part of the soul and explaining how a healthy man manages the demands of all the soul's parts (571d–572b), Socrates addresses the opposing case. He explains first the process by which a young man is drawn to tyranny and then the end result. Tyrannized by eros and plagued by endless need, the young man "will stick at no terrible murder, or food, or deed" (574e). As it comes to light in Socrates' description, the tyrant's life, we might say, is "*essentially* appropriation, injury, overpowering of what is alien and weaker; suppression, hardness, imposition of one's own forms, incorporation and at least, at its mildest, exploitation." We might say; Nietzsche *does* say: the quoted words are of course his. Yet he offers them not as a definition, let alone an indictment, of the tyrant; rather they are the words he uses in section 259 to define the essence of "*life itself*" (my emphasis). What we see in 259, and in 257 (the reference to beastliness), is Nietzsche offering

20. Perhaps it would be more accurate to say that Plato's philosophers depend on or are even constituted by the sublimation of carnivorousness: they come from the meat-eating class that was absent from the city of pigs and are likened to dogs.

subtle *refutative* responses to a key premise of Socrates' whole discussion in book 9. Where Socrates distinguishes between the philosopher and the tyrant and sets them up as opposing spiritual poles, Nietzsche insists on the philosopher's being a kind of tyrant. The "essence" of "life itself" is nothing other than the stuff of tyranny; and the philosopher, as the most alive of all men, must necessarily be a great tyrant.

The third probable reference to the *Republic* in the early sections of part 9 appears in section 260, where Nietzsche introduces by name his (in)famous distinction between master and slave moralities. This may correspond to Socrates' declaration that the tyrant, who of course is ostensibly a master, is in truth a kind of slave (576a). Socrates had already spoken of the tyrannic man's being tyrannized by love (eros) (574e). But that claim, strictly speaking, applied only to the man who was on his way to becoming a tyrant. Socrates didn't quite say there that the tyrannic man as such, in his fully developed state, is a slave. That claim isn't made until 576a, where Socrates declares: "The tyrannic nature never has a taste of freedom or true friendship." With his introduction of the distinction between master and slave moralities Nietzsche offers his own polarity. Having denied the distinction between philosopher and tyrant, he certainly does not want to deny the distinction between aristocracy and demos. Yet even here his polarity is more than a polarity. For it turns out that "in all the higher and more mixed cultures" and, indeed, "even in the same human being, within a *single* soul," these two moralities and the psychic forces that give rise to them are found together, in dynamic and creative tension. There can be no doubting Nietzsche's particular love and advocacy of master morality and all that belongs to it. But surely at least some of his emphasis arises from his desire to oppose modern democracy's disparagement of aristocracy. And surely the highest natures, like all higher cultures, house elements associated with both moralities. Slave morality, with its hostility toward the healthy and its utilitarian cast, is disdained by Nietzsche. But the highest nobility, that is, the *philosopher's* nobility, owes something to the slave—and not just historically or developmentally, but in the present. Such is the inference I draw from what Nietzsche introduces as "[a] final fundamental distinction" between the two moralities: "the longing for *freedom,* the instinct for the happiness and the refinements of the feeling of freedom, belong just as necessarily to slave morality and morals as the art of reverence and devotion and the enthusiasm for them are the regular symptom of an aristocratic way of thinking and valuating."[21] Does Nietzsche himself not exhibit the instinct that he here attributes to slave morality? Isn't it precisely this instinct that permits him to infuse the qualities born of master morality with the depth and imagination that characterize the philosopher's value creation? (Imaginative creativity, after all, is more the province of slaves than of masters.) If so, then *Nietzsche's philosopher, like Socrates' tyrant, is not only a master but also a slave.* Perhaps that is why Nietzsche calls himself a man of duty (226), and why the philosopher can be a complementary man (207) who leaves everyone he touches richer for the touch (295).

It is not only on the basis of the line just quoted that I call Nietzsche's philosopher a slave. Throughout his mature corpus Nietzsche depicts the philosopher as one who submits to a calling and to the truth about life. Something of this, in fact, is conveyed in the line that immediately follows the line I just quoted: "This makes it clear without further ado why love *as passion*—it is our European specialty—absolutely must be of aristocratic origin." Passion, to one who knows it and to one who knows about the Greek origin of the word, signifies bondage. It is useful to note this peculiar usage whereby the greatest of commanders is a slave, for it might make us more amenable to the peculiarity of Nietzsche's use of "master" as well. I have no intention of entering into apologetics. I will only point out, because it matters to a proper interpretation and because it appears in section 260, that Nietzsche's self-affirming master is a philanthropist—and that he is so precisely *because* he is so properly self-affirming. His ruling is giving, sometimes solicitous giving: "In the foreground [of the noble type of man] there is the feeling of fullness, of power that seeks to overflow, the happiness of high tension, the consciousness of wealth that would give and bestow: the noble human being, too, helps the unfortunate, but not, or almost not, from pity, but prompted more by an urge begotten by excess of power."

At the heart of book 9 of the *Republic*, which is the culmination of the long night's argument (book 10 being or at least appearing to be a kind of addendum), is Socrates' direct comparison of the tyrant's life with that of the philosopher. He offers three "proofs" of the latter's superiority. The first proof is an analogical thought experiment aimed at unveiling the tyrant as a slave. Socrates instructs his interlocutors to consider the condition of a wealthy private man who is removed from the protection of the city and placed with

---

21. Hollingdale translation.

his family in a remote place accompanied only by his slaves and domestics. The man will be overwhelmed by fear and compelled to fawn on his slaves and flatter his servants. And things would only get worse if antislavery neighbors were to settle around him, whereupon he would be "watched on all sides by nothing but enemies" (579b). The tyrant is bound in just such a prison, "full of many fears and loves" and unable to go abroad or see what men desire to see. The "real tyrant is, even if he doesn't seem so to someone, in truth a real slave to the greatest fawning and slavery, and a flatterer of the most worthless men; and with his desires getting no kind of satisfaction, he shows that he is most in need of the most things and poor in truth" (579d–e). The second proof is an inference made from a postulated epistemological capability. The (three) different kinds of men prefer (three) different kinds of life. The only person able to make an adequate judgment of these preferences would be the one who has tasted the pleasures of each. That person, says Socrates, is the philosopher. He alone has the experience, the prudence, and the arguments by which to weigh the respective claims, for the pleasures of wealth and honor are widely accessible while "the kind of pleasure connected with the vision of what *is* [i.e., the pleasure of the philosophic life] cannot be tasted by anyone except the lover of wisdom" (582c). What this lover of wisdom chooses, of course, is the life devoted to the fulfillment of that love. The third proof gets directly to the heart of the matter, comparing the experiences—the pleasures—of the different kinds of human beings. Socrates begins by stating the conclusion: "Observe that the other men's pleasure, except for that of the prudent man, is neither entirely true nor pure but is a sort of shadow painting" (583b). *Pure* pleasure, we learn, is not preceded by and dependent on pain. *True* pleasure is that which comes of filling oneself with what *is:* those who fill themselves with that which *is not* are insatiable and hence violent toward one another.

Nietzsche, it seems to me, offers something in response to each of these proofs. To Socrates' first proof, according to which the tyrant is actually a slave, he responds with the discourse on mastery and slavery that we just examined. In response to the second proof, which is based on the purported unique ability of the philosopher to judge the pleasures of different lives, Nietzsche demonstrates his own ability to judge different kinds of souls. Souls, he says, can be "tested" by the passing-by of something that is of the first rank but unprotected (263). A refined soul will respond with reverence and will show "delight in the nuances of reverence." Base souls may feel hatred;

or they may respond with abashed recognition of that which is above their level. (263). The point is that Nietzsche, like Socrates' philosopher, has what it takes to judge different kinds of lives. The judging itself is the stuff of Socrates' third proof and of Nietzsche's response to it. Like Socrates, Nietzsche accords highest rank to the philosopher. Yet whereas Socrates bases his judgment on the standard of pleasure, Nietzsche pointedly abjures that standard in favor of what looks like its opposite: "it almost determines the order of rank of *how* profoundly human beings can *suffer*" (270; second emphasis added). To be sure, one's depth of suffering doesn't tell everything: we shouldn't overlook Nietzsche's "almost." But it does tell a lot, and it does so because "profound suffering" doesn't just correlate with nobility, it "makes noble; it separates." This is hardly everything there is to know about Nietzschean nobility. One need only recall his emphasis on cheerfulness and dance to understand that suffering is only an *instrumental* good. But an instrumental good is still a good, and to lose sight of this good is to risk missing the path to the most refined enjoyments of life, not to mention the highest affirmation, the love of life, that emerges only after one has passed through the depths of suffering (56).[22]

Finally, a few observations from the latter parts of the respective ninth chapters. Socrates continues to address the inner lives of the tyrant and the philosopher (or king) and the implications thereof even after concluding his third proof at 585e, until almost the very end of book 9. Highlights of this continuing discussion include his calculation that the kingly man lives 729 times more pleasantly than the tyrant (587e) and his threefold or three-form image of the soul (a many-headed beast, a lion, and a human being [588b–e]). Similarly, Nietzsche devotes the second half of part 9 to the inner life of the philosopher-tyrant. He offers a series of personal reflections that *show*, more than explain, his response to the question that part 9 announces with its title, "What Is Noble?" And amid these personal reflections we find what may be responses to the two highlights of Socrates' account I just mentioned. (1) In connection with Socrates' arithmetical calculation, let us consider the follow-

---

22. Section 271 seems to me Nietzsche's response to Socrates' discourse on pure pleasures. "What separates two people most profoundly," he begins, "is a different sense and degree of cleanliness [*Reinlichkeit*; note that the primary meaning of *rein* is "pure"]." Indeed, within a line he is speaking of smell, just like Socrates, except that Socrates refers to "the pleasures of smells" (584b) while Nietzsche invokes a less pleasant scenario: " 'They can't stand each other's smell!' " In light of his frequent charge of uncleanliness against those who lie too easily or prettily, the reference may well be aimed directly at Socrates' "plebian"-hedonistic argument.

ing. Seven hundred and twenty-nine is a number with many significances. One of these is that it equals what the Greeks took to be the number of days and nights in a year. And in fact this is alluded to by Socrates only a line or so later when, following a remark by Glaucon, he says: "And yet the number is true and appropriate to lives too, if *days and nights* and months and years are appropriate to them" (emphasis added).[23] These lines appear a few pages from the end of book 9. Might Nietzsche be nodding to this passage when, several pages from the end of his own ninth chapter, he mentions "a man [who] has been sitting alone with his soul in confidential discord and discourse, year in and year out, *day and night*" (289; emphasis added)? It is impossible to say, but it may be worth noting that this solitary, both in his way of life and in his beliefs and doubts, bears a striking resemblance to the philosopher—to *Nietzsche*. This hermit, for example, "does not believe that any philosopher . . . ever expressed his real and ultimate opinions in books. . . . Indeed, he will doubt whether a philosopher could *possibly* have 'ultimate and real' opinions."

(2) There is a passage in Nietzsche that is perhaps just evocative enough to make it a plausible response to Socrates' famous threefold image of the soul. In section 291, which appears in more or less the "right" place (that is, late in the chapter), Nietzsche speaks of man as "a manifold, mendacious, artificial, and opaque animal"—an animal, moreover, who wishes in his shrewdness "to enjoy his soul for once as *simple.*" How striking a formulation in light of Socrates's image, which represents man as a manifold (i.e., three-formed) behind a facade that makes him appear simple, a facade that thereby might be called mendacious and that certainly is artificial and makes man opaque. In Nietzsche's formulation the means of creating a false front of simplicity is morality, which he calls "a long undismayed forgery." In light of Nietzsche's ongoing critique of Socratic morality, does it not seem plausible, indeed more than plausible, that Nietzsche would interpret Socrates' use of the image as an exercise in just such forgery? (The image itself, though, does not strike me as especially objectionable from a Nietzschean standpoint. Whatever morality it is meant to serve, the image represents just the things that a truly scientific

---

23. Bloom offers the following explanatory note (p. 470n11): "Philolaus, the pre-Socratic . . . calculated that there were 364½ days in the year. If there are a similar number of nights, the number would be 729. He also held that there is a great year of 729 months. It is probably this to which Socrates refers. In what way the number 729 would express years is unknown."

psychology would seem to acknowledge: the account even has the lion in the central place among the three forms.)

Finally, there is section 295, which, as we have seen, seems to invoke Socrates in one form or another—the historic Socrates, the Platonic Socrates, and/or the musical Socrates who here wears the mask of Dionysus.[24] Nowhere else does Nietzsche so strikingly embrace Socrates, even as he goes beyond the historic and Platonic versions by fulfilling the musical impetus that Socrates began to act upon only on his deathbed.

We turn finally to the part 10 that Nietzsche does not include and the *Nachgesang* that he does. In being a sort of addendum, the Aftersong is like book 10 of the *Republic:* both the *Republic* and *Beyond Good and Evil* had seemed to come to fit conclusions at the ends of their respective ninth chapters. Beyond that, though, the parallels seem to end. In book 10 of the *Republic* Socrates reopens the apparently settled question of poetry, offering a new critique—this one from a philosophic rather than a civic perspective (though he also invites the poets to argue their way back into the city). Then he proves the immortality of the soul. And then, by way of illustrating this immortality and providing grounds both for morality and, especially, philosophy, he concludes the dialogue by telling the myth of Er. With no part 10 properly speaking, *Beyond Good and Evil* does not seem to respond to any of this. Or does it? Where Socrates criticizes poetry, Nietzsche offers a poem.[25] In place of Socrates' proof of the soul's immortality, Nietzsche sings of change from the past and longing for a new future—all within the bounds of a single, mortal lifetime. And in place of Er and a call to philosophy as the only way to avoid the thousand-year descent into hell, Nietzsche gives us Zarathustra, the philosopher and complementary man, whose message offers the only redemption available to humanity. Where Er had shown the way to avoid the nether regions and ascend to heaven, Nietzsche anticipates the overcoming of the moral world order with the wedding of darkness and light.

---

24. See Chapter 7, note 15.

25. Does Nietzsche's replacement of Socrates' criticism of poetry with a poem signify that he has resolved the conflict between philosophy and poetry, or has chosen poetry over philosophy? Certainly Nietzsche embraces poetry with much less reservation than does Socrates, to say the least. Then again, Socrates himself allows for poetry to petition for admission to a philosophically governed regime, so perhaps Nietzsche is only doing what Socrates suggested might be done.

A concluding word now on the general character of *Beyond Good and Evil*. The purpose of the foregoing analysis has been to establish that *Beyond Good and Evil* is Nietzsche's response to the *Republic*, architecturally, thematically, and politically (i.e., as a political act)—indeed, not only a response but Nietzsche's *own Politeia*. All of the evidence I have adduced on behalf of this claim is internal to the book. I am aware of nothing from Nietzsche's correspondence or notebooks that supports my interpretation (though I cannot claim deep knowledge of these resources). This lack of external evidence is presumably one reason why scholars have not recognized the book's relation to the *Republic*. Another reason may be the evidence from Nietzsche's correspondence that seems to speak *against* my interpretation. But a quick look at that evidence will show that the opposite is true.

The evidence to which I refer are the indications from Nietzsche's correspondence that *Beyond Good and Evil* was originally conceived as a revised version of *Human, All Too Human*, an earlier book also of nine parts along with a preface and a concluding poem.[26] As the new book progressed it became too different to remain a revision of the old one. Yet there are still notable parallels between them, as a look at *Human, All Too Human*'s contents list will readily reveal. The third part of that book is called "Religious Life"; the seventh, "Woman and Child"; the eighth, "A Look at the State"; and the ninth, "Man Alone with Himself." In its final form *Beyond Good and Evil* is constructed in significant part along the same lines as *Human, All Too Human*. Surely, then, if *Beyond Good and Evil* parallels any book, that book is not the *Republic* but Nietzsche's own earlier effort. So we must conclude—unless, perhaps, *Human, All Too Human* was *itself* constructed with the *Republic* in mind.

Which, as it turns out, is likely. I will not engage in a textual analysis of *Human, All Too Human* here. It seems to me that my textual analysis of *Beyond Good and Evil* must and should suffice for the case I am making. But I will at least point out two facts that render plausible the claim that *Human, All Too Human* was itself written as a response to the *Republic* (though whether it was meant to be *as much* a response as *Beyond Good and Evil* is doubtful). First, it is clear that Nietzsche had already arrived at his exalted (i.e., Platonic) conception of the philosopher's task by the time he wrote *Human, All Too Human*: his understanding of the philosopher's greatness and the greatness of his task, which he almost undoubtedly learned from the

---

26. See Lampert, *Nietzsche's Task*, pp. 5–6.

Republic, is evident even as early as his essay on "Schopenhauer as Educator." Second, the account Nietzsche gives in *Ecce Homo* suggests that *Human, All Too Human* had its origin and purpose in his discovery of a *Republic*-like task—that is to say, a task (like that of *Beyond Good and Evil*) that is *Republic*-like in shape and scope while anti-Platonic, that is, anti-idealist, in content. In the opening section of *Ecce Homo*'s commentary on *Human, All Too Human* Nietzsche depicts the book as the beginning of a campaign, a "war without powder and smoke," against idealism (*EH*, Books, "HAH" 1). He then proceeds to recount the origins of the book in his discovery and owning up to his own (Platonic) potential: After spending too many years both ideologically and professionally fettered, "all at once it became clear to me in a terrifying way how much time I had already wasted—how useless and arbitrary my whole existence as a philologist appeared in relation to my task. I felt ashamed of this *false* modesty" (*EH*, Books, "HAH" 3). And there can be no mistaking the grandeur, *the Platonism,* of the task he was now undertaking: "How I thought about myself at this time (1876), with what tremendous sureness I got hold of my task and its world-historical aspect—the whole book bears witness to that" (*EH*, Books, "HAH" 6). It turns out, then, that the relation of *Beyond Good and Evil* to *Human, All Too Human* does not undermine but rather testifies that *Beyond Good and Evil* is a response to the *Republic.*

Nietzsche clearly did not wish to advertise the relation of *Beyond Good and Evil* to the *Republic*. His brief account of *Beyond Good and Evil* in *Ecce Homo,* while rich, highlights the book's negative or critical character and its subservience to *Thus Spoke Zarathustra,* the book that immediately preceded it. In *Ecce Homo* Nietzsche describes *Beyond Good and Evil* as the first of his "fish hooks" (*EH*, Books, "BGE" 1), the first of his efforts to entice readers and lead them to *Zarathustra,* a book whose greatness and strangeness required this kind of recruitment. But in this account Nietzsche at least leaves room for greater unspoken dimensions. One of the characteristics he cites is *Beyond Good and Evil*'s foreground "refinement"—"in form, in intention, in the art of *silence*" (*EH*, Books, "BGE" 2). This silence, it seems to me, refers not only to what may be hidden between the lines but also to the broader character and purpose of the book. As we have already noted, Nietzsche wrote in a letter to his esteemed friend Jacob Burckhardt that *Beyond Good and Evil* "*says the same things as Thus Spoke Zarathustra* but differently, very differently" (emphasis added). Now consider: Nietzsche calls *Zarathustra* "the greatest present that has ever been made to [humanity] so far," "the highest book there is" and also "the *deepest*" (*EH*, Preface 4).²⁷ If he is at all in earnest in this assessment, it is hard to deny *Beyond Good and Evil* comparable importance. To be sure, insofar as the two books say the same thing *Zarathustra* must be granted superior rank for coming first and for accounting for its teaching in a way that *Beyond Good and Evil* does not. (*Zarathustra* shows us the education of the one who discovered eternal return.) But insofar as *Beyond Good and Evil* says the same things *differently*—and insofar as it *does* different things—it seems to me to gain an extraordinary stature and greatness of its own. *Zarathustra* had ended with a philosopher ready to take up the task of founding and legislating. *Beyond Good and Evil* is where the philosopher undertakes that task. In *Zarathustra* Nietzsche had articulated a comprehensive perspective on life and shown how he had come to that perspective. In *Beyond Good and Evil* he initiates the appropriate political response to that perspective, in the process revealing more about philosophy and its ground²⁸ than he does in any other book and reflecting on the relation between philosophy and politics. In all of this, the book stands with—and against—the *Republic*.²⁹

Why *against*? Having seen the Platonic parallels and echoes in *Beyond Good and Evil*, it is time to ask: How should we understand the quarrel between Nietzsche and Plato? The question is important not so much for genealogical reasons but because it is through exploring the quarrel with Plato that we can reach the heart of Nietzsche's vision. Nietzsche tells us in *Ecce Homo* that besides being "in all essentials a *critique of modernity*," *Beyond Good and Evil* also includes "pointers" to a positive vision (*EH*, Books, "BGE" 2). My suggestion is that the positive vision toward which these pointers beckon can best be understood and evaluated if one begins with Nietzsche's quarrel with Plato. The relation between *Beyond Good and Evil* and the *Republic* points us toward the defining depths and peaks of Nietzsche's thought.

27. For citations to some of Nietzsche's other exalted claims on behalf of *Zarathustra*, see Berkowitz, *Nietzsche*, pp. 127 and 291–92n4.

28. See Lampert, *Nietzsche's Teaching*, p. 247.

29. That *Beyond Good and Evil* initiates what was intended to be a full-scale attempt at philosophic legislation is confirmed by *The Antichrist*, the only completed part, the projected first part, of Nietzsche's incomplete second *Hauptwerk*, *The Will to Power*. There we find a conception of the work of the legislator and an articulation of the natural tripartition of humanity that echo the *Republic* uncannily (57)—or so one would say if one didn't know that these same themes were first echoed in *Beyond Good and Evil*.

9

WILL TO POWER VERSUS EROS, OR A BATTLE OF ETERNITIES

In trying to apprehend the basis of Nietzsche's quarrel with Plato we are beset by the problem with which we began: a good part of Nietzsche's opposition to Plato needs to be understood as strategic or prescriptive as opposed to philosophic or diagnostic. As we have seen, the mature Nietzsche was inclined to separate Plato a good deal from Platonism; he attributed a large part of Plato's idealism to a well-intended even if catastrophic judgment about what was needed to ground morality and a decent politics. Yet Nietzsche was not prepared to attribute Plato's "error" *entirely* to a political (mis)calculation. And for that matter, even insofar as strategic political considerations did guide Plato's actions, that Plato would be guided by such considerations itself implies a deeper difference with Nietzsche: strategic political judgments, though not as deep as such pre-political matters as the character of existence, the (non)existence of the divine, the meaning of human flourishing, and so on, at least reflect such matters. So even if Nietzsche *were* prepared to attribute Platonism entirely to a political calculation, his abhorrence of Platonism would still testify to a deeper antagonism with Plato. The contours of this pre-political, deep-level antagonism are not hard to see. Where Plato gives us a realm of being and eternity, Nietzsche speaks of the exclusivity of becoming and the inescapability of time. Where Plato gives us a morally governed cosmos and a world that will yield to human understanding and perhaps even to human correction, Nietzsche lauds tragic or Dionysian pessimism. Where Plato sees eros as the animating core of the soul, Nietzsche discovers will to power. Each of these disagreements and much else besides is implicated in the relation of *Beyond Good and Evil* to the *Republic*. But each of these disagreements is not equally prominent or accessible. As I explained above, the two books share a political character: each addresses a number of deep themes but does so in light of an overarching question, the question of the best regime. Each treats that question, moreover, as the question of how best to deal with the soul's leading or even comprehensive force: where Plato's Socrates constructs a regime aimed at the proper education and satisfaction of *eros,* Nietzsche does the same with respect to *will to power.* Given this shared political character, the disagreement that is most fully addressed by the two books—and the one that provides entree into the others—is the question of will to power versus eros.

This question is endlessly deep and endlessly complicated. What *is* will to power? What does it seek? In what does it find satisfaction? (Does such a question even make sense?) What leads to, and what constitutes, its perfection? These questions can hardly be settled by the limited analysis I am attempting here. Yet it seems to me that the comparison of *Beyond Good and Evil* to the *Republic* provides the seed of an answer to the last question—which also, incidentally, carries with it the seeds to the answers to the other questions. Interestingly that seed, or at least its husk, its *name,* is the same for both Nietzschean will to power and Platonic eros. The thing that signifies the perfection of both will to power and eros—and therewith life's highest fulfillment, both for Nietzsche and for Plato—is the embrace of *eternity.* The way to see this is to examine will to power and eros by way of their highest or most perfect exemplar, the philosopher.[1]

Will to power and eros are not comparable in every sense, even if considered only as psychic forces.[2] They *are* comparable in the sense that each occupies the central place in the economy of the soul and might almost be said to constitute the soul. Yet whereas eros is depicted as a desire, or metadesire, such that it might attain fulfillment with the acquisition of the right object or experience (i.e., insight), will to power is depicted by Nietzsche as an eruption

---

1. Looking to the highest exemplar to discover the nature of a species may sound like a Platonic procedure, and it is; but it is also a Nietzschean procedure, as indicated by Nietzsche's embrace of the idea that a "return to nature" would be a "*going-up*" to nature (*TI,* Skirmishes, 48). To be sure, one who seeks understanding must also study the average (*BGE* 26). But the reason to do so (besides the need to understand the practical power of the many) is to find pointers toward the high, just as Socrates seeks to understand perfect virtue by way of investigating its imperfect versions. Hence Nietzsche's allusion to Socrates amid the very aphorism in which he insists on the need to investigate the average. *Unlike* Socrates, though, Nietzsche emphasizes his intense distaste at such investigation.

2. In keeping with the political character of *Beyond Good and Evil,* my concern here is with will to power only as manifest in human beings, that is, as a physiopsychic force. As we have seen, Nietzsche goes further than this, suggesting that "*all* efficient force . . . the world defined and determined according to its 'intelligible character'" is "'will to power' and nothing else" (36). In this he goes beyond anything Plato says about eros—or, rather, beyond anything Plato has *Socrates* say.

rather than as a teleologically guided force.[3] Will to power does this and that, but it is not naturally oriented or drawn toward any particular end. Thus will to power seems a different *kind* of thing from Plato's eros, not just a different desire or a different kind of desire. But to leave the matter there is to overstate the distance between Nietzsche and Plato. For even if will to power is not by nature oriented toward any particular end, it still admits of greater and lesser development and fulfillment in consequence of different kinds of pursuits. Will to power does this and that, but "this" may well be better than "that"—*naturally* better. For Nietzsche as for Plato there exists a hierarchy of ways of being and of human types. The human types are defined and ranked according to their proper ways of being and according to the extent to which they do or don't take up their proper ways of being. More specifically, and again like Plato, for whom the character of one's eros is definitive, Nietzsche ranks ways of life and human types according to their development and fulfillment of will to power. (If Nietzsche subscribes to a natural hierarchy of human types, is will to power not teleological after all? It is not, at least not if we take teleology to entail either a natural inclination or a felt or otherwise experienced directedness toward an end, for there is none of this in Nietzsche's conception will to power.) Indeed, the same person sits atop Nietzsche's hierarchy as Plato's: just as in Plato the philosopher exemplifies the fullest development and satisfaction of eros, so in Nietzsche the philosopher exemplifies the fullest development and satisfaction of will to power. And as I have already mentioned—and as we will now consider—both Nietzsche and Plato speak of the core of philosophic longing and the peak of philosophic attainment in terms of eternity.[4]

The Platonic philosopher is one who grasps or seeks to grasp what *is*, and

---

3. The nonteleological character of will to power should be evident to anyone who has read any of Nietzsche's myriad descriptions of this force. Nietzsche succinctly explains the basis of this characterization, that is, his guiding psychointerpretive principle, in section 360 of *The Gay Science*: "I have learned to distinguish the cause of acting from the cause of acting in a particular way, in a particular direction, with a particular goal. The first kind of cause is a quantum of dammed-up energy that is waiting to be used up somehow, for something, while the second kind is, compared to this energy, something quite insignificant, for the most part a little accident in accordance with which this quantum 'discharges' itself in one particular way—a match versus a ton of powder. Among these little accidents and 'matches' I include so-called 'purposes.'"

4. Is it really plausible to contend that Nietzsche and Plato are referring to "the same person" when they speak of the philosopher? It is, and not only because both of them see the philosopher as being oriented toward eternity. More important, and more simply, Nietzsche and Plato seem to have same historic persons and the same types in mind when they speak of philosophers—starting with Socrates and Plato themselves.

his quest culminates or would culminate in apprehension of the timeless Good. The Nietzschean philosopher, of course, denies any such timeless realm; yet he, too, seeks and gains a kind of eternity in his embrace of the idea of eternal return. It is no overstatement to refer to eternal return as *the good* for Nietzsche, for it is only by embracing eternal return—only by willing all that has been and all that is, willing that it should all recur endlessly—that one can overcome the spirit of revenge and love life completely. (I will expand on this logic below.) Nietzsche does not fully articulate the eternal return teaching in *Beyond Good and Evil*. *Zarathustra* is the book of eternal return, which is why, even though it is enormously important in its own right, *Beyond Good and Evil* is still a hook by means of which Nietzsche intends to lead readers to *Zarathustra*. (See the last lines of the Aftersong—the last lines of the book.) Yet if the eternal return teaching isn't fully articulated in *Beyond Good and Evil*, it still is present—in two ways. First and more narrowly, it is flashed, so to speak, in section 56, where Nietzsche speaks of "the ideal of the most high-spirited, alive, and world-affirming human being who has not only come to terms and learned to get along with whatever was and is, but who wants to have *what was and is* repeated into all eternity, shouting insatiably *da capo*."

Second, the teaching of eternal return informs the entirety of *Beyond Good and Evil*. Behind every political enterprise is some conception of the good, and Nietzsche's political enterprise, by pointing the way to a new nobility, also points the way to *da capo*, for one would not be able to will all the horrors and nonsense of the past and present unless one saw them as indispensable parts of a story that includes redemptive (i.e., noble) peaks.[5] Just as the *Republic* treats the education and governance of eros more than it inquires directly into eros' nature (it's the *Symposium* that takes up *that* inquiry), so *Beyond Good and Evil* fundamentally addresses the education and governance of will

---

5. To speak of a single good for all human beings might sound too egalitarian for Nietzsche and might lead one to wonder whether eternal recurrence really could be the good for all. Lomax, in fact, contends that the "doctrine" of eternal return is a noble lie taught by the philosopher of the future but not believed by him. Lomax's reason lies in an objection not to a common good, however, but to the idea that the philosopher, a skeptic, would embrace a faith in something that he cannot know to be true. To Lomax I would reply that it seems reasonable that Nietzsche's philosopher can will what he does not know to be true because he understands his willing as just that—willing, not believing. And in response to the suggestion that Nietzsche could not subscribe to a single good for all, I would say that it is misleading to refer to eternal return as the common good. It is common only in the sense that it is the good for human beings as such. It is very *un*common in the sense that only very few human beings will be able either to will eternal return or to understand it, let alone both.

to power toward and in light of the good, eternal return. To be sure, eternal return figures less prominently in *Beyond Good and Evil* than does the Good, or the *idea* of the Good, in the *Republic*. And Nietzsche's treatment of the education and governance of will to power is less overtly connected to eternal return than Plato's corresponding treatment is to his Good. Indeed, unlike Plato, Nietzsche does not lay out an educational program. These differences, however, do not undermine the parallel I am asserting between the respective tasks of the two books. If eternal return is less prominent than it "should" be and is less clearly the end toward which education should be oriented, that is because it cannot be taught usefully until Nietzsche's readers have first been prepared: as Heidegger's reading of Nietzsche demonstrates, the eternal return can sound almost Platonic, like a reification of becoming into timeless Being.[6] If Nietzsche had seen this danger—and he often did show a keen awareness of the ways in which the prejudices of modern readers could work against his purposes—he would have understood that such a reading would drive away the skeptical "free minds" whom he was trying to reach, as well as attract unwanted true believers. Finally, the need to submerge the good also plausibly accounts for Nietzsche's "failure" to lay out an educational program à la the *Republic*. Because he must remain taciturn about the good, it would make no sense for Nietzsche to lay out an educational program in the way that Socrates does in book 7. In fact, though, Nietzsche does seek to educate his readers toward the good—in just the way that Plato seeks to educate *his* readers. After all, it is the citizens of a utopian *kallipolis* whose education is depicted in book 7. Plato's *readers*, like Nietzsche's, receive the beginnings of a subtler but perhaps more comprehensive education—something worthier of the title *paideia* or *Bildung*—through their encounter with the philosopher-poets whose books they are reading.

I have already indicated that the formal difference between will to power and eros, that is, the difference implied by the distinction between (nonteleological) will and (teleological) desire, is less than it initially appears. With the discovery of eternity as the fulfillment of both forces, we have encountered a

---

6. Heidegger has propounded an influential interpretation according to which Nietzsche's embrace of eternal return represents only the final stage of the metaphysics that Nietzsche meant to overcome. In my view Heidegger rightly appreciates the place of eternal return in Nietzsche's thought but wrongly (for reasons to be reviewed briefly below) views eternal return as a teaching born of the spirit of revenge. See his *Nietzsche, Volume I: The Will to Power as Art*, pp. 200–10; also see "The Word of Nietzsche: 'God is Dead,'" in *The Question Concerning Technology and Other Essays*, pp. 53–112.

substantive convergence. Indeed, a substantive kinship at a very deep level: this shared place of eternity in Nietzsche and Plato, though the last of our parallels, is really the first, the deepest. In fact, in retrospect a substantive kinship between will to power and eros has been suggested throughout *Beyond Good and Evil*, beginning with the opening line of the preface. Philosophy, though later defined in terms of will to power (9), is also—indeed first—linked to what can only be called eros: "Supposing truth is a woman—what then?" The link is repeated more than once, as we have seen. But isn't will to power palpably *unerotic*? Isn't it closer to what Socrates in the *Republic* calls spiritedness (*thymos*)? Indeed, doesn't Nietzsche effectively repudiate the very existence of eros, as seen, for example, in his assertion of a natural antagonism between men and women? I would say no, at least if one takes the measure of will to power from its highest (i.e., its most powerful) exemplars. For the embrace of eternal return is the apotheosis of the love of life, a love that Nietzsche depicts as spirited but not waspish, as open-hearted and full of awe and grace. And this highest love is continuous with love that surely does deserve to be called erotic: in *Zarathustra* Nietzsche symbolically depicts the embrace of eternal return as Zarathustra's, that is, a man's, love for Life, a woman. If there is antagonism between true lovers, it's an antagonism that sustains love and renders it lively and that doesn't preclude gratitude and trust, though it does preclude full and secure possession. Of course there is something to the reading of will to power as *thymos*. But as I suggested in Chapter 1, thymos itself is an expression, indeed I would say a variant, of eros.[7]

Yet another substantive kinship is indicated amid Nietzsche's and Plato's divergent conceptions of the philosopher and his characteristic activity. For

---

7. For Zarathustra's love affair with Life, see *Zarathustra* III, "The Other Dancing Song." That erotic love in Nietzsche's view need not preclude gratitude and trust is indicated at *GS* 363. That the (male) lover can never fully possess his (female) beloved, at least where the lovers are refined, is also indicated at *GS* 363 and perhaps suggested, as we have seen, at the center of the central part (part 5) of *Beyond Good and Evil* (194–95). Not everyone agrees with this reading regarding the erotic character of, or at least eros' kinship with, will to power. Understandably so, given Nietzsche's talk of power instead of beauty and of antagonism rather than love. Perhaps, too, the anerotic interpretation of will to power has been encouraged by the uses to which Nietzsche has been put by those inclined to interpret romance as real or potential exploitation. The prevalence of the anerotic interpretation of will to power probably also owes something to Heidegger's influence. Lampert, by contrast, in each of his commentaries strongly advances the view that Nietzsche's conception of philosophy, that Nietzsche himself, and thus that will to power *itself* are all fundamentally erotic.

the divergence, it turns out, is less a matter of different activities than of different *emphases*. Nietzsche emphasizes the philosopher's doing and making, that is, his commanding and legislating, but this doing and making follow from, and indeed are dictated by, his *knowing*. Similarly, Plato defines the philosopher primarily as a knower, but he gives us a philosopher whose knowing is followed by doing, even *making*. In the *Republic* the philosopher not only knows, but also rules, and does so by making a new city and a new people out of new religious teachings; and in the *Symposium*, the other dialogue in which philosophy is depicted as erotic, the philosopher, precisely because he *is* erotic, *gives birth*.

But to repeat, a deep difference remains: Nietzsche's good and Plato's good are not identical. The shared identification of eternity as the good implies a kinship at a very deep level, but this remaining difference is at an even deeper, indeed the deepest possible, level: when human beings are conceived essentially as willing or desiring beings, nothing is deeper than the question of what it is they want and what would satisfy them. Thus as Nietzsche and Plato have come closer together, the locus of their quarrel has come into view. The contest between them, or at least between their public teachings, is at bottom a contest between competing understandings of eternity.

If this esoteric-sounding question of eternity is the deepest of human matters, it may well prove to be the most consequential as well. It is time to break open the husk and investigate the kernel. (1) What does Nietzsche mean by eternity? (2) What does it mean that he adopts a term with a connotation so different from his own meaning? (3) What accounts for his new and different understanding, that is, can this most basic of views be understood in light of some other characteristic of his thought? (4) And what are the consequences of Nietzsche's eternity for life and for politics? Only by making progress at these four questions will we be able to begin to consider a fifth question: Is Nietzsche right about the good? These questions are no less difficult than the "endlessly deep and endlessly complicated" question of will to power versus eros. But they are at least a little narrower, which permits, if not a more comprehensive inquiry, perhaps a more directed and thus a deeper downward plunge.[8]

---

8. This approach is meant to be consistent in spirit with Nietzsche's own way: "I approach deep problems like cold baths: quickly into them and quickly out again" (*GS* 381). Scholars are not philosophers, but perhaps Nietzsche scholarship ought to imitate its subject in this regard.

(1) What does Nietzsche mean by eternity? I must begin with a caution to those who read Nietzsche in English translation. On some occasions (one of which has already been noted), both Kaufmann and Hollingdale have turned German words that signify *eternity* (*ewig, Ewigkeit, Verewiger, verewigen*), which means apartness from time, into English words that signify *immortality*, which of course is something very different. That Nietzsche does sometimes speak of immortality (*unsterblich, Unsterblichkeit*) makes matters worse, since the mistranslation muddies an important distinction that Nietzsche has clearly thought about. In what follows I will retranslate where necessary.

Nietzsche denies what is usually signified by "eternity." He rejects the existence of a realm of pure Being that is beyond time. Rather, the word for him typically signifies the endlessness of time: to will the eternal recurrence of all that is and has been means to will an *endless* repetition. "Eternity" for Nietzsche most often means "forever" or "sempiternity" or encompassing all of time, with the important addition that one presumes the endlessness of time. Thus one can see why Kaufmann and Hollingdale might do as they have done: according to the usual way of thinking about eternity, Nietzsche is *not* really talking about eternity when he uses the word. Nevertheless "immortality" remains a bad substitution, for a key part of Nietzsche's eternity-cum-sempiternity is the willing acceptance of mortality. Time goes on without end; the individual and the species do not.

(2) Why, then, use so loaded and potentially misleading a word? Perhaps because what we *experience*, both in our highest moments and in our moments of deepest longing, *is* in fact eternal, that is, timeless, or at least points to or intimates timelessness. If Nietzsche most typically means by "eternity" sempiternity, or persisting in and through time, he nevertheless attaches another meaning to the term on other occasions—a meaning that warrants use of the term in a way that eternity-as-sempiternity does not. In *Twilight of the Idols*, which appeared within two years of *Beyond Good and Evil*, Nietzsche speaks of "eternal joy"—"the eternal joy of creating" and "the eternal joy of becoming" (Ancients, 5). And in the last lines of the last song in *Zarathustra* he writes that "all joy wants eternity—wants deep, wants deep eternity" (IV, Drunken Song 12). "Eternal joy" seems to signify a sense of consummation or perfection that is, by virtue of being such, something timeless. The line from *Zarathustra* can be interpreted simply as meaning that we wish our greatest moments to last forever, that is, as a longing for "eternity" under-

stood as sempiternity. But if one reflects on such longing one sees that what's desired is more than just continuation but also an apotheosis, a validation and enshrining that adds something more, another element, to the experience. That element, I think, is the sense of being beyond time—rather, the actual *experience* of being beyond time. This *is* a kind of eternity, even if all experience, including the experience of a timeless moment, takes place within time. Thus Nietzsche is right to use the old word. Indeed, in using it he not only does justice to his own view but also offers an implicit explanation and critique of those who use it in the older way. The older usage reflects one kind of error or another. Moved either by the experience of eternity or by the longing for the experience, human beings typically—and mistakenly, in Nietzsche's view—interpret their experience as signifying a timeless *realm*. That is the more innocent reason for the older usage of the word. Other reasons are less healthy by Nietzsche's lights. People postulate an eternal realm because they seek compensation for life's disappointments; and they postulate immortality out of a desire for revenge against those who do well in this world.[9] And this, too, is made clear by comparing Nietzsche's use of "eternity" with the more common usage.[10]

(3) With the question of what accounts for Nietzsche's understanding of eternity we come to what may be the most perilous part of the present inquiry. It may be difficult to resist the temptation to reductive psychological explanation as we examine characteristics of Nietzsche's thought that are connected

---

9. Nietzsche also acknowledges something like the phenomenon I attributed to Socrates' three uncomprehending lovers (Aristodemus, Apollodorus, and Alcibiades) in Chapter 4, that is, the mistranslation of *eternity* as *immortality*. On Nietzsche's account it is Jesus who lived and loved eternity and it is his apostles who, for reasons of limited capacity and shattering grief (after the Crucifixion), mistranslated eternity into immortality. Like Plato on my reading, Nietzsche connects the mistranslation of eternity into immortality to unfortunate political tendencies. See *Antichrist* 33–43.

10. Some of Nietzsche's literary devices can perhaps be understood as ways of representing and stimulating the experience of eternity. Consider the two works I have just cited. Zarathustra's songs, like all Dionysian music, seem to want to remove the "listener" from ordinary time and, in a sense, from time itself. And just a few pages before his invocation of "eternal joy" in *Twilight*, Nietzsche writes the following about his preferred form of writing: "The aphorism, the apothegm, in which I am the first among the Germans to be a master, are the forms of 'eternity'; it is my ambition to say in ten sentences what everyone else says in a book—what everyone else does *not* say in a book" (Skirmishes, 51). The quotation marks around "eternity" may signify irony on Nietzsche's part. But the concluding remark suggests that the real irony is that Nietzsche *does* embrace the experience of timelessness even while rejecting the meaning that others attach to it.

to the universal ideal of eternal return: these characteristics, besides relating to the matter at hand—indeed, *because* they relate to the matter at hand—are also quite personal. It doesn't help matters that Nietzsche himself routinely engaged in such reductive explanation, even giving it a name: "the *backward inference* from the work to the maker, from the deed to the doer, from the ideal to those who *need it,* from every way of thinking and valuing to the commanding need behind it" (GS 370; first emphasis added). I have no intention of employing backward inference here. The characteristics I am about to note are not offered as insights into Nietzsche's psyche. They do, however, concern psychological phenomena. So we will steer clear of Nietzsche's psyche, but we will continue to wade—more deeply, I hope—into Nietzschean psychology.

It seems to me that there are four primary factors that, together, give rise to Nietzsche's embrace of the ideal of eternal recurrence: (a) the longing for eternity; (b) the life-justifying experience of eternity; (c) the implausibility (as Nietzsche sees it) of a separate eternal "realm" or eternal structures; and (d) the harmfulness (again, as Nietzsche sees it) of believing in such a realm. A moment's reflection will show that these four factors, by postulating a deep desire, a felt solution, and the impossibility of other solutions, constitute a powerful logic on behalf of eternal recurrence as the good. But these four factors do not arise from nothing. They are themselves produced or at least shaped and enlarged by several other, deeper factors.

What chiefly underlies the first two factors (a and b) is yet another factor: (e) the sense that life and existence need to be redeemed. (By "chiefly underlies" I do not mean that [a] and [b] arise entirely from [e], but rather that [e] contributes mightily to them and accounts for much of their intensity.) Life is so full of baseness and ugliness, so much dominated by nonsense and injustice, that one could hardly hope to resist being driven to the spirit of revenge without knowledge or a faith that somehow finds the grounds on which to affirm life. (Manifestations of the spirit of revenge include both otherworldly and secular idealism—the latter including virtually the whole range of modern political aspirations—and even, among certain kinds of higher spirits, renunciation of the will, or the will to nothingness [GM III 28].) To find or create such knowledge or faith is what I mean by redemption. It is not obvious that every thinker of high rank has felt the need for redemption or imputed it to others. Among those who seem far from Nietzsche in this regard are several whom Nietzsche particularly admires for their affirmative stance toward life but in whom affirmation gives no sign of having had to fight through despair or nihilism: think of Aristophanes, or Nietzsche's favorite Roman poets, or perhaps Machiavelli or Montaigne, figures who could hardly be accused of denying the hard facts of life yet for whom life seems as it were automatically self-justifying, *already* justified. (One wonders whether the same isn't true of Socrates and Plato, notwithstanding their solicitude for the neediness of others.) Indeed, the search for redemption belongs far more to Judea than to Rome.[11] Yet the need is surely postulated (and felt) by Nietzsche and is evident in all his books. And no doubt Nietzsche would say of the figures I have cited that, to the extent they fall short of willing eternal return, they themselves still need to be redeemed, whether they recognize it or not. The redemption of humankind is the last note sounded in *Beyond Good and Evil*'s concluding poem.

What underlies the third factor (c) is (f): Nietzsche's rejection of the "fundamental faith of the metaphysicians," which he defines as *"the faith in opposite values"* (*BGE* 2). The faith in opposite values leads people to believe that the "higher things" (love, creativity, virtue, etc.) must have their origins somewhere other than in the lower things, since nothing, they suppose, "could originate out of its opposite." Hence the need for an eternal realm. Nietzsche, to the contrary, questions the existence of any kind of opposites and insists that intellectual probity demands the denial of opposite values: he suggests that at the root of the high—and not only at the root—we find low and even savage passions (cruelty, rapaciousness, etc.).

One who wishes to understand and come to a decision about Nietzsche's vision should critically consider just these "subfactors": (e) *Does* life need to be redeemed? Is it really impossible to love life and overcome revenge without anything like willing eternal return? And (f) is Nietzsche's repudiation of the

---

11. Löwith and Lomax (whose views on this matter seem variants of Heidegger's) also note that in postulating the need for redemption Nietzsche is on common ground with Christianity. They go much farther than this, though, asserting that Nietzsche's thought has a Christian character not only in asserting the need for redemption but also in its teaching about the fulfillment of that need, that is, the embrace of eternal recurrence. As Heidegger argues that Nietzsche never frees himself from the Platonic metaphysical tradition, Löwith argues that he never frees himself from a Christian (and simultaneously anti-Christian) worldview. And Lomax argues that the "doctrine of eternal return" is akin to Christianity in its effort to glorify the self and achieve vengeance against indifferent nature by winning immortality for the self. See Lomax, *The Paradox of Political Education*, pp. 83–86. (It should be noted, though, that in the end—in the "surprise finish" of his study—Lomax separates Nietzsche from the doctrine of eternal recurrence and therewith from Christianity.)

metaphysicians' faith truly a requirement of intellectual probity? In raising these questions (raising, not answering) I will try to show that both these features of Nietzsche's thought, both the positing of a need for redemption (e) and his rejection of the "metaphysicians' faith" (f), arise from yet another, even more basic feature: (g) his commitment to a newly conceived ideal of nobility (*Vornehmheit*).

(e) Most of those who believe in the need for redemption do so on Scriptural grounds, though they find ample confirmation of Scripture in what they see around them. Human beings are sinful and, absent redemption through divine grace, are headed toward damnation. Nietzsche's grounds are of course different. It is not sin and damnation but the spirit of revenge from which human beings need to be delivered. His argument is strictly naturalistic or empirical, though psychological and therefore difficult to prove. We are creatures of will and can only reconcile ourselves fully with life and the world if we are able to align our will with what it did not bring about and indeed does not like: only by willing all that is and has been can we bring our will in accord with life and thus prevent it from resenting or warring against life. Lest this sound either psychosophistical or too much like surrender to chance, it is important to note that in Nietzsche's view one won't, and indeed shouldn't, align one's will with all that has been until one comes to see the baser parts of life as parts of a story that includes glorious peaks—*justifying* peaks. What constitutes a peak is nobility, or affirmation of life and self. The peaks of the peaks, as it were, are those affirmations that come about by transfiguring the ugly and base into the beautiful and noble—such as one finds in Greek tragedy (as Nietzsche sees it). It is for the sake of the peaks that one wills the baser parts of life. This does *not* mean, however, that the present is to be justified by the future or the past by the present. Such thinking would be but a "progressive" form of vengefulness. Life is justified by its peaks, but those peaks may be, indeed have been, scattered throughout time.[12]

---

12. See *WP* 708: "The present must not under any circumstances be justified by a future, nor must the past be justified for the sake of the present." Also see *GM* III 27 and *WP* 1. Heidegger asserts that Nietzsche does rely on a future in order to redeem the present; and this is one reason why Heidegger, seeming to turn Nietzsche against himself, accuses him of merely overturning rather than overcoming nihilistic metaphysics and thus remaining caught in the spirit of revenge. See *Nietzsche, I*, pp. 200–10; also see "The Word of Nietzsche: 'God is Dead.'" But Heidegger discounts passages of the sort I have just cited as well as (more important) the particular character of Nietzsche's sought-after future, with its *embrace of* rather than escape from suffering and

To come to a judgment about this postulated need for redemption would require that one consider as well as one can—which means subjectively and intersubjectively—Nietzsche's psychoempirical presuppositions. I will not attempt to perform the analysis here, though I will point out the apparent closeness between Nietzsche's ideal and the similarly all-embracing ideals of various religious and contemplative traditions. Nietzsche, however, would insist on the differences between his ideal and theirs. What he calls for is a Yes to life that denies neither the reality nor the badness of the bad, which is why pronouncing this Yes requires a heroic overcoming. By contrast, the religious versions of the Yes, in his view, either say Yes only after saying No to the things of this world, that is, after denying the reality of this world, in which case they have actually demoted and devalued life; or else say Yes too indiscriminately, that is, without having first discerned the truly high and low, which has the effect of devaluing the high by equating it with the low. Among the former, in his view, fall much of Christianity as well as Buddhism; his chief exemplar of the latter is Jesus (A 28–35).

(f) Now to Nietzsche's rejection of the metaphysicians' faith. How is one to think about this? The first thing to note is that while Nietzsche repudiates

---

mortality. Nietzsche's sought-after future, in other words, is a future whose essential difference from the present would be that people would accept life as it is. To be sure, there are many passages in Nietzsche's mature works that speak of a better future and thus seem, particularly to ears steeped in Scripture or in progressivism, to promise justification of the present by the future. But these passages can be explained by reference to literary or rhetorical considerations. When Zarathustra speaks of a future that will justify the present—as he does, for example, in his prologue—he has not yet understood eternal recurrence. And the passages in post-*Zarathustra* books can plausibly be accounted for by considering the rhetorical demands of Nietzsche's project. Recall that these books are all fish hooks (*EH*, Books, "BGE" 1), which means that Nietzsche is trying to reach readers where they currently are; and many are currently "mired" in "progressivism." As Socrates had pretended that his way was consistent with conventional piety, so does Nietzsche. (What's different is that the piety of Nietzsche's intended audience is secular progressivism.) See Lampert, *Nietzsche's Teaching*, pp. 255–86, for a more extensive account and refutation of Heidegger's critique. In sum, and as I have already noted, Nietzsche does look upon life as something that needs to be redeemed, but what can redeem it are peaks—human peaks—that can appear and have appeared in every era. The point of his project is to preserve and enhance the possibility of such peaks in the future. (Having taken Nietzsche's side against the accusing Heidegger, perhaps I may be permitted to offer an exculpatory thought on behalf of some of those whom Nietzsche accuses: If Nietzsche's forward-looking project can be defended against the charge of vengefulness because it is based on love of life as it is, then perhaps those monotheists who see the world as infused with a redeeming godliness are entitled to the same defense. Indeed, there are interesting resemblances between Nietzsche's interpretation of being, time, and the good and those of certain kinds of religionists—as Nietzsche seems to have known [37].)

the faith in opposite values, he nevertheless incessantly makes opposite valuations. High and low may be inextricably intertwined, but there is such a thing as high and low. Surely no one insists on this more than Nietzsche.[13] The question concerns the relation of the high to the low, that is, the nature and extent of the high's *dependence* on the low. Does intellectual conscience demand, as Nietzsche says it does, that we resist attributing the high to anything other than the low—that we resist recourse to something like Plato's *eidē*? Nietzsche makes a powerful and by now familiar case for the reliance of the high on the low, not only developmentally but also even in the subsistence of the high: sublimation is an ongoing process. Yet one might accept this much but still part company with Nietzsche. One might well hold that the "material cause" of the high *is* in fact the low—for example, that the will to truth is the product of the spiritualization of cruelty—while still believing that there is, indeed needs to be, a separate "formal cause," some set of structures or forms that preexist the development of the high. Conceived thus, such structures or forms (*eidē*) would necessarily be in some sense higher than the material cause. Or rather, the existence of such forms would necessarily amount to the natural existence, priority, and pre-givenness of the high.

Nietzsche, of course, denies just this. He insists that the formal cause of something high, if indeed he would accept such a thing as a formal cause, is no higher that the material out of which the thing developed. The high (e.g., the will to truth) is produced "from below," as it were—by the mysterious, creatively self-organizing force called will to power. Nietzsche subscribes to a principle of method that demands that one eschew recourse to "superfluous teleological principles" (*BGE* 13) and exhaust a single kind of causality before assuming other kinds (*BGE* 36). And he suggests that a single kind of causality, "causality of the will," is sufficient to explain nothing less than "the world defined and determined according to its 'intelligible character'" (36).[14] The question with which we are faced is whether Nietzsche isn't claiming too much. For even if the development of the high out of the low can somehow be represented in terms of will-causality, is it really being *explained*? And if

---

13. To be clear: "High" and "low" refer, respectively, to the more complex and refined and conscious—or, in short, the more powerful—and the less. Will to power is itself neither high nor low. Or, rather, it is both, since all activity, high, low, or in between, expresses will to power.

14. As noted above, section 36 states a hypothesis based on a thought experiment that it proposes but does not run. It does seem clear, though, both from the larger context of the book as well as from Nietzsche's extensive notes for his planned next *Hauptwerk*, that he had performed the experiment to his own satisfaction.

not, doesn't Nietzsche's denial of another kind of causality amount to an assertion of something he cannot know? Is he not propounding a mirror image of the metaphysicians' faith? (The quarrel between Nietzsche and Plato really may turn on the question of the metaphysicians' faith, the relation of the high to the low, just as Nietzsche suggests. It is not for nothing that Nietzsche raises the issue in section 2 of *Beyond Good and Evil*, preceding it only with section 1's raising the question of the value of truth, which is the only issue more basic than this one but one on which Nietzsche and Plato agree.) Nietzsche himself acknowledges the ultimately mysterious character of creative, form-giving will to power. How then can he know that no other kind of causality is at work or that will to power itself isn't more than he thinks? Why not confess not-knowing rather than assert nonbeing? Nietzsche's harsher critics might convict him of hubris. But perhaps a fairer explanation, if indeed an explanation is wanted, would point to a more refined kind of pride, a pride based on the demanding virtue of intellectual probity: a pride connected to the demands of nobility.

(g) I have suggested that Nietzsche's new ideal of nobility (*Vornehmheit*) lies behind his insistence on the need for redemption (e) and his rejection of the "faith of the metaphysicians" (f). The structure of *Beyond Good and Evil*, its culmination in a section titled "What is Noble?" indicates that nobility is the lodestar of Nietzsche's political project.[15] Nobility is also the ideal that informs *Beyond Good and Evil*'s philosophic work per se, in that philosophy itself is for Nietzsche the peak of nobility. What *is* noble? Nietzsche's new conception is too subtle and multifaceted to be fully communicated by any formula—indeed, this is part of its newness. (Primitive nobility, while affirmative, tends toward simplicity.) But Nietzsche himself uses formulas—if not to communicate the full meaning of nobility, then at least to point to or represent its essence. One of these appears in section 212 of *Beyond Good and Evil*, where "being noble" (*Vornehm-sein*) is summarized as "wanting to be by oneself, being able to be different, standing alone and having to live independently." Readers will recognize that these characteristics distinguish both the philosopher and the free minds, though of course the former more than the latter, from the rest of humanity. (This itself testifies to the newness of Nietzsche's conception of nobility. Traditional conceptions of nobility are

---

15. I call part 9 the culmination of *Beyond Good and Evil* because it addresses the being, the life, of the highest being (the philosopher), along with the regime that favors his appearance and his work—and which will *be* his work.

surely in some tension with philosophy, with its willingness and even eagerness to look behind every curtain without regard for shame or the strictures of conventional piety. Compare the curiosity of the "plebian" Socrates, even to the point of dubious taste, with the self-regarding and thus self-restraining dignity of Aristotle's great-souled man. Nietzsche himself notes the inhibitions imposed by nobility upon thought and artistic receptiveness: "men of a noble culture" find it difficult to appreciate that which is alien to them; "we" moderns, on the other hand, have access to a wide variety of things—"We enjoy Homer again, for example"—only because of our *ignoble* historical sense [224].) Readers might also notice that, accordingly, these same qualities characterize the very investigations undertaken by this philosopher for the free minds who are reading his book.[16] But how does this new ideal of nobility account for the felt need for redemption (e) and the rejection of the metaphysicians' faith (f)?

Answers begin to emerge when we take note of the word itself. What has been rendered here (and by leading translators and interpreters) as *noble* is the German *vornehm*. Unlike *edel*, which is also typically rendered as *noble*, *vornehm* refers to standing or status and particularly to being well-born or aristocratic. (*Edel*, by contrast, is closer to beauty, or moral beauty. The difference between *vornehm* and *edel* is similar to the difference in ancient Greek between *gennaios* and *kalos*.) As such, *Vornehmheit* as an ideal seems to me to contribute to the need for redemption in two ways. First, perfect nobility *requires* redemption, for the core and essential expression of this nobility is affirmation of oneself and the world, and such affirmation is only possible for one who has overcome the spirit of revenge by willing eternal recurrence. Second, one whose ideal is *Vornehmheit* will feel the need for such redemption with particular acuteness, for his very consciousness of nobility, his proclivity to notice and assign to things their proper rank, will only make him more aware of and more oppressed by the baseness that predominates in human life. True, the noble person will show a certain solicitude and courtesy toward

---

16. Whether the ideal of nobility equally informs Nietzsche's other mature works would be an interesting question to investigate. Like Plato, Nietzsche has written his *Politeia* from a political standpoint, which turns out in his case to mean from a standpoint that takes its bearings from the ideal of nobility. We might expect, then, to find his other works, his less political works, less nobility oriented. Or perhaps Nietzsche's mature works are *all* as political as *Beyond Good and Evil*? In fact they seem so to me, and this reading is consistent with Nietzsche's conception of the philosopher as an *essentially* political (i.e., legislative) actor.

those whom he finds beneath his own level. But that will not lessen the severity with which he *sees* or, consequently, the oppression that he feels.

The influence of *Vornehmheit* on Nietzsche's rejection of the faith of the metaphysicians (f) is probably more evident than its influence on the felt need for redemption (e). Nietzsche presents his rejection of the metaphysicians' faith as a matter of intellectual conscience, as surely it is. But this conscience and its peculiar intensity surely owe something to an ideal of nobility that prizes independence and the ability to be different. I suggested above that where some of Nietzsche's critics might see his rejection of "higher structures" as hubris I would connect it to a different, more refined pride. The pride of which I am speaking is a pride that insists on the utmost severity upon oneself: no giving oneself the benefit of the doubt and, most especially, no giving in to the wishes of the heart. Heart must be tethered to mind—must be *sacrificed* to mind.[17] The question, though, as I have already stated, is whether Nietzsche doesn't claim too much, that is, whether he doesn't illicitly convert not-knowing into nonbeing. Or, to put it in terms more appropriate to the present discussion, the question is whether he isn't led by his proud severity to the mirror image of wishful thinking.

Consider section 50 of the *Antichrist*, in which Nietzsche articulates "a psychology of 'faith'" and distances himself from "'believers.'" In answer to the claim that "Faith makes blessed: *hence* it is true," Nietzsche offers the following: "Let us suppose, with some leniency that it was proved that faith makes blessed. . . . Would blessedness—or more technically speaking, *pleasure*—ever be a proof of truth? This is so far from the case that it almost furnishes a counterproof; in any event, the greatest suspicion of a 'truth' should arise when feelings of pleasure enter the discussion of the question 'What is true?'" That which pleases or fulfills the wishes of the heart warrants extreme "suspicion."[18] Indeed, by the end of the aphorism suspicion has become conviction: "What does it mean, after all, to have *integrity* in matters of the mind? That one is severe against one's heart, that one despises 'beautiful sentiments,' that one makes of every Yes and No a matter of conscience. Faith

---

17. This principle is repeated over and over in Nietzsche's many books. In *Beyond Good and Evil* see particularly part 2, "The Free Mind." To get a sense of the degree of Nietzsche's severity, consider his view that even scientific hypotheses "may be granted admission and . . . value in the realm of knowledge" only on condition that they remain "under police supervision, under the police of mistrust" (*GS* 344). How much more mistrust, then, must be due beliefs that please the heart.

18. Also see *BGE* 33 and *GM* III 24.

makes blessed: consequently it lies." Gone from this final formulation is the "almost" of the prior one. One cannot help but wonder—or at least I cannot help but wonder—whether this severity hasn't overcorrected for wishful thinking. Of course, there is good reason to proceed as Nietzsche does, and very few people are even capable of it. It is better for a thinker to err on the side of severity, particularly where the matter at hand touches the deepest longings of the heart. It is almost certainly *nobler* to err on the side of severity. But better still from the standpoint of truth is not to err at all; and it's not clear that Nietzsche, by making a ruling passion of severity cum self-denial, hasn't let his love of *Vornehmheit* make *him* "the human being who has flown highest yet and gone astray most beautifully" (60).[19]

Having identified the ideal of *Vornehmheit* as a major force behind Nietzsche's emphasis on redemption and (via his severe intellectual conscience) his identification of eternal recurrence as the good, I need to pause here to introduce a caution. His embrace of the ideal of *Vornehmeit* is the moral foundation or ground of his stance toward life. As such it goes a long way toward explaining the other features of his thought that I have mentioned and, indeed, the general character of his thought.[20] Nietzsche himself instructs us to look to the moral ground of a thinker's work as its motive spring: "the moral (or immoral) intentions in every philosophy constituted the real germ of life from which the whole plant had grown" (6). But a moral foundation doesn't stand alone. For one thing, it has its own submoral sources in psychophysiology. (I will not enter into this except to note that Nietzsche sees "great health" as the psychophysiological source of his ideal of *Vornehmheit*). And it is bound up with cognitive and ontological assumptions, "pre-valuative" assumptions, that determine what one can see and the terms in which one interprets

---

19. Section 50 of *The Antichrist* is perhaps unrepresentative in the extremity of its formulation, but it is continuous with Nietzsche's general theme. In section 39 of *Beyond Good and Evil*, for example, Nietzsche warns against the error of supposing an idea to be false simply because it makes people unhappy and evil. He makes no mention, however, of the opposite error, that is, supposing an idea to be *true* because it leads to unhappiness and evil—this despite his awareness that there are people, cynics, who tend in just this direction (26). Arguably the free minds to whom Nietzsche means to speak are at least as likely to imitate the cynic as the idealist. Why, then, no warning against the cynics' error? Unless, perhaps, such a warning would alienate free minds by sounding too idealistic.

20. The influence of this ideal on the general character of Nietzsche's thought may be what Leo Strauss had in mind with his final word on Nietzsche—the closing line of his posthumously published study of *Beyond Good and Evil*: "Die vornehme Natur ersetzt die göttliche Natur." "Note on the Plan of Nietzsche's *Beyond Good and Evil*," in *Studies in Platonic Political Philosophy* (originally appeared in *Interpretation: A Journal of Political Philosophy* 3, nos. 2 and 3 [1973]).

and names what one sees. Chief among this class of assumptions, it seems to me, is Nietzsche's belief in the inescapability of time, or the nonexistence of the atemporal. If the ideal of *Vornehmheit* is the fundamental *moral* feature of Nietzsche's thought, his understanding of time may be its fundamental *ontological* feature. Nietzsche's awareness of time is one of the outstanding features of his thought in general, manifesting most clearly in his historical or developmental approach to matters both social and personal.

What is the relation between these two great features of Nietzsche's thought? Nietzsche's emphasis on the moral impetus behind thought might suggest that we interpret a fundamental ontological principle such as his own understanding of the relation between being and time as a consequence of his even more basic moral project. And indeed, such an interpretation is plausible. Surely, as a general matter, a thinker's moral intention and its psychophysiological substrate shape and limit what he concludes about the character of being. And with respect to Nietzsche on being and time, it is not hard to see a causal connection between the embrace of *Vornehmheit* and a keen awareness of humanity's enmeshment in time. One who embraces the ideal of *Vornehmheit* will be given to severe self-judgment and will aspire to render his life as perfect as possible, as if it were an artwork; and this will make him particularly conscious of time. Yet the causal connection between the embrace of *Vornehmheit* and a keen awareness of time might just as plausibly be seen in the opposite way: maybe the awareness of time contributes to the embrace of *Vornehmheit*. An awareness of time is an awareness of the past, of all that needs to be justified or made right or redeemed. What's more, although Nietzsche emphasizes the primacy of the moral intention in a thinker's thought, he does so predominantly where the thought at issue is erroneous. The story is typically one in which a psychological or physiological weakness gives rise to a moral intention that in turn leads to ontological error. Where a thinker writes out of great health, though, there is less reason to suppose that his ontological principles will be in error or even that they are the direct products of a moral intention. Great health combined with intellectual rigor doesn't so much give rise to or create ontological principles as allow one to approach an independently existing ontological truth.[21] Finally, it may be that

---

21. By "independently existing ontological truth," I don't mean truth that is free of human interpretation—such a thing doesn't exist in Nietasche's view—but rather the clearest sight or best interpretation of the world as it presents itself to us, which for Nietzsche is the only world there is.

the causality between the embrace of *Vornehmheit* and Nietzsche's view of being and time is mutual, and that neither of these two features of his thought is prior to the other. In the end, we must judge Nietzsche's and Plato's conceptions of the good on their own terms and not by any inferred moral intention. Even if their conceptions of the good are the result of prior moral intentions, those intentions cannot be evaluated except in light of the resulting teachings about the good. It is only by the fruit that one can really know the tree.

Which takes us to our next question.

(4) The last of the questions I laid out above concerns the consequences of Nietzsche's conception of eternity for politics and for life. To answer this question would require nothing short of an assessment of the entirety of Nietzsche's political and moral teaching. For as I will explain below, the question of eternity, as the question of the good, surely gives rise to or at least shapes every aspect of Nietzsche's political and moral thought. I raise the question here, though, for three reasons. First, I want to highlight just that fact. Those who are interested in Nietzsche as a political thinker ought to recognize the rootedness of his thought in this deepest and apparently most apolitical of questions; and those whose attention is drawn not to politics but to eternal recurrence ought to know that that question is deeply connected to politics and indeed (as I will argue below) is best approached by way of Nietzsche's political thought. To miss this connection is to sunder Nietzsche's good from his legislative project, which can only lead to a skewed interpretation of the character of that project.

Second, I wish to offer an observation about the character or structure of Nietzsche's political and moral thought. I have asserted that for Nietzsche, willing eternal recurrence of the same is the good. To will eternal return is to overcome the spirit of revenge and thoroughly affirm life. That's what's so good about it. But another way of describing its goodness is to say that to will eternal return is to will as robustly and as extensively as possible, to experience one's will as unobstructed and hence in some way godlike. Eternal recurrence is good, is *the* good, because it most fully satisfies will to power. This "most fully" is important, for it enables us to understand more fully what else is good, that is, lesser goods, and wherein their goodness lies. Absent awareness of eternal recurrence as the crowning good, one would be able to perceive that Nietzsche's conception of will to power provides the basis for a moral and political hierarchy. One would be able to see that, for Nietzsche, the goodness of goods lies in the experience of power they bring and that this relation to power constitutes the basis for a natural ranking or hierarchy of goods. ("What is good? Everything that heightens the feeling of power in man, the will to power, power itself. What is bad? Everything that is born of weakness" [A 2].)[22] And one would be able to see that the way to promote the good, that is, the thrust of healthful politics, would be to promote a culture that stimulates contest and striving. But one would miss something equally important and more than likely end up with a partial and thereby distorted conception of moral and political good: for it is only by understanding that eternal recurrence is the crowning good, and why this is so, that one will understand the meaning of power and the way to power for Nietzsche.[23] Only then will one be in a position to speak with some soundness about a Nietzschean politics, or the content and character of Nietzsche's legislative project. (For all that he follows Plato, Nietzsche says comparatively little about the specifics of a good regime: we can say as a general principle that Nietzsche seeks a politics that is true to nature, even an ascent to nature, but with respect to specifics we must either conjecture or try to work out the meaning of this principle ourselves.)[24] That eternal recurrence is the good indicates that for Nietzsche the "maximal feeling of power" is achieved by reconciling oneself and one's will with what

---

22. Notice that the criteria of good and bad are not strictly comparable. The former concern the *causes* of power, the latter the *effects* of weakness. The subsequent line demonstrates that Nietzsche's moral thought is indeed naturalistic and even eudaimonistic after a fashion: "What is happiness? The feeling that power is *growing*, that resistance is overcome." Also see *Twilight Errors* 2. The moral and political consequences of will to power—along with those of Platonic eros and Rousseau's "desire to extend our being"—will be addressed again in Chapter 10.

23. That will to power must be understood in light of its essential connection to eternity has been argued most notably by three interpreters, who make widely varying judgments of the connection. Heidegger saw in this connection an indication of Nietzsche's supposed vengefulness and continuation and completion of metaphysics. Löwith "tried to establish the idea of eternity as the center of [Nietzsche's] philosophy" but saw eternity and will to power as ultimately incompatible. Lampert argues for the connection without subscribing to either of the foregoing critiques. See respectively Heidegger, *Nietzsche*, esp. volume I; Löwith, *Nietzsche's Philosophy of the Eternal Recurrence of the Same* (the quote, which refers to the volume I have cited, appears in Löwith, *Mein Leben in Deutschland vor und nach 1933*); and Lampert, *Nietzsche's Teaching*. Lampert reviews the stances of some of Nietzsche's more prominent interpreters on this question at p. 335n102.

24. Why *is* Nietzsche less forthcoming than Plato about the good regime? Perhaps there is more than one legitimate regime. Or perhaps modernity, with its multiple competing strands and its self-consciousness, makes postmodernity and its possibilities less knowable. Or perhaps Nietzsche *isn't* less forthcoming than Plato, who, after all, is quite specific about regimes that are *not possible* and perhaps not even desirable.

is; and it suggests that a political and moral hierarchy true to Nietzsche's conception could be much more humane than is typically thought.²⁵ This is of more than theoretical interest: as long as Nietzsche continues to fascinate and inspire, he stands to influence political life. And to the extent that his ideal of eternal recurrence is not understood, that influence threatens to be utopian and vengeful and *in*humane.

Finally, Nietzsche's eternity certainly has implications for what one might call the politics of the soul—that is, for readers' efforts at self-cultivation. Like the *Republic*, *Beyond Good and Evil* concerns itself centrally with the soul. What we conventionally think of as political—regime types, the education of rulers, the political uses of religion, and so on—is addressed for the sake of individuals, particularly the best individuals. In the *Republic* this prioritization becomes clear at the end of book 9, when Socrates states that the city in speech, though it may never come into being, can serve the psychic development of those who have contemplated it (592). In *Beyond Good and Evil* this is made explicit early in part 9, though it is not so difficult to discern throughout the book. Many of Nietzsche's readers, including prominent ones, have been so struck—and attracted—by the implications of his thought for the project of personal cultivation that they have effectively disregarded his political teaching (which they don't like) or have discounted Nietzsche's claim that optimal personal development requires a more favorable politics than liberal-

---

25. The words in quotation marks come from what might be the most succinct of Nietzsche's published descriptions of will to power: "Every animal . . . instinctively strives for an optimum of favorable conditions under which it can expend all its strength and can achieve its maximal feeling of power; every animal abhors . . . every kind of intrusion or hindrance that obstructs or could obstruct this path to the optimum (I am *not* speaking of its path to happiness, but its path to power, to action" (*GM* III 7). My point, to repeat, is that the state of being that most fully satisfies this criterion is one of acceptance and affirmation of what is. A fair question, though, is to what extent the humaneness of Nietzsche's crowning good pervades the secondary heights of the hierarchy of goods. Does a partial ability to say *da capo* necessarily outweigh, say, the satisfactions of being a not very spiritual tyrant? More concretely, do the satisfactions of being a mediocre Nietzschean (a scholar, say) outweigh the satisfactions of being a Borgia? And if not, isn't there something dangerous about the will-to-power teaching, even—or especially—if it's true? Here, perhaps, we glimpse something of the political difference between Nietzsche and Plato. Read closely, the Platonic Socrates establishes the inferiority of the tyrannical life only to the philosophic life, not to any other lives. Yet he speaks as if he has established the inferiority of the tyrannical life to *all* other lives. (To be sure, the tyrannical *soul* Socrates describes in book 9 is the worst of all the souls he depicts. But Socrates never quite eliminates the possibility of someone being a tyrant without having a tyrannical soul.) I will return to this theme in the next chapter.

ism.[26] In this they do Nietzsche a disservice even as they make Nietzsche palatable for late modern or postmodern liberal taste. (Not the least of the consequences of this apolitical reading of Nietzsche is that it obscures his affinity with Plato.) But the disservice isn't total, for Nietzsche does mean to educate his readers as individuals. Indeed, he must educate them *first*, in order that he may thereafter enlist them in his political project. And, caring as he does for those with the highest spiritual potential, presumably he also means to offer guidance irrespective of any larger political project. For that matter the apolitical reading may not be a disservice to Nietzsche after all, even if it does fall short of the truth. For if a liberal mask is what it takes to allow readers who wouldn't otherwise come to Nietzsche to enter his thought and ultimately support his project, then Nietzsche's end is served by those who have constructed that mask, notwithstanding that they may have done so because they never endorsed or perhaps even saw that end. (Some might suppose that Nietzsche wouldn't be interested in reaching readers who wouldn't approach him unless he were wearing a liberal mask. But this seems too harsh a judgment, especially in light of the respect Nietzsche shows for the spiritual depths and heights of all sorts of antagonists.)[27]

26. Among those who have effectively discounted the connection between Nietzsche's teachings about self-cultivation and his political views are some of his more prominent interpreters, including Kaufmann in his landmark *Nietzsche: Philosopher, Psychologist, Antichrist*, and Nehemas in *Nietzsche: Life as Literature*. Neither Kaufmann nor Nehemas is unaware of Nietzsche's political concerns, but they treat these concerns as effectively detachable from the other parts of Nietzsche's thought—Kaufmann because he thinks those other parts stand on their own and can be fully apprehended without reference to politics, Nehemas because he denies that Nietzsche even has a positive or legislative political teaching. Prominent postmodern theorists, meanwhile, sharing Nietzsche's disdain for bourgeois society and wanting to make use of his teachings about self-cultivation, have often seen the connection between those teachings and Nietzsche's political project but have taken it upon themselves to sever the connection. In their hands Nietzsche's politics are *made* detachable. Thus does Foucault, for example, assert that "the only valid tribute to thought such as Nietzsche's is precisely to use it, to make it groan and protest," and that "being unfaithful to Nietzsche" is of no concern to him; see "Prison Talk" in *Power/Knowledge*, p. 54. Similarly, Rorty, while appropriating Nietzsche as a model of self-creation, breezily decrees that Nietzsche's political views may be disregarded as irrelevant to that model; see *Contingency, Irony, and Solidarity*, pp. 65 and 98–103. Indeed, Rorty speaks for many when he accuses Nietzsche of betraying the principles that inform his teachings on personal cultivation—principles such as perspectivism and acceptance of the contingency of life—with his assertive, hierarchical political teaching.

27. Ah, but those antagonists have in common a passion or stature that is far removed from the spirit of modern and postmodern liberalism. Yet, as both Plato and Nietzsche note, democracy—for which we may substitute liberalism—is marked by a plethora of human types. Surely, then, Nietzsche would acknowledge that many who subscribe to liberalism nevertheless

Nietzsche has much to say by way of guiding his sympathetic readers in their efforts at self-cultivation—regarding the chaotic strivings of our drives and the need to order them; regarding will to power as the source of this order even as it is the source of the original disorder; regarding the need to master passions by sublimating them; and so forth. It is not for nothing that Nietzsche is widely recognized as the source of much subsequent psychological theory, including clinical theory.[28] Yet just as those who do not appreciate the meaning or place of eternity in Nietzsche's thought will tend toward a distorted view of will to power and hence his politics, so, too, they will tend toward a distorted view of self-cultivation and hence his psychic politics or his conception of the good life. Those who do not appreciate the meaning and place of eternity will certainly be able to see and make some kind of sense of Nietzsche's conceptions of probity, creativity, and "'giving style' to one's character" (GS 290). And they should even be able to appreciate Nietzsche's teaching about revenge and the need to overcome it: although that teaching is finally anchored in the teaching on eternal recurrence, it is presented repeatedly and accessibly. But because eternal return is (in Nietzsche's view) the only way truly—that is, fully—to overcome the spirit of revenge, those who do not appreciate the teaching not only won't overcome revenge, they won't understand that they haven't and can't overcome it. And they will likely be led to the personal analogue of political idealism, that is, utopian projects of self-cultivation that risk delusion and demoralization and that must in any case fail. This is not a dire-sounding prospect. Certainly it is less troubling than the *political* utopianism that would result from an attempt to create a Nietzschean politics without understanding the meaning and place of eternity in Nietzsche's thought. Yet the two utopianisms are not without a practical connection, if only because those who have failed in their misconceived attempts at Nietzschean self-cultivation would seem susceptible to the siren song of a misconceived Nietzschean politics.

---

display a spirit or the germ of a spirit of independence and pride. Indeed, surely many of the "free minds" to whom Nietzsche especially means to speak in *Beyond Good and Evil* fit this description.

28. Ellenberger devoted a section of *The Discovery of the Unconscious*, "The Prophet of a New Era: Nietzsche," to detailing the many ideas that rendered Nietzsche "the common source of Freud, Adler and Jung," among others. Also see May, "Nietzsche's Contributions to Psychology," and Ginsberg, "Nietzschean Psychiatry." Kaufmann has also effectively made the case for Nietzsche's power and worth as psychic guide both in his *Nietzsche* and in the more exclusively psychological *Discovering the Mind, Volume Two*, in which Nietzsche figures as both model and teacher of self-knowledge and self-cultivation.

CONCLUSION

Leo Strauss is reported to have said that, given the choice, he would have chosen to live when he did because with access to Nietzsche's writing he had access to the greatest philosophic contest: Plato had given the deepest and most comprehensive account of the whole, and Nietzsche had given the most comprehensive critique of that account.[29] I won't presume to make so sweeping a comparative judgment myself (and not only because it would be too inelegant in the present context to leave Rousseau unmentioned): Who knows what depths might exist in other thinkers, beyond scholars' awareness, or at least beyond mine? But I do subscribe wholeheartedly to the gist of Strauss's statement. Plato gives a staggeringly deep and broad account of things, and Nietzsche gives a comparably deep and broad rebuttal. What makes this antagonism even more amazing, though, is that there is so much in common between the two thinkers. Not just formally—motivational monism, and so on—but substantively, right down to the identification of eternity as the good. I have argued in these pages that the nub of the antagonism between Nietzsche and Plato is found in the interior of this most basic similarity, that is, in their respective understandings of eternity. Both thinkers see the embrace of eternity as the good, but what they mean by this embrace are two very different things. If this is correct then perhaps I have clarified the antagonism. But clarifying a question is worthwhile only if it helps us address it. So let me conclude by raising anew the question of Nietzsche versus Plato. (5) Who, if either, is right? And how shall we judge?

If the heart of the Nietzsche–Plato antagonism is in fact where I have located it, perhaps we can best move toward a judgment by inquiring into the source of the antagonism: *Why* does Plato advocate an understanding according to which the good life involves insight into eternal *eidê* and a good that is beyond being and intelligibility? And why does Nietzsche repudiate these very things? I will treat Nietzsche here only as critic: if one is persuaded to Plato's view of the *eidê* and the good, then the issue is settled; if one is not persuaded by Plato, then, given Nietzsche's agreement with Plato on the longing for eternity, the issue is settled in Nietzsche's favor, since no other eternity besides eternal recurrence is possible. (An interesting question that I cannot take up here is whether and to what extent Nietzsche's way to eternity would satisfy

---

29. Grant, *Technology and Justice*, p. 90.

us even if Plato is right. Would the embrace of eternal return reconcile one to the goodness of life and open the highest possibilities? Or would the denial of eternal structures inhibit the highest experiences and *prevent* one from affirming all that is?)

Nietzsche, of course, offers his own interpretation of Platonism. As I mentioned at the outset, Nietzsche interprets Plato's advocacy of Platonism as something politic and insincere—not in toto, but to a considerable extent: Platonism was perpetrated as a noble lie—or, rather, a *holy* lie (*pia fraus*). And what Nietzsche does not attribute to such lying, he attributes to Plato's desire "to prove to himself that reason and instinct of themselves tend toward one goal, the good, 'God'" (191)—a desire born of an unfortunate seduction, but a seduction of a noble and powerful mind. These explanations are explanations of Plato's *error*: for reasons outlined in *Beyond Good and Evil* (especially section 36 but also the whole of part 1) and reviewed briefly above, Nietzsche finds Plato's conceptions of eternity and eternal *eidê* both wrong and unnecessary—wrong *because* unnecessary: all that can be explained can be explained by recourse to will-causality (36). Positing a higher causal realm is at best a fictional explanation that doesn't really explain.

But those inclined to accept Nietzsche's critique must reckon with an important fact: Plato's conception of eternity, like Nietzsche's, is grounded on an interpretation of *experience*. Platonic metaphysics are not speculative, or at least no more so than any interpretation of private experience is speculative. The *eidê* are not deductions by Plato so much as the names he has assigned, on the basis of reasoned interpretation, to things he has *seen* (i.e., intellected). Such at least is the picture given us in the dialogues. And such has been the view of Platonists through the ages, who have recognized in Plato a persuasive account and interpretation of their own experience.[30] A fair consideration of the contest between Nietzsche and Plato must therefore proceed as an analysis and judgment of experiences and their interpretation.

How does one choose between such contestants? How can one judge the experiential judgments of others? Exactly as one always does: by attending to the phenomenology of the experience insofar as possible (i.e., by seeking to apprehend the other's experience as fully and directly as one can) and then considering the explicit and implicit grounds for the other's interpretation of

---

30. Plotinus, for example, seems to have believed he saw in Plato representations of experiences (insights) that he, Plotinus, had independently had.

his experience.[31] I should also add that one should abide all the while by "the conscience of *method*" (36), though as I noted above, it is not clear whether the content with which Nietzsche fills this term amounts to a healthy conscience or a hypertrophied one.

Even leaving aside the special demands of Nietzschean intellectual conscience, there is nothing easy about assessing experiential judgments. Interpreting one's own experience, let alone the experience of others, is a very tricky business. Indeed, one cannot begin to judge another person's experiential claim with any adequacy unless one has had the same experience, or something close to it, oneself. And needless to say this requirement of intersubjectivity becomes more daunting when, as here, what is at issue are claims of rare insights into the highest things.[32] Absent some sense of shared experience with the one whose claim is under consideration, one is thrown back on some kind of faith or trust in others—not blind trust, at least not necessarily,

---

31. A somewhat more complete summary of this process and its underlying principle is offered by Ken Wilber as part of a defense of the "contemplative sciences," a term that is meant to embrace Plato's work, among others. "It dawns on few interpreters that these systems are, through and through, from top to bottom, the results of actual contemplative apprehensions and direct developmental phenomenology. The higher levels of these systems cannot be experienced or deduced *rationally*, and nobody from Plotinus to Aurobindo thinks they can. However, *after the fact* of direct and repeated experiential disclosures, they can be rationally reconstructed and presented as a 'system.' But the 'system,' so called, has been discovered, not deduced, and checked against direct experience in a community of the like-minded and like-spirited. . . . There is absolutely nothing 'metaphysical' about these systems: they are empirical-phenomenological developmental psychology at its most rigorous and most comprehensive, carried straightforwardly and openly into the transpersonal domains via the experimental instrument of contemplation" (*Sex, Ecology, Spirituality*, p. 336; emphasis in the original.) Also see Wilber pp. 264–76, where the same point is elaborated and objections are answered. To what may be the most commonly voiced objection to this approach, namely, "that these mystical states are private and interior and cannot be publicly validated," Wilber answers: "This is simply not true; or rather, if it is true, then it applies to any and all nonempirical endeavors, from mathematics to literature to linguistics to psychoanalysis to historical interpretation. Nobody has ever seen, 'out there' in the 'sensory world,' the square root of a negative one" (p. 266).

32. Nietzsche, we should note, does not shrink from offering his own interpretations of the experiences that others have believed to be insights into eternal being. He finds Platonism to be grounded in dubious interpretation. This is what he refers to in *Beyond Good and Evil* as the "faith of metaphysicians" (2). The matter is treated somewhat more extensively in *Twilight of the Idols*, where Nietzsche highlights confusions (e.g., "confusing the last and the first") and false inferences (e.g., a doer from the deed) as well as the falsifying effects of grammar ("I am afraid we are not rid of God because we still have faith in grammar"; "Reason" 4, 5). And against those who claim direct experience of or union with the eternal (i.e., the divine), he responds with a series of debunking counterinterpretations, running the nihilistic gamut from an unmet yearning for love (Jesus) to autohypnosis (priests, fakirs, Brahmins) to more "colorful" varieties of pathology (various saints and mystics) (*A* 28–35; *GM* I 6; *GM* III 17).

but trust all the same, that is, reliance on those who seem best positioned to know.

To some this reliance will not be not so troubling, for one finds that many gifted individuals separated by vast distances of time and space have reported experiences and insights that are remarkably similar to those which make up the core of Platonism. Doesn't the existence of similar experiential claims by individuals from dissimilar times and places testify to the credibility of their claims? Perhaps. (Wilber thinks so: "Are the mystics and sages insane? Because they all tell variations on this same story, don't they? The story of awakening one morning and discovering that you are one with the All, in a timeless and eternal and infinite fashion.")[33] But there is an answer to this argument-by-numbers, and no one has made it more powerfully than Nietzsche, who recognizes that a shared human nature—shared longings, shared needs, and shared linguistic structures—can as easily result in shared *error* as in shared insight (20; also, *GM* III 17). Not even the high intelligence and nobility of an idea's adherents prove its truth. If nobility ensured truth, then the "worst, most durable, and most dangerous of all errors so far" (Preface) could not have been the work of the philosopher whose "way of thinking . . . was a *noble* [*vornehme*] way of thinking" (14); nor could "the noblest and most remote feeling attained among men," the feeling embodied in the injunction to "love man *for God's sake*," have been a going "astray" (60). If even nobility does not guarantee truth, there is nothing left but to consider the thing itself—the experience and its competing interpretations—with the utmost rigor and sensitivity. Hardly an easy task, to say it again, and not least because the demands of intellectual conscience must themselves be worked out (what *is* rigor in such a case? what *is* sensitivity?).

To carry out this task is beyond what I can attempt here. But perhaps I have at least clarified the work to be done. And perhaps I can clarify it further by offering a countervailing note. For all that I have just said about the question at issue between Nietzsche and Plato being a matter of interpreting experience, that is, being subjective or at best intersubjective, there may well be a more objective approach to it—a *political* approach. Although the question of eternity is not a political question, one's view of this matter does eventuate in a political teaching. Might it not be the case, then, that their political teachings can help us understand and judge between Nietzsche and Plato at the

---

33. Wilber, *A Brief History of Everything*, p. 42.

more basic, pre-political level at which their antagonism begins? This political approach is not an easy one. The objective path is as extensive as the subjective approach is intensive—too extensive even to begin here. But before the beginning comes the commitment. So let me conclude by making the case for the political approach to the contest between Nietzsche's and Plato's eternities.

The political consequence of a nonpolitical doctrine cannot prove the doctrine true or false. But not all nonpolitical doctrines are equally removed from politics. Now consider: We do (and should) judge the truth of political doctrines at least in part by their consequences—one needn't be a pragmatist but only a kind of ethical or political naturalist to believe so. This being the case, might not those nonpolitical doctrines that are close to politics—doctrines that assert a claim about human well-being—also be properly judged by their practical consequences? But is the question of eternity really anything close to a political question? Yes, as it happens. For the competing views of eternity are not matters of metaphysical speculation but rather claims about experiences that are held up by these thinkers as human perfection and thus a general standard of goodness. The antagonism concerns what is wanted and what is good for the soul. Which begins to sound awfully political: What is politics, for Plato or for Nietzsche, if not "the art whose business it is to care for souls" (*Laws* 650b)?[34]

Another way of formulating the case for a political approach to the question of competing eternities is to say that, for both Nietzsche and Plato, the truth of a doctrine about human life needs to be tested against the standard of nature. Now what can this mean except to test it against a vision of health? To be sure, we do not understand health entirely: as Nietzsche says, we still need to *uncover* the basic text of *homo natura* (230). But we do know *something* about what's entailed by health. There are things that all of us save the severely impaired can recognize as good and bad, as signs of flourishing or evidence of dysfunction. And this is particularly so at the macrolevel of society, where injustice and antinaturalism and even to some extent their opposite numbers are "big" enough to see. There is much truth in Socrates' seemingly ridiculous claim that the city, being big, will show us things we wouldn't see at the microlevel of the individual (*Republic* 368d–e). So if we were to accept

---

34. Nietzsche's "great politics" (*großen Politik*, rendered by Kaufmann as "large-scale politics"; 208) primarily concerns conflict over matters cultural and spiritual, that is, the care of souls.

one philosopher's political teaching as preferable based on an assessment of the health it seems to promote, we would have grounds for supposing that the same philosopher's understanding of the good, that is, his understanding of eternity and our relation to it, may also be true. Not conclusive grounds, but at least something suggestive.

To judge the truth of a teaching by its effects seems terribly slippery. And so it is. But slipperiness is no objection when there is only one kind of path. Yes, only one kind of path: to think about the question of eternity, which I have identified as *the* issue between Nietzsche and Plato, is necessarily to engage in *political* reflection, for the question of eternity is a question about the well-being of the soul. The question of eternity turns out to be not so much a nonpolitical question as a pre-political one—which makes it in some ways *simply* political. What I referred to above as the subjective path is indeed different from the path I have just now been speaking of—that is, looking at political consequences—but it, too, turns out to be a kind of political path, for it centers on a judgment of what is good for oneself, or for human beings, which is a judgment belonging to the art whose business it is to care for souls. The good as seen by Plato and Nietzsche may be something that transcends politics, but it can be inferred—to the extent that it can be inferred—from the political teaching to which it has given rise. Perhaps, then, the objective political approach isn't as slippery as it first seems, or at least no more so than any other approach.

There is yet one more reason to approach the quarrel between Nietzsche and Plato through consideration of their political teachings. Both philosophers' political teachings are far more than just a statement of principles and proofs. They are *poetic:* they educate the heart and spirit along with the mind and thereby prepare readers, as nothing else could, to apprehend and judge their underlying conceptions of eternity. We normally think of the political as the realm of the ephemeral. Yet high-level political poetry—the construction of a beautiful city or a new vision of nobility—is the gateway into the precincts of eternity.

EPILOGUE:
ONE OR MANY?

The question might be put a little more precisely: One, Two, or Three? Do Plato, Rousseau, and Nietzsche give accounts of the soul's preeminent force that are consistent and complementary, the differences signifying divergent perspectives on what is regarded as essentially the same thing, or do they give fundamentally different accounts? The answer, of course, is *both*. But the question is worth raising because it invites us to consider the philosophers in relation to one another and thus to reconstruct a three-party dialogue. As I suggested at the outset of this investigation, Plato, Rousseau, and Nietzsche not only speak to the same phenomena but also, by virtue of seeing those phenomena so similarly, effectively speak to *one another* on the question of what to make of it all—and, I might now add, on the question of what to *do*. As we have seen most clearly in Nietzsche's confrontation with Plato, differences become clearer, and are sometimes shown to be deeper, precisely as common ground is established and shown to be more extensive than it had seemed. That is to say, real differences become clearer as merely apparent ones are washed away. Those remaining differences can then become our focus as we each consider the question that it has been my purpose to clarify, namely, the question of who (if anyone) among the three thinkers, to what extent and in what respects, is right. In what follows I want to call attention, first, to a few ways in which the three philosophers oppose one another in their treatments of eros, ways that recall some of the more evident general distinctions between different epochs in the history of political philosophy; then, to a few ways in which they differ yet complement and even mutually illumine one another; and finally, to a few ways in which they agree and thus impress us with the practical import of their arguments (surely where three such thinkers agree, there must be some presumption of correctness). But such thinkers, being philosophers in the strictest sense of the word, cannot *simply* agree on anything of theoretical import, for such agreement would require a doctrinal certainty that true philosophy disavows. Awareness of the impossibility of such certainty—a *glad* awareness—and the belief that we must pursue these questions as if they *could* be settled, are the marks of a true philosopher and hence the most basic agreements between Plato, Rousseau, and Nietzsche.

PSYCHOLOGY ANCIENT AND MODERN: DIFFERENCES

Perhaps no differences are as apparent to contemporary students of political philosophy as those which seem to mark a philosopher as an "ancient" or a "modern."[1] And indeed, several key differences between the three philosophers' accounts of eros[2] fit with what one might expect from figures associated with—who *initiated*—their respective philosophic epochs.[3] We see, for example, Plato affirming the reality of the "high" and making it the focus of desire with his talk of the Good and the *eidê*, neither of which is embraced, by these names or any others, by Rousseau or Nietzsche. The trajectory runs, if I may oversimplify, from Plato's Good and the *eidê* to Rousseau's embrace of *ideals* that are generated by the imagination to Nietzsche's outright repudiation of all of these things as falsehoods whose appeal is born of, and whose effect is to promote, vengeance against life. Or to put it in more phenomenological terms, the trajectory runs from timeless or eternal objects of contemplation (Plato) to timeless reverie (Rousseau) to the embrace of eternity conceived as endlessly repeating time (Nietzsche).

We also see a trajectory with respect to rhetoric, from Plato's reticence to Rousseau's and Nietzsche's ever greater boldness of expression if not frankness. This is evident even in their chosen terminologies. With *erōs* Plato

---

1. The distinction between ancients and moderns, a cause célèbre in past centuries, has probably been taught most powerfully in recent times by Leo Strauss—so powerfully that many who reject the rest of Strauss's legacy accept this part. Less widely accepted is Strauss's subdivision of the history of modern political philosophy into "three waves." See, for example, "The Three Waves of Modernity," in *An Introduction to Political Philosophy*, pp. 81–98.

2. As in the Introduction, I will sometimes employ "eros" generically, to refer to Plato's *erōs*, Rousseau's desire for more being, and Nietzsche's will to power.

3. By Strauss's reckoning Rousseau initiated the "second wave" of modernity and Nietzsche the third. (The initiator of the first wave, and thus of modernity as such, was Machiavelli.) It might seem dubious to credit Plato with initiating a philosophic epoch insofar as he was a student of Socrates. But it was Plato who began the *written* classical tradition; and given the potency and, even more, the added philosophic dimensions that come with Platonic writing, Plato does emerge as a founder alongside Socrates.

adopts a word in wide currency and thus already rich with subphilosophic and complicating connotations. Rousseau, by contrast, speaks the clinically descriptive language of the "desire to extend our being," though he speaks little, leaving the meaning of the term to be teased out of his thought by close reading. Nietzsche, finally, coins a phrase that is broad but clear; and if "will to power" proves a more slippery term than it at first appears, Nietzsche undertakes to unpack it. Not that Rousseau and Nietzsche are simply frank—far from it. Both write artistically and with delicacy. Neither wants to be too easily or widely understood, and both go so far as to affirm what must appear by today's standards as out-and-out deception: consider Rousseau's justification of "fictions" (which, by virtue of their just results, are not to be considered lies) and Nietzsche's embrace of and delight in "masks."[4] Nietzsche, moreover (and perhaps Rousseau as well), joins Plato in seeing the deepest insights as inexpressible by discursive speech (*BGE* 296). Yet by writing in their own names and in spelling out *why* they endorse deception, Rousseau and Nietzsche equip their persistent readers with the ability to apprehend their meanings with greater certainty than Plato allows. In any case they make, in their own names, bold pronouncements that directly challenge moral, political, and religious orthodoxy.

Finally, the three philosophers occupy "appropriate" points on a trajectory with respect to eros' scope. ("Appropriate" to their respective epochs.) For all that I have claimed that eros is for Plato the soul of the soul, the single preeminent psychic force, Plato presents it, ostensibly, less as *the* force than as *a* force—indeed, as a *desire*, one among many. This is true both in the *Republic*, where Socrates initially assigns eros to one part of the soul, and in the *Symposium*, where Socrates pointedly does not join his more cosmologically minded companions in depicting eros as a force pervading the cosmos. These ostensible limits to the range and power of eros are not misrepresentations. Eros emerges as the soul's preeminent force, but it remains a specific desire. It can dominate the soul as a tyrant, which is to say it can draw other desires into alliance or service (*Republic* 572e–573b). But those other desires remain just that, *other;* they are not incorporated into eros or described by eros the way that Rousseau's expansiveness or Nietzsche's will to power describes the entirety of human being. Rousseau, of course, also speaks of a "*desire* to extend

---

4. Rousseau's justification of fictions appears in his extended reflections on truth and lying in the "Fourth Walk" of the *Reveries*. For Nietzsche's remarks about masks, including both their inevitability and their desirability, see especially *Beyond Good and Evil* 4, 5, and 40.

our being." But this desire is clearly a manifestation of a more general, indeed thoroughgoing, expansiveness that characterizes human being as such and is its fundamental disposition. Recall the passage from the *Dialogues* in which self-love is likened to a magnet. Nothing so sweeping appears in Plato. Nietzsche, finally, hypothesizes and seems to subscribe to the view that will to power explains *everything*.[5] Human beings are but moments of will to power, albeit the highest (i.e., the most complex and most spiritual) moments. True, in *Beyond Good and Evil* Nietzsche proposes this only as a hypothesis, as we have seen (36). But he also gives instructions regarding the testing of the hypothesis, and it seems fairly clear from all he says—and from all he planned to say in the unfinished *The Will to Power*—that he had performed the test to his own satisfaction, at least enough to accept "cosmic" will to power as a working hypothesis and certainly enough to regard will to power as the essential reality of all *human* behavior.

What does this expansion of explanatory scope from Plato to Rousseau to Nietzsche have to do with the question of philosophic epochs? First, it parallels and indeed partakes of the spirit of modern science. For all its rigor and principled tentativeness—its insistence on falsifiability, and so on—modern science is extraordinarily expansive in its view of its own possibilities. And this expansiveness arises from its "new," simplified view of the stuff of reality. By reducing phenomena to the kinds of things that *can* be scientifically examined, that is, matter and energy, it can confidently speak to everything it regards as real. Second, if Tocqueville is to be believed, as I think he is, democratic people, for which we may substitute *modern people* since democracy is the predominant fact of modernity, tend to discount the significance of difference and to be drawn to ideas with greater and greater generality and application.[6] Whether one joins Tocqueville in suspecting that this is a distorting prejudice stemming from democracy or sees it instead as the overcoming of a prior, *aristocratic* prejudice, it does seem to describe modernity—and we do see it, or so it seems to me, in the movement from Plato to Rousseau to Nietzsche.

5. "Suppose, finally, we succeeded in explaining our entire instinctive life as the development and ramification of *one* basic form of the will—namely, of the will to power, as *my* proposition has it; suppose all organic functions could be traced back to this will to power and one could also find in it the solution of the problem of procreation and nourishment—it is *one* problem—then one would have gained the right to determine *all* efficient force univocally as—*will to power*. The world viewed from inside, the world defined and determined according to its 'intelligible character'—it would be 'will to power' and nothing else.—" (*BGE* 36)

6. See, for example, *Democracy in America*, pp. 411–16, 425–26, and 640–43.

There is an irony at work here if I'm right—two ironies, in fact, though Nietzsche would instruct us to see them as two facets of a single one. In characterizing Nietzsche as I have just done I am effectively putting him forward, in this respect at least, as our chief exemplar, first, of democratic modernity, and second, of Socratism and Platonism: in purporting to have insight into the character of all existence, notwithstanding the necessarily provisional nature of that and indeed every insight, Nietzsche is effectively asserting, to a grand extent, the knowability of being, which is the very assertion, along with the assertion of the correctability of being, for which he criticized both Socratism (and Platonism)[7] and modern science throughout his career. (Nietzsche regarded modern science as a species of Platonism precisely for sharing these same two presumptions.) But these ironies are not unknown to Nietzsche, who does not mean to repudiate everything about either modernity or Platonism. To the contrary, his well-known advocacy of intellectual conscience is an embrace of *science*. What are sometimes understood as repudiations of science are elements of a dialectical critique, a critique of science as currently practiced from the standpoint of what he considers a truer or more scientific science.[8] Moreover, what I have described as modern in Nietzsche is also a *return* to ancient, or pre-Socratic, ways. In the case of each of the three trajectories I have cited, Plato, following Socrates, reversed the prevailing philosophic tendencies. This is evident in the dialogues themselves, including the

---

7. Nietzsche does not simply equate Socratism and Platonism, but he does see Platonism as sharing these defining traits of Socratism. Regarding the relation between Socratism and Platonism, see Dannhauser, *Nietzsche's View of Socrates*, chap. 4.

8. Nietzsche's embrace of science is nowhere more evident than in the book to which he gave the title, *Die Frohliche Wissenschaft*, and has been helpfully explained by Lampert in his commentary on book 5 of that work in *Nietzsche and Modern Times*. It is striking that Nietzsche, who is rightly seen as the culmination of the modern critique of reason and who rejects the idea of an ordered, knowable cosmos, nevertheless hypothesizes about the character of all being. Some might say that he is liberated to venture so boldly because he understands knowledge to be created rather than discovered by the thinker. But this, I think, is overstating the degree to which Nietzsche sees knowledge as invention: all knowledge may be interpretation, but interpretations are not all equal, and what separates them is the degree to which they are *not* mere invention, i.e., the degree to which they comprehend *what is*, remembering that for Nietzsche *what is* means *the world that appears or shines forth to us*. It may be, though, that he is able to hypothesize as broadly as he does because of his skepticism, that is, his insistence on holding all "truth" as probability rather than certainty, which is related to but distinct from the view that knowledge is mere invention. Another source of his ability to hypothesize so broadly may be his view of human beings—the part of Being into which he has the greatest and most direct access—as continuous with the rest of Being. This is a positive legacy of the "true but deadly" doctrines that have supplanted Christian anthropology in late modernity (*UD* 9).

Symposium, in which eros is conceived by some interlocutors as a cosmic force whose mythic depiction was but a dressed-up scientific totalism. So, as much as Nietzsche exemplifies tendencies associated with democratic modernity and Socratism, he also, and perhaps more importantly, can be seen as reviving a very ancient outlook—and supplementing it with the methodological and substantive advances of modern science, thereby pointing the way to a postmodern epoch.

Such are some of the more apparent and thematic differences between Plato, Rousseau, and Nietzsche on the question of eros. But how deep do they go? The rhetorical artistry of the three philosophers makes it impossible to accept any of these trajectories at face value, that is, as accurate and proportional expressions of substantive differences.[9] Plato's classical characteristics (embrace of a moral order, writing characterized by indirection and reticence, comparatively moderate claims of explanatory power) and Rousseau's and Nietzsche's progressively more modern characteristics *could* indicate fundamentally different outlooks, but they could also indicate only that the three philosophers meant to appeal to the different sensibilities of their respective contemporaries or even that they meant to *propound* different sensibilities in accordance with the needs and perils of their respective eras. The only way to make a determination about these differences is to grapple with each of the philosophers in turn, locating and weighing in each case—which is to say, in the case of each claim or idea—the grounds for skepticism. I have tried in the preceding chapters to offer something toward that end, and have expressed my own view of the magnitude of the differences indicated by the trajectories I have just cited. To the extent that one comes to regard these differences of presentation as expressing substantive differences, one will have gained another avenue by which to approach the merits of the three philosophers' respective interpretations. For these three sets of differences, the three trajectories I have just identified—perhaps these three above all others—speak to the most basic questions of what *is* and our capacity to know what *is.* That Nietzsche, who goes furthest in seeming to disavow the possibility of knowledge, somehow makes the most sweeping claims about what *is,* is worthy of reflection. So, too, is the fact that Plato, who speaks of a unitary Good that is beyond Being, is able to accommodate the noetic heterogeneity of

---

9. It bears noting that the ancients/moderns divide that so many have learned from Strauss is at times ignored by Strauss himself, and thus arguably shown to be either a partial truth or even a somewhat dubious exoteric teaching. See Lenzner and Kristol, "Leo Strauss: An Introduction."

Being. And even if one discounts the three trajectories as the products only of strategic or rhetorical considerations, still one cannot dismiss them as philosophically unimportant, if only because one can learn much from philosophers' attempts to shape readers' sensibilities. From "merely" strategic projects, from the choice of aims and measures, one can infer much about the strategists' views of various kinds of human beings and even, if qualifiedly, about human nature as such.

COMPLEMENTARY VIRTUES

There is much in Plato's, Rousseau's, and Nietzsche's respective treatments of the soul's preeminent force that differs from but complements the other treatments. The complementarity arises partly from divergent perspectives or avenues of approach and partly from different foci. The complementary insights and virtues are many. I wish only to cite a few that seem to me particularly important.

Plato, as I noted above, does not claim for eros the same scope of "operations" that Rousseau claims for the desire for expanded being or, especially, that Nietzsche claims for will to power. Paradoxically, though—or perhaps it is not paradoxical: from a Platonist's perspective it is not—Plato arguably gives the most comprehensive account of the Whole, of which his treatment of eros is but part, albeit the central part.[10] For by situating eros with respect to that which is beyond the soul, by defining eros as a desire whose true objects are the *eidê* and the Good, Plato makes of psychology something transpsychic, something metaphysical or even theological. (These *objects*, we recall, are the means by which eros achieves its *aim* of embracing eternity.) One could object, of course, that Plato gives the most comprehensive account only if his account is *true*, only if eros is in fact the desire for these objects, which is far from an incontrovertible claim—indeed, as we have seen, some doubt whether even Plato sees the matter thus. But this objection is not quite sound, for Plato's account, whatever its ontological accuracy, is *phenomenologically* true: whether or not one subscribes to the existence of the *eidê* and

---

10. Eros is central to the Whole in that it mediates between the human or the finite and the divine or the infinite and as such binds the Whole together. So at least says Socrates, quoting Diotima, though Socrates speaks of "mortal" and "immortal" rather than of finite and infinite (*Symposium* 202d–203a).

the Good, his account still holds true in the sense that in being erotic, in loving and longing, we seek eternity and thus *presuppose* the existence of the *eidē* and the Good or something like them. (Indeed, Socrates says just this [517b, 533a].) Thus Plato's special virtue, even from the standpoint of a skeptic, is to articulate the understanding or worldview that eros itself subscribes to and without which eros would not be able to sustain itself—indeed, without which eros would not be eros.

Rousseau, who sees human being as such as expansive, shows us the pervasiveness and the multifariousness of this expansiveness and how it accounts for the political problem—and, accordingly, how it must be accounted for by any political solution. This much one can say on the basis of what we've already seen. Beyond this I would cite two more unique virtues. First, with his focus on human development, both in the species but especially in the individual (think here of his accounts of the genesis and development of *amour-propre*), Rousseau reveals much about the developmental stages and possibilities of the desire for extended being. If I have not attended much to this contribution in this study, that is only because Rousseau's treatment of the development of self-love has been addressed extensively elsewhere. I needed only to establish and underscore that self-love on Rousseau's account is in fact expansive, which I tried to do in Chapter 5.

Second, it seems to me that Rousseau teaches the most about how to relate lesser goods to the greatest good, or how to translate the recognition of a single comprehensive good into a hierarchy of particular goods. He is clearest about what makes a good good. Or at least he makes an understanding of these things more readily available than does Plato or Nietzsche. All three philosophers provide the ground on which to recognize a hierarchy of goods. And all three, it seems to me, allow us to surmise from an examination of the highest goods what makes *any* good good, that is, wherein lies goodness as such. But neither Plato nor Nietzsche allows us to do so as easily or with as much confidence as does Rousseau. Plato's lesser goods (e.g., the demotic virtues) prove to be so far beneath the highest goods as to obscure the connection between the two classes. The same is true of Nietzsche's goods. Although Nietzsche provides the common currency of goodness (i.e., power) and would therefore seem to establish the connection between lower and higher goods à la Rousseau, he so denigrates the lower as to follow Plato in all but severing that connection. Rousseau, by contrast, by showing that being (or the feeling of being) is the defining stuff of goodness at every level, provides the common currency of goodness and *uses* it to show that lesser goods really are good, and why. Indeed, if it's true that Plato and Nietzsche are like Rousseau in seeing a single good as somehow constitutive of all goodness, it is Rousseau's example that helps us see this is so. Rousseau may teach less than Plato or Nietzsche about the Whole and the essential meaning of eros (or eros' place in the whole), but he teaches more about the practical implications of his phenomenological and empirical insights. And he helps us learn more from Plato and Nietzsche, especially concerning the practical implications of their insights. For this alone, I think, Rousseau belongs in this dialogue. (We will return to practical implications—and applications—below.)

Like Rousseau, Nietzsche highlights the pervasiveness and multifariousness of a single psychic drive. And more than Rousseau, he explains why its multifariousness does not contradict its singularity—which is to say, Nietzsche makes the fullest case for motivational monism. In so doing, he also does the most to make plausible the existence of a single comprehensive good and hence the shared goodness of all goods (though as I noted above, his disdain for lower goods somewhat obscures this groundwork) and their hierarchic ordering (this he does not obscure). Furthermore, Nietzsche reveals the most about what he aptly names sublimation (*sublimieren*),[11] that is, the development of the refined and civilized out of the primordial and savage, and the persistence of the latter in the former. (Sublimation does not mean extirpation.) Consider, for example, his treatment of cruelty and its role in culture, including (especially) high culture. Consider, too, his depiction of the philosopher as a tyrant. Here one might lodge an objection similar to the one I addressed with respect to Plato. Surely, one might argue, Nietzsche's account of sublimation has value only if its underlying metaphysical basis is right, that is, only if the process of refinement is without any natural teleological basis. But that is not so. Even if one were to reject Nietzsche's metaphysics in favor of something as far distant as Christian Platonism, Nietzsche's account of sublimation could still be *phenomenologically* true. His metaphysics and their causal explanation of sublimation are separable from his description or narrative of sublimation. Finally, with his exploration of vengefulness, Nietzsche alone does for sickness and weakness what all three philosophers do for health and strength: he shows the unity behind the variety. Plato points toward the

---

11. For an extensive account of the development and novelty of Nietzsche's teaching regarding sublimation, see Kaufmann, *Nietzsche*, pp. 211–56.

Good, as do Rousseau and Nietzsche in their own ways. Nietzsche alone, with his extraordinary dissection of the spirit of revenge and its psychophysiological sources, gives us the Bad. But let me not risk giving the wrong impression. If Nietzsche attends to the bad, that is because, as he sees it, the bad is ascendant in late modernity. Like Plato—and like all affirmative spirits (*BGE* 260)—he begins, and takes his bearings, from health, from strength, from the good, from *eternity*.

SHARED PRACTICAL WISDOM

Eternity isn't the most politically salient of terms, notwithstanding that it can, and for us does, refer to desire and experience. Yet as we saw in the *Symposium*, the longing for eternity can have enormous political consequences. And if we substitute for "the longing for eternity" the more neutrally descriptive term, "the soul's expansiveness," the political consequences become even more evident. The soul's expansiveness is both the source of aggression and imperialism and the psychological "stuff" of vigorous patriotism and virtue. But as obviously value laden as these terms are, all of my observations and analyses thus far have been largely descriptive and explanatory; and insofar as we have encountered clear political implications, the implications have been largely negative, particularly from the standpoint of modern liberalism, which requires above all that political eros be rendered lawful and moderate. (Not that negative lessons are less important than positive ones. One need not be a Hobbesian or a conservative to recognize political eros' endless potential for disaster.)[12] We have yet to explore the possibility of deriving *positive prescriptive* lessons from Plato's, Rousseau's, and Nietzsche's treatments. Here I will only offer one general suggestion, based on what I take to be common ground among the three philosophers. My suggestion, though based on common

---

12. An appreciation of the disastrous potential of political eros does tend to lead, though, if not necessarily to conservatism, at least to moderation. Plato's utopianism *in thought* only underscores his appreciation of the need to recognize limits in practice. Rousseau, too, though abstract and thus in a sense "perfectionist" in his articulation of the principles of political right, eschews revolution and radical reform (at least in the ordinary senses of these words) in practice. Nietzsche of course stands out as an exception in this regard. For him there was no question of protecting an even marginally defensible order. Nietzsche believed that a crisis was developing that would result either in the reassertion and enthronement of nobility or in its final defeat and extirpation. Rather than look askance at eros in politics, he put his own political eros on display and hoped thereby to enlist and direct that of his readers.

ground among philosophers who are not notably friendly to modern liberalism, does not seem to me in any way hostile to liberalism.[13] It may even indirectly support and enrich liberalism. The common ground is at the level of phenomenology: Plato, Rousseau, and Nietzsche are alike in seeing human beings as pursuing *more being*—this irrespective of their divergent interpretations of the ultimate meaning and the deep sources of this shared end. Furthermore, the three philosophers effectively indicate that human beings are right to pursue more being—or rather, *would* be right if they understood wherein being does and does not lie, for all goods *are* good because and to the extent that they yield more being. Hence my suggestion: in subscribing to all this, the three philosophers each point to the grounds for a naturalistic morality and politics. This has particular relevance to our own time, which has seen a resurgence of moral and political naturalism—or, as it is more commonly called, ethical naturalism—but a resurgence, in my view, that is hampered by a missing piece. It is just this piece that Plato, Rousseau, and Nietzsche provide.

Moral and Political Naturalism: the Problem

By moral and political "naturalism" I mean an understanding of the good as the desirable and the desirable as that which we already in fact desire. This is in contrast to approaches that determine the good by some sort of deduction or abstract reasoning. Traditionally one has looked to Aristotle and to the "moral sense" theorists of the Scottish Enlightenment as sources of naturalistic theory. The resurgence of naturalism in our own time supplements these older sources with the findings of contemporary social and biological science, both of which speak with power born of empirical research—social science by ascertaining or verifying that various desires and moral dispositions are present across cultures, biology and psychology by offering accounts of the basis and evolution of these desires and dispositions. Ethical naturalism seeks

---

13. If one doubts the compatibility of psychic and moral monism with democratic liberalism, mention of Spinoza should at least suffice to make one reconsider. Spinoza's psychology, which is centered on the doctrine of the *conatus,* is as monistic as any that we have considered here and arguably as expansionist; and his politics are undeniably liberal-democratic, even if scholars disagree on both the character of the *conatus* (*is* it expansive?) and, consequently, the grounds of his liberal political theory. An inquiry into the implications for liberal democracy of the soul's expansiveness could do no better than to take Spinoza as its starting point.

to identify needs and desires that are found in human beings generally[14] so that it might thereby propound as human goods the objects of these desires. And it claims some success in its seeking. Thus one finds a leading theorist proclaiming the naturalness of some twenty goods based on twenty natural desires, ranging from sexual mating and familial bonding to friendship and justice-as-reciprocity to religious and intellectual understanding, and finding in these goods a natural basis for political aspiration and standards.[15] These efforts are impressive and may even mark the rebirth, on new grounds, of the principle of natural right.

But not even a perfectly comprehensive catalogue of such desires would suffice as the basis for determining the human good. The good may be the desirable, but surely we cannot suppose that whatever one desires at any moment is good. Some desires are too obviously harmful. Others may be perfectly benign in themselves but may be in conflict with other, equally benign desires. What's needed is a principle or set of principles by which we may judge and order the multitude of desires and determine which are in conflict with our well-being. One might suppose that such a principle could be found "pragmatically," through a prudential, consequentialist inquiry: that we already can agree that some desires under some circumstances lead to bad results suggests that prudence can take us some way toward the principle(s) we seek. And surely we employ a kind of prudence when choosing among rival benign desires all the time. As these considerations indicate, prudential reasoning is clearly necessary to the conduct of life even on the most naturalistic view. But in the end—indeed, from the beginning—prudence must refer to something beyond itself. *On what basis* are we to choose this good over that? On what basis are we to evaluate claims of goodness? We are thrown back to our need for a principle by which to order the desires, which means, a principle by which to weigh them. The problem is not so much to determine our

---

14. Why "generally" rather than "universally"? The guiding premise of ethical naturalism is that the existence of individuals who do not share particular desires does not undermine the claim that these desires are constituents of a general human nature—so long as the exceptional individuals are indeed exceptional, that is, relatively rare. See Larry Arnhart, *Darwinian Natural Right*, pp. 30–31.

15. See Arnhart, *Darwinian Natural Right*. The twenty desires are listed on pages 29 to 36; discussion of their ability to serve as the source of political aspiration and standards occupies the rest of the book. Arnhart's is perhaps the most comprehensive and succinct of recent efforts to advance ethical naturalism and to bring it to bear on politics and political philosophy. Other contemporary figures whose work aims to uncover a natural basis for moral and political practice include Robert McShea, James Q. Wilson, and Roger Masters.

stance toward desire as to determine what is *truly* desirable, what it is that we most want and that would yield the greatest and most comprehensive satisfaction. The guiding practical premise of such an inquiry is that a fuller happiness and a securely decent moral and political order require a better grasp of the deepest and most powerful human longings.[16] Only by identifying these most consequential needs and longings can we discover the principle(s) by which to order our desires and make possible a truer and more coherent naturalism.

. . . and a Solution?

In their treatments of eros, Plato, Rousseau, and Nietzsche take us closer to just such a principle, notwithstanding that none of these three has normally been associated with ethical naturalism.[17] For not only do they each identify a single preeminent psychic force or desire and a corresponding good, but furthermore, that good is such that it manifests itself and is attainable in different objects to varying degrees and is the very source of all goods, that is, the stuff of goodness (for human beings) as such. *That* good? Surely, as we have seen, the three philosophers do not subscribe to the same understanding of the good? In one important respect they do. Notwithstanding their different interpretations of eros' aim and its ontological meaning and context, Plato, Rousseau, and Nietzsche all see human beings as pursuing, and the good life as marked by, what one can fairly describe as *more or maximum being*, understanding by this term just what Rousseau clearly meant by it: that

---

16. The guiding *theoretical* premise of such an inquiry (apart from the assumption that the knowledge needed may be available to us) is the commensurability of all human goods. Commensurability does not mean compatibility: certainly one needs to choose among competing goods. What it means is that there exists some measure or standard by which all goods can be judged. Needless to say, this premise and consequent pursuit of a single principle or set of principles by which to validate and weigh desires is at odds with modern pluralism's rejection of the legitimacy of a unified account of human goods. But our pluralism, which has never been quite as opposed to a unified account as it has liked to think—it has never shrunk from making its own unified and even hierarchical claims—shows signs of a growing willingness to acknowledge the legitimacy of a unified account, so long as the account can accommodate a great diversity of goods. On pluralism's professed rejection of a unified account of goods, see Kochin, *Gender and Rhetoric in Plato's Political Thought*, p. 133. On its penchant to grant itself exemptions from this rejection, see Wilber, *Sex, Ecology, Spirituality*, pp. 22–31; also Taylor, *Sources of the Self*.

17. It seems to me, though I will not develop the point here, that Aristotle's naturalism effectively employs something approaching such a principle, though perhaps not so specifiable a one as can be found in Plato, Rousseau, and Nietzsche.

is, maximum *feeling* of being. And if the good life is universally *marked* by greater being, it also seems fair to say that it somehow *consists* in greater being. By subscribing to a single comprehensive good that constitutes the goodness of all goods, each of the three philosophers effectively points to the principle required for a coherent moral and political naturalism—the *same* principle, namely, that what is good is what maximizes the feeling of being. To be sure, the deep differences of interpretation are not to be discounted. But practical or political life is commonly marked by agreement among parties whose deepest reasons are at variance. If Plato, Rousseau, and Nietzsche agree that living well, indeed all life's goods, are somehow constituted by maximizing one's being, then they might each be brought to bear on the project of moral and political naturalism. Bringing them to bear on this matter, even formulating a principle such as I have just done, does not mean that we can hope to ascertain a detailed practical formula for ranking and choosing among goods, or anything close to that. That would be impossible even if we were addressing just one of these figures, let alone all three. Moral and political naturalism neither claims nor seeks to dispense with case-by-case practical reasoning in moral and political deliberation. Specific cases, though, unless they are to be arbitrarily decided, entail recourse to a general principle such as the one provided, if not advocated, by these philosophers.

But *do* Plato, Rousseau, and Nietzsche agree that maximized being is what constitutes living well? And can a principle as abstract as the one I have stated really be meaningful? I can address these questions briefly, since my responses will be based on the more detailed inquiries of Parts One through Three.

Only Rousseau among the philosophers we have been considering speaks in terms of human *being*. Only he teaches explicitly that being, or the feeling of being, is the substance and the measure of living well. By doing so Rousseau provides us with a way of understanding goods and assimilating them into a hierarchy. My contention, though, is that Plato and Nietzsche effectively teach the same thing. True, the three accounts differ in their interpretations of the ultimate sources or metaphysical substrates of being, with Plato connecting maximized being to entities or principles (the *eidê*) whose existence is unacknowledged by Rousseau and denied by Nietzsche. The accounts also differ, at least in their respective emphases, with respect to the means by which being can be maximized: where Plato emphasizes contemplation, Nietzsche emphasizes creative activity, with Rousseau perhaps splitting the difference. Yet on the basis of all we have seen in this study, it is reasonable to say that each presents those who live well as somehow enjoying a greater degree of being.

With respect to Rousseau this should be obvious. In any case, I cannot add anything to what I argued in Chapter 5. Nietzsche, too, offers a fairly clear case in key respects. Nietzsche does not explicitly speak of magnitudes of "being," not even in the limited way that Plato does. Yet it does not seem alien to Nietzsche's meaning to say he effectively does speak of being when he speaks of power. For *to be* is to be *active,* and to be active is to feel and expend power. By speaking the language of power Nietzsche simply highlights wherein being lies or consists—wherein *all* being consists. Much of what might strike us from the outside as passive experience is in fact active and thus appropriately thought of in terms of power. This is seen best by considering the affirmation of eternal return, which *seems* to be the pinnacle of passivity (in that one affirms what already is and has been) but which is, after all, an active *willing,* and an utterly unfettered willing at that. The embrace of eternity, Nietzsche's highest good, is good because it gives to will to power endless expanse, endless *being.*

It is Plato on whom this goodness-as-maximum-being interpretation might seem most dubious. My central argument with respect to Plato was of course that eros is directed toward *eternity,* even if the longing for eternity is typically mistranslated into the pursuit of immortality. But whichever of these one is seeking, whether eternity or immortality, one is also—even more palpably—pursuing more *being.* The philosopher contemplating what *is* is thereby "filled with" what *is,* that is, with that which has more being. And those whose erotic pursuits are more ordinary, who seek immortality through children or fame, are also seeking more being: What is immortality to the one who pursues it if not inextinguishable *being?* Thus while embrace of eternity is eros' true object and immortality its most common object, *maximum being* seems the best way to express (1) what is experienced and (2) what is sought in or through these objects. Indeed, *being* is in some ways an easier or more obvious interpretation of the end of eros than is either eternity or immortality. Consider the example of Alcibiades, whose chief aspiration seems less to achieve everlasting fame than to fill the world with himself—which also means incorporating the world *into* himself—in the present.[18]

How should we understand the relation in Plato's thought between eter-

---

18. Plato, *Alcibiades I.*

nity and being (i.e., felt being)? Do we seek eternity (or, more typically, immortality) for the sake of greater being? Or do we seek greater being for the sake of eternity? It may be that the question is ill put and that the two words express two aspects of the same thing, *eternity* expressing eros' goal with an eye toward its object and aim, *being* expressing its goal with respect to experience or phenomenology. Or perhaps *being* is the more general object of desire, indeed the universal object of desire, so that eros, like every other desire, is a species of the desire for more being. (Recall that Plato never assigns to eros the scope that Rousseau and Nietzsche assign to their versions.) Whatever the case, *being* seems to me the thing the lover experiences or hopes to experience. Plato does not communicate any of this definitively. But it is no imposition of foreign categories to speak of Platonic eros in this way: we need only notice in Plato's treatments of eros, indeed in his treatments of great desire of any kind, his characters' repeated use of the vocabulary of fullness and aliveness and consummation, a vocabulary that expresses a sense of enlarged *being*—when they aren't speaking explicitly of being. As we saw in Part One, the promise of greater being is key, both substantively and rhetorically, to both the explicit and the deeper accounts of eros conveyed in the *Republic* and the *Symposium*.

In the end, though, the plausibility of thinking of eros in this way—not to mention the utility of thinking of eros in this way—depends on whether the goodness of particular goods, as presented by the philosopher, can be shown to lie in their somehow increasing our degree of felt being. The completion of this task is beyond what I can offer in this brief discussion, whose purpose is only to make a general suggestion. But it is possible to imagine the outlines. For example, the goodness of philosophy (for the philosopher)[19] might be shown to consist in an increase in being that comes from apprehending and abiding with the *eidê* (if we think in terms of the philosopher as Socrates *describes* him, especially in the *Republic*); or it might be shown to consist in an increase in being that comes from transcendence of defensive partiality and from self-forgetting openness to the wonders of being (if we think in terms of the philosopher as Socrates *exemplifies* him). The goodness of civic virtue (for the individual practitioner) would similarly be shown to lie in an increase of one's being, albeit a less considerable enlargement than that

---

19. Much else, not immediately relevant to our inquiry, might be said of what is good or not good about philosophy *for society*.

brought by the philosophic life. One might show that the citizen increases the degree of his being by participating in and identifying himself with something larger than himself (the polis) and perhaps, too, by the extension of his will over others (if he has a share in rule) and over himself, for civic virtue surely entails self-mastery and discipline.[20] And so on with respect to other goods, such as friendship, music, honor, athletics, and the rest. Can the goodness of these goods (when they are in fact goods, i.e., when they're pursued in the right form) really be interpreted in this way? Is it sensible to understand multifarious concrete goods according to a single, abstract measure? Though less directly than Rousseau or Nietzsche, Plato suggests that it is.

Why then have these three philosophers not been put to use in this way by proponents of ethical naturalism? Part of the explanation may be that no need has been felt. Many of those whose approach to morality and politics centers on empirically determinable needs and desires seem to suppose that there is no need to look beyond what is immediately palpable, no need to interpret desire by imputing some overarching principle to it. Indeed, a search for such a principle is apt to smack of "metaphysics" or some other dubious or fantastic pursuit. And in any case they might suppose that to reach for an ordering principle before first discovering all that needs to be ordered is a dubious thing, not only intellectually but also morally and politically. (As admittedly it is, though to seek this principle by identifying an underlying chief desire seems much less dubious, and may in fact be necessary for understanding the many particular desires in the first place.) But another part of the answer probably lies in the three philosophers themselves, in what they are each seen to be doing.

The relative neglect of Plato by ethical naturalists is paradoxical but understandable. Paradoxical because Plato seems to offer the basis for just the sort of principle we have been discussing. He suggests in more than one dialogue that our desires point to, that they already reach for, a single object. In the *Republic* the Platonic Socrates says of "the Good": "Now this is what every soul pursues and for the sake of which it does *everything*" (*Republic* 505d-e;

---

20. Democratic people have often had difficulty understanding how one gains, either in freedom or in happiness—or in *being*—from restraint. For current purposes let it suffice to say that self-restraint involves both being restrained and doing the restraining. Part of the self is ruler and part is ruled, and everything depends on which is which. If the part of the self that we consider our essential self, or closer to our essential self, (i.e., the rational part of the self) is ruling, then we are gainers.

emphasis added). But the neglect of Plato is understandable because, even if we disregard the discrepancies between the dialogues in question, few believe they understand, and fewer still agree on, what the Good described by Plato actually *is*. Indeed, it is not clear that the Good is in any practical sense an "object" or condition to which we might aspire. Some take it to be a principle to regulate our inquiry more than our striving. Others interpret it as something metaphysical or ontological without significance for how we live.[21] Still others, mindful that something good must be good *for someone*, hold that the Good, since it must be understood as the good-in-itself, is unintelligible.[22] Moreover, even if one does take the Good to be the real and appropriate object of our aspiration, it is not clear how this ought to direct the conduct of those (almost all of us) who lack the requisite nature and training to apprehend the Good.[23] The Good may be that for the sake of which the soul does everything, but, with the possible exception of the philosopher, the soul doesn't quite know what it's doing: "The soul divines that it [the Good] is something but is at a loss about it and unable to get a sufficient grasp of just what it is, or to have a stable trust as it has about the rest" (505e). Thus our ability to discover in Plato the basis for a principle by which to order the desires would seem minimal at best.

Yet if Plato is especially difficult and reticent in his treatments of the Good, he is somewhat less so in his treatments of the *desire* for the good, as we have seen.[24] By understanding eros as the longing for eternity, we learn about what does and does not satisfy our deepest desire; and by understanding desire and the appeal or "reward" of eternity in terms of enhanced being, we are given a basis on which to determine what is good and how to rank the various goods. If one equates the good with the desirable, then it is perfectly acceptable, indeed incumbent upon one who wishes to find a ground for politics and morality, to inquire into desire itself.

---

21. See, for example, Lachterman, "What is 'The Good' of Plato's *Republic?*"; and Miller, "Platonic Provocations," pp. 163–93.

22. This is Nietzsche's position. Also see Leibowitz, "The Moral and Political Foundations of Socratic Philosophy," pp. 138–39n170.

23. Cf. Aristotle, *Eudemian Ethics* I.8, 1217b25: "Even if there were a form or single look of the good, it would not be of any use for the [humanly] good life or for practical conduct."

24. As explained in Chapter 3, note 3, when I capitalize "Good" I am referring to the Good as such, that is, that which is beyond and the source of both being and knowing. Lowercase "good," by contrast, signifies the good for us, for human beings. There may well be a connection between the two (if indeed there *is* a Good). The good, or the good for us, may entail sight of the Good. Still, the two meanings are distinguishable.

Rousseau, too, has been neglected by contemporary ethical naturalists. Rousseau is understood to have been a penetrating explorer of the soul and is seen as a discoverer of the historicity of human nature, and in these senses he *has* informed contemporary naturalism. But one tends to regard his prescriptive thought as being limited to the propagation of abstract principles of political right, which, whatever their value, are not particularly relevant to the enterprise of determining and ranking goods. Only when we appreciate what has not yet been widely appreciated, that is, his view of the expansiveness of being, can we see Rousseau's much more significant potential contribution to the naturalistic enterprise.

Unlike Plato and Rousseau, Nietzsche explicitly offers his thought as the basis for a naturalistic set of values. Recall his proclamation in the *Antichrist*: "What is good? Everything that heightens the feeling of power in man, the will to power, power itself. What is bad? Everything that is born of weakness" (2).[25] Contemporary theorists have not availed themselves of Nietzsche's offer, however, undoubtedly because of the character of Nietzschean morality and politics. Surely Nietzsche's formula leads to a regime utterly at odds with democratic liberalism? And what is its embrace of power as the good if not the *overturning* of morality? Yet the connection between Nietzsche's formula and antidemocratic politics should not be overstated. The formula speaks only to the meaning or content of goodness. It does not say anything about the distribution of goods, about *whose* feeling of power is to be preferred to whose. Nietzsche's views on that may be detachable from the formula quoted above. And although the highest power, that of the philosopher, is political, it is so refined, so cultural or spiritual in its means, that it could conceivably be exercised (as perhaps it *has* been exercised) behind or above and even on behalf of a liberal regime. (Not altogether unlike Jefferson's "natural aristocracy," albeit in an extended and more remote sense.) I don't mean to suggest that Nietzsche's political thought is liberal or democratic. I do mean to suggest, though, that he joins Plato and Rousseau in providing a basis for determining and ranking values that may not *in principle* be incompatible with liberalism. And in so explicitly articulating a principle by which to determine and rank goods, Nietzsche offers the most powerful testimonial to the possibility of a true and coherent naturalism.

---

25. A similar claim is made at *A* 11: "An action demanded by the instinct of life is proved to be right by the pleasure that accompanies it"; also see *Twilight* Errors 2.

The three philosophers' common ground vis-à-vis naturalism is limited—not only theoretically but practically as well. Even if each embraces *being* in the ways I have described, they posit divergent paths to that end. One need only recall in this regard Nietzsche's call for agonistic striving versus Plato's and Rousseau's promotion of attuning oneself to a harmonious order. The three also differ with respect to how people should be encouraged to conceive of their place in the Whole—Nietzsche promoting the idea that humanity must aspire to overcome itself, Rousseau and Plato warning of the danger of just such an aspiration. But the common ground, if limited, is also very elevated. What one accepts as the "stuff" of living well will necessarily define one's mental landscape.

HUMANITY, PHILOSOPHY, DIVINITY: CODA

Whatever the prospects of finding in Plato, Rousseau, and Nietzsche a basis for moral and political naturalism, the foregoing discussion should at least have reminded us of the practical importance of the three treatments of eros. I should say, the *inevitable* practical importance, for eros is one of those matters of theoretical interest whose study cannot but touch, and probably more than just touch, the sources of our most fundamental moral and political attitudes. There can be little doubt that each of the three philosophers counts on just this. Each clearly seeks to shape or reshape his readers' basic judgments, even if it is not so clear (at least to judge from disagreements among interpreters) how broad an effect they think they can achieve. We may therefore speak of Plato's, Rousseau's, and Nietzsche's expected—indeed, their *intended*—practical effects. What precisely these effects are varies from case to case, according to both the philosopher's assessment of the nature of eros and his judgment of the current and future situation. But the philosophers' respective practical projects share at least two important features. First is an acceptance of divisions among basic human types. As reflected in their multilayered writing and in numerous substantive teachings, none of them imagines that his teachings would, or should, affect all classes of people in the same way. Even Rousseau, the sole democratic political theorist among the three, writes in the happy expectation of being understood differently (or not at all) by different sorts of people. Rousseau routinely differentiates between different types of human beings, sometimes according to intellectual inclination or capacity (as in *Emile*'s distinction between those who think and those who don't [408] and the *First Discourse*'s distinction between the few true geniuses and the many pretentious mediocrities),[26] and sometimes according to other criteria, such as political potency and skill (as in the *Social Contract*'s depiction of the legislator and even in its distinction between statesmen and ordinary citizens).

Second, in interpreting the philosopher as the highest human type, the one in whom the soul's preeminent force has been developed most fully and in whom humanity has thereby reached its most perfect and natural expression, Plato, Rousseau, and Nietzsche each effectively advocate the philosophic life for those for whom it is possible.[27] And not only advocate, but initiate. Here the relation between theory and practice forms a perfect circle, with *theoretical* insight into eros yielding as its chief *practical* implication the choiceworthiness of the *theoretical* life. The call to philosophy is chief among practical implications because it has first-order implications for everyone—not just (1) the few philosophers or potential philosophers, but also (2) that greater number of those who, while falling short of the philosophic nature themselves, might still take their bearings from these exemplars (Plato's gentlemen, Rousseau's faithful friends, Nietzsche's "free minds"), as well as (3) the many who will be educated and thereby in a real sense ruled by philosophers, however indirectly.

---

26. The distinction cited in *Emile* is the effect of education or its lack; the one cited in the *First Discourse* is attributed to nature and ties Rousseau to the Socratic tradition. Regarding Rousseau as a practitioner of multilayered writing, consider the following from the "Preface of a Second Letter to Bordes," in which Rousseau defends his *First Discourse*: "I had to take some precautions at first, and I did not want to say everything in order to make sure that everything got a hearing. I unfolded my ideas only successively and always to only a small number of Readers. I spared not myself, but the truth, in order to have it pass more readily, and make it more useful. . . . The majority of my Readers must often have found my discourses poorly structured and almost entirely disjointed for want of perceiving the trunk of which I only showed them the branches. But that was enough for those capable of understanding, and *I never wanted to speak to the others*" (Bordes 115; emphasis added). Did Rousseau really not want to speak to the others? Certainly he did not want to try to persuade them to see the truth as he saw it. But just as surely he attempted to impart salutary beliefs and wholesome judgments to a broader readership. Also consider the inegalitarian implications of Rousseau's defense of "fictions" in his investigation of truth and lying in the "Fourth Walk" of the *Reveries*, as well as the "Notice on the Notes" that precedes the main body of the *Second Discourse*, where Rousseau effectively discourages less qualified readers from encountering the passages that contain his most radical ideas.

27. This is evident in the case of Plato and Nietzsche, even if the numbers of people to whom this applies are small. (The number of people who fall short of philosophy but might live lives of learning is greater.) Rousseau's advocacy of philosophy (and of learning more generally) is less clear but still real, if my interpretation of the place of philosophy in his thought (in Part Two) is correct.

There is a limit, of course, to this similarity between Plato, Rousseau, and Nietzsche. If philosophy is defined and is rendered choiceworthy by virtue of its status vis-à-vis eros or extended being or will to power, respectively, then insofar as eros, extended being, and will to power are different, so too will philosophy's nature and goodness be seen differently. Hence the three philosophers' divergent portraits of true philosophy. Plato's emphasis is on contemplation of what *is*, that is, on what lies outside and especially "above" the self and its ephemera. The soul is an object of inquiry, indeed the preeminent object of inquiry. But the soul must be understood with respect to that overarching or surrounding context, since what it wants and is directed to lies beyond its own confines, at least as it typically understands its confines. Rousseau, by contrast, emphasizes the essential inwardness or self-oriented nature of philosophy. What the soul needs or what would satisfy it most fully is a return to or withdrawal into the self, where, free of the alienating influences of society, it can rest content in its own sufficiency or else prepare to "spread" itself over the natural order. Even the true philosopher's discursive analysis, at least to judge from Rousseau's own example, will often be directed at himself. And even when his gaze is directed outward, for example in his political analyses, his motivation is "selfish": he either seeks recognition ("the wise man . . . is not insensitive to glory" [*FD* 58]) or revels in the exercise of his powerful faculties. Nietzsche, finally, emphasizes above all the philosopher's creating and commanding, his cultivation and exercise of *power*.

But emphases do not tell the whole story, and as I suggested in earlier chapters, there is more overlap in the three philosophers' depictions of philosophy than is initially evident. The relations among their respective accounts are a bit like the relations among certain Platonic dialogues, each highlighting or pointing to what is apparently but not wholly absent from the others, thereby helping us to see in the others what we otherwise would have missed. That's not to say that the differences among the three accounts of philosophy are negligible or simply functions of different vantage points rather than real conflicts. (For that matter, we shouldn't assume that Platonic dialogues don't conflict with one another in some ways.) It is to say, though, that the differences are narrower than they appear.

I have already discussed the overlap between Plato's and Nietzsche's portraits of the philosopher's activity with respect to *knowing* versus *making*. Plato gives us the philosopher as lover and knower; Nietzsche, as maker and ruler. Yet it is Plato who first articulates the "Nietzschean" idea of rule by philosophers; indeed, he *depicts* such rule, albeit on a small scale, within the dialogues themselves. And in propounding new teachings on the gods and the very structure of Being he arguably undertakes creation and ruling himself. Nietzsche, on the other hand, gives us a philosopher who creates and rules, yet who is *called* to create and rule only on the "Platonic" basis of his prior *knowing*—a knowing, moreover, that is propelled by loving, à la Plato. As for Rousseau, while I have not considered his depiction of philosophy explicitly with respect to these poles, it is not difficult to discern their copresence in his conception of his own task and thus the philosopher's task as such.

More difficult than reconciling knowing and making is reconciling Plato's emphasis on what lies beyond the soul, or the soul's situatedness within a cosmic order, with Rousseau's and Nietzsche's more self-oriented account of philosophy's nature and goodness.[28] But the case can be made—from both sides. For one can reasonably interpret Platonic contemplation of the *eidê* as a return to and an abiding with one's true self. To see the philosopher's objects of contemplation as lying beyond him is to view those objects from the standpoint of the self in its ordinary or egoic form. Yet the achievement of the philosopher, the very ascent to philosophy, can be understood as the transcendence of this very self, as we have seen. The philosopher, as philosopher, is *constituted* by the *eidê*; and if he and indeed all of us are by nature *directed* to the *eidê*, then there is no reason why we shouldn't conceive of philosophy as an ascent to one's true self. Indeed, by sometimes depicting philosophy as recollection or return, Plato encourages us to conceive of the matter in just this way. If we often resist this instruction, that is probably because we don't habitually think of the true self as the common self. Our more common tendency is to conceive of the true self as unique and idiosyncratic rather than common. The conception of the true self as unique and idiosyncratic is typical of modernity and seems to find support in Rousseau's and Nietzsche's respective varieties of radical individualism. In fact, though, Rousseau and Nietzsche both belie this modern tendency. Or to be more precise, they follow it so far as to overcome it. Rousseau seeks to be true to himself in all his uniqueness yet ends identifying with all of being. Nietzsche embraces the willing of all

28. Is Nietzschean philosophy aptly described as self-oriented? The Nietzschean philosopher's commanding and legislating is obviously "outward" activity. But Nietzsche's emphasis is more on the commander and legislator than on the commands and legislation, and although I've maintained that Nietzsche's philosopher takes his bearings from nature, nature is far less prescriptive for him that it is for Plato's philosopher. Nietzsche's philosopher is as unfree but also as free as an artist.

that is and has ever been, in all its particularity; yet if each of us embraces *all* particularity then each of us is willing precisely the same thing—so for him, too, the highest individuality becomes universal, or common.

The three philosophers still differ, of course, with respect to the character of the Whole and our relation to it (e.g., the question of the *eidê*), which means that they still differ—decisively—with respect to the proper interpretation of philosophy. But in what we have just considered we see that there is much common ground among them with respect to the *phenomenology* of philosophy, and thereby the phenomenology of eros as well.

There is one more similarity between Plato's, Rousseau's, and Nietzsche's respective depictions of the philosopher, one that crowns and thus in a sense comprehends the rest and in so doing brings to light what may be the most basic *difference*. The similarity is that each presents philosophy as somehow divine and the philosopher as godly or godlike. The difference lies in the grounds of this presentation and in what constitutes divinity. For Plato the philosopher partakes of divinity by ascending to the eternal. As we saw in Chapter 4, the experience can be depicted both "negatively," that is, as overcoming the (ordinary or egoic) self, and "positively," that is, as "filling" the self with eternal Being, since it is the nature of the soul to be informed by the objects to which it attends. For Rousseau, by contrast, what makes the contemplator "like God" is his perfect self-sufficiency amid solitary reverie (*Reveries* 69). One might suppose that this godlike self-sufficiency arises from the content of the reverie, that is, from the self's identification with or absorption in nature or being, and thus that the content itself is somehow divine. And perhaps, too, the insights that arise from meditation on the reveries are divine. But Rousseau does not refer to either of these as divine. Only self-sufficiency is accorded that designation. Rousseau conceives of divinity in terms that are more active and political than Plato's. The same is true, to an even greater extent, of Nietzsche, who attributes to the philosopher the tasks belonging to the biblical God: creating worlds, sustaining them, legislating for human beings and even blessing and sheltering them; and lest these not suffice to elevate the philosopher to divinity, Nietzsche also gives us a god who philosophizes (*BGE* 295).

Undoubtedly these characterizations of philosophy as divine are intended to highlight philosophy's beauty and splendor and thereby inspire interest and respect. Almost as surely, though, they also reflect Plato's, Rousseau's, and Nietzsche's sincere estimates of their own activity, in which case the differences between the three depictions of the philosopher boil down to divergent conceptions of what is divine, of what divinity *is*. The question of the philosopher, and therewith the question of eros, is the question of humanity's relation to the divine or the infinite. In a sense this question is only a reformulated version of the question of eternity, which has already come into sight as the matter at issue among Plato, Rousseau, and Nietzsche. But the question of humanity's relation to the divine casts the question of eternity in a new light. The differences among the three conceptions of embracing eternity now come to light as the differences among *partaking* of divinity via contemplation of the eternal, versus *imitating* (or *rivaling*) divinity by achieving perfect self-sufficiency "like God," versus *appropriating* divinity by creating, sustaining, lawgiving, and blessing. Which of these is the most plausible conception of the divinity open to human beings? Is it even necessary to choose?[29] Does it make sense to think that philosophy, or indeed any human activity, is in *any* sense divine? And how shall we judge?

To the last question, at least, I can offer the following. As a version of the question of eternity, the question of humanity's relation to the divine is at bottom a matter of interpreting experience. One must interrogate one's experience—one's longing or expansiveness; the objects of one's desire and ends of one's aspiration; one's felt connection to God or one's sense of transcendence or liberation or ascent—both in itself and in light of accounts offered by philosophers such as Plato, Rousseau, and Nietzsche. And one must do one's best to consider philosophers' accounts that are beyond one's own experience but that speak to it, or claim to. The experience at issue, concerning as it does the interaction between humanity and the divine, is daemonic—which means that the question of humanity's relation to divinity, the question of eros, is also a question *for* eros. Daemonic Eros must speak for itself, and we can do no better than to attend to its testimony. The highest matters cannot be interrogated from above.[30]

---

29. Theologians, at least, have often supposed that the three conceptions I have just identified—divinity as the ground of being, as perfect self-sufficiency, and as creator, sustainer, and lawgiver—are not mutually exclusive but rather compatible and continuous aspects or moments of divinity.

30. Eros, as the highest thing in us, cannot be interrogated from above. Yet it affords a view of that which is even higher than itself. According to Diotima's report, Eros "ferr[ies] . . . to human beings things from gods" (202e), which might be understood to mean that the way to gain sight of the Good is through understanding the desire for the Good. Or in the less guarded words of a not altogether alien tradition: "Infinity does not abide being known. . . . The only one who knows, yet without knowing, is highest desire" (*Sefer ha-Zohar* 3:26b).

REFERENCES

Ahrensdorf, Peter J. 2000. "The Fear of Death and the Longing for Immortality: Hobbes and Thucydides on Human Nature and the Problem of Anarchy." *American Political Science Review* 94, no. 3: 579–93.
Alfarabi. 1969. *Alfarabi's Philosophy of Plato and Aristotle.* Trans. Muhsin Mahdi. Ithaca: Cornell University Press.
Anastaplo, George. 1964. "Human Being and Citizen." In Joseph Cropsey, ed., *Ancients and Moderns: Essays on the Tradition of Political Philosophy.* New York: Basic Books.
Annas, Julia. 1981. *An Introduction to Plato's* Republic. Oxford: Oxford University Press.
Aristophanes. 1984. *Clouds.* Trans. Thomas G. West and Grace Starry West. In *Four Texts on Socrates.* Ithaca: Cornell University Press.
———. 1984. *The Complete Plays of Aristophanes.* Ed. Moses Hadas. New York: Bantam Books.
Aristotle. 1962. *Nicomachean Ethics.* Trans. Martin Ostwald. Indianapolis: Library of Liberal Arts.
———. 1984. *The Politics.* Trans. Carnes Lord. Chicago: University of Chicago Press.
———. 1986. *De Anima.* Trans. Hugh Lawson-Tancred. New York: Penguin Books.
———. 1992. *Eudemian Ethics.* Trans. Michael Woods. New York: Oxford University Press.
Arnhart, Larry. 1998. *Darwinian Natural Right.* Albany: SUNY Press.
Benardete, Seth. 1989. *Socrates' Second Sailing: On Plato's Republic.* Chicago: University of Chicago Press.
———. 2001. "On Plato's *Symposium.*" In Plato's *"Symposium."* Trans. Seth Benardete with commentaries by Bloom and Benardete. Chicago: University of Chicago Press.
Berkowitz, Peter. 1995. *Nietzsche: The Ethics of an Immoralist.* Cambridge, Mass.: Harvard University Press.
Bloom, Allan. 1968. "Interpretive Essay." In *The Republic of Plato.* Trans. Bloom. New York: Basic Books.
———. 1977. "Response to Hall." In *Political Theory* 5, no. 3: 315–30.
———. 1993. *Love and Friendship.* New York: Simon and Schuster.
———. 2001. "The Ladder of Love." In Plato's *"Symposium,"* trans. Seth Benardete

with commentaries by Bloom and Benardete. Chicago: University of Chicago Press.

Bolotin, David. 1979. *Plato's Dialogue on Friendship: An Interpretation of the* Lysis, *with a New Translation.* Ithaca: Cornell University Press.

Bowery, Anne-Marie. 1998. "Responding to Socrates' Pedagogical Provocation." In "The Paideia Project Online," papers presented at the Twentieth World Congress of Philosophy, Boston, August 10–15, 1998. http://www.bu.edu/wcp/Main Anci.htm.

Brann, Eva. 2004. *The Music of the Republic.* Philadelphia: Paul Dry Books.

Bruell, Christopher. 1994. "Introduction." In Xenophon, *Memorabilia,* trans. Amy L. Bonnette. Ithaca: Cornell University Press.

Burger, Ronna, ed. 2002. *Encounters and Reflections: Conversations with Seth Benardete.* Chicago: University of Chicago Press.

Butterworth, Charles. 1979. "Interpretive Essay." In *Reveries of the Solitary Walker,* trans. Butterworth. Indianapolis: Hackett Publishing, 1979.

Cantor, Paul A. 1985. "The Metaphysics of Botany: Rousseau and the New Criticism of Plants." *Southwest Review* 70: 362–80.

Cassirer, Ernst. 1954. *The Question of Jean-Jacques Rousseau.* Ed and trans. Peter Gay. Bloomington: Indiana University Press.

———. 1963. *Rousseau, Kant, and Goethe.* Trans. James Gutmann et al. New York: Harper and Row.

Cicero. 1945. *Tusculanae Disputationes.* Trans. J. E. King. Cambridge, Mass.: Harvard University Press.

Colli and Montinari. 1968. *Nietzsche Werke: Kritische Gesamtausgabe* (*Sechste Abteilung, Zweiter Band*) Berlin: Walter de Gruyter.

Conway, Daniel W. 1997. *Nietzsche and the Political.* New York: Routledge.

Cooper, Laurence D. 1999. *Rousseau, Nature, and the Problem of the Good Life.* University Park: Penn State University Press.

———. 2001. "Beyond the Tripartite Soul: The Dynamic Psychology of the *Republic.*" *Review of Politics* 63: 341–72.

Craig, Leon Harold. 1994. *The War Lover: A Study of Plato's* Republic. Toronto: University of Toronto Press.

———. "Strange Images: Nietzsche's Perplexing Guide to *Beyond Good and Evil.*" Paper presented at the 1984 Annual Meeting of the American Political Science Association, Washington, D.C.

Davis, Michael. 1999. *The Autobiography of Philosophy: Rousseau's* The Reveries of the Solitary Walker. Lanham, Md.: Rowman and Littlefield.

Dannhauser, Werner J. 1974. *Nietzsche's View of Socrates.* Ithaca: Cornell University Press.

Derathé, Robert. 1948. *Le Rationalisme de Jean-Jacques Rousseau.* Paris: Presses Universitaires de France.

Eden, Robert. 1983. *Political Leadership and Nihilism: A Study of Weber and Nietzsche.* Tampa: University Presses of Florida.

Ellenberger, Henri. 1970. *The Discovery of the Unconscious.* New York: Basic Books.

Ellis, Madeleine. B. 1977. *Rousseau's Socratic Aemilian Myths: A Literary Collation of* Emile *and the* Social Contract. Columbus: Ohio State University Press.

Foucault, Michel. 1972. *Power/Knowledge.* Trans. and ed. Colin Gordon. New York: Pantheon Books.

Gillespie, Michael Allen. 1988. "Nietzsche's Musical Politics." In Gillespie and Tracy B. Strong, eds., *Nietzsche's New Seas: Explorations in Philosophy, Aesthetics, and Politics.* Chicago: University of Chicago Press.

Ginsberg, Mitchell. 1973. "Nietzschean Psychiatry." In Robert Solomon, ed., *Nietzsche: A Collection of Critical Essays.* Notre Dame: University of Notre Dame Press.

Grace, Eve Noirot. 2000. "Conscience: The Ambiguous Science of 'Simple Souls.'" Paper presented at the Annual Meeting of the American Political Science Association, August 31–September 3, Washington, D.C.

———. 2001. "The Restlessness of 'Being': Rousseau's Protean Sentiment of Existence." *History of European Ideas* 27: 133–51.

Grant, George. 1986. *Technology and Justice.* Notre Dame: Notre Dame University Press.

Griswold, Charles. 1988. "Plato's Metaphilosophy: Why Plato Wrote Dialogues." In Griswold, ed., *Platonic Writings, Platonic Readings.* New York: Routledge.

Gurvitch, Georges. 1932. *L'idée du droit social. Notion et système du droit social. Histoire doctrinal depuis le XVIIe siècle jusqua'à la fin du XIXe siècle.* Paris: Libraire du Receuil Sirey.

Hegel, G. W. F. 1977. *The Phenomenology of Spirit.* Trans. A.V. Miller. New York: Oxford University Press.

Heidegger, Martin. 1977. *The Question Concerning Technology and Other Essays.* Trans. William Lovitt. New York: Harper Torchbooks.

———. 1979. *Nietzsche, Volume I: The Will to Power as Art.* Trans. David Farrell Krell. New York: Harper and Row.

Hirschman, Albert O. 1978. *The Passions and the Interests.* Princeton: Princeton University Press.

Hobbes, Thomas. 1994. *Leviathan.* Ed. Edwin Curley. Indianapolis: Hackett Publishing.

———. 1839–45. *The English Works of Thomas Hobbes,* 11 vols. Ed. William Molesworth.

Howland, Jacob. 1993. *The Republic: The Odyssey of Philosophy.* New York: Twayne Publishers.

Hyland, Drew A. 1990. "Plato's Three Waves and the Question of Utopia." In *Interpretation* 18, no. 1: 91–109.

———. 1995. *Finitude and Transcendence in the Platonic Dialogues.* Albany: SUNY Press.

Joseph, H. W. B. 1935. *Essays in Ancient and Modern Philosophy.* Oxford: Oxford University Press.

Kaufmann, Walter. 1974. *Nietzsche: Philosopher, Psychologist, Antichrist,* 4th ed. Princeton: Princeton University Press.

———. 1980. *Discovering the Mind, Volume Two: Nietzsche, Heidegger, and Buber.* New York: McGraw Hill.

Kelly, Christopher. 1987. *Rousseau's Exemplary Life: The "Confessions" as Political Philosophy.* Ithaca: Cornell University Press.

———. 2003. *Rousseau as Author: Consecrating One's Life to the Truth.* Chicago: University of Chicago Press.

Klein, Jacob. 1965. *A Commentary on Plato's Meno*. Chapel Hill: University of North Carolina Press.

Kochin, Michael S. 2002. *Gender and Rhetoric in Plato's Political Thought*. New York: Cambridge University Press.

Koziak, Barbara. 2000. *Retrieving Political Emotion:* Thumos, *Aristotle, and Gender*. University Park: Penn State University Press.

Lachterman, David. 1989–90. "What is 'The Good' of Plato's *Republic*?" In *Four Essays on Plato's "Republic"*: *Saint John's Review* 39, nos. 1 and 2: 139–71.

Lampert, Laurence. 1986. *Nietzsche's Teaching: An Interpretation of* Thus Spoke Zarathustra. New Haven: Yale University Press.

———. 1993. *Nietzsche and Modern Times: A Study of Bacon, Descartes, and Nietzsche*. New Haven: Yale University Press.

———. 1996. *Leo Strauss and Nietzsche*. Chicago: University of Chicago Press.

———. 2001. *Nietzsche's Task: An Interpretation of* Beyond Good and Evil. New Haven: Yale University Press.

Leibowitz, David Mark. 1996. "The Moral and Political Foundations of Socratic Philosophy: A Study of Plato's *Apology*." Ph.D. diss., Harvard University.

Lenzner, Steven J., and William Kristol. 2004. "Leo Strauss: An Introduction." In *Perspectives on Political Science* 33, no. 4: 204–14.

Levine, Andrew. 1976. *The Politics of Autonomy: A Kantian Reading of Rousseau's Social Contract*. Amherst: University of Massachusetts Press.

Lomax, J. Harvey. 2003. *The Paradox of Philosophical Education: Nietzsche's New Nobility and the Eternal Recurrence in* Beyond Good and Evil. Lanham, Md.: Lexington Books.

Löwith, Karl. 1986. *Mein Leben in Deutschland vor und nach 1933: Ein Bericht*. Stuttgart: J. B. Metzlersche Verlagsbuchhandlung.

———. 1997. *Nietzsche's Philosophy of the Eternal Recurrence of the Same*. Trans. J. Harvey Lomax. Berkeley and Los Angeles: University of California Press.

Lutz, Mark J. 1998. *Socrates' Education to Virtue: Learning the Love of the Noble*. Albany: SUNY Press.

Machiavelli, Niccolò. 1985. *The Prince*. Trans. Harvey C. Mansfield Jr. Chicago: University of Chicago Press.

MacIntyre, Alasdair. 1988. *Whose Justice? Which Rationality?* South Bend: University of Notre Dame Press.

Marks, Jonathan. 2005. *Perfection and Disharmony in the Thought of Jean-Jacques Rousseau*. New York: Cambridge University Press.

Masters, Roger D. 1968. *The Political Philosophy of Rousseau*. Princeton: Princeton University Press.

May, Rollo. 1974. "Nietzsche's Contributions to Psychology." *Symposium: A Quarterly Journal in Modern Foreign Literatures*. Syracuse: Syracuse University Press.

McGuire, David. "Beyond Good and Evil: A Prelude to a Philosophy of the Past." *Examined Life On-Line Philosophy Journal* 3: 11. http://examinedlifejournal .com/articles/template.php?shorttitle=beyondgood&authorid=70.

Melzer, Arthur M. 1990. *The Natural Goodness of Man: On the System of Rousseau's Thought*. Chicago: University of Chicago Press.

Miller, Mitchell. 1985. "Platonic Provocations: Reflections on the Soul and the Good in the *Republic*." In *Platonic Investigations*, ed. Dominic J. O'Meara. Washington, D.C.: Catholic University of America Press.

Montaigne, Michel de. *The Complete Essays of Montaigne.* Trans. Donald M. Frame. Stanford: Stanford University Press.

Nehamas, Alexander. 1985. *Nietzsche: Life as Literature.* Cambridge, Mass.: Harvard University Press.

Newell, Waller R. 2000. *Ruling Passion: The Erotics of Statecraft in Platonic Political Philosophy.* Lanham, Md.: Rowman and Littlefield.

Nichols, Jr., James. H. 1995. "Platonic Reflections on Philosophic Education." In Michael Palmer and Thomas L. Pangle, eds., *Political Philosophy and the Human Soul: Essays in Memory of Allan Bloom.* Lanham, Md.: Rowman and Littlefield.

Nichols, Mary P. 1984. "The *Republic*'s Two Alternatives: Philosopher-Kings and Socrates." *Political Theory* 12, no. 2: 252–74.

———. 1988. "Spiritedness and Philosophy in Plato's *Republic.*" In *Understanding the Political Spirit: Philosophical Investigations from Socrates to Nietzsche,* ed. Catherine H. Zuckert. New Haven: Yale University Press.

Nietzsche, Friedrich. 1968. *Nietzsche Werke. Kritische Gesamtausgabe.* Berlin: Walter de Gruyter.

———. 1954. *The Antichrist.* In *The Portable Nietzsche,* trans. and ed. Walter Kaufmann. New York: Penguin Books.

———. 1954. *Thus Spoke Zarathustra.* In *The Portable Nietzsche,* trans. and ed. Walter Kaufmann. New York: Penguin Books.

———. 1954. *Twilight of the Idols.* In *The Portable Nietzsche,* trans. and ed. Walter Kaufmann. New York: Penguin Books.

———. 1966. *Beyond Good and Evil: Prelude to a Philosophy of the Future.* Trans. Walter Kaufmann. New York: Vintage Books.

———. 1967. *Ecce Homo.* Trans. Walter Kaufmann. New York: Vintage Books.

———. 1967. *On the Genealogy of Morals.* Trans. Walter Kaufmann and R. J. Hollingdale. New York: Vintage Books.

———. 1967. *The Will to Power.* Trans. Walter Kaufmann and R. J. Hollingdale. Ed. Kaufmann. New York: Vintage Books.

———. 1968. *The Birth of Tragedy.* In *Basic Writings of Nietzsche,* trans. and ed. Walter Kaufmann. New York: Modern Library.

———. 1968. *Nietzsche Werke, Kritische Gesamtausgabe.* Herausgegeben von Giorgio Colli und Mazzino Montinari. Berlin: Walter de Gruyter.

———. 1973. *Beyond Good and Evil: Prelude to a Philosophy of the Future.* Trans. R. J. Hollingdale. New York: Penguin Books.

———. 1974. *The Gay Science.* Trans. Walter Kaufmann. New York: Vintage Books.

———. 1983. *Untimely Meditations.* Trans. R. J. Hollingdale. New York: Cambridge University Press.

———. 1996. *Human, All Too Human: A Book for Free Spirits.* Trans. R. J. Hollingdale. New York: Cambridge University Press.

Nussbaum, Martha. 1986. *The Fragility of Goodness: Luck and Ethics in Greek Tragedy and Philosophy.* New York: Cambridge University Press.

Orwin, Clifford. 1994. *The Humanity of Thucydides.* Princeton: Princeton University Press.

———. 1998. "Rousseau's Socratism." *Journal of Politics* 60: 174–87.

Pangle, Thomas L. 1976. "The Political Psychology of Religion in Plato's *Laws.*" *American Political Science Review* 70: 1059–77.

Pippin, Robert B. 1997. *Idealism as Modernism: Hegelian Variations*. New York: Cambridge University Press.
Plato. 1968. *The Republic of Plato*. Trans. Allan Bloom. New York: Basic Books.
———. 1980. *The Laws of Plato*. Trans. Thomas L. Pangle. Chicago: University of Chicago Press.
———. 1987. *Alcibiades I*. Trans. Carnes Lord. In *The Roots of Political Philosophy: Ten Forgotten Socratic Dialogues*, ed. Thomas L. Pangle. Ithaca: Cornell University Press.
———. 1987. *Cleitophon*. Trans. Clifford Orwin. In *The Roots of Political Philosophy: Ten Forgotten Socratic Dialogues*, ed. Thomas L. Pangle. Ithaca: Cornell University Press.
———. 1987. *Critias*. Trans. A. E. Taylor. In *The Collected Dialogues of Plato, Including the Letters*, ed. Edith Hamilton and Huntington Cairns. Princeton: Princeton University Press.
———. 1987. *Letters*. Trans. L. A. Post. In *The Collected Dialogues of Plato, Including the Letters*, ed. Edith Hamilton and Huntington Cairns. Princeton: Princeton University Press.
———. 1987. *Phaedo*. Trans. Hugh Tredennick. In *The Collected Dialogues of Plato, Including the Letters*, ed. Edith Hamilton and Huntington Cairns. Princeton: Princeton University Press.
———. 1987. *Timaeus*. Trans. Benjamin Jowett. In *The Collected Dialogues of Plato, Including the Letters*, ed. Edith Hamilton and Huntington Cairns. Princeton: Princeton University Press.
———. 1998. *Gorgias*. Trans. James H. Nichols Jr. Ithaca: Cornell University Press.
———. 1998. *Phaedrus*. Trans. James H. Nichols Jr. Ithaca: Cornell University Press.
———. 2001. *Plato's "Symposium."* Trans. Seth Benardete. Chicago: University of Chicago Press.
Plutarch. 1998. "Alcibiades." In *Greek Lives*. Trans. Robin Waterfield. New York: Oxford University Press.
Robinson, T. M. 1970. *Plato's Psychology*. Toronto: University of Toronto Press.
Roochnik, David. 1997. "Irony and Accessibility." In *Political Theory* 25, no. 6: 869–85.
———. 2003. *Beautiful City: The Dialectical Character of Plato's* Republic. Ithaca: Cornell University Press.
Rorty, Richard. 1989. *Contingency, Irony, and Solidarity*. New York: Cambridge University Press.
Rosen, Stanley. 1965. "The Role of Eros in Plato's *Republic*." *Review of Metaphysics* 18: 452–75.
———. 1987. *Plato's* Symposium. South Bend: St. Augustine's Press.
———. 1993. *The Question of Being: A Reversal of Heidegger*. New Haven: Yale University Press.
Rousseau, Jean-Jacques. 1959–69. *Œuvres complètes*, 4 vols. Vol. 3. Paris: Gallimard, Bibliothèque de la Pléiade.
———. 1959–69. *Œuvres complètes*, 4 vols. Vol. 4. Paris: Gallimard, Bibliothèque de la Pléiade.
———. 1964. *First Discourse (Discourse on the Sciences and Arts.)* In *The First and Second Discourses*. Trans. Roger D. and Judith R. Masters. New York: St. Martin's Press.

———. 1964. *Second Discourse (Discourse on the Origin and Foundations of Inequality Among Men)*. In *The First and Second Discourses*. Trans. Roger D. and Judith R. Masters. New York: St. Martin's Press.

———. 1978. *On the Social Contract*. In *On the Social Contract with Geneva Manuscript and Political Economy*. Ed. Roger D. Masters. Trans. Judith R. Masters. New York: St. Martin's Press.

———. 1979. *Emile, or on Education*. Trans. Allan Bloom. New York: Basic Books.

———. 1986. *Considerations on the Government of Poland*. In *Political Writings*. Ed. and trans. Frederick Watkins. Madison: University of Wisconsin Press.

———. 1986. *Constitutional Project for Corsica*. In *Political Writings*. Ed and trans. Frederick Watkins. Madison: University of Wisconsin Press.

———. 1986. *Last Reply by J.-J. Rousseau of Geneva*. In *The First and Second Discourses Together with the Replies to Critics and Essay on the Origin of Languages*. Ed. and trans. Victor Gourevitch. New York: Harper and Row.

———. 1990. *Rousseau, Judge of Jean-Jacques: Dialogues*. Trans. Judith R. Bush, Christopher Kelly, and Roger D. Masters. Hanover: University Press of New England.

———. 1992. *Reveries of the Solitary Walker*. Trans. Charles E. Butterworth. Indianapolis: Hackett Publishing.

———. 1995. *The Confessions and Correspondence, Including the Letters to Malesherbes*. Trans. Christopher Kelly. Hanover: University Press of New England.

———. 1997. *Julie, or the New Heloise*. Trans. Philip Stewart and Jean Vaché. Hanover: University Press of New England.

Santas, Gerasimos. 1988. *Plato and Freud: Two Theories of Love*. New York: Basil Blackwood.

Sayre, Kenneth M. 1988. "Plato's Dialogues in Light of the *Seventh Letter*." In *Platonic Writings, Platonic Readings*, ed. Charles L. Griswold Jr. New York: Routledge.

Schwartz, Joel. 1984. *The Sexual Politics of Jean-Jacques Rousseau*. Chicago: University of Chicago Press.

Siverthorne, M. J. 1973. "Rousseau's Plato." In *Studies on Voltaire and the Eighteenth Century* 116: 235–49.

Segal, Charles. 1978. "'The Myth Was Saved': Reflections on Homer and the Mythology of Plato's *Republic*." *Hermes* 106, no. 2: 315–36.

Sorenson, Leonard. 1990. "Natural Inequality and Rousseau's Political Philosophy in His *Discourse on Inequality*." *Western Political Quarterly* 43, no. 4: 763–88.

Strauss, Leo. 1964. *The City and Man*. Chicago: University of Chicago Press.

———. 1983. *Studies in Platonic Political Philosophy*. Chicago: University of Chicago Press.

———. 1989. *An Introduction to Political Philosophy: Ten Essays by Leo Strauss*. Ed. Hilail Gildin. Detroit: Wayne State University Press.

———. 1989. *The Rebirth of Classical Political Rationalism: An Introduction to the Thought of Leo Strauss*, selected and introduced by Thomas L. Pangle. Chicago: University of Chicago Press.

———. 2001. *On Plato's* Symposium. Chicago: University of Chicago Press.

Taylor, Charles. 1989. *Sources of the Self*. Cambridge, Mass.: Harvard University Press.

Thucydides. 1996. *The Peloponnesian War*. Trans. Richard Crawley. In *The Landmark Thucydides*, ed. Robert B. Strassler. New York: Free Press.

Tocqueville, Alexis de. 2000. *Democracy in America*. Trans. Harvey C. Mansfield and Delba Winthrop. Chicago: University of Chicago Press.
Xenophon. 1994. *Memorabilia*. Trans. Amy L. Bonnette. Ithaca: Cornell University Press.
———. 1996. *Apology of Socrates to the Jury*. Trans. Andrew Patch. In *The Shorter Socratic Writings: Apology of Socrates to the Jury, Oeconomicus, and Symposium*, ed. Robert C. Bartlett. Ithaca: Cornell University Press.
Wilber, Ken. 1995. *Sex, Ecology, Spirituality: The Spirit of Evolution*. Boston: Shambhala.
———. 1996. *A Brief History of Everything*. Boston: Shambhala.
Zakopoulos, Athenagoras N. 1975. *Plato on Man*. New York: Philosophical Library.
Zuckert, Catherine. 1996. *Postmodern Platos: Nietzsche, Heidegger, Gadamer, Strauss, Derrida*. Chicago: University of Chicago Press.
Zuckert, Catherine, ed. 1988. *Understanding the Political Spirit: Philosophical Investigations from Socrates to Nietzsche*. New Haven: Yale University Press.

INDEX

Achilles, 81n. 13
activity
   of Alcibiades, 3n. 2, 55–56, 112–17, 121–27, 129–32
   of Apollodorus, 55–56, 112–19, 120–21, 125–27, 129–32
   of Aristodemus, 55–56, 112–17, 119–21, 125–27, 129–32
   desire and, 65–66, 147–49, 166–69
   dialogue as, 55–56, 57–61
   egoic consciousness and, 167–69
   eros and, 11–12, 55–56, 57–61, 65–66, 97–102, 112–32
   extended being and, 147–49, 154–64, 166–69
   faculties and, 148, 166–67, 168
   intellectual activity, 154–64
   Nietzsche on, 252–60, 280–81
   philosophers and, 97–102, 280–81, 326–28
   of philosophy, 252–60
   Plato on, 55–56, 57–61, 65–66, 97–102, 112–32, 256–57, 280–81
   politics and, 112–32
   possession compared, 166–69
   progeny and, 99–101
   Rousseau on, 147–49, 166–69
   self-love and, 116–17, 146n. 14, 147–49
   of Socrates, 55, 83–86, 97–102, 106–7, 112–32
   truth and, 55–56
   will to power and, 172
Adeimantus
   city of pigs of, 47
   eros of, 77n. 10
   on justice, 229–30
   on philosophers, 246
   Socrates and, 26–27, 219–21, 235n. 40
Aeschylus, 220–21
Agathon, 58n. 6, 59, 61, 77n. 10, 81n. 13
age, 150

Alcibiades
   activity of, 3n. 2, 55–56, 112–17, 121–27, 129–32
   being and, 105
   eros and, 62n. 11, 112–17, 121–27, 129–32
   eros of, 77n. 10
   politics and, 112–17, 121–27, 129–32
   Socrates and, 46, 112–17, 121–27, 129–32
   thymos of, 60–61
Alfarabi, 98, 105n. 12
amour de soi, 137n. 2, 145–49, 150–51, 154, 158–59, 165–69
amour-propre
   activity and, 116–17
   death and, 169n. 46
   desire and, 144–49, 150–51, 154, 165–69
   education of, 116n. 31, 168–69
   egoic consciousness and, 158–59
   eros and, 116–17, 118–19
   extended being and, 144–49, 150–51, 154, 158–59, 165–69
   goods and, 165–69
   morality and, 125n. 42
   power and, 165
   reveries and, 158–59
   self-consciousness and, 158–59
   terminology of, 137n. 2
   thymos and, 116n. 31, 117–18, 144
anger, 113, 117–19, 129
The Antichrist (Nietzsche), 291–92
aphorisms, 215n. 11
Apollodorus, 55–56, 60–61, 112–19, 120–21, 125–27, 129–32
Apology (Plato), 57n. 3, 104n. 11, 115
aristocracy, 262–66
Aristodemus
   activity of, 55–56, 112–17, 119–21, 125–27, 129–32

Aristodemus (*continued*)
  beauty and, 81n. 14
  eros and, 112–17, 119–21, 125–27, 129–32
  eros of, 77n. 10
  politics and, 112–17, 119–21, 125–27, 129–32
  religion and, 113, 119–21, 129–30
  thymos of, 60–61
Aristophanes
  Birds, 221
  on desire, 61
  dialogue of, 59
  on eros, 60, 61, 62, 62n. 11, 63, 66, 100
  eros of, 77n. 10
  Frogs, 59n. 9
  love and, 88
Aristotle
  on desire, 138n. 3
  as dialectical, 58n. 7
  on eros, 49
  on *eudaimonia*, 155
  on Good, 322n. 23
  naturalism of, 317n. 16
  on politics, 171n. 49
Arnhart, Larry, 316n. 15
Athens, 3n. 2, 90–91, 114, 115n. 29, 122–24, 127n. 47, 128–29

beauty
  Aristodemus and, 81n. 14
  being and, 85
  death and, 55
  education on, 131
  egoic consciousness and, 163
  eidê and, 88n. 19, 194
  eros and, 55, 61–62, 63, 64, 65, 69–83, 92, 95–97, 110–11, 115–17, 162, 172, 193–94
  extended being and, 163
  gender and, 221
  Good and, 70–71
  goods and, 78, 79–83, 92
  happiness and, 80–81
  intellectual activity and, 163
  love and, 80–83, 95–97, 163n. 39, 179–80
  Nietzsche on, 37n. 32, 221
  nonidentity with the good, 78, 79–83, 92
  philosophers and, 88–89, 99–102
  philosophy and, 163, 193–94
  Plato on, 61–62, 63, 64, 65, 69–83, 95–97, 99–102, 110–11, 115–17, 193–94
  politics and, 55
  Rousseau on, 163n. 39, 172–73
  Schopenhauer on, 37n. 32
  self-consciousness and, 163
  of Socrates, 115–17, 122, 125
  Socrates on, 69–83
  thymos and, 81–82
  truth and, 88–89
being. *See also* Being; extended being
  Alcibiades and, 105
  beauty and, 85
  Being and, 33, 106–11
  Cave allegory and, 108n. 16, 109
  character types and, 139, 141–42
  citizenship and, 320–21
  death and, 319–20
  desire and, 141–43, 317–24
  education of, 142–43
  egoic consciousness and, 86n. 16, 103–11
  eidê and, 106, 107–8, 162–63
  Emile and, 141, 142
  eros and, 68–76, 92–93, 100, 103–11, 162, 315, 317–24
  eternity and, 284–87, 290–92, 319–20, 322
  experience of, 138–39, 141–43
  extended being and, 315, 317–24
  Good and, 106–11
  goods and, 139–41, 171, 317–24
  infinity and, 103, 145
  knowledge of, 309–11
  life and, 284–87, 290–92
  love of, 147
  morality and, 293–94
  Nietzsche on, 284–87, 290–92, 293–94, 315, 317–24
  nonbeing and, 75–76
  nothing and, 105–11
  philosophers and, 100, 319
  philosophy and, 319
  Plato on, 68–76, 100, 103–11, 171, 315, 317–24
  politics and, 142
  progeny and, 109
  question of, 138–43
  Rousseau on, 138–43, 145, 171, 315, 317–24
  self-interest and, 103–11
  self-love and, 142–43
  society and, 142
  Socrates on, 68–76, 119
  terminology of, 137n. 2
  thymos and, 43–44, 109
  time and, 293–94
  truth and, 108–9, 175
  will to power and, 315, 317–24
Being, 33, 48–49, 68–72, 106–11, 309n. 8

INDEX   341

Benardete, Seth, 42n. 40, 115
Beyond Good and Evil (Nietzsche)
  activity in, 252–60
  Aftersong in, 214, 270
  aristocracy in, 262–66
  beauty in, 221
  Cave allegory in, 252–56
  character types in, 210–14, 233–35
  democracy in, 219–21, 224, 261–62
  desire in, 227
  divinity in, 248
  education in, 213–14, 249–51
  eros in, 223
  eternity in, 216–17
  gender in, 219–21, 241–42, 253, 258–60
  gods in, 219
  goods in, 212
  happiness in, 213, 234
  Human, All Too Human (Nietzsche) compared, 271–72
  justice in, 226–27
  knowledge in, 227–28, 229–30, 256–58
  morality in, 213, 239–40, 244–45, 252–56, 265–66, 269–70
  nature in, 226–27, 239–40, 244–45, 258, 259–60
  part 1, 224–27
  part 2, 227–30
  part 3, 230–35
  part 4, 235–38
  part 5, 239–45
  part 6, 245–52
  part 7, 252–60
  part 8, 261–62
  part 9, 262–70, 289
  philosophers in, 212, 226, 230, 232–35, 240–41, 245–52, 256–58, 262–70
  philosophy in, 216–17, 223, 224–27, 229, 252–60
  politics in, 208–10, 213–14, 243–44, 247–49, 261–70
  possession in, 219–21, 241–44
  power in, 221, 225–26
  preface of, 214, 222–24
  pride in, 219
  psychology in, 227
  reason in, 244–45
  religion in, 231, 232–35
  Republic (Plato) compared generally, 13–15, 17, 205–14, 271–73, 275–81
  rule in, 210–14, 226, 232–35, 240–41, 247–49
  science in, 224–27, 246, 291n. 17
  section 65, 215, 218–22
  section 73, 215, 218–22
  section 237, 215, 218–22
  section 274a, 222n. 22
  section 295, 216
  section 296, 215–17
  sexuality in, 227, 259–60
  skepticism in, 247–48
  soul in, 211–12, 238, 243–44, 267–70, 296
  spiritedness in, 230, 231–32
  structure of, 214–22
  suffering in, 267–68
  themes of generally, 210–14
  title of, 223n. 25
  truth in, 226, 253, 258–60
  tyrants in, 261–70
  virtue in, 237, 250–51, 252–60
  will to power in, 208–10, 227, 245, 259–60, 275–81
  wisdom in, 225–26
Birds (Aristophanes), 221
Bloom, Allan, 26n. 13, 44–45, 63n. 14, 81n. 13, 179–80, 269n. 23
body, 19, 25, 27, 29–30, 36–38
botany, 155, 155n. 25, 156
Brann, Eva, 87n. 18, 88n. 20, 89n. 21, 98n. 3, 108n. 16
Bruell, Christopher, 114n. 25
Burckhardt, Jacob, 251n. 8, 272
Burns, Timothy, 63n. 14

Callicles, 75
Cave allegory
  being and, 108n. 16, 109
  Nietzsche on, 252–56
  philosophers and, 36n. 31
  politics and, 98
  reckoning in, 45n. 44
  sublimation and, 72
  thymos in, 61–62
Cephalus, 24n. 10, 25, 225
chapter overview, 10–16
character types. *See also* human nature
  being and, 139, 141–42
  death and, 169n. 46
  desire and, 141–42, 146–47, 149–51, 173–74
  eros and, 324–25
  extended being and, 146–47, 149–51, 173–74, 324–25
  faculties and, 141–42
  goods and, 173–74

character types (*continued*)
   Nietzsche on, 210–14, 233–35, 324–25
   Plato on, 210–14, 324–25
   power and, 173–74
   Rousseau on, 139, 141–42, 146–47, 149–51, 169n. 46, 173–74, 324–25
   self-consciousness and, 151
   self-love and, 146–47, 149–51
   will to power and, 277, 324–25
Charmides (Plato), 90
children, 242–43. *See also* family
Christianity, 283n. 9, 285n. 11
Cicero, 20n. 2
citizenship, 178n. 2, 320–21
city. *See also* politics
   building, 227–28
   Cave allegory and, 36n. 31
   education and, 182–83
   eros and, 47–48
   goods and, 26n. 15
   philosophy and, 90–91
   soul and, 23–24, 39, 184, 237–38, 243–44
   thymos and, 39, 47–48
Cleitophon, 222n. 27
communism, 182, 185, 239–40, 241–44, 263
compassion, 153
Confessions (Rousseau), 159n. 31
consciousness. *See* egoic consciousness
contemplation, 83–86, 106–7. *See also* meditation
courage, 45–46
Craig, Leon Harold, 29n. 21, 48n. 48, 116n. 32, 207n. 4

Dannhauser, Werner J., 207n. 4
death
   beauty and, 55
   being and, 319–20
   character types and, 169n. 46
   desire and, 169n. 46
   egoic consciousness and, 3–4, 83–86
   eros and, 55, 69–72, 74–76, 77–78, 79–80, 92, 95–97, 111, 126, 129, 319–20
   eternity and, 83–86, 282, 283
   freedom and, 83–86, 119
   insight and, 83–86
   Nietzsche on, 282, 283
   philosophers and, 45–46, 83–87, 100–102
   philosophy and, 89–90, 127
   politics and, 55
   power and, 3–4
   Rousseau on, 169n. 46

   self-love and, 169n. 46
   of Socrates, 119
   Socrates on, 69–72, 74–76, 77–78, 79–80, 83–86, 116–17, 128
   soul and, 131, 270
   truth and, 84–86, 89–90
democracy, 219–21, 224, 261–62, 308, 321n. 20
desire. *See also* extended being
   activity and, 65–66, 147–49, 166–69
   Agathon on, 61
   Aristophanes on, 61
   being and, 141–43, 317–24
   body and, 29–30, 36–38
   character types and, 141–42, 146–47, 173–74
   and compassion, 153
   death and, 169n. 46
   egoic consciousness and, 30, 167–69
   Emile and, 141, 151
   eros and, 24–25, 27–38, 43–44, 56–57, 61–66, 68–76, 80, 95–97, 276–77, 307–8
   eternity and, 282–83, 284–85, 314–15
   extended being and, 136–38, 143–51, 152–55, 165–75, 180, 193, 307–8, 312
   faculties and, 166–67, 168
   for family, 153–54
   for freedom, 265–66
   for Good, 321–22
   goods and, 135–38, 143–44, 165–75, 315–24
   human nature and, 169–71
   intellectual activity and, 154–55
   Kant on, 135
   for knowledge, 154, 179, 192–93
   for love, 154
   naturalism and, 315–24
   nature and, 136, 169–71
   Nietzsche on, 227, 276–77, 282–83, 284–85, 307–8, 315–24
   objects of, 4, 24–25, 28–38, 40–41, 56, 61–66, 68–76, 95–97
   and patriotism, 153
   philosophers and, 29–30, 32–38, 179, 189–90
   philosophy and, 29–31, 34–38
   Plato on, 20–25, 27–38, 38–44, 61–66, 95–97, 276–77, 307–8, 315–24
   possession and, 152, 166–69, 173–74
   power and, 3–4, 146–47, 149–51, 153, 173–74
   for prestige, 152–53
   reason and, 24–25, 38–39
   Rousseau on, 136–38, 141–51, 152–55, 165–75, 307–8, 312, 315–24
   savages and, 150–51

self-consciousness and, 145–46, 147, 151
self-interest and, 149
self-love and, 137, 144–51, 154, 165–69
Socrates on, 61, 63–66
soul and, 20–25, 31–38, 307–8, 314–15, 321–22
terminology of, 138n. 3
thymos and, 24–25, 38–44
truth and, 29–30, 175, 179
tyrants and, 29–30
and virtue, 153
will to power and, 171, 227, 276–77, 307–8
dialogue, 7–9, 55–56, 57–66, 305–6
Dialogues (Rousseau), 147–49
diaretic activity, 45
Die Frohliche Wissenschaft (Nietzsche), 309n. 8
Dionysus, 59, 59n. 9
Diotima
  Athens and, 128–29
  attribution to, 63
  on eros, 61–62, 69, 72, 80–83, 87, 95–97, 110, 127–32, 329n. 30
  on fame, 57n. 5
  on philosophy, 89
  Plato on, 69, 72
  politics and, 127–32
  power and, 128–29
  on sublimation, 32n. 26
Divided Line, 108–9, 249, 250–51
divinity, 248, 328–29
dogmatism, 224n. 27
doing. *See* activity

Ecce Homo (Nietzsche), 272, 273
ecstasy, 156–57, 159n. 31, 178n. 2
Eden, Robert, 208n. 5, 237n. 42
education
  on beauty, 131
  of being, 142–43
  city and, 182–83
  of Emile, 142, 151, 154, 168–69, 179–80, 188–201
  eros and, 78–80, 111–12, 182–83, 185–86, 209–10, 278–79
  eternity and, 278–79
  extended being and, 168–69, 177–80
  gender and, 182, 184–85, 186–91
  goods and, 177–78, 181–83, 278–79
  gymnastics in, 230–32
  human nature and, 180–81
  love and, 182, 191–94
  morality and, 196–97, 198–99
  music in, 31, 230–32
  Nietzsche on, 6n. 5, 213–14, 249–51, 278–79
  by philosophers, 97–102
  of philosophers, 249–51, 252, 254
  philosophy and, 87, 91, 111–12, 130–32, 177–83, 185–201, 249–51
  Plato on, 6n. 5, 78–80, 178–79, 193–94, 209–10, 213–14, 230–32, 249–51, 252, 254, 278–79
  politics and, 6n. 5, 123–24, 130–32, 195–96, 213–14
  possibility of, 179, 181–83, 197–201, 250–51
  by Rousseau, 325n. 26
  Rousseau on, 6n. 5, 142–43, 168–69, 177–83, 185–201
  of self-love, 116n. 31, 168–69
  by Socrates, 97–102, 123–24, 181–82, 184–85
  Socrates on, 6n. 5
  sublimation and, 191–94
  of *thymos*, 48n. 47
  will to power and, 278–79
egoic consciousness. *See also* self-consciousness
  activity and, 167–69
  beauty and, 163
  Being and, 106–11
  being and, 86n. 16, 103–11
  death and, 3–4, 83–86
  desire and, 30, 167–69
  eros and, 86n. 16, 96, 100–111, 120, 124–25, 172
  extended being and, 158–59, 161–64, 167–69
  Good and, 106–11
  infinity and, 103
  intellectual activity and, 161–64
  Nietzsche on, 327–28
  philosophy and, 161–64
  Plato on, 100–111, 116–17
  possession and, 167–69
  progeny and, 109
  reveries and, 158–59
  Rousseau on, 158–59, 161–64, 167–69, 172–73, 327–28
  self-consciousness and, 158–59, 162–64
  self-love and, 158–59
  Socrates and, 116–17
  thymos and, 109
  transcendence of, 92–93, 100–111, 116–17, 158–59, 161–64
  truth and, 108–9
eidê. *See also* truth
  beauty and, 88n. 19, 194

eidê (continued)
  being and, 106, 107–8, 162–63
  Cave allegory and, 36n. 31
  eros and, 32–33, 34, 311–12
  experience of, 87n. 18
  extended being and, 164
  Good and, 70–71, 106
  goods and, 299–300
  philosophers and, 327–28
  philosophy and, 164
Ellenberger, Henri, 298n. 28
Ellis, Madeleine B., 183n. 7
Emile
  being and, 141, 142
  desire and, 141, 151
  education of, 142, 151, 154, 168–69, 179–80, 188–201
  extended being and, 151, 179–80
  faculties and, 141
  gender and, 188–91
  happiness of, 174
  love and, 191–94
  meditation by, 192–93
  as philosopher, 179, 189–90
  philosophy and, 179–80, 188–201
  power of, 149
  self-love and, 151
Emile (Rousseau)
  character types in, 324–25
  desire in, 143, 145
  education in, 178–83, 185–201
  eros in, 179–80, 185–86, 192
  extended being in, 143, 145, 178–80, 193
  family in, 182
  gender in, 182, 186–91
  goods in, 73n. 8, 143, 181–83
  human nature in, 180–81
  life in, 182–83
  love in, 182, 191–94
  morality in, 196–97, 198–99
  philosophers in, 189–91
  philosophy in, 178–83, 185–201
  politics in, 195–96
  power in, 149
  Republic (Plato) compared, 17, 178–83
  rule in, 182
  self-love in, 145
  truth in, 187–88, 190–91, 195–97
Er, 270
eros. *See also* extended being; will to power
  activity and, 11–12, 55–56, 57–61, 65–66, 97–102, 112–32

  of Adeimantus, 77n. 10
  Agathon on, 61
  Alcibiades and, 62n. 11, 77n. 10, 112–17, 121–27, 129–32
  anger and, 113, 117–19, 129
  Apollodorus and, 112–19, 120–21, 125–27, 129–32
  Aristodemus and, 77n. 10, 112–17, 119–21, 125–27, 129–32
  Aristophanes and, 60, 61, 62, 62n. 11, 63, 66, 77n. 10, 100
  Aristotle on, 49
  beauty and, 55, 61–62, 63, 64, 65, 69–83, 92, 95–97, 110–11, 115–17, 162, 172, 193–94
  Being and, 68–72, 106–11
  being and, 68–76, 92–93, 100, 103–11, 162, 315, 317–24
  beneficiaries of, 77n. 10
  body and, 19, 25, 27, 29–30, 36–38
  character types and, 324–25
  city and, 47–48
  communism and, 185
  contemplation of, 83–86, 106–7
  death and, 55, 69–72, 74–76, 77–78, 79–80, 92, 95–97, 111, 126, 129, 319–20
  desire and, 24–25, 27–38, 43–44, 56–57, 61–66, 68–76, 80, 95–97, 276–77, 307–8
  dialogue on, 57–66
  Diotima on, 61–62, 69, 72, 80–83, 87, 95–97, 110, 127–32, 329n. 30
  education and, 78–80, 111–12, 182–83, 185–86, 209–10, 278–79
  egoic consciousness and, 86n. 16, 96, 100–111, 120, 124–25, 172
  eidê and, 32–33, 34, 311–12
  ends of, 27–36, 40–42, 44–50, 61–66, 68–76, 95–97
  of Eryximachus, 77n. 10
  eternity and, 92, 95–97, 126, 129, 276–81, 314–15, 319–20, 322
  evil and, 26–27, 30–31
  extended being compared, 4–5, 56–57, 136–37, 144, 162–64, 169–73, 179–80, 305–29
  gender and, 66n, 185
  of Glaucon, 47–48, 77n. 10
  Good and, 32–33, 35, 54, 70–72, 74–75, 106–11, 311–12
  goods and, 26–27, 30–31, 54, 63, 64–65, 69, 73–74, 78–83, 92, 95–97, 110–11, 115, 144, 210, 312–13
  health and, 102, 111–12, 209–10

imperialism and, 3
infinity and, 55, 95–97, 103
justice and, 210
life and, 71n. 5, 92–93
love and, 80–83, 95–97, 192
naturalism and, 315–24
Nietzsche on, 223
ordinary, 86–91, 95–97, 100–101, 102, 104, 125–26, 129, 131, 327, 328
origins of, 40–44
overt account of, Socrates', 67–80, 91–93
overview of, 10–12
of Pausanias, 77n. 10
Phaedrus on, 60
of philosopher-kings, 30n. 22, 34, 70n. 1
philosophers and, 25–27, 29–30, 32–38, 49, 68–80, 97–102, 144n. 11, 184, 185, 210, 276–81, 325, 326–28
philosophic epochs and, 306–11
philosophy and, 29–31, 34–38, 44–49, 68–80, 86–93, 95–97, 98–99, 100–101, 102–3, 113, 117–19, 126–32, 179–80, 185–86, 193–94, 223, 324–29
of Plato, 114
Platonic account of generally, 10–12, 67–68, 76–93, 95–97
pleasure and, 74–76, 101
of Polemarchus, 77n. 10
politics and, 10–11, 12, 16, 17–20, 41, 53–56, 69, 78–80, 97–102, 111–32, 209–10, 314–15
power and, 126, 130
progeny and, 69, 72, 99–101, 109
question of, 11, 27–31, 56–57, 61–66, 68–76
Rousseau on, 179–80, 185–86, 192
rule and, 185
self-interest and, 58, 65, 96, 100–111, 162
self-love and, 116–17, 118–19, 124–26
sexual, 36–38, 64–65, 74
of Socrates, 34–35, 41–42, 47, 70n. 1, 89, 95, 104, 106–7
Socrates on, 11, 19–20, 25–27, 27–38, 44–49, 57, 60, 61, 62–66, 67–93, 95–112, 112–32
Socratic account of, 67–80, 91–93, 95–97
soul and, 24–27, 31–38, 40–50, 56–57, 210, 307–8
sublimation and, 30–38, 43–44, 71–76, 191–94
terminology of, 5n. 4
thymos and, 20, 38, 40–50, 57, 59–61, 61–62, 81–82, 102–3, 109, 124–25, 210
truth and, 11, 29–30, 57–61, 65–66, 70, 78–80, 100–101, 102–3, 108–9, 111–12, 125–26, 162, 326–28
tyrants and, 25–27, 29–30, 32, 76–77, 108, 112, 144n. 11, 210
unity of, 91–93, 95–97, 110–11
will to power compared, 4–5, 13–15, 56–57, 125–26, 173, 209–10, 227, 259–60, 275–81, 305–29
wisdom and, 192
Eryximachus, 77n. 10, 128–29
eternity. *See also* time
being and, 284–87, 290–92, 319–20, 322
death and, 83–86, 282, 283
desire and, 282–83, 284–85, 314–15
divinity and, 328–29
education and, 278–79
eros and, 92, 95–97, 126, 129, 276–81, 314–15, 319–20, 322
experience of, 83–86, 87, 96, 284–85, 300–303, 329
extended being and, 314–15
faith and, 284–86, 287–89, 290–92
goods and, 277–79, 281, 284, 291–96, 298, 299–304
infinity and, 328–29
life and, 284–87, 290–92, 294–98
love and, 280
morality and, 294–96
nature and, 303–4
Nietzsche on, 216–17, 276–304, 314–15
nobility and, 278–79, 286, 289–94
philosophers and, 100–101, 277–79, 281, 328–29
philosophy and, 216–17, 328–29
Plato on, 95–97, 100–101, 216–17, 276–81, 299–304, 314–15, 319–20, 322
politics and, 278–79, 294–98, 302–4, 314–15
psychology and, 283–94
question of, 281–83
realm of, 284–85
redemption and, 284–87, 290–92
Rousseau on, 314–15
soul and, 296–98, 303–4
translation of, 217n. 17, 282, 319
truth and, 84–86
will to power and, 276–81, 294–96, 298, 314–15
eudaimonia, 155
Euthyphro (Plato), 90
evil, 26–27, 30–31, 313–14. *See also* goods
existence. *See* being

existential longing. *See* psychic force
experience
   of being, 138–39, 141–43
   divinity and, 329
   of *eidê*, 87n. 18
   of eternity, 83–86, 87, 96, 284–85, 300–303, 329
   of extended being, 155–60
   of Good, 87n. 18
   Nietzsche on, 284–85, 300–303
   of philosophers, 262–70
   Plato on, 300–303
   of soul, 172–73
extended being. *See also* eros; will to power
   activity and, 147–49, 154–64, 166–69
   beauty and, 163
   being and, 315, 317–24
   character types and, 146–47, 173–74, 324–25
   compassion and, 153
   desire and, 136–38, 143–51, 152–55, 165–75, 180, 193, 307–8, 312
   in *Dialogues* (Rousseau), 147–49
   education and, 168–69, 177–80
   egoic consciousness and, 158–59, 161–64, 167–69
   eidê and, 164
   Emile and, 151, 179–80
   in *Emile* (Rousseau), 143, 145, 178–80, 193
   eros compared, 4–5, 56–57, 136–37, 144, 162–64, 169–73, 179–80, 305–29
   eternity and, 314–15
   experience of, 155–60
   faculties and, 166–67, 168
   family and, 153–54
   God and, 158, 159n. 30
   goods and, 12, 136–38, 143–44, 165–75, 177–78, 312–13
   happiness and, 157–58
   health and, 168, 173, 174
   human nature and, 161, 169–71
   intellectual activity and, 154–64
   knowledge and, 154, 193
   love and, 154
   meditation and, 156–62
   naturalism and, 315–24
   nature and, 161, 169–71
   overview of, 12–13
   patriotism and, 153
   philosophers and, 12–13, 100, 325, 326–28
   philosophic epochs and, 306–11
   philosophy and, 12–13, 160–64, 177–80, 324–29
   Plato on, 152n. 19
   politics and, 164n. 41, 168–69, 312, 314–15
   possession and, 152, 166–69, 173–74
   possibility of, 179
   power and, 146–47, 149–51, 153, 173–74
   prestige and, 152–53
   question of, 144–51
   reveries and, 166
   savages and, 150–51
   self-consciousness and, 145–46, 147, 151, 155–59, 162–64
   self-interest and, 149
   self-love and, 137, 144–51, 154, 158–59, 165–69
   soul and, 160–61
   transcendence and, 158–59, 161–64
   truth and, 175, 326–28
   virtue and, 153
   will to power compared, 4–5, 305–29
   writing and, 156–62

faculties, 141–42, 148, 166–67, 168, 170
faith, 284–86, 287–89, 290–92
family, 153–54, 182. *See also* children
finitude. *See* infinity
First Discourse (Rousseau), 198–99, 325
Foucault, Michel, 297n. 26
freedom. *See also* transcendence
   from anger, 118n. 34
   death and, 83–86, 119
   desire for, 265–66
   philosophers and, 83–86, 179, 189–90
   from prejudice, 179
   of Socrates, 124–25
Frogs (Aristophanes), 59n. 9

The Gay Science (Nietzsche), 277n. 3, 280n. 7
gender
   beauty and, 221
   communism and, 263
   democracy and, 219–21
   education and, 182, 184–85, 186–91
   Emile and, 188–91
   eros and, 66n, 185
   love and, 241–42
   Nietzsche on, 219–21, 241–42, 253, 258–60, 280
   philosophers and, 185
   philosophy and, 186–91
   Plato on, 182, 184–85, 219–21, 239–40, 241–42, 244–45, 263
   possession and, 219–21, 241–42
   power and, 221

Rousseau on, 182, 186–91
truth and, 188n. 18, 223, 253, 258–60
Gillespie, Michael, 237n. 42
Glaucon
  desire of, 33
  eros of, 47–48, 77n. 10
  on justice, 229
  Socrates and, 21, 210, 229
  thymos and, 42, 47–48
God, 88n. 18, 106, 158, 159n. 30
gods, 219
Good. *See also* goods
  beauty and, 70–71
  being and, 106–11
  desire for, 321–22
  egoic consciousness and, 106–11
  eidê and, 70–71, 106
  eros and, 32–33, 35, 54, 70–72, 74–75, 106–11, 311–12
  experience of, 87n. 18
  goods and, 54
  self-interest and, 106–11
  sight of, 110–11
  Socrates on, 70–72, 74–75
  soul and, 48, 321–22
  terminology of, 70n. 3, 322n. 24
  as unity, 110–11
goods. *See also* evil; Good
  Achilles and, 81n. 13
  Agathon on, 81n. 13
  beauty and, 78–80, 79–83, 92
  being and, 139–41, 171, 317–24
  character types and, 173–74
  citizenship and, 320–21
  city and, 26n. 15
  commensurability of, 317n. 16
  desire and, 135–38, 143–44, 165–75, 315–24
  education and, 177–78, 181–83, 278–79
  eidê and, 299–300
  eros and, 26–27, 30–31, 54, 63, 64–65, 69, 73–74, 78–83, 92, 95–97, 110–11, 115, 144, 210, 312–13
  eternity and, 277–79, 281, 284, 291–96, 298, 299–304
  extended being and, 12, 136–38, 143–44, 165–75, 177–78, 312–13
  faculties and, 170
  Good and, 54
  happiness and, 80–81, 140–41
  health and, 313–14
  human nature and, 26–27, 169–71

Kant on, 135, 137
life and, 170–71, 182–83, 294–96, 298
love and, 80–83
naturalism and, 315–24
nature and, 136, 169–71
Nietzsche on, 26n. 15, 81n. 12, 212, 277–79, 281, 284, 291–94, 294–96, 298, 299–304, 312–14, 315–24
nonidentity with the beautiful, 78, 79–83, 92
philosophers and, 212, 277–79, 281, 319
philosophy and, 90, 119, 177–78, 181–83, 249–51, 319
Plato on, 21, 26–27, 63, 64–65, 69, 73–74, 78–83, 95–97, 110–11, 115, 144, 212, 277–79, 281, 295n. 24, 299–304, 312–13, 315–24
politics and, 16, 210, 278–79, 294–96, 298, 302–4
possession and, 173–74
power and, 173–74
question of, 135–38
Rousseau on, 73–74, 136–38, 139–41, 143–44, 165–75, 177–78, 181–83, 312–13, 315–24
rule and, 212
self-love and, 165–69
Socrates on, 21, 26–27, 69, 73–74, 78–83
soul and, 21
terminology of, 70n. 3, 322n. 24
thymos and, 81–82
virtue as, 140
will to power and, 13–15, 171, 294–96, 312–14
Gorgias (Plato), 53, 75
Grace, Eve Noirot, 159n. 31
gymnastics, 230–32

happiness
  beauty and, 80–81
  extended being and, 157–58
  goods and, 80–81, 140–41
  morality and, 213
  Nietzsche on, 213, 234
  of philosophers, 157–58, 160
  Plato on, 213
  religion and, 234
  reveries and, 157–58
  Rousseau on, 140–41, 157–58, 174
  self-consciousness and, 157–58
Hauptwerk, The Will to Power (Nietzsche), 14n. 8, 209n. 7, 228n. 34, 273n. 29, 288n. 14, 308
having. *See* possession
health
  of aristocracy, 262–63
  eros and, 102, 111–12, 209–10

health (*continued*)
  extended being and, 168, 173, 174
  goods and, 313–14
  nature and, 164, 303–4
  politics and, 294–96, 303–4
  soul and, 23–24, 25, 149n. 17, 164, 172, 195, 211–12, 303–4
  truth and, 293
Hegel, G. W. F., 156n. 27
Heidegger, Martin, 208n. 5, 279, 280n. 7, 285n. 11, 286n. 12, 295n. 23
Hobbes, Thomas, 3–4, 7–8, 153
Homer, 42–43
honor, 44, 46–47
Howland, Jacob, 28n. 17, 31
Human, All Too Human (Nietzsche), 271–72
human nature. *See also* character types
  desire and, 169–71
  education and, 180–81
  evil and, 26–27
  extended being and, 161, 169–71
  goods and, 26–27, 169–71
  intellectual activity and, 161
  Nietzsche on, 8, 302
  philosophy and, 161
  Plato on, 26–27, 169–70, 244–45
  psychic force in, 8
  Rousseau on, 8, 161, 180–81
  thymos in, 42–43
  unity of, 244–45
hunger, 227
hunting, 45, 186

idleness, 154–55
ignorance, 57
Iliad (Homer), 42–43
immortality. *See* death
imperialism, 3
infinity, 4, 55, 95–97, 103, 145, 328–29
insight, 83–86, 87, 96
intellectual activity, 154–64

Jefferson, Thomas, 323
Jesus, 283n. 9
Jews, 242–43
justice, 210, 224–27, 229–30, 235–37

Kant, Immanuel, 135, 137
Kaufmann, Walter, 297n. 26, 298n. 28
Kelly, Christopher, 160n. 34, 160n. 35, 163, 169n. 46, 187n. 15

knowledge. *See also* truth
  of being, 309–11
  building, 227–28
  desire for, 154, 179, 192–93
  extended being and, 154, 193
  love of, 245–46, 326–27
  morality and, 224n. 26
  Nietzsche on, 227–28, 229–30, 256–58
  philosophers and, 179, 189–90, 245–46, 256–58, 281, 326–27
  of Socrates, 57
Kochin, Michael S., 185n. 13

Laches (Plato), 90
Lampert, Laurence
  on *Beyond Good and Evil* (Nietzsche), 239n. 1
  on Nietzsche generally, 205n. 1, 208n. 5, 214n. 10, 280n. 7
  on philosophy, 29n. 21
  on politics, 261n. 18
  on science, 309n. 8
  on truth, 226
  on will to power, 295n. 23
Laws (Plato), 74, 86n. 16
Leibowitz, David Mark, 57n. 3, 104n. 11
Leontius, 41
liberalism, 6–7, 130–32, 296–98, 314–15, 323
life
  being and, 284–87, 290–92
  eros and, 71n. 5, 92–93
  eternity and, 284–87, 290–92, 294–98
  faculties and, 170
  family and, 182
  goods and, 170–71, 182–83, 294–96, 298
  love and, 182, 280
  morality and, 292–94, 294–96
  Nietzsche on, 284–87, 290–92, 294–98
  nobility and, 292–94
  philosophers and, 178, 191n. 24
  philosophy and, 119, 191n. 24
  Plato on, 71n. 5
  Rousseau on, 178, 182–83
  will to power and, 277, 294–96
Locke, John, 153
Lomax, J. Harvey, 207n. 4, 237n. 42, 278n. 5, 285n. 11
love. *See also* self-love
  beauty and, 80–83, 95–97, 163n. 39, 179–80
  of being, 147
  desire for, 154
  ecstasy of, 178n. 2

education and, 182, 191–94
Emile and, 191–94
eros and, 80–83, 95–97, 192
eternity and, 280
extended being and, 154
gender and, 241–42
goods and, 80–83
of knowledge, 245–46, 326–27
life and, 182, 280
of order, 163n. 39
philosophers and, 179, 189–90, 326–27
of philosophy, 126
Plato on, 95–97, 115
possession and, 241–42
of power, 130
Rousseau on, 182, 191–94
of Socrates, 112–32
truth and, 179, 258
of wisdom, 192–93, 195, 258, 267
Löwith, Karl, 285n. 11, 295n. 23

maker, 256, 281, 326–27
manifest lovers. *See* activity
martyrdom, 229
master and slave morality, 265–67
Masters, Roger D., 183n. 7
McGuire, David, 207n. 4, 227n. 30, 234n. 38
meditation, 155n. 25, 156–62, 192–93. *See also* contemplation
modeling, 97–102
modernity, 306–11
modesty, 16
Montaigne, Michel de, 183
morality
being and, 293–94
education and, 196–97, 198–99
eternity and, 294–96
happiness and, 213
knowledge and, 224n. 26
life and, 292–94, 294–96
master and slave and, 265–66
naturalism and, 315–24
nature and, 239–40, 244–45
Nietzsche on, 213, 239–40, 244–45, 252–56, 265–66, 269–70, 275–76, 292–94, 294–96, 315–24
nobility and, 292–94
philosophy and, 196–97, 198–99, 252–56
Plato on, 213, 315–24
politics and, 275–76, 294–96
reason and, 244–45

Rousseau on, 196–97, 198–99, 315–24
self-love and, 125n. 42
society and, 254–55
soul and, 269–70
time and, 293–94
truth and, 196–97
virtue and, 252–56
will to power and, 245, 294–96
music, 31, 230–32, 237n. 42

naturalism, 315–24
nature. *See also* human nature
desire and, 136, 169–71
eternity and, 303–4
extended being and, 161, 169–71
goods and, 136, 169–71
health and, 164, 303–4
intellectual activity and, 161
justice and, 226–27
morality and, 239–40, 244–45
Nietzsche on, 14–15, 16, 226–27, 239–40, 244–45, 258, 259–60, 295, 303–4
philosophers and, 258
philosophy and, 161, 258, 259–60
Plato on, 16, 169–70, 240, 303–4
politics and, 136, 295, 303–4
power and, 128–29
Rousseau on, 16, 136, 156–57, 161, 169–71
self-consciousness and, 156–57
sexuality and, 259–60
soul and, 303–4
Nehemas, Alexander, 297n. 26
Newell, Waller R., 105n. 12
Nichols, Mary P., 41n. 39
Nietzsche, Friedrich. *See also Beyond Good and Evil*; will to power
on activity, 252–60, 280–81
The Antichrist, 291–92
aphorisms of, 215n. 11
on aristocracy, 262–66
on beauty, 37n. 32, 221
on being, 284–87, 290–92, 293–94, 309–11, 315, 317–24
on Being, 309n. 8
on Cave allegory, 252–56
on character types, 210–14, 233–35, 324–25
on children, 242–43
correspondence of, 251n. 8, 271–73
on death, 282, 283
on democracy, 219–21, 224, 261–62
on desire, 227, 276–77, 282–83, 284–85, 307–8, 315–24

Nietzsche (*continued*)
  dialogue with Plato and Rousseau, 7–9, 305–6
  Die Frohliche Wissenschaft, 309n. 8
  on divinity, 248
  dogmatism and, 224n. 27
  Ecce Homo, 272, 273
  on education, 6n. 5, 213–14, 249–51, 278–79
  on egoic consciousness, 327–28
  on eros, 223
  on eternity, 216–17, 276–304, 314–15
  on experience, 284–85, 300–303
  on faith, 284–86, 287–89, 290–92
  The Gay Science, 277n. 3, 280n. 7
  on gender, 219–21, 241–42, 253, 258–60, 280
  on gods, 219
  on goods, 26n. 15, 81n. 12, 212, 277–79, 281, 284, 291–94, 294–96, 298, 299–304, 312–14, 315–24
  on happiness, 213, 234
  Hauptwerk, The Will to Power, 14n. 8, 209n. 7, 228n. 34, 273n. 29, 288n. 14, 308
  Human, All Too Human, 271–72
  on human nature, 8, 302
  on Jews, 242–43
  on justice, 226–27
  on knowledge, 227–28, 229–30, 256–58, 309–11
  on life, 284–87, 290–92, 294–98
  on master and slave, 265–67
  on morality, 213, 239–40, 244–45, 252–56, 265–66, 269–70, 275–76, 292–94, 294–96, 315–24
  music and, 237n. 42
  naturalism and, 315–24
  on nature, 14–15, 16, 226–27, 239–40, 244–45, 258, 259–60, 295, 303–4
  on nobility, 213, 216, 262, 265–66, 268, 278–79, 286, 289–94, 302
  numbers and, 214n. 10
  on opposite values, 285, 287–89
  as philosopher, 250–51
  on philosophers, 26n. 14, 212, 226, 230, 232–35, 240–41, 245–52, 256–58, 262–70, 276–81, 325, 326–28
  philosophic epochs and, 306–11
  on philosophy, 216–17, 223, 224–27, 229, 252–60, 290n. 16, 324–29
  on Plato, 205–6, 223–24, 275–76, 299–304, 309–11
  on pleasure, 291–92
  on politics, 98, 208–10, 213–14, 243–44, 247–49, 261–70, 275–76, 278–79, 290n. 16, 294–98, 302–4, 314–15, 315–24
  on possession, 219–21, 241–44
  on power, 149n. 15, 221, 225–26
  pride and, 219, 291
  psychology of, 227, 283–94
  reading of, 14–15
  on reason, 244–45
  on redemption, 284–87, 290–92
  on religion, 231, 232–35
  on revenge, 284, 286, 298, 313–14
  on rule, 210–14, 226, 232–35, 240–41, 247–49
  scholarship on, 207n. 4, 208n. 5
  "Schopenhauer as Educator," 272
  on science, 224–27, 246, 291n. 17, 309–10
  on sexuality, 227, 259–60
  skepticism and, 247–48, 309n. 8
  on Socrates, 81n. 12
  on soul, 211–12, 238, 243–44, 267–70, 296–98, 303–4
  on spiritedness, 230, 231–32
  on sublimation, 288, 313
  on suffering, 267–68
  Thus Spoke Zarathustra, 250–51, 272–73, 278, 280, 282–83, 287n. 12
  on time, 293–94
  on truth, 226, 253, 258–60, 291–92, 302, 309n. 8, 326–28
  Twilight of the Idols, 282, 283n. 10
  on tyrants, 26n. 14, 261–70
  on virtue, 237, 250–51, 252–60
  on wisdom, 225–26
  on writing, 222n. 22, 283n. 10
nobility
  eternity and, 278–79, 286, 289–94
  life and, 292–94
  morality and, 292–94
  new, 213, 216
  philosophers and, 262, 265–66, 268
  truth and, 302
noble lie, 232–35, 300
nonbeing, 75–76
nothing, 105–11, 115–16
numbers, 214n. 10
Nussbaum, Martha, 62n. 11

Oedipus, 225
opposite values, 285, 287–89
order, 163n. 39
Orwin, Clifford, 127n. 47

patriotism, 153
Pausanias, 77n. 10

Pericles, 90–91, 115n. 29, 127n. 47
Phaedrus, 60, 77n. 10
Phaedrus (Plato), 37, 53, 103–4
philosopher-kings
  eros of, 30n. 22, 34, 70n. 1
  rule by, 126n. 44, 182, 185, 206–7, 239–41, 240–41, 247–49
philosophers. *See also* philosopher-kings; philosophy
  activity of, 97–102, 280–81, 326–28
  Adeimantus on, 246
  beauty and, 88–89, 99–102
  being and, 100, 319
  candidates to be, 91n. 23, 131–32, 245–52, 325
  Cave allegory and, 36n. 31
  courage of, 45–46
  death and, 45–46, 83–87, 100–102
  desire and, 29–30, 32–38, 179, 189–90
  divinity and, 248, 328–29
  education by, 97–102
  education of, 249–51, 252, 254
  eidê and, 327–28
  Emile as, 179, 189–90
  epochs of, 306–11
  eros and, 25–27, 29–30, 32–38, 49, 68–80, 97–102, 144n. 11, 184, 185, 210, 276–81, 325, 326–28
  eternity and, 100–101, 277–79, 281, 328–29
  experience of, 262–70
  extended being and, 12–13, 100, 325, 326–28
  freedom and, 83–86, 179, 189–90
  gender and, 185
  goods and, 212, 277–79, 281, 319
  happiness of, 157–58, 160
  infinity and, 328–29
  insight of, 83–86, 87, 96
  knowledge and, 179, 189–90, 245–46, 256–58, 281, 326–27
  life and, 178, 191n. 24
  love and, 179, 189–90, 326–27
  as maker, 256, 281, 326–27
  modeling by, 97–102
  nature and, 258
  Nietzsche as, 250–51
  Nietzsche on, 26n. 14, 212, 226, 232–35, 240–41, 245–52, 256–58, 262–70, 276–81, 325, 326–28
  nobility and, 262, 265–66, 268
  Plato on, 12–13, 22, 25–27, 29–30, 32–38, 68–80, 97–102, 144n. 11, 162, 190, 199–200, 212, 231, 232–35, 239–41, 245–52, 254, 256–57, 276–81, 296n. 25, 325, 326–28
  pleasure and, 36–37, 46–47, 101, 267
  as poets, 9–10
  politics and, 97–102, 247–49
  prejudice and, 179, 189–90
  progeny and, 99–101
  qualities of, 179, 189–90, 245–46, 250–51
  reading of, 9–10, 14–15, 67–68, 183–84
  reason and, 179, 189–90
  religion and, 232–35
  Rousseau on, 12–13, 160, 178, 187n. 15, 189–91, 325, 326–28
  rule by, 97–102, 126n. 44, 182, 185, 199–200, 206–7, 212, 226, 231, 232–35, 239–41, 247–49, 326–27
  skepticism and, 247–48
  Socrates as, 97–102, 250–51, 256–57
  Socrates on, 22, 68–80, 162, 246
  soul and, 22, 32–38, 162, 184, 185
  sublimation and, 32–38
  suffering and, 267–68
  thymos and, 49, 230
  truth and, 29–30, 45–46, 88–89, 96, 97–98, 179, 189–90, 190–91, 245–52
  tyrants and, 25–26, 29–30, 32, 210, 262–70, 296n. 25
  virtue and, 250–51
  will to power and, 276–81, 325, 326–28
philosophy. *See also* philosophers
  activity of, 252–60
  anger and, 113, 117–19, 129
  Apollodorus and, 113
  beauty and, 163, 193–94
  being and, 319
  candidates for, 91n. 23, 131–32, 245–52, 325
  city and, 90–91
  death and, 89–90, 127
  desire and, 29–31, 34–38
  Diotima on, 89
  divinity and, 328–29
  education and, 87, 91, 111–12, 130–32, 177–83, 185–201, 249–51
  egoic consciousness and, 161–64
  eidê and, 164
  Emile and, 179–80, 188–201
  epochs of, 306–11
  eros and, 29–31, 34–38, 44–49, 68–80, 86–93, 95–97, 98–99, 100–101, 102–3, 113, 117–19, 126–32, 179–80, 185–86, 193–94, 223, 324–29
  eternity and, 216–17, 328–29
  extended being and, 12–13, 160–64, 177–80, 324–29

philosophy (*continued*)
  gender and, 186–91
  goods and, 90, 119, 177–78, 181–83, 249–51, 319
  honor and, 46–47
  human nature and, 161
  infinity and, 328–29
  life and, 119, 191n. 24
  love of, 126
  morality and, 196–97, 198–99, 252–56
  nature and, 161, 258, 259–60
  Nietzsche on, 216–17, 223, 224–27, 229, 252–60, 290n. 16, 324–29
  Plato on, 12–13, 29–31, 34–38, 44–49, 68–80, 86–93, 95–97, 113, 178–79, 193–94, 199–200, 206–7, 216–17, 221–22, 324–29
  politics and, 127, 129–32, 164n. 41, 195–96, 206–7, 290n. 16
  possibility of, 179, 181–83, 197–201, 250–51
  power and, 119, 121
  psychic force and, 7–8
  Rousseau on, 12–13, 160–64, 177–83, 185–201, 324–29
  self-consciousness and, 162–64
  sexuality and, 259–60
  Socrates on, 44–45, 68–80, 86–93
  soul and, 160–61
  sublimation and, 34–38
  theology and, 206–7
  thymos and, 44–49, 221–22
  transcendence and, 161–64
  truth and, 88–91, 100–101, 102–3, 126, 131–32, 187–88, 190–91, 195–97, 326–28
  tyrants and, 127
  victory and, 46–47
  virtue and, 252–60
  will to power and, 259–60, 324–29
Plato. *See also* eros; *Republic*; *Symposium*
  on activity, 55–56, 57–61, 65–66, 97–102, 112–32, 256–57, 280–81
  Apology, 57n. 3, 104n. 11, 115
  on beauty, 63, 64, 65, 69–83, 95–97, 99–102, 110–11, 115–17, 193–94
  on being, 68–76, 100, 103–11, 171, 315, 317–24
  on Being, 68–72, 106–11
  on body, 19, 25, 27, 29–30, 37–38
  on character types, 210–14, 324–25
  Charmides, 90
  on city, 23–24, 39, 47–48, 182–83, 227–28, 237–38, 243–44
  on communism, 182, 185, 239–40, 241–44, 263
  on death, 69–72, 74–76, 77–78, 79–80, 83–86, 95–97, 100–102, 116–17, 270
  on democracy, 219–21, 261–62
  on desire, 20–25, 27–38, 38–44, 61–66, 95–97, 276–77, 307–8, 315–24
  dialogue with Nietzsche and Rousseau, 7–9, 305–6
  on Diotima, 69, 72
  on divinity, 248
  on education, 6n. 5, 78–80, 178–79, 180–85, 193–94, 209–10, 213–14, 230–32, 249–51, 252, 254, 278–79
  on egoic consciousness, 100–111, 116–17
  on *eidē*, 194, 299–300, 311–12
  eros of, 114
  on eternity, 95–97, 100–101, 216–17, 276–81, 299–304, 314–15, 319–20, 322
  Euthyphro, 90
  on evil, 26–27
  on experience, 300–303
  on extended being, 152n. 19
  on gender, 182, 184–85, 219–21, 239–40, 241–42, 244–45, 263
  on gods, 219
  on Good, 70–72, 74–75, 106–11, 311–12, 321–22
  on goods, 21, 26–27, 63, 64–65, 69, 73–74, 78–83, 95–97, 110–11, 115, 144, 212, 277–79, 281, 295n. 24, 299–304, 312–13, 315–24
  Gorgias, 53, 75
  on gymnastics, 230–32
  on happiness, 213
  on human nature, 26–27, 169–70, 244–45
  on infinity, 95–97, 103
  on justice, 224–27, 229, 235–37
  Laches, 90
  Laws, 74, 86n. 16
  on life, 71n. 5
  on love, 95–97, 115
  on morality, 213, 315–24
  on music, 230–32
  naturalism and, 315–24
  on nature, 16, 169–70, 240, 303–4
  Nietzsche on, 205–6, 223–24, 275–76, 299–304, 309–11
  noble lie of, 232–35, 300
  on nothing, 105–11, 115–16
  Phaedrus, 37, 53, 103–4
  on philosophers, 12–13, 22, 25–27, 29–30, 32–38, 68–80, 97–102, 144n. 11, 162, 190, 199–200, 212, 230, 231, 232–35, 239–41, 245–52, 254, 256–57, 262–70, 276–81, 296n. 25, 325, 326–28

philosophic epochs and, 306–11
on philosophy, 12–13, 29–31, 34–38, 44–49, 68–80, 86–93, 95–97, 113, 178–79, 180–85, 193–94, 199–200, 206–7, 216–17, 221–22, 324–29
on pleasure, 74–76, 101
on politics, 23–24, 36–38, 39, 41, 53–56, 69, 78–80, 97–102, 111–32, 206–7, 209–10, 213–14, 261–70, 295n. 24, 302–4, 314–15, 315–24
politics of, 114n. 26
on possession, 219–21, 241–44
on power, 115–17, 119, 121, 225–26
on pride, 219
on progeny, 69, 72, 99–101, 109, 185
on property, 234
reading, 67–68, 183–84
on reason, 20–25, 37, 38–39, 58–59
on rule, 182, 199–200, 210–14, 231, 232–35, 239–41, 247–49
rule by, 206
scholarship on, 207n. 4
on self-interest, 65, 100–111
Seventh Letter, 46n. 45
on sexuality, 74
Socrates and, 114
Sophist, 89n. 21
on soul, 18–19, 20–27, 31–50, 56–57, 103–4, 162, 164, 191, 211–12, 237–38, 243–44, 264, 269–70, 296, 303–4, 307–8, 327–28
Statesman, 45n. 44
on sublimation, 30–38, 43–44, 71–76, 191–94
on theology, 206–7
on *thymos*, 18, 19, 20–27, 38–50, 57, 59–61, 61–62, 81–82, 102–3, 109, 221–22, 230
on truth, 29–30, 55–56, 65–66, 70, 78–80, 108–9, 226, 326–28
on tyrants, 25–27, 29–30, 32, 39, 76–77, 108, 112, 144n. 11, 261–70, 296n. 25
on unity, 244–45
on virtue, 235–37
on wisdom, 195, 225–26
Platonism, 205–6, 223–24, 275–76, 299–304, 309–11
pleasure, 36–37, 46–47, 74–76, 101, 267, 291–92
Plotinus, 87n. 18, 106, 300n. 30
pluralism, 317n. 16
poetry, 9–10, 270, 304
Polemarchus, 77n. 10, 225–26
politics. *See also* city; rule
  activity and, 112–32
  Alcibiades, 112–17, 121–27, 129–32

Apollodorus, 112–19, 120–21, 125–27, 129–32
Aristodemus, 112–17, 119–21, 125–27, 129–32
Aristotle on, 171n. 49
beauty and, 55
being and, 142
Cave allegory and, 98
death and, 55
Diotima on, 127–32
education and, 6n. 5, 123–24, 130–32, 195–96, 213–14
eros and, 10–11, 12, 16, 17–20, 41, 53–56, 69, 78–80, 97–102, 111–32, 209–10, 314–15
eternity and, 278–79, 294–98, 302–4, 314–15
extended being and, 164n. 41, 168–69, 312, 314–15
goods and, 16, 210, 278–79, 294–96, 298, 302–4
health and, 294–96, 303–4
infinity and, 55
limits of, 6–7
morality and, 275–76, 294–96
naturalism and, 315–24
nature and, 136, 295, 303–4
Nietzsche on, 98, 208–10, 213–14, 243–44, 247–49, 261–70, 275–76, 278–79, 290n. 16, 294–98, 302–4, 314–15, 315–24
philosopher-kings and, 126n. 44
philosophers and, 97–102, 247–49
philosophy and, 127, 129–32, 164n. 41, 195–96, 206–7, 290n. 16
of Plato, 114n. 26
Plato on, 17–20, 23–24, 36–38, 39, 41, 53–56, 69, 78–80, 97–102, 111–32, 206–7, 209–10, 213–14, 261–70, 295n. 24, 302–4, 314–15, 315–24
psychic force and, 5–7
Rousseau on, 136, 142, 195–96, 312, 314–15, 315–24
Socrates on, 69, 78–80, 97–102, 112–32
soul and, 18–19, 23–24, 39, 243–44, 296–98, 303–4
theology and, 206–7
thymos and, 18, 19, 20, 39, 41
truth and, 55–56, 195–96
will to power and, 208–10, 278–79, 294–96, 298, 314–15
possession, 152, 166–69, 173–74, 219–21, 241–44
power. *See also* will to power
  character types and, 173–74
  death and, 3–4
  desire and, 3–4, 146–47, 149–51, 153, 173–74

power (*continued*)
    Diotima and, 128–29
    of Emile, 149
    eros and, 126, 130
    extended being and, 146–47, 149–51, 153, 173–74
    gender and, 221
    goods and, 173–74
    Hobbes on, 3–4, 7–8
    imperialism and, 3
    love of, 130
    nature and, 128–29
    Nietzsche on, 149n. 15, 221, 225–26
    philosophy and, 119, 121
    Plato on, 115–17, 119, 121, 225–26
    Rousseau on, 146–47, 149–51, 165, 173–74
    self-interest and, 149
    self-love and, 146–47, 149–51, 165
    of Socrates, 115–17, 122, 124–25
    of soul, 33n. 28, 139n. 5, 149
    truth and, 226
    wisdom and, 225–26
prejudice, 179, 189–90
prestige, 152–53
pride, 219, 291
progeny, 69, 72, 99–101, 109, 185
Prometheus Bound (Aeschylus), 220–21
property, 234
psychic force, 3–9. *See also* eros; extended being; power; will to power
psychology, 227, 283–94
Pythagoreans, 20n. 2

reading, 9–10, 14–15, 67–68, 183–84
reason
    desire and, 24–25, 38–39
    morality and, 244–45
    Nietzsche on, 244–45
    philosophers and, 179, 189–90
    Plato on, 20–25, 37, 38–39, 58–59
    reveries and, 156
    self-interest and, 58–59
    in soul, 20–25, 37, 38–39
    thymos and, 38–39
    truth and, 58–59
redemption, 284–87, 290–92
religion, 113, 119–21, 129–30, 231, 232–35
Republic (Plato)
    activity in, 97–102, 256–57
    beauty in, 69–83, 95–97, 99–102, 110–11, 193–94
    Being in, 68–72, 106–11

being in, 68–76, 100, 103–11
Beyond Good and Evil (Nietzsche) compared generally, 13–15, 17, 205–14, 271–73, 275–81
body in, 19, 25, 27, 29–30, 37–38
book 1, 224–27
book 2, 227–30
book 3, 230–35
book 4, 235–38
book 5, 239–45
book 6, 245–52
book 7, 252–60
book 8, 261–62
book 9, 262–70
book 10, 270
character types in, 210–14
city in, 23–24, 39, 47–48, 182–83, 227–28, 237–38, 243–44
communism in, 182, 185, 239–40, 241–44, 263
death in, 69–72, 74–76, 77–78, 79–80, 83–86, 95–97, 100–102, 270
democracy in, 219–21, 261–62
desire in, 20–25, 27–38, 38–44, 95–97
diaretic activity in, 45
divinity in, 248
education in, 78–80, 178–79, 180–85, 193–94, 209–10, 213–14, 230–32, 249–51, 252, 254, 278–79
egoic consciousness in, 100–111
Emile (Rousseau) compared generally, 17, 178–83
eros in, 18, 19–20, 24–38, 40–50, 53–54, 56–57, 61–62, 64–65, 67–93, 95–112, 144, 193–94, 209–10, 275–81
eternity in, 95–97, 100–101, 216–17
evil in, 26–27
gender in, 182, 184–85, 219–21, 239–40, 241–42, 244–45, 263
gods in, 219
Good in, 70–72, 74–75, 106–11
goods in, 21, 26–27, 69, 73–74, 78–83, 95–97, 110–11, 144, 212
gymnastics in, 230–32
happiness in, 213
human nature in, 26–27, 244–45
infinity in, 95–97, 103
justice in, 224–27, 229, 235–37
life in, 71n. 5
love in, 95–97, 115
morality in, 213
music in, 230–32

nature in, 240
noble lie in, 232–35
nothing in, 105–11
philosophers in, 22, 25–27, 29–30, 32–38, 68–80, 97–102, 144n. 11, 162, 190, 199–200, 212, 230, 231, 232–35, 239–41, 245–52, 254, 256–57, 262–70
philosophy in, 29–31, 34–38, 44–49, 68–80, 86–93, 95–97, 178–79, 180–85, 193–94, 199–200, 206–7, 216–17, 221–22
pleasure in, 74–76, 101
politics in, 17–20, 23–24, 36–38, 39, 41, 53–54, 69, 78–80, 97–102, 206–7, 209–10, 213–14, 261–70
possession in, 219–21, 241–44
power in, 225–26
preface of, 224n. 27
pride in, 219
progeny in, 69, 72, 99–101, 109
property in, 234
reading, 67–68
reason in, 20–25, 37, 38–39
rule in, 182, 210–14, 231, 232–35, 239–41, 247–49
self-interest in, 100–111
sexuality in, 74
soul in, 18–19, 20–27, 31–50, 56–57, 103–4, 162, 191, 211–12, 237–38, 243–44, 264, 269–70, 296
Stephanus pagination of, 216
structure of, 214–22
sublimation in, 30–38, 43–44, 71–76, 191
Symposium (Plato) complements, 17–18, 32n. 26, 37–38, 53–54, 60–61, 61–62, 64–65, 67–68, 72n. 6, 76–77, 108–9
themes of generally, 210–14
theology in, 206–7
thymos in, 18, 19, 20–27, 38–50, 57, 60–61, 61–62, 81–82, 102–3, 109, 221–22, 230
truth in, 29–30, 70, 78–80, 108–9, 226
tyrants in, 25–27, 29–30, 32, 39, 76–77, 108, 112, 144n. 11, 261–70
unity in, 244–45
virtue in, 235–37
wisdom in, 195, 225–26
restraint, 321n. 20
revenge, 284, 286, 298, 313–14
reveries, 155–64, 166
Reveries (Rousseau), 155–60
Roochnik, David, 22n. 5
Rorty, Richard, 297n. 26

Rosen, Stanley, 35n. 30
Rousseau, Jean-Jacques. *See also Emile*; extended being
on activity, 147–49, 166–69
on beauty, 163n. 39, 172–73
on being, 138–43, 145, 171, 315, 317–24
on botany, 155, 155n. 25, 156
on character types, 139, 141–42, 146–47, 169n. 46, 173–74, 324–25
on compassion, 153
Confessions, 159n. 31
on death, 169n. 46
on desire, 136–38, 141–51, 152–55, 165–75, 307–8, 312, 315–24
Dialogues, 147–49
dialogue with Plato and Nietzsche, 7–9, 305–6
on ecstasy, 156–57, 159n. 31
on education, 6n. 5, 142–43, 168–69, 177–83, 185–201
education by, 325n. 26
on egoic consciousness, 158–59, 161–64, 167–69, 172–73, 327–28
on eros, 179–80, 185–86, 192
on eternity, 314–15
on faculties, 166–67, 168
on family, 153–54, 182
First Discourse, 198–99, 325
on gender, 182, 186–91
on God, 158, 159n. 30
on goods, 73–74, 136–38, 139–41, 143–44, 165–75, 177–78, 181–83, 312–13, 315–24
on happiness, 140–41, 157–58
happiness of, 174
on human nature, 8, 161, 180–81
idleness of, 154–55
on infinity, 145
on intellectual activity, 154–64
on life, 178, 182–83
on love, 182, 191–94
meditation of, 155n. 25, 156–62
on morality, 196–97, 198–99, 315–24
naturalism and, 315–24
on nature, 16, 136, 156–57, 161, 169–71
on patriotism, 153
on philosophers, 12–13, 160, 178, 187n. 15, 189–91, 325, 326–28
philosophic epochs and, 306–11
on philosophy, 12–13, 160–64, 177–80, 185–201, 324–29
Plato read by, 183–84
on politics, 136, 142, 195–96, 312, 314–15, 315–24

Rousseau (*continued*)
  on possession, 166–69, 173–74
  on power, 146–47, 149–51, 165, 173–74
  Reveries, 155–60
  reveries of, 155–64, 166
  on rule, 182
  on savages, 150–51
  on self-consciousness, 145–46, 147, 151, 155–59, 162–64
  on self-interest, 149
  on self-love, 116–17, 118n. 34, 125n. 42, 137, 142–43, 144–51, 158–59, 165–69
  Social Contract, 200n. 36, 325
  on soul, 160–61, 164, 172–73
  on transcendence, 158–59, 161–64
  on truth, 187–88, 190–91, 195–97, 326–28
  on virtue, 140, 153
  of writing, 156–62
  writing of, 155n. 25, 183–84
rule
  democracy and, 321n. 20
  eros and, 185
  goods and, 212
  Nietzsche on, 210–14, 226, 232–35, 240–41, 247–49
  by philosophers, 97–102, 126n. 44, 182, 185, 199–200, 206–7, 212, 226, 231, 232–35, 239–41, 247–49, 326–27
  by Plato, 206
  Plato on, 182, 199–200, 210–14, 231, 232–35, 239–41, 247–49
  by religion, 232–35
  Rousseau on, 182
  by Socrates, 97–102
  Socrates on, 232–35

savages, 150–51
Schlosser, Joel, 237n. 42
Schopenhauer, 37n. 32
"Schopenhauer as Educator" (Nietzsche), 272
science, 224–27, 246, 291n. 17, 308–10
self-consciousness, 145–46, 147, 151, 155–59, 162–64. *See also* egoic consciousness
self-interest, 58–59, 65, 75–76, 96, 100–111, 149, 162. *See also* self-love
self-love, 116–19, 124–26, 137, 142–51, 154, 158–59, 165–69. *See also* self-interest
Seventh Letter (Plato), 46n. 45
sexes. *See* gender
sexuality, 36–38, 64–65, 74, 227, 259–60
Sicily, 3n. 2, 114, 115n. 29, 122–24
sight, 110–11

skepticism, 247–48, 309n. 8
slave morality, 265–67
Social Contract (Rousseau), 200n. 36, 325
society, 142, 254–55
Socrates
  activity of, 55, 83–86, 97–102, 106–7, 112–32
  Adeimantus and, 26–27, 219–21, 235n. 40
  Alcibiades and, 46, 112–17, 121–27, 129–32
  Apollodorus and, 112–19, 120–21, 125–27, 129–32
  Aristodemus, 112–17, 119–21, 125–27, 129–32
  on beauty, 69–83
  beauty of, 115–17, 122, 125
  on being, 68–76, 119
  on Being, 68–72
  city and, 227–28
  on death, 69–72, 74–76, 77–78, 79–80, 83–86, 116–17, 128
  death of, 119
  on democracy, 219–21
  on desire, 61, 63–66
  dialogue of, 59, 61–66
  on education, 6n. 5
  education by, 97–102, 123–24, 181–82, 184–85
  egoic consciousness and, 116–17
  on eros, 11, 19–20, 25–27, 27–38, 44–49, 57, 60, 61, 62–66, 67–93, 95–112, 112–32
  eros of, 34–35, 41–42, 47, 70n. 1, 89, 95, 104, 106–7
  freedom of, 124–25
  Glaucon and, 21, 210, 229
  on gods, 219
  on Good, 70–72, 74–75
  on goods, 21, 26–27, 69, 73–74, 78–83
  on hunger, 227
  ignorance of, 57
  on justice, 224–27, 229, 235–37
  knowledge of, 57
  love of, 112–32
  modeling by, 97–102
  Nietzsche on, 81n. 12
  noble lie of, 232–35
  as philosopher, 97–102, 250–51, 256–57
  on philosophers, 22, 68–80, 162, 246
  on philosophy, 44–45, 68–80, 86–93
  Plato and, 114
  on pleasure, 74–76
  on politics, 69, 78–80, 97–102, 112–32
  power of, 115–17, 122, 124–25
  on pride, 219
  on progeny, 69, 72

reading, 67–68
religion and, 113, 120
on rule, 232–35
rule by, 97–102
self-interest of, 104
on soul, 21–27, 31–38, 57, 162, 237–38
soul of, 116–17
on sublimation, 31–38, 71–76
on *thymos*, 38–50, 57
thymos of, 41–42, 47
on truth, 60, 70, 78–80
on tyrants, 76–77
Socratism, 309–11
Sophie, 191–94
Sophist (Plato), 89n. 21
Sophocles, 25
Sorenson, Leonard, 161n. 36
soul
  Being and, 48–49
  city and, 23–24, 39, 184, 237–38, 243–44
  death and, 131, 270
  desire and, 20–25, 31–38, 307–8, 314–15, 321–22
  eros and, 24–27, 31–38, 40–50, 56–57, 210, 307–8
  eternity and, 296–98, 303–4
  evil and, 26–27
  experience of, 172–73
  extended being and, 160–61
  Good and, 48, 321–22
  goods and, 21
  health and, 23–24, 25, 149n. 17, 164, 172, 195, 211–12, 303–4
  intellectual activity and, 160–61
  morality and, 269–70
  nature and, 303–4
  Nietzsche on, 211–12, 238, 243–44, 267–70, 296–98, 303–4
  partition of, 18, 20–27, 38–39, 48–50, 56–57, 103–4, 109, 164, 238, 264
  philosophers and, 22, 32–38, 162, 184, 185
  philosophy and, 160–61
  Plato on, 18–19, 20–27, 31–50, 56–57, 103–4, 162, 164, 191, 211–12, 237–38, 243–44, 264, 269–70, 296, 303–4, 307–8, 327–28
  politics and, 18–19, 23–24, 39, 243–44, 296–98, 303–4
  reason in, 20–25, 37, 38–39
  Rousseau on, 160–61, 164, 172–73
  of Socrates, 116–17
  Socrates on, 21–27, 31–38, 57, 162, 237–38
  strength of, 33n. 28, 139n. 5, 149
  sublimation and, 31–38, 191–94
  thymos in, 18, 19, 20–27, 38–50
  tyrants and, 32, 39
  unity of, 48–50
  wisdom and, 195
Spinoza, Benedict, 315n. 13
spiritedness, 230, 231–32. *See also thymos*
Statesman (Plato), 45n. 44
Strauss, Leo
  on Aristophanes, 59n. 9
  on body, 37n. 33
  on Diotima, 57n. 5
  on eros, 63n. 12, 65n. 16
  on goods, 81n. 14
  on Nietzsche, 292n. 20, 299
  on philosophic epochs, 306n. 1, 306n. 3, 310n. 9
  on philosophy, 47n. 46
  on *thymos*, 43
sublimation
  Nietzsche on, 288, 313
  Plato on, 30–38, 43–44, 47, 71–76, 191–94
suffering, 267–68
Sun image, 108, 249–50
Symposium (Plato)
  activity in, 55–56, 57–61, 65–66, 97–102, 112–32
  beauty in, 61–62, 63, 64, 65, 69–83, 95–97, 99–102, 110–11, 115–17
  Being in, 68–72, 106–11
  being in, 68–76, 100, 103–11
  death in, 69–72, 74–76, 77–78, 79–80, 83–86, 95–97, 100–102, 116–17
  desire in, 61–66, 95–97
  education in, 78–80
  egoic consciousness in, 100–111, 116–17
  eros in, 53–56, 57–66, 67–93, 95–132, 185
  eternity in, 95–97, 100–101
  Frogs (Aristophanes) compared to, 59n. 9
  Good in, 70–72, 74–75, 106–11
  goods in, 63, 64–65, 69, 73–74, 78–83, 95–97, 110–11, 115
  infinity in, 95–97, 103
  life in, 71n. 5
  love in, 95–97
  nothing in, 105–11, 115–16
  philosophers in, 68–80, 97–102
  philosophy in, 68–80, 86–93, 95–97, 113
  pleasure in, 74–76, 101
  politics in, 53–56, 69, 78–80, 97–102, 111–32

Symposium (continued)
   power in, 115–17, 119, 121
   progeny in, 69, 72, 99–101, 109, 185
   reading, 67–68
   reason in, 58–59
   Republic (Plato) complements, 17–18, 32n. 26, 37–38, 53–54, 60–61, 61–62, 64–65, 67–68, 72n. 6, 76–77, 108–9
   self-interest in, 58–59, 65, 100–111
   sexuality in, 74
   soul in, 103–4
   structure of, 59n. 8, 64, 72n. 6, 128n. 50
   sublimation in, 32n. 26, 71–76
   thymos in, 49n. 49, 59–61, 81–82, 102–3, 109
   truth in, 55–56, 65–66, 70, 78–80, 108–9
   tyrants in, 76–77

theology, 206–7
thinking. *See* contemplation; intellectual activity; meditation; reason
Thrasymachus, 48n. 47, 77n. 10, 225
Thucydides, 3, 55, 115n. 29
Thus Spoke Zarathustra (Nietzsche), 250–51, 272–73, 278, 280, 282–83, 287n. 12
thymos
   beauty and, 81–82
   being and, 43–44, 109
   in Cave allegory, 61–62
   city and, 39, 47–48
   desire and, 24–25, 38–44
   dialogue on, 47–48, 59–61
   education of, 48n. 47
   egoic consciousness and, 109
   ends of, 40–42, 44–50
   eros and, 20, 38, 40–50, 57, 59–61, 61–62, 81–82, 102–3, 109, 124–25, 210
   goods and, 81–82
   honor and, 44, 46–47
   in human nature, 42–43
   origins of, 40–44, 60
   philosophers and, 49, 230
   philosophy and, 44–49, 221–22
   politics and, 18, 19, 20, 39, 41
   question of, 38–42, 60
   reason and, 38–39
   self-interest and, 109
   self-love and, 116n. 31, 117–18, 144
   of Socrates, 41–42, 47
   Socrates on, 38–50, 57
   in soul, 18, 19, 20–27, 38–50
   sublimation of, 43–44
   tyrants and, 39

   victory and, 40–41, 43, 44, 46–47
   will to power and, 280
time, 293–94. *See also* eternity
Tocqueville, Alexis de, 111, 125, 308
transcendence, 75–76, 92–93, 100–111, 116–17, 158–59, 161–64. *See also* freedom
truth. *See also* eidê
   activity and, 55–56
   beauty and, 88–89
   being and, 108–9, 175
   death and, 84–86, 89–90
   desire and, 29–30, 175, 179
   dialogue and, 57–61
   egoic consciousness and, 108–9
   eros and, 11, 29–30, 57–61, 65–66, 70, 78–80, 100–101, 102–3, 108–9, 111–12, 125–26, 162, 326–28
   eternity and, 84–86
   extended being and, 175, 326–28
   faith and, 291–92
   gender and, 188n. 18, 223, 253, 258–60
   health and, 293
   love and, 179, 258
   morality, 196–97
   Nietzsche on, 226, 253, 258–60, 291–92, 302, 309n. 8, 326–28
   nobility and, 302
   philosophers and, 29–30, 45–46, 88–89, 96, 97–98, 179, 189–90, 190–91, 245–52
   philosophy and, 88–91, 100–101, 102–3, 126, 131–32, 187–88, 190–91, 195–97, 326–28
   Plato on, 29–30, 55–56, 65–66, 70, 78–80, 108–9, 226, 326–28
   pleasure and, 291–92
   politics and, 55–56, 195–96
   power and, 226
   reason and, 58–59
   religion and, 233
   Rousseau on, 187–88, 190–91, 195–97, 326–28
   self-interest and, 108–9
   Socrates on, 60, 70, 78–80
   terminology of, 70n. 2
   virtue and, 237
   will to power and, 326–28
Twilight of the Idols (Nietzsche), 282, 283n. 10
tyrants
   desire and, 29–30
   eros and, 25–27, 29–30, 32, 76–77, 108, 112, 144n. 11, 210
   Nietzsche on, 26n. 14, 261–70
   philosophers and, 25–26, 29–30, 32, 210, 262–70, 296n. 25

philosophy and, 127
Socrates on, 76–77
soul and, 32, 39
sublimation and, 32
thymos and, 39

unity, 48–50, 91–93, 95–97, 110–11, 244–45

vertical descriptors, 31n. 24, 70n. 2
victory, 40–41, 43, 44, 46–47
virtue, 140, 153, 235–37, 250–51, 252–56

wakefulness, 224n. 27
Wilber, Ken, 301n. 31, 302
will to power. *See also* eros; extended being
  activity and, 172
  being and, 315, 317–24
  in *Beyond Good and Evil* (Nietzsche), 208–10, 227, 245, 259–60, 275–81
  character types and, 277, 324–25
  desire and, 171, 227, 276–77, 307–8
  education and, 278–79
  eros compared, 4–5, 13–15, 56–57, 125–26, 173, 209–10, 227, 259–60, 275–81, 305–29
  eternity and, 276–81, 294–96, 298, 314–15

extended being compared, 4–5, 305–29
faith and, 288–89
goods and, 13–15, 171, 294–96, 312–14
life and, 277, 294–96
morality and, 245, 294–96
naturalism and, 315–24
opposite values and, 288n. 13
overview of, 4–5, 13–15
philosophers and, 276–81, 325, 326–28
philosophic epochs and, 306–11
philosophy and, 259–60, 324–29
politics and, 208–10, 278–79, 294–96, 298, 314–15
psychology and, 227
self-love compared, 125–26
sexuality and, 227, 259–60
thymos and, 280
truth and, 326–28
wisdom, 29n. 21, 192–93, 195, 225–26, 258, 267
writing, 155n. 25, 156–62, 183–84, 222n. 22, 283n. 10

Xenophon, 114

Zarathustra, 250, 270, 280, 283n. 10, 287n. 12

www.ingramcontent.com/pod-product-compliance
Lightning Source LLC
Chambersburg PA
CBHW032127010526
44111CB00033B/152